Dynamics of Growth

DYNAMICS OF GROWTH

An Economic Profile of Texas

Edited by
LOUIS J. RODRIGUEZ
Vice Chancellor and Provost
University of Houston at Clear Lake City

MADRONA PRESS – AUSTIN, TEXAS

ISBN 0-89052-023-2
Library of Congress Catalog Card No. 77-84107
Copyright 1978 by Louis J. Rodriguez
FIRST EDITION
Manufactured in the United States of America

DYNAMICS OF GROWTH
seventeenth book produced by Madrona Press
has been printed on Nekoosa Natural paper.
Type used for text is eleven-point Journal Roman, two-point
leaded, set on the IBM Electronic Selectric Composer.
Type used for display is Lydian.
Printing: Capital Printing Company, Austin
Binding: Custom Bookbinders, Austin

MADRONA PRESS, INC.
BOX 3750
AUSTIN, TEXAS 78764

*To my Mother and Father
for their unwaivering faith in the
values of education.*

ACKNOWLEDGMENTS

I am indebted to a number of individuals for their assistance with this volume. The writers of these essays demonstrated a collective cooperation and commitment to time schedules which was extraordinarily commendable. Mrs. Colleen Farrington, in the face of a heavy workload, accepted without complaint the additional burden of retyping the complete manuscript. The University of Houston Foundation provided support which helped to make this work possible. I am grateful to Dr. Alfred R. Neumann, Chancellor of the University of Houston at Clear Lake City, for his interest, encouragement, and assistance in making the publication of this book a reality.

PREFACE

In the post-World War II era, considerable attention has been directed toward economic development at the state and local levels. There has been active competition among states and regions to increase their tempo of economic information by state and local organizations. In the beginnings of this period, it was often discovered that while a considerable amount of national economic information was available, much less had been gathered and analyzed at regional levels. Business people attempting to make decisions in terms of where to locate new production facilities and government officials and students of regional economic growth often found their activities limited by a dearth of economic information. There still exists an absence in many states of adequate sources to which individuals may turn to obtain an overall evaluation of a particular state's economy. While much data have been gathered, a great deal still needs to be done in terms of analyzing and presenting this information in a usable manner.

This collection of essays dealing with the Texas economy is an attempt to make available to interested business people, government officials, legislators, educators, and students a summary of the major developments and the chief components of the Texas economy in the post-World War II era. The objective is to present and analyze developments in a concise, readable manner so that these essays can be read and understood by individuals without formal training in economics.

Nineteen writers, each with a thorough knowledge and background of the Texas economy, have contributed to this collection. In "The Theory of Economic Development and the Challenge of A Developmental Policy," Thomas DeGregori sets the stage for the remainder of the essays by presenting and analyzing the factors which go into a region's economic development. His presentation uses Texas as a setting in which to apply the concepts pertinent to economic expansion.

In "The Evolution of the Texas Economy," I present an overall view of Texas economic development in the post-World War II era. Texas' performance is compared with that of the nation and factors in the state's economic development are evaluated. Economic strengths and weaknesses in this period of Texas economic evolvement are analyzed.

Jared E. Hazleton, in "Natural Resources in Texas," examines the natural resource base in Texas, and analyzes the past and possible future contributions of these resources to Texas economic growth. The interaction of technological developments and resource utilization as they apply to the future are presented.

Allen Commander, Mary C. Schiflett, and John V. Zuckerman are the authors of "Texas—The Energy Economy." They take a thorough, analytical, and realistic look at past, present, and future energy needs of the Texas economy. The writers project energy sources and needs to the year 1985 and make some policy recommendations in this area.

Human resource development in Texas is analyzed by Antonio Furino and William S. Franklin. This study includes education, training, retraining and rehabilitation, labor market information and mobility, health care supportive services, and children of working parents. The authors present the major public efforts leading to the development of human resources in Texas and identify several problem areas that will need greater attention in the future.

In "Organized Labor in Texas," Allan G. King and Robert W. Glover study the unionization movement in Texas. Areas covered are factors causing workers to organize in the state, a comparison of labor organization in Texas with the nation, problems faced by the labor movement in Texas, and the projection of possible unionization efforts in the state during the 1970s.

Stanley A. Arbingast is the author of "Manufacturing in Texas," which presents the composition of major industries in Texas using data relating to employment, output, sales, and income. The importance of manufacturing to the state is analyzed, and factors influencing manufacturing developments in the state are evaluated and future possibilities are considered.

In "The Agricultural Economy of Texas," Thomas J. Stanly

discusses the major aspects of the state's agricultural economy. Special attention is given to the role of the agricultural sector as it relates to the other components of the economy. Location and diversification of major products, structural changes in the nonfarm sector of the agricultural economy as well as financing considerations are discussed. Possible future trends are presented.

Vernon E. Sweeney, Jr. presents and analyzes the role of Texas financial institutions and their contributions to the economic development of the state in "The Financial System of Texas." Specifically, the role played by these instutions in the formation of capital in Texas is considered.

Dale B. Truett, Paul N. Bartlett, Jr., and Lila Flory in "Texas in International Trade," examine the importance of international commerce to the Texas economy. Major product lines traded, chief trading partners, financing aspects, and transportation facilities are analyzed. A future outlook in terms of potential for this ares is presented.

Daniel C. Morgan, Jr., author of "A Fiscal Profile of Texas," looks into trends in state and local government financing in Texas. Amounts and sources of revenue and areas of expenditures are analyzed. Comparisons are made between Texas and other states in terms of revenue and expenditure areas. Current financing problems are evaluated and possible future solutions are presented.

Lorna A. Monti, in "The Texas Economy in Space," discusses the functional economic regions of Texas, income growth, division of labor by areas, and Texas' ties to national economic patterns.

Robert H. Ryan, in "The Future is Today," presents a brief summary of some possible future economic development trends in the state. Among the major areas examined are urbanization, education, agriculture, trade, resource utilization, transportation, and manufacturing.

It is our expectation that this collection of essays will be utilized as classroom and reference source material as well as be of value to anyone interested in the economic development of Texas.

Louis J. Rodriguez

CONTENTS

Acknowledgments vi
Preface vii

1. The Theory of Economic Development and the Challenge of a Developmental Policy
   Thomas R. DeGregori 1

2. The Evolution of the Texas Economy
   Louis J. Rodriguez 15

3. Natural Resources in Texas
   Jared E. Hazleton 41

4. Texas—The Energy Economy
   Allen Commander, Mary C. Schiflett, and John V. Zuckerman 77

5. Human Resource Development in Texas
   Antonio Furino and William S. Franklin 97

6. Organized Labor in Texas
   Robert W. Glover and Allan G. King 136

7. Manufacturing in Texas
   Stanley A. Arbingast 157

8. The Agricultural Economy of Texas
    Thomas J. Stanly 169

9. The Financial System of Texas
    Vernon E. Sweeney, Jr. 196

10. Texas in International Trade
    Dale B. Truett, Paul N. Bartlett, Jr., and Lila Flory 222

11. A Fiscal Profile of Texas
    Daniel C. Morgan, Jr. 244

12. The Texas Economy in Space
    Lorna A. Monti 272

13. The Future is Today
    Robert H. Ryan 289

Contributors 295
Bibliography 301
Index 307

Dynamics of Growth

ONE

THE THEORY OF ECONOMIC DEVELOPMENT AND THE CHALLENGE OF A DEVELOPMENTAL POLICY

Thomas R. DeGregori

GROWTH AND DEVELOPMENT

Economic growth is relatively easy to define. Growth means getting bigger, and economic growth means an increase in gross national product (or in gross regional or state product). Since other items also grow, such as population and prices, gross product must be adjusted for changes in population and prices in order to arrive at some concept of the "real" per capita change in product. Thus, we can specify several concepts of economic growth, state them with precision, and evolve increasingly refined and sophisticated methods of measuring and comparing various forms of growth. Economic development, a larger concept, is more difficult to define. Growth is an element of development, though in the future it is possible that a developmental policy might seek to limit growth. Development is much more than growth; it involves qualitative structural changes.

Growth is not only a component of development, but it is normally the major causal factor in the qualitative changes that define development. Developmental distinctions are implied when we speak of transitions from agricultural to industrial economies, from rural to urban societies, or from industrial to post-industrial societies. Each of these is caused by growth, and therefore each has a set of quantitative indices that particularly define it. The quantitative indices, though, are not enough. Denmark and New Zealand are not industrial countries; nevertheless, their highly productive agriculture gives them a high standard of living and most of the other attributes of industrial economies. Similarly, urbanization in Texas ranks at about the national average. However, the pattern of the development of most Texas cities and the large number of first generation urbanites give Texas cities a different political and cultural orientation than most cities in the United States.

Economic development hinges on a variety of quantitative and qualitative changes. In a sense, it is a twentieth-century variant of the eighteenth-century concept of progress. Growth and development are good; at least that is how they are commonly perceived. To be an underdeveloped region of the United States, such as the South, is to be a backward region, as it is assumed that everyone wants growth and development. Similarly, some of the previously leading industrial states of the United States are experiencing slower rates of growth, and this is cited as evidence of decadence and decline by Southerners.

Though we frequently speak of both growth and development as being good, the value issue is different in each case. We can, in fact, speak of the issue of growth apart from its "goodness" or "badness."[1] A theory of development cannot in any meaningful way be separated from its value components because it is in reality a theory of desirable change.

The assumptions that growth is development and that growth and development are good have merit for most of human history. In the post-World War II era, as countries or states and regions of countries gained control of their destinies, economic improvement—growth—became the major policy objective.

The values implicit in the economic activity of tool-using provide a framework for a retrospective analysis of the economic process itself. From stone axes to rockets, one can find a prescription for a system of economic values. Tools are additive. Steel axes are better than stone axes. What can be done with one set of tools can be done better with their successors. The use of new tools must overcome a pattern of conservatism of established skills and social practices, and the eventual adoption of inventions signifies the acceptance of a technological "betterness."

The improvement of new tools can be achieved in many areas, by adding greater precision, greater speed, more power, and so on. In aggregate, the economic impact has been greater production. Greater production historically has meant more regularized food supplies, improved shelter, and consequently, greater individual longevity and total population. In recent times, economic development has meant increased literacy, greater access to the arts, and more leisure. Contrary to some romantic opinions, the advance of science and material and immaterial technology has not been antithetical to the arts. In sum, economic development means more: more goods and, central to the economist's way of thinking, more choice.

Today we speak of development and underdevelopment, but, strangely enough, few speak of overdevelopment. The latter concept, though, does follow logically. If we have a value system that defines economic product in terms of human needs, such as nutrition, health, shelter, and so on, and in which more is better than less, then there is an implicit concept of sufficiency that can be achieved and surpassed. Orthodox economists speak of infinite wants and finite means, but our modern economic experience increasingly belies this concept. Since wealth is not evenly distributed, it is possible for some segments of a population to be overdeveloped while others are underdeveloped. In fact, as we shall show, the two concepts and conditions are intricately related.

In looking at the causal factors for development of a region or a state, such as Texas, one must analyze conditions and policies at two levels. First, what are the forces for development operating at the national level that establish the framework for development of all its components? Second, what are the resource endowments and the policy options for development available to state and local governmental units?

DEVELOPMENT FORCES

Obviously, in the first case, the most important factor for the economic development of Texas was that most of its peoples came from cultural areas that were in the throes of industrial transformation. Furthermore, politically, the state became part of a country that was moving into the first rank of industrial nations. Walter Prescott Webb describes the barriers that the arid and semi-arid plains of Central and West Texas constituted against settlement and development.[2] Throughout a good part of the nineteenth century, Texas was a frontier. As Webb suggests, one aspect of a frontier is "an advance against nature." The very implements of this advance against nature were the western science and technology brought in by the settlers in Texas as part of their cultural baggage.[3] The area that now constitutes Texas had been inhabited for some time prior to the predominantly Anglo-Saxon settlement from the United States. The earlier Indian (and to a lesser degree, the Spanish) settlers lacked the skills and technology in agriculture, husbandry, metalworking, literacy, and so forth, to develop Texas much beyond what it was in 1820. More important than the technology itself were those habits of tinkering, those elements of curiosity and the conviction that problems are soluble. Settlers brought with them from their parent culture the traits which enabled them to carry technology and continually adapt it to changing environmental conditions. The movement of people into different climatic regions is not a simple matter. Technology that is merely carried into a region without being adapted is not likely to be very productive and will probably facilitate a stagnation or crystallization of the economy at a very low level of development.[4]

At the time that settlers from the United States arrived in what was to become Texas, there were two basic resources: the grassland for stock raising and the river bottoms for cotton and other agricultural pursuits. Both are still important in the Texas economy. Both were a function of the body of skills and technology that allowed for their exploitation. This is particularly true of cotton, which was in the throes of rapid expansion as the leading export of the United States following the development of the cotton gin and the series of technological transformations of the English textile industry. There was plenty of room for expansion (growth) of these two endeavors. However, even here, development (as distinct from growth) to current levels of sophistication in these businesses required continued application of new technology. For example, cattle raising went from the open range to various forms of fencing, and then to the feedlots. Development continued from selective breeding by merely gelding less prized bulls to premium studs, and artificial inseminzation. For transportation, the evolution was from cattle drives to boat or rail, to trucks, to local slaughterhouses and then by refrigerated railcar or truck to market.

It was the dynamic interaction between humans and their environment that constituted the basic force for development. The primary factor was the cultural and mental heritage of a people. For, in some sense, material technology, the techniques of tool and implement using, and the organization of political and economic pursuits, are all the embodiment of ideas. Too frequently, economists and others speak of development as a process of material accumulation, the acquisition of some ill-defined stuff called capital, and the employment of pre-existing resources, when in fact the primary developmental resource is what goes on in people's heads. Initiating development is largely a process of changing people's ways of thinking, making it both easier and more difficult than generally conceived. More difficult because changing people's ways of thinking is difficult; cultures resist change. Easier because alternate techniques of accumulation, which assume pre-existing wealth and long passages of time, can be overcome if the cultural factors are conducive to development.

The early settlers to Texas brought little that the economists would call capital, and they found few resources, but they did initiate a process of development. Even in those cases where they found resources for cotton growing or cattle raising, they changed them. For, as Erich Zimmermann has pointed out, resources are not fixed, they are not a natural part of the environment; they are in fact a functional relationship between man and the environment.[5] The raw materials were there before settlement, but they became resources due to the skill and ingenuity and technology of the settlers. The same is true, of course, for those "resources," such as oil, that originally were either not known to exist or for which there was not then a major economic use.

As important as cultural heritage for Texas was the political incorporation that became the immediate source of its scientific and technological capability. Political integration facilitated the free movement of people and ideas into Texas. Some of the important resource-creating inventions that we have mentioned came from outside Texas and could be exploited because they created products that could be shipped and sold throughout a large national market. The very progress of development tends in itself to be a sustaining force. Success breeds success, and one gain in development reinforces others. Though we may not be able to isolate the causal factors, it is clear that Texas has also received a number of intangible benefits from being a politically integrated part of a developing economy.

When we consider the evolution and/or diffusion of tools, skills, and knowledge as the critical elements in growth and development, then we can see even more the developmental importance of political integration. For, as Wendell Gordon has noted, "technical knowledge can move only" from where it is to where it is not.[6] Equally important is how it moves. Whenever there is contact between peoples of different levels of technological achievement, there is most frequently some technical transfer. In the nineteenth and twentieth centuries, however, the period of Texas development, the industrial and scientific revolutions were acquiring a sophistication that made technological diffusion difficult except as a conscious process. Between countries, it most generally took the form of foreign investment.

The purpose of foreign investment was profitability, either profitability from extracting a raw material or profitability from the sale of finished products to the local inhabitants. At best, technical diffusion was an accidental by-product of this process, and it was generally minimal. Thus, it gave rise to advanced sectors of export mining or plantation agriculture in the midst of overall economic backwardness. The very concentrated focus of foreign investment minimizes cultural contact and the possibilities of economic transformation. The recipient countries rarely receive enough of the vital scientific and technological components of industrialization to give them the capability of sustaining development on their own initiative. In a word, foreign investment generally brings limited and concentrated growth but not development.

Political integration and cultural continuity bring foreign investment from more developed regions of the country. There are important differences, though. The investment will tend to draw skilled personnel, some of whom will become permanent residents. They will demand and help to create educational institutions for their children. In a foreign country the tendency is to create a school solely for the expatriate children or to send these children to the mother country for their education. In less developed regions of one's own country, schools are created for the benefit of almost everyone.

There are vast numbers of cultural items in addition to education that are important for development. Expatriates are unlikely to be a moving force in their creation except for a few amenities that are directly beneficial to them. Those brought to a new region of their country can be a force for the creation of an infrastructure of schools, roads, libraries, and so on, not only because they can benefit from it but also because it is "their" town or state.

Though political integration has been important for development in Texas, there have been some drawbacks. These were particularly important in the post-Civil War period. The industrialization that was creating the large population centers that were consuming Texas beef was predicated on high tariffs. These tariffs were designed, as are all tariffs, to keep out cheaper foreign products. Most of the industries thus benefited were in the Northeast and upper Midwest. Consumers in all sections of the country were hurt, but the citizens of the South and West who did not experience any compensatory development as a result of the tariff policy were particularly damaged.

POLICY

From the Civil War to 1933, the national government was dominated by Republicans and Northerners. This does not mean that the South was ravished by the Union Army in carrying out Reconstruction policies. Though this myth is still in common currency, most reputable historians find that the one thing that the North failed to do for any sustained time was to carry out any genuine Reconstruction policy, giving the freed slaves even a modest chance for advancement. Such efforts were to wait nearly a century and are as yet incomplete. Texas and Southern economic development was slowed by national economic policy that favored industrialization at the expense of other sectors of economic life.

Many Southern Bourbon or Tory politicians supported these policies in their desperate bid to find external allies in their continuing efforts to suppress the supposedly freed blacks. The compromise of 1876 was the likely result of such an alliance. The results of the presidential election of that year were contested, although it is likely that Samuel Tilden, the Democrat, did in fact defeat Rutherford B. Hayes, the Republican. The "compromise" that gave Hayes the presidency involved withdrawing the last remnant of Union troops, giving the South complete internal control in social policy (a near return to slavery). This action assured Republicans and Northerners of the control of national economy for another generation.

Despite alliances between Republicans and Southern Tory Democrats, Texas and the South remained solidly Democratic from the Civil War to 1933 and then on to 1952. At times, toward the end of the nineteenth century, the Populists were more of a threat to this one-party dominance. Being Democratic meant that Texas and the South were in the minority in the national government. Even had they been Republican, it is unlikely that Texas or other Southern states would have significantly altered Northern industrial dominance of national economic policy. If the protective policy of tariffs hurt Texas and the South, so did the relatively hands-off internal policy. The very feedback mechanism of development made it likely that regions that were economically ahead would stay that way. Skilled labor, transportation networks, sources of supply, and markets for products all give an established industrial region opportunity for further industrialization. The cartelization that was allowed to persist in many industries meant that financial control of industry would remain in the Northeast even after some of the plant and production were dispersed into other regions.

Corporate economic policies that were allowed free reign for long periods of time were damaging to Texas and the South. For example, freight rates were much higher in the South and Southwest, making goods shipped into the region bear a higher transit cost and making it more difficult for Southern manufacturers to compete in national markets. Monopoly pricing, such as the Pittsburgh plus system, tended also to discriminate against the South. While this system operated, all steel was priced according to a set list plus freight costs from Pittsburgh to its destination. Thus, if a Birmingham, Alabama manufacturer bought steel from a Birmingham steel plant, he paid the set price plus freight costs from Pittsburgh to Birmingham. Since the freight charge was for nonexistent transportation, it was called phantom freight. Consequently, Northeastern manufacturers closer to Pittsburgh paid lower prices for steel, no matter where they bought, and those in Texas and the South paid more, no matter where they bought it or how much it cost.

The direct economic impact of national economic policy on Texas began to change for the better in 1933, when the state became part of the ruling coalition in the Democratic Congress and in the executive power of Franklin D. Roosevelt. A Texas Democrat and former Speaker of the United States House of Representatives, John Nance Garner, was vice-president, and his protege, Sam Rayburn, would become House Speaker in a few years. Lyndon B. Johnson became majority leader of the Senate in 1955, vice-president in 1961, and president from 1963 to 1969. During the last forty years, it has almost become a cliché that Texas has more political power on the national level than any other state.

The Texas economy has benefited from the political influence in activist interventionist government. Texas and Southern congressmen were key members of the farm state coalitions that helped to rescue Southern agriculture from the doldrums of the 1930s. Texas has always received its share of the public works from the national Democratic governments. When the war came, Texas received more than its share of military bases and defense plants. In the cold war aftermath of World War II, Texas continued to obtain a large measure of defense spending, even moving into the aerospace field with the Manned Space Center in Houston. These plants and installations gave rise to secondary supply industries and in many cases became part of the nucleus of growing industrial centers, such as Houston or the Dallas-Fort Worth metroplex.

Following World War II, large industries began to disperse their plants by building them closer to their markets. The less developed regions, such as Texas and the South, were the most obvious beneficiaries of this trend. It was greatly facilitated by the move of the national government to eliminate regional railroad freight rate disparities. This was at precisely the time that the Democratic Party began to lose strength in the South, largely over the race question. Conservative economic and social philosophies were often raised as an explanation for Texas' support of Eisenhower or national Republican policies. However, these can hardly be the explanation, as Texas and the rest of the South had always done poorly under such national economic policies. The state moved into the ranks of the more rapidly growing regions under the stimulus of interventionist Democratic regimes.

Texas and the South began to turn to more conservative economic policies for development in the 1950s and 1960s. That does not mean that they turned their backs on the largess of the national government. It does mean that Texas began a vigorous campaign at the state and local levels to attract private industries. Different locations have different strengths for drawing investment. Houston east to Port Arthur had, among other things, good rail and ship transportation opportunities and oil for a petrochemical industry. One common denominator does run through the various promotions for industrial investment: low taxes and low wages. Underdevelopment within a country has become one of the most attractive features for investors. There is an ironic twist to such policies: the way to get rich is to stay poor. Texas and other Southern states have favored "right to work" and other anti-union measures to keep wages down so as to bring in industry, presumably to raise wages. Conversely, it is argued by some that progressive firms that wish to settle in an area and import managerial personnel prefer a better paid highly motivated work force and good schools, roads, and other social services to low wages and low taxes.

IMPACT OF GROWTH

New industry in a locality or region is not an unmixed blessing.[7] The very policies used to attract them, low taxes and low wages, are certainly not desired by wage earners or those who need the benefits of social services. Secondly, it calls into question the very purpose of growth and development. States and localities love to boast of new industries and the payrolls and products they generate. While the payrolls are beneficial to the recipients and to the merchants where they trade, it is highly questionable whether aggregate figures on the growth of state or regional products are of much value as indicators of development. The very low wage, low tax policies result in a smaller portion of the product being left behind to stimulate the local economy. In some cases there are initial tax holidays, public bond issues to fund capital construction, and other financial inducement. With the tax holidays and tax subsidies, who is going to pay the taxes for the social services that economic growth necessitates?

The era of competitive bidding by local and state governments for investments will probably continue for some time. It has been thus far the major policy option for development available to local authorities, that is, other than the exercise of political influence at the national level. There are definite countervailing trends, however, in the offing. A western state invites tourists to visit but not to stay. A city in California seeks to limit growth and is sued by developers. The city is supported by other cities and the developers are joined by associations of their compatriots. An industrial east coast state opposes a port and industrial park development. The battle is joined from coast to coast, as conservationists and others do battle to protect the environment and show more concern for the quality of life rather than quantity.

Though environmentalists make news throughout the nation, their victories are few and not always lasting. The recent energy shortage, renewed commitment to an Alaskan pipeline, and a relaxation of pollution control indicate that in a crisis, maintenance of material living standards takes precedence over maintenance of the quality of life. Though their victories be few, however, the environmentalists have raised issues that must be faced. The very crisis that bodes some gains and many losses for the conservation movement is in itself the strongest argument for conservationist policies. While economists and business leaders were talking about continued unlimited growth, conservationists were recognizing the limits of our environment. While oil and automobile companies were promoting the private automobile and pressuring government to create the roads and freeways, environmentalists were talking about mass transit, bikeways, and the like. Our crises are in a sense the product of expansionist policies, and not only did the conservationists correctly forecast our current difficulties, they also provided the philosophical basis for the way out of them.

Let us look at some areas of Texas as an illustration of the contending attitudes toward growth. Texas has several fast growing metropolitan centers, preeminent among them the Dallas-Fort Worth and Houston-Galveston areas. Conservation movements are alive and well in these areas but politically insignificant. It would not be wrong to say that boosterism prevails: getting bigger is getting better. New population, new industries, and new jobs are counted gleefully, and if the federal census shows these cities to have fewer citizens than the locale imagined, a howl is raised. The question is, who benefits? Even in conventional terms it is highly questionable if any significant portion of the population benefits. New jobs bring new people. To be beneficial, it would have to be shown that the unemployed gain employment or that the currently employed find better employment. New industries mean more tax revenue (even considering tax holidays). However, they also mean a greater need for expenditures, particularly capital expenditures for schools, roads, sewers, parks, and so on. Taxes to pay for most of these capital expenditures, or to retire the bonds that paid for them, are levied district or city wide. Thus it is possible that residents in established neighborhoods are subsidizing the capital expenditures of the newcomers. Even with new roads, traffic congestion increases in metropolitan areas as population is spread out, increasing the distance from home to work or to private and public amenities. More people, traffic, and industry also mean more pollution. Under these circumstances, it would appear that for some sizable portion of the population, growth has meant a decline in the quality of life.

New payrolls mean more paying customers for business enterprises. For the small store or service station owner, however, population growth brings more business for a limited time only, until a new competitor enters the market. Few small businesses benefit by growth, except those whose circumstances allow them to grow bigger or who offer some specialty items predicated on selective minority tastes. The only clearly definable beneficiaries of growth are those enterprises that cater to city-wide or regional markets and therefore have a competitive advantage to expand with the population. As would be expected, this latter group are leading boosters in Texas and in cities across the nation. What is less understandable is that boosterism remains an endemic part of the belief system of most Americans.

It is argued that the immigrants to the cities benefit by urban growth policies. After all, they migrate voluntarily, do they not? Obviously, urban growth reflects the cumulatively better economic opportunities of these areas. Further, many rural areas of Texas are suffering economic decline. Given these factors, the truism of voluntary migration has a limited meaning. Bountiful versus bleak economic opportunities can and obviously do outweigh other factors in population migration. It does not indicate, though, where people would prefer to reside if they could earn a livable income. Until this question can be answered, any assertion about benefits to migrants is meaningless. All it says is that, given current economic policy and established market structures, it is easier for people to earn income in some areas and not in others. It does not mean that these policies and structures cannot be altered if there are good social reasons to do so.

On the assumption that large numbers of rural to urban migrants would rather not move (an assumption for which there is considerable evidence in Texas cities, such as Houston), it is quite likely that the net social costs exceed the social and economic benefits. We have already seen where urban sprawl and overcrowding are being questioned by many. Conversely, many rural areas with already small populations find their numbers diminishing. Many capital facilities, such as schools and stores, are utilized little or not at all, while urban areas are forced to build new ones to accommodate new rural to urban migrants. Reduced population means a reduced tax base to service the debt on these already created capital facilities. This frequently can cause an increase in taxes with no increase in services. Further, many of the out-migrants are the younger, more productive, mobile members of the community. Just as there are cumulative forces for growth, there are also cumulative forces of decline. Increasing taxes with constant or declining services and minimum economic opportunity lead to out-migration, which lowers the tax base, and so on.

CONCLUSIONS

What are the solutions to the economic problems facing Texas and other states? Basically, Texas has been pursuing a policy of growth. Virtually all indices of economic change are growth indices. Development has tended to follow as a natural concomitant because Texas was a part of an economy and culture that was undergoing social transformations that can justifiably be called development. We have now reached a point in the state and in the nation, however, where growth

Conclusions

and development diverge. That does not mean that we still do not need economic growth. There is still considerable poverty in Texas, and we clearly need more product to solve it. Much of the economic growth in the last decade has done little to benefit some of the very poor, such as migrant farm workers in the lower Rio Grande Valley. We need growth there, but we need economic growth that is part of a developmental process that transforms existing social and economic relations, allowing the needy to participate.

Overall, the economic conditions of the 1970s, with problems of urban crowding, pollution, and resource and environmental limitations, require economic development policies that foster growth in some instances but not in others. What is needed are economic policies that are predicated on a theory of economic development that weighs costs and benefits other than those of the market and that recognize the constellation of economic forces and structures. Policies that have brought us to a current state of well-being could have increasingly adverse consequences if blindly carried forward.

We have already seen in the last few years evidence of deterioration in the quality of life for the affluent of Texas and the nation. For the poor in the ghettos of our Texas cities, small increases in income have been matched by breakdowns in social structures and public safety, congestion and the decline of public transit for those without cars, and increasing pollution. The decline in public safety has meant that the affluent have been acquiring more wealth and greater fear of losing it. More growth alone cannot solve these problems.

Unfortunately, there are no easy "development" solutions that can be found in textbooks or that can be expressed in models or other formulas. The first step in a development policy is to recognize the inadequacy of existing formulations. In Texas, and across the nation, there is a growing sense that our economic policy is not working. Whether this malaise can be translated into effective economic development policy depends upon the people and their leaders. Ultimately, this is the most important resource of a state or nation. The true test of the greatness of Texas and Texans will be the ability to respond creatively to the challenge of our time.

NOTES

1. Even here there are hidden value-laden assumptions. Economists speak of the production of "goods," not "bads" or "neutrals." Further, measurement requires that some items be counted and others

not. And items change in quality through time; how can they be quantitatively compared? Government is included in the production of "goods," to the consternation of some. Conversely, there is a definite value assumption concerning market judgments. If an item is legally produced for sale in the market, it is counted. If it is produced for personal use, it generally is not counted. Most introductory textbooks in economics note that maid services are counted for GNP; a wife's services are not. Most of these problems are well known and though it can be argued that growth theory is not as free of value judgments as most of its practitioners would like to think, the thrust of the theorizing in this area is away from any kind of value inquiry.

2. Walter Prescott Webb, *The Great Plains*; idem, *The Great Frontier*.

3. The role of science and technology in creating resources and opening frontiers can be found in the writings of two of Webb's colleagues at The University of Texas and in one of my works. See C. E. Ayres, *The Theory of Economic Progress*, Chapters VI and VII; Erich W. Zimmermann, *World Resources and Industries: A Functional Appraisal of the Availability of Agricultural and Industrial Materials*, Chapter I; and Thomas R. DeGregori, *Technology and the Economic Development of the Tropical African Frontier*, Chapter I.

4. See George M. Foster, *Culture and Contact: America's Spanish Heritage*, Chapters II and XVII, for an analysis of the diffusion and crystallization of an ill-adapted technology at a low level of productivity.

5. Zimmerman, op. cit., Chapter I.

6. Wendell C. Gordon, "Foreign Investments," *Business Review*, p. 14.

7. Probably the best single source on the problems involved in foreign investment can be found in Gordon, op. cit. Though Gordon is writing about investments between countries, most of what he says has significant application to investment within counties.

TWO

THE EVOLUTION OF THE TEXAS ECONOMY

Louis J. Rodriguez*

The post-World War II era, probably as a result of the "Revolution of Rising Expectations," has witnessed a pronounced world-wide preoccupation with economic development. In the United States this thrust has been emphasized at the national, regional, state, and local levels. Most Americans are familiar with our national race to keep ahead of the Russian economy and the efforts of state chambers of commerce to push their states to the forefront in economic growth. Additionally there has been intensive competition among cities to court industries considering relocation or expansion of their facilities. Concern with ecological factors has reduced some of the intensive competition for industry which is not considered to be compatible with environmental needs. Nevertheless, the race for economic growth is still intense. Texas, like other states, has been actively engaged in promoting the growth of its economy. Promotion has taken the form of improvement of the quality of human resources, better utilization of natural wealth and the expansion of social overhead capital such as transportation and power facilities. Government efforts at the state and local levels to promote economic expansion have been considerable.

In generally describing and evaluating Texas' economic growth in the post-World War II era, I will present a brief historical sketch of

---

*The writer is indebted to Dr. Sam Bruno and Dr. Edna Kilgore of the University of Houston at Clear Lake City for their comments on the rough draft of the manuscript. Student Assistant James Price provided much valuable research assistance.

the Texas economy, compare major indicators of economic growth in Texas with the indicators in the United States as a whole, analyze the economic development in the state as it relates to the major positive and negative factors of economic growth, and present an overview of the current status of the Texas economy.

EARLY DEVELOPMENTS

As in most of the United States, the Texas economy evolved from an agricultural base.

> *Cotton, corn and cattle used to be the widespread basis of the Texas economy. Then came oil; next commerce and industry. In deep southeast Texas today rice and sugar cane are staple crops while in the northwest part, especially in the Texas Panhandle, wheat is the money crop. Like most of the United States, industrialization has caused Texas cities to grow at astounding rates. Most Texans today live in cities, but farms, ranches, and oil are still important. In a Texas sunset you can still see the outline of a Brahma bull standing next to a drilling rig.*[1]

To illustrate this, total Texas oil production in 1900 was less than a million barrels, by 1937, it had increased to 510,318,000 barrels, and by 1940 amounted to 493,126,000 barrels.[2]

The movement to develop the Texas economy began before the twentieth century. In 1889 Governor Joseph D. Sayre predicted a continued bleak future for the state if factories were not established. He named dependence upon external industry as one of the apparent reasons that people in the state were having difficulty meeting their obligations. In 1900 commercial clubs in various cities throughout Texas were working for the establishment of local manufacturing plants. During this time of industrial cultivation, the prime effort was to attract textile mills, which were considered especially helpful in bringing wealth and prosperity. Canning factories were also deemed desirable. In 1903 many local clubs formed the Federated Commercial Clubs of Texas, with the major objective of sponsoring and promoting industrial development through the creation of new factories. To attract factories, this group recommended that the state legislature empower cities to grant tax exemptions. The Texas Industrial Congress (TIC) created in 1910, sponsored the development of manufacturing industries.[3]

After World War I, industrial promotion was a chief activity of chambers of commerce. Normally organized along regional bases, they cooperated to the benefit of the entire state. The Texas Planning Board, created in 1935 and limited to a four-year life span, functioned to develop the state's resources. The Board made surveys of the state's economic potential and sought ways to improve social and economic conditions in Texas.[4]

Texas manufacturing plants, increasing in importance, produced approximately $100 million in goods in 1929 and $1.5 billion in 1939, by which time there were 5,376 manufacturing operations in the state. New plants built during 1939 totaled 289, and factory employment increased to 156,787. In terms of the number employed by industry, the state jumped from a national rank of 23 in 1900 to 11 in 1937.

The depression took its toll on Texas industry and the number of producing industrial firms decreased from 5,198 in 1929 to 3,648 by 1933. This decline in the number of units was accompanied by a reduction in the value of manufactured products from $1.45 billion to $687 million. During the same period, 1929-33, the number of wage and salary earners dropped from 156,143 to 91,374.[5]

The Texas economy is commonly identified with oil. While oil is one of the mainstays of the economy, it was not until approximately 1900 that the quest for oil in Texas was more important than the search for water. Frequent efforts, for example, were made to case off the nuisance oil when drillers struck oil in the search for water. Historically, other industries such as shipbuilding, petroleum refining, manufacturing of oil machinery and tools, production of nonferrous metals, milling of flour and other grains, bakery and dairy industries, chemicals, farm equipment, and cotton have played important roles on the Texas economic scene.[6] Possessing excellent natural resources and coastwise shipping for transportation, the state has, over the years, prepared for economic growth. Nevertheless, it required the impact of World War II and promise of government contracts to bring the attention of Texas and out-of-state financial interest to the sleeping economic giant—Texas. Although industry was developing before World War II, truly rapid progress was not realized. This is evidenced in the data in Figure 2-1 and Table 2-1 which present a survey of the sources of income in Texas during 1929-43. It can be noted from the data that petroleum and farm income increased markedly, and total income rose from $1.7 billion in 1929 to $5.8 billion in 1943.

A major trend in the evolution of the Texas economy has been the shift of the state's population from rural areas to urban centers. For example, 3.6 percent of the population in 1850 was urban and 96.4

percent rural. By 1972 the figures were 79.8 percent urban and 21.2 percent rural. The impact of this movement toward the cities has been the creation of a large labor market, essential for attracting and sustaining industrial development. With industrialization came an expansion of organized labor and its influence. Rapidly expanding metropolitan populations have brought problems in transportation, health, and education. The demands upon government have changed rapidly and the base of the economy has been altered. With the location of the Lyndon B. Johnson Space Center in Houston and the orientation toward space research, the Texas economy was greatly influenced by the economics and politics of the space age which meant an era of new economic activity in the state. Historically, each major phase of economic activity—cattle, cotton, oil, industry, and space exploration—has left its imprint upon the Texas socio-economic system.

INDICATORS OF ECONOMIC GROWTH

Indicators of economic advancement include per capita income, personal income, total employment, unemployment, and education of employees. In some instances, the percentage of income derived from manufacturing versus that obtained from agriculture is also an indicator of advancement. This results from the fact that incomes from agriculture generally tend to be lower than those created by industry. One of the best measures of economic performance of an area is real per capita income, for it reflects economic factors such as population, total production, productivity, educational levels, natural resources, and technology.

Table 2-2 presents the performance of the Texas economy in several of the above mentioned categories for selected years, and compares the results in Texas with those of the nation. Significant advances were registered in every category of the Texas economy during the 1950-75 period. The Texas performance can convey meaning, however, only when related to what took place in the rest of the United States.

An analysis of data in Table 2-2 reveals that during 1950-75, personal income increased 600 percent in Texas compared with 654 percent in the United States.[7] The largest single source of personal income in Texas in 1975 was wages and salaries, followed by property income and transfer payments. Between 1950 and 1970, personal income in Texas advanced at an annual compounded rate of 6.9 percent, which was 0.4 of one percentage point greater than in the United

TABLE 2-1

TRENDS OF INCOME IN TEXAS BY PRINCIPAL SOURCES
1929-1943

(In thousands of dollars)

	Value of Minerals:				Farm Cash Income	Farm Subsidies	Value Added by Manufacturing	Total Non-Agricultural Pay Rolls Except Mgf. and Mining	Total
	Petroleum	Natural Gas (At Well)	Sulphur	Other Minerals (Including Natural Gasoline)					
1929	$328,926	$15,343	$43,811	$39,226	$ 665,759	$............	$460,307†	$1,100,973	$2,677,625
1930	288,786	18,644	35,768	49,823	500,300	....	362,398	1,039,001	2,318,065
1931	176,685	10,221	24,760	30,513	349,447	....	272,935	831,970	1,716,062
1932	251,941	10,050	19,946	20,455	285,979	....	254,974	589,022	1,451,156
1933	225,688	11,414	27,139	23,834	360,722	69,534	237,307	570,000	1,665,220
1934	332,826	13,265	23,448	27,310	350,280	40,953	269,987	685,141	1,763,717
1935	356,701	13,490	24,374	31,901	369,879	55,082	306,700	695,959	1,876,538
1936	434,091	16,895	29,353	40,980	425,966	40,683	370,048	788,060	2,171,190
1937	584,427	19,655	36,546	44,337	557,212	35,182	439,854	980,000	2,724,078
1938	537,999	19,414	22,116	29,867	417,043	97,610	446,480	928,000	2,535,429
1939	477,555	20,568	28,498	46,720	439,064	84,321	453,105	935,000	2,512,580
1940	492,833	19,144	32,145	36,514	469,083	75,356	415,357	967,578	2,539,265
1941	560,411	21,726	45,488	63,168	627,095	52,945	529,449	1,219,000	3,146,515
1942	564,000*	22,000*	41,000*	93,000*	990,110	37,642	636,638	1,758,570	4,142,960
1943	714,000*	24,000*	41,000*	95,000*	1,162,000	35,000*	650,000*	2,850,000*	5,571,000*

* Tentative estimate. † From original Census report.
Source: *Texas Looks Ahead: The Resources of Texas*, Vol. 1, University Cooperative Society, Austin, Texas, 1944.

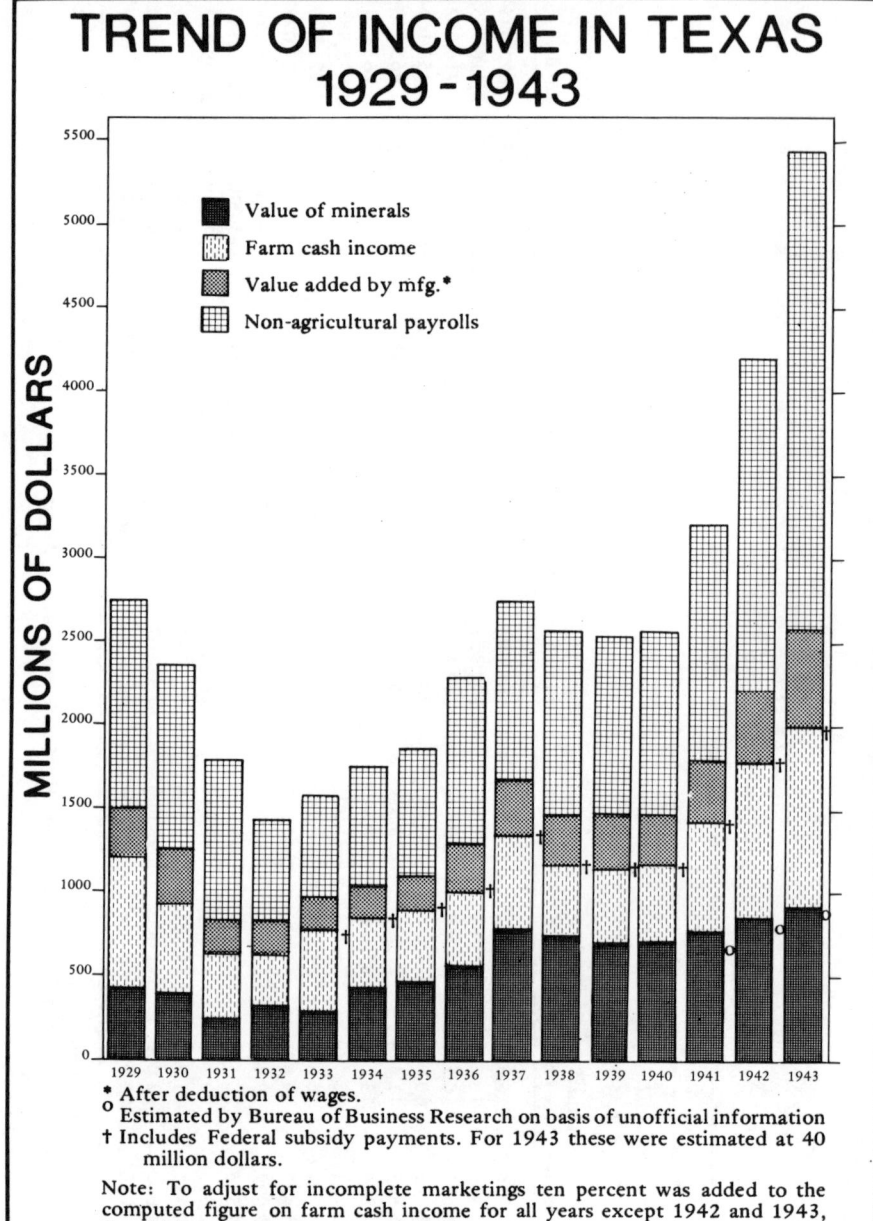

FIGURE 2-1

Source: *Texas Looks Ahead: The Resources of Texas*, Vol. 1, University Cooperative Society, Austin, Texas, 1944. p. 34.

TABLE 2-2

SELECTED ECONOMIC INDICATORS FOR TEXAS AND THE UNITED STATES
1950-1975*

Geographical Area	Years						
	1950	1960	1970	1972	1973	1974	1975
TEXAS							
Personal Income[1]	11	19	41	48	54	60	66
Per Capita Income[1]	1,349	1,931	3,606	4,102	4,632	5,106	5,631
Unemployment[2]	112	182	168	178	194	221	325
Percent	3.9	5.3	3.6	3.7	3.9	4.3	6.1
Employment[3]	1,921	2,532	3,636	3,890	4,146	4,353	4,463
UNITED STATES							
Personal Income[4]	191	325	616	943	1,520	1,153	1,250
Per Capita Income[5]	1,501	2,219	3,935	4,513	5,049	5,486	5,902
Unemployment[6]	3,288	3,852	4,088	4,840	4,304	5,076	7,830
Percent	5.3	5.5	4.9	5.6	5.2	6.1	9.1
Employment[6]	45,222	54,234	70,920	73,714	76,896	78,413	76,301

*Personal income is in billions of dollars; unemployment and employment are in thousands, and per capita income is in dollars. All of the data except the percentage figures have been rounded to the nearest dollar.

Sources:

[1] *Statistical Abstract of U. S. 1973, 1976*, U. S. Department of Commerce, Bureau of the Census, Washington, D. C., 1973, 1976, p. 326, 431.

[2] Ibid., p. 225. "Survey of Current Business," 1976, Summer.

[3] The data is for non-agricultural employment—*Statistical Abstract of the U. S. 1971, 1976*, U. S. Department of Commerce, Bureau of the Census, Washington, D. C., 1971, p. 218 (For 1960 and 1970), 1976, p. 690; Texas Employment Commission (Non-Agricultural Employment), *Employment and Earnings Bulletin No. 1370-8. Statistical Abstract of U. S. 1961*, Department of Commerce, Bureau of Census, Washington, D. C. 1961, p. 211 (for 1960); and *Statistical Abstract of U. S. 1955*, p. 190 (for 1950). For 1950 data includes agricultural employment (2,758).

[4] *Statistical Abstract of U. S. 1973, 1976*.

[5] Ibid., p. 323, p. 405.

[6] Ibid., 1976, p. 1-2.

States. Of the increases during 1950-70 approximately 15 percent were absorbed by population growth, and 35 percent were needed to offset price increases. During 1970-75, personal income increased 61 percent in Texas and 103 percent in the United States.[8]

Personal income between 1950-70 experienced five different cycles, which generally corresponded with the movement of the United States economy. During 1950-52, rapid expansion was experienced in personal income with an annual increase of 10.6 percent. The 1952-54 recession was felt in Texas, and expansion of personal income declined to an annual rate of 2.6 percent. Rapid growth in this economic indicator took place from 1954 to 1957, the annual income increment being 7 percent. For 1954-63, a period which recorded two national recessions, the rate of expansion declined to 4.5 percent. The 1963-70 period registered a marked 9 percent annual increase in personal income in Texas, and 8 percent nationally. During 1950-63, the Texas annual expansion of 5.7 percent was equal to the national average and in 1963-70, the rate increase was nearly 1 percent higher than in the United States. A major development took place during 1950-70 in terms of the origins of income. Whereas agricultural income accounted for 12 percent of the state's total in 1950, this figure dropped to 5 percent by 1963, and contined to diminish into the 1970s.

In terms of unemployment, Texas had a smaller portion of its labor force out of work during the years under study than did the United States. In 1975, for example, the difference was considerable with 6.1 percent of the Texas labor force unemployed as compared with 9.1 percent of the total United States. The data reveal a favorable economic growth pattern for Texas relative to the United States. This reflected in a percentage increase in total employment in Texas between 1950-75 of 132 percent compared with the United States figure of 69 percent. However, in terms of the very important per capita income component, Texas actually lost ground during some of this time, and the situation in 1972 was very similar to what it had been in 1950. This condition can be explained by the population expanding more rapidly in Texas than in the nation.

Of the economic indicators in Table 2-2, per capita income, as has been stated, is the best for conveying a comprehensive view of economic growth. Per capita income in Texas was lower than that of the United States for each of the years presented in Table 2-2. Expressed as percentages of the national average, Texas personal income per capita was 89.9 in 1950, declined to 86.2 in 1970, and increased to 95 in 1975. Over the two decades 1950-70, annual per capita income increased by 4.9 percent in Texas compared with 5 percent nationwide. For the period 1963-70, however, Texas registered annual percentage increases of 7.5 compared with 6.9 for the United States. The situation in 1963-70 is explained primarily by a more rapid increase in personal income and a slower increment in population in Texas when compared with the national rate. Per capita income in Texas was 14 percent less than the national average in 1963, 10 percent less in 1970, and 5 percent less by 1975.

When adjustments in per capita income are made for inflation, the result is an indication of real buying power. For the 1950-70 period, real per capita income in Texas rose by 2.5 percent compounded annually and during 1950-63 the rate was 1.4 percent or $336 in terms of 1958 prices. A sharp rise took place during 1963-70 when annual increases in wages averaged 4.4 percent, or a rise of $711. Over the twenty-year period, 1950-70, the total increment was $1,047, but the national real per capita income increased by $1,202, or $155 more than Texas. Thus the level of income in Texas continued to more closely resemble that of the United States.

Table 2-3 presents information pertaining to the origin of income in Texas. It can be noted from the data that wages and salaries were responsible for 60 percent of total income in 1950 and 65 percent in 1970. Wages and salaries in 1950 accounted for 4 percent more of personal income in the nation than in Texas; however, by 1970 this figure had declined to less than 1 percent. By 1970 manufacturing sources in Texas were responsible for 5 percent less of personal income than for the United States as a whole, but the difference had narrowed since 1950.

Farm wages had dropped from being more important in Texas than

TABLE 2-3

COMPOSITION OF ANNUAL INCOME IN TEXAS
SELECTED YEARS 1950, 1960, 1970
(In percents)

ORIGIN	1950	1960	1970
Wages and Salaries	60	63	65
Proprietors Income	21	14	9
Property Income	11	14	13
Transfer Payments	6	6	9
Other Labor Income	1	3	4
Total	100	100	100

Source: Bower, Leonard: "Personal Income in Texas Accelerates at Rate Faster Than the Nation's." *Texas Resources and Industries,* Bureau of Business Research, Austin, Texas, 1971, pp. 47-52.

in the nation to equal importance by 1970. While mining was more important in Texas than in the United States in 1970, it had declined in relative importance. Government and trade were more important in Texas than in the United States by the end of 1970, but the difference was small. Proprietorships, which had been a much more important source of income in Texas in 1950 than for the United States, were only slightly more significant by 1970. Payments in the form of interests, rents, and dividends were rapidly expanding income components in Texas.

Several trends are discernible from a study of personal income data in Texas during the 1950 to 1970 period. (1) Proprietary organizations such as farms, small businesses, and self-employed workers became relatively less important. (2) Large corporations became more important, and these organizations paid interest, dividends, and large salaries to the managerial group, which helps to explain the leveling off of the growth of proprietary income and the rise in property income. (3) Transfer payments expanded markedly with the two major categories being welfare and unemployment compensation. Increases in contributions to pay for these benefits averaged 13 percent per year. Income from wages and salaries, the most important contributor to personal income, averaged annual compound increases of 7.4 percent. (4) During 1950-70, finance, insurance, and real estate registered the largest annual compound increase in wages and salary income of 9 percent. (5) Services rose at an annual rate of 8.8 percent. (6) Personal income from manufacturing increased by 8.5 percent annually. (7) Payroll income from some sources expanded slowly, with mining, for example, rising at the rate of 4.1 percent yearly over a twenty-year period. This rate declined to 2.8 percent during the 1960-70 decade. (8) Farm wages decreased annually at an average rate of 1.9 percent with most of this decline taking place during the 1950s. The sixties registered some recovery in farm income in Texas.

Overall there was rapid industrialization and urbanization during the 1950 to 1975 period in Texas. By 1975 the state economy more closely resembled that of the nation than in 1950. For 1950-63, Texas generally lagged behind the United States and between 1960-75 the state expanded more rapidly than the nation. The 1950-60 period is explained by a rapid decline in agriculture. A recovery of the farm economy plus rapid industrialization explains the favorable Texas position during 1963-75.

TEXAS ECONOMIC GROWTH FACTORS

The Texas economy possessed several major strengths in its economic growth during the 1950-75 period. As has been previously stated, the state's per capita income increased. The percentage of unemployment was annually lower in Texas than in the nation. Total employment increased at a much more rapid rate in Texas, although some of this expansion probably resulted from a smaller numerical base. Personal income in Texas increased at a faster rate than in the United States. The increased industrialization of the state and the ensuing wage difference between rural and urban areas caused a considerable amount of labor to move from the declining farming areas to rapidly expanding manufacturing regions. This resulted in higher earnings and in 1960, for example, incomes in cities averaged 40 percent more than in rural areas. During the 1960-75 period, while farm workers accounted for about 33 percent of the labor force in rural counties, they registered 85 percent of the decrease in employment.

Population

The strong and rather powerful performance of the Texas economy relative to the national scene and the rapid growth of the Texas economy may, to a large extent, be explained by the increase in population. Table 2-4 presents Texas population for years 1850 to 1975.[9]

According to the data in Table 2-4, between 1960-75, the population of Texas expanded from 9,579,677 to 12,127,000, an increase of 27.7 percent compared with 18.8 for the United States. Texas' net population gain of 1,617,053 during the sixties was the third largest of any state in the United States, surpassed only by California and Florida. In 1960, Texas was the sixth largest state in the nation, and by 1970 it had climbed to fourth position in terms of total population among the states. Of the population increase during the sixties, 98 percent occurred in the state's standard metropolitan statistical areas (SMSA), which reflects the continuous urbanization and industrialization of Texas. Accompanying the increase of population in the metropolitan areas was a decline in the population outside of the SMSAs. Approximately 85 percent of the population increase from 1960-70 took place in SMSAs of 500,000 or more, which in the state included Dallas, Fort Worth, Houston, and San Antonio. These four major metropolitan areas by 1970 accounted for 46 percent of the population as compared with 40 percent in 1960 and 34 percent in 1950.

TABLE 2-4

TEXAS POPULATION, 1850-1975

Year	Population	Increase Over Preceding Decade	Percentage Increase In Decade	Population Per Square Mile
1850	212,592	N/A	N/A	0.8
1860	604,215	391,623	184.2	2.3
1870	818,579	214,364	35.5	3.1
1880	1,591,749	773,170	94.5	6.1
1890	2,235,527	643,778	40.4	8.5
1900	3,048,710	813,183	36.4	11.6
1910	3,896,542	847,832	27.8	14.8
1920	4,663,228	766,686	19.7	17.8
1930	5,824,715	1,161,487	24.9	22.1
1940	6,414,824	590,109	10.1	24.3
1950	7,711,194	1,296,370	20.2	29.3
1960	9,579,667	1,868,483	24.2	36.4
1970	11,196,730	1,617,053	16.9	42.6
1975	12,237,000	1,039,270*	9.3*	45.8

*This represents only a five-year period, 1970-75.

Sources: *Texas Almanac 1972-1973*, The Dallas Morning News, Dallas, Texas, 1973, p. 146; *Historical Statistics of the United States Colonial Times*, Washington, D. C., U. S. Department of Commerce Bureau of the Census, 1960, pp. 12-13; *World Almanac-1977*, Newspaper Enterprise Association, Inc., New York, 1977, p. 701.

The population growth in non-metropolitan counties of Texas during the 1960s registered a very modest 1.3 percent increase, considerably less than the 16.9 percent average for the state. The Panhandle area may be characterized by a loss in population, a few counties in the western and northern boundaries excepted. The data reveal for 1960-70 that 146 of the 254 counties in Texas lost population. By 1970, the population of the state was heavily concentrated along a north-south metropolitan axis extending from Sherman-Dennison in the north to Austin-San Antonio in the south, as well as a southeastern complex including Houston, Galveston-Texas City, and Beaumont-Port Arthur-Orange.

A major component in population changes is the fertility rate. Between 1960-70 about 2,246,200 babies were born to mothers living in Texas. This was offset by 843,600 deaths, leaving a net gain of 1,402,600. During 1960-70 there were 108,200 fewer babies born to Texas mothers than for the comparable period of 1950-60. Texas thus experienced the same general decline in fertility as the United

States after 1957. Accompanying the decline in the birth rate was an increase in the death rate. In the 1960s approximately 161,800 more deaths occurred than had been the case in the 1950s, which represented an increase in mortality of about 23.7 percent.

The net balance between fertility and mortality was a decline in the natural increase of 270,000 (16.1 percent). This resulted in a smaller increase in Texas' population during the 1960s as compared with the 1950s. During the 1960s approximately 213,200 immigrants came to Texas. Birth rates were greater than death rates in all except twenty-nine counties during the 1960s.

Rural-Urban Shift

Among the major factors accounting for the movement of people from the rural to urban areas in Texas was the shift from an agricultural to an industrial society.[10] As previously stated, urban incomes averaged about 40 percent higher than rural earnings in 1960. Additionally, farm workers received on the average only two-fifths as much income as other production workers, whether urban or rural. As farm workers moved from rural to urban areas, wage differences should have been reduced. However, this did not take place. While the emigration from the farms undoubtedly reduced the increase in difference between urban and rural wages, it did not reverse the trend. This is explained by the expanding demand for workers in urban areas and decreased demand in rural areas for traditional types of unskilled labor resulting from the increasing application of technology in agriculture.

Between 1959-68, for example, wages of manufacturing workers in Texas increased nearly twice as much as wages of farm workers. For employment in the average size rural county of Texas not to have declined, the value of the county's agricultural production would have had to increase about fifteen million dollars during the 1960s. The actual results were increases in the neighborhood of two million dollars over this time span. Additional factors accounting for the wage differences were the scarcity of water, particularly in West Texas, and the preference of farm workers for other than agricultural employment in the rural areas. In 1958 farm labor comprised approximately 31 percent of the work force in the rural counties, a proportion declining to 26 percent by 1968.

Farm workers in rural areas are increasingly employed primarily in enterprises that are: (1) supplying goods and business services that are related to agriculture production in the area; (2) in activities supplying goods and business services to residents in local industries; (3) manufacturing concerns that ship outside the area. Between 1958-68 approximately two thousand manufacturing plants were established in rural counties, a development partly explained by the desire of manufacturers to take advantage of low wage levels. Characteristically, these manufacturing plants were small, with three-fourths of them in 1968 employing less than twenty workers. These operations tended to be

TABLE 2-5

INFANT DEATH RATE FOR THE UNITED STATES,
TEXAS AND PLANNING REGIONS
1968-1971*

Geographical Areas	1968	1969	1970	1971
Panhandle	18.7	22.6	26.2	12.6
South Plains	25.1	27.6	23.8	25.9
North Texas	26.4	23.0	22.5	23.0
North Central Texas	22.7	22.5	21.8	19.3
North East Texas	21.8	21.7	21.9	18.2
East Texas	25.9	21.3	23.6	25.9
West Central Texas	18.3	20.8	22.8	21.7
Upper Rio Grande	18.7	18.8	18.6	16.1
Permian Basin	24.7	24.1	25.2	18.8
Concho Valley	22.4	20.2	24.0	25.0
Central Texas	26.7	21.7	24.0	22.6
Capitol	22.1	22.3	19.5	18.2
Brazos Valley	24.0	18.8	26.0	23.7
Deep East Texas	22.7	22.6	19.6	21.7
South East Texas	21.3	22.2	22.2	18.7
Gulf Coast	22.3	20.8	20.5	19.4
Golden Crescent	20.6	18.4	22.7	22.2
Alamo	23.5	23.8	20.0	19.6
South Texas	19.9	14.8	18.4	14.9
Coastal Bend	22.5	19.5	20.2	17.7
Lower Rio Grande	20.1	18.1	19.9	21.1
TEXAS	22.4	21.7	21.4	20.0
UNITED STATES	21.7	20.7	19.8	19.2

*The infant death rate is the number of deaths under 1 year of age divided by the number of live births multiplied by 1,000.

Sources: Texas Health Data Institute. Texas Department of Health, *Vital Statistics*, 1968, 1969, and 1970. Department of Health, Education and Welfare, Public Health Service: Monthly Vital Statistic Report, Vol. 19, No. 12. Texas Office of Economic Opportunity, *Poverty in Texas*, Austin, Texas, 1974, pp. 150-52.

labor intensive, producing such items as apparel, food products, lumber and other building materials. Additionally, these were the types of industries that were geared to reducing transportation costs, with plants being located near the sources of raw materials or near markets for bulky items, such as cement.[11]

The population increase in Texas, by providing labor essential to expanding metropolitan areas, has also provided an incentive for the location of certain types of industries in rural areas. In the absence of these developments the decline of agriculture could possibly have presented a problem to the state as a whole. Such was not the case, however, since manufacturing filled the void created by the decline.

Population Quality

The quality of population in the state was also enhanced during the years under consideration. For example, in 1960, 39.7 percent of the

TABLE 2-6

STATE FISCAL YEARS 1968-1976 BY GROUP
TEXAS COMMUNITY FOOD PROGRAMS

Group	1968	1969	1970	1976
Total Food Stamp Program	34,030	39,349	114,779	983,297
Total Commodity Distribution				
Program	1,395,043	1,464,620	1,525,985	1,733,305
Schools	1,091,511	1,093,747	1,104,119	1,544,289
Welfare (needy individuals)	239,005	277,204	330,714	N/A
Institutions	31,949	32,708	30,620	19,233
Summer Camps	26,078	28,686	29,838	28,479
Child Care Centers (includes				
Head Start)	6,500	27,855	21,718	N/A
Supplemental Food Program	–	4,420	8,976	N/A
Total Food Stamp and Commodity				
Distribution Programs	1,429,073	1,503,969	1,640,784	2,716,602

Source: Texas Department of Public Welfare, *Annual Reports*, 1968, 1969, 1970, 1976. Texas Office of Economic Opportunity. *Poverty in Texas*, Austin, 1972, pp. IX-15.

individuals living in Texas twenty-five years and over had less than an eighth grade education. This figure was reduced to 29.9 percent by 1970. While 24.6 percent of Texans, age twenty-five years or over, were high school graduates in 1960, 25 percent were graduates by 1970; 7.7 percent were college graduates in 1960, and 11.1 percent in 1970. In addition to the positive relationship apparent between education and income, there is the reality that sophisticated skills are more significant in an industrialized society than in rural areas. The rise in the educational level as the population increased aided the economic expansion of the state during 1950-70.[12]

Health is another aspect of population significantly affecting economic activity. In a given population, there appears to be a relationship between the level of income and the health of its individuals. For example, the United States Department of Health, Education, and Welfare in its report, *Delivery of Health Services for the Poor*, indicated that:

Among persons of family incomes less than $2,000, about 29 percent have chronic conditions with limitations of activity, as contrasted with 7.5 percent among persons with a family income of $7,000 or more. Persons with family income of less than $2,000 have more than double the days of restrictive activity a year than persons on incomes of $7,000 or more. In the working age group, 45-64, the lower income group has three and one half times as many disability days, 39.5 in the under $2,000 income group as compared to 14.3 in the over $7,000 income group. A larger portion of persons who lived in lower income families had multiple hospital episodes than those in higher income groups. The length of hospital stay is longer for the poor . . . and they are more often hospitalized for nonsurgical conditions. This exists in spite of the fact that the poor are much less likely to have hospital insurance to cover bills.[13]

One of the indicators of the health of a population is the infant death rate. Table 2-5 presents the Texas death rate of infants in 1968, 1969, 1970, and 1971 according to geographical areas, to the entire state, and to the United States. During 1968, the infant rate in Texas was 22.4; by 1969 it was 21.7; in 1970 it was 21.4; and in 1971, 20.0. But also, in 1971 the infant death rate in Texas was 17.9 for the Anglo population, 19.3 for the Latin, and 29.4 for the Black. To reduce the high percentage of infant deaths caused by communicable diseases and to improve the general health and private medical and dental care, the state increased free public health resources. To improve the nutritional standards of its population, the state has sponsored food stamp and school lunch programs, as shown in Table 2-6. During 1968, 1,395,045 people received surplus commodities in Texas, and 34,030 received food stamps. During the fiscal year 1976, surplus commodities were issued to 1,733,305 and food stamps to 983,297. During 1968-76, the total participation in food distribution programs increased from 1,429,073 to 2,716,602 individuals, a 90.1 percent jump.[14]

Natural Resources

Natural resources have been another major component helping the economic expansion of Texas.[15] The state has a wide variety of mineral resource in the production of approximately twenty-five types of basic rock minerals. The two basic categories are mineral fuels and non-fuel minerals, which include chemical raw materials, low unit value raw materials, industrial mineral raw materials, and full metallic minerals. Mineral resource industry production/value expanded from a modest beginning in the middle of the 1800s to one billion dollars by the early 1940s and to $13.8 billion by 1974. By far the most important in this group during the last three or four decades has been the production of oil and gas. The value of production of non-fuel minerals, still relatively insignificant compared with the output of fuel minerals, has been increasing at a faster rate than that of oil and gas in recent years. Much of this production is the result of population and industrial growth in Texas.

Oil and gas production account for about 90 percent of the total value of mineral output in Texas. Not only valuable in their own right, these minerals also support many industrial activities by providing either basic raw materials or industrial fuels. The value of mineral fuel production increased markedly during 1950-58. Output, however, declined in the late fifties, remained relatively steady throughout the early 1960s, and has made modest annual increases since 1964. International crises have put a new importance on the production of these two particular minerals in Texas.

Coal is another mineral fuel found in Texas, expecially along the coastal plain. At the turn of the century more than one hundred mines were operating in the state, but with the introduction of natural gas, most of these operations were closed. At present three large lignite mines operate in East Texas. At Rockdale in Milam County, the plant uses considerable quantities of lignite to generate power for processing aluminum brought in from foreign sources via the Texas Gulf coast. In Limestone County, another operation is using large quantities of lignite as industrial fuel for generating power for electric utilities. South of Marshall, lignite is used for processing a non-fuel material—activated carbon. Estimates on the size of reserves of coal and lignite in Texas range from ten to twenty billion tons. Given the new development in terms of energy, these deposits are assuming unprecedented importance. It appears that there are sufficient coal sources to supply Texas' electrical needs for three hundred years.

Uranium is found in South Texas. First developed in the 1950s, uranium operations lessened with the closing of a major mill in Karnes County, but increased again in 1968 with major uranium exploration. When the Karnes County plant was opened several new deposits were discovered, and mills were constructed. Major reserves of uranium are probably restricted to the South Texas area, because efforts to extend South Texas mining trends eastward have been unsuccessful. Uranium deposits in other parts of Texas, especially in Northwest Texas, are marginal, and appear to be economically unfeasible.

There is a group of non-ferrous minerals available in Texas. Chemical raw materials include sulphur, limestone, shell for lime, dolomite, salt, and natural sodium sulfate. Sulphur production has been cyclical since 1950, partly caused by variations in world supply and demand. Current estimates suggest one hundred seventy million long tons in the entire Gulf coast, with approximately one half located in coastal Texas, and a hundred million ton reserve in West Texas. Recovery of sulphur from sour gas is a secondary source.

The second important raw material produced in the state and used by the chemical industry is salt. Essential for the manufacture of chemicals, salt production in 1971 was approximately fifteen times that of 1950. Lime is another important chemical in industrial processing. Its production in 1971 amounted to approximately $22 million, about ten times the value of the 1950 output.

Shell, sand, gravel, coarse stones, and ceramic clays are also available in the state of Texas. Metallic raw minerals while not currently important, in terms of volume include lead, zinc, silver, molybdenum, mercury, and manganese, all found in the central Texas mineral region and in parts of Trans Pecos Texas. Operations in these areas tend to be minor because of small deposits and marginal quality. Some copper is mined in North Texas and low-grade iron ores are found in East and Central Texas. Siderite and limonite ores in East Texas have been used in steel making. Mining of these deposits has been hindered by the lack of local coking coal although new technological processes may alter the situation. It is possible that the high-alumina clays of East Texas may be future sources of aluminum.

The Texas economy is dependent to a large degree on minerals, primarily the output of crude oil and natural gas, for its well-being.

For approximately forty years, mineral fuels have been responsible for over 90 percent of the total value of minerals in Texas. But in the last twenty years, the production of non-ferrous minerals within the state has risen at a faster rate than that of fuel minerals, indicating development of the Texas mineral industry on a broader base. The current output in terms of value on non-fuel minerals is 2.6 times greater than in 1950 and the production of mineral fuel approximately twice that of 1950.[16]

Texas has a land area with a considerable amount of variety in terms of agricultural diversity. Forests are important, and the restoration in Texas to combat the exhaustion of timber resources has been one of the state's major victories of the twentieth century. Before 1930 timber resources were widely exploited. Since the thirties, public and private efforts have reduced forest fires, increased tree planting, and fostered natural growth of timbers. As a result, annual tree growth in principal forest areas of East Texas exceed harvests by approximately 28 percent per year.

Conservation of Texas' forest resources has been the concern of federal bureaus, state agencies, district and county governments, timber producers, processors, and wood products manufacturers. This resource has been a major plus in the economic expansion of the state.[17]

Water is an important natural resource. The rainfall in many parts of the state however, is insufficient. Were it evenly distributed, the annual rainfall in Texas would be adequate. Reservoirs of water underlie more than half of the surface area of Texas. Long a major source of municipal water supplies, these reservoirs now depend increasingly on surface water because of the depletion of aquifer sources. Over one half of the total Texas crop values are produced with irrigation, primarily from the Ochlala formation on the high plains. There are approximately thirty-seven hundred running streams with a combined length of eighty thousand miles draining 263,513 square miles within the state of Texas. Additionally, many smaller streams are present within the state. A major development in this century has been the increase in the number of Texas reservoirs, which have helped to improve water conservation and supplies.

Wildlife is abundant in the state. It has more than 540 species of birds—three-fourths of all different species to be found in the United States are identified in Texas. Among states, Texas ranks third in sales of fishing licenses, fourth in hunting permits, and with its 142 species of mammals, ranks third.

Because of its great size, Texas offers great climatic diversity that is generally favorable for a wide variety of human activity. However, the unpredictable fluctuations in rainfall, temperature, and wind continually challenge agriculturalists, businessmen, and public officials. Agriculture is nevertheless a big business in Texas and the agribusiness industry annually contributes approximately $10.1 billion to the economy of the state. Although only about 3.8 percent of the state's population is engaged in actual farm production, agriculture and related activities employ approximately 25-30 percent of the labor force.[18] In addition to the uncertainty of water sources mentioned above, temperatures are often a problem to producers, particularly growers of fruits and vegetables. Freezing temperatures in the lower Rio Grande Valley, in 1961 and 1962, were disastrous. Improvements in forecasting techniques have minimized some of the unfavorable effects of capricious weather on economic activities in the state, but adverse climate remains a negative factor in many parts of the state.

Government

The public sector has been actively involved in the post-World War II spurt of economic development.[19] The Texas Industrial Commission (TIC), intent on promoting the economic development of the state, has sponsored a variety of instructional programs:[20]

1. Assistance in training industrial development teams

2. Texas Industrial Planning Seminars (TIPS) to design the initial steps that a community should take to organize a program to attract industry

3. Clinics on economic development for communities wishing to attract industry

4. Project simulations permitting local industrial development teams to practice presentations and techniques in selling a community

5. Special seminar programs to cover the needs and topics identified by the requesting organization

6. Seminars in business opportunities to assist small minority business owners or prospective owners

7. State procurement seminars held four times yearly in small Texas cities to instruct minority business owners on doing business with state and federal agencies and private business firms

8. Special seminars for minority business operations conducted with the Small Business Administration (SBA) with people provided

by Texas colleges and universities.

In addition to its educational services, TIC offers these consulting services: (1) community analysis clinics to pinpoint specific advantages or disadvantages of a community, as compared to cities of similar size; (2) industrial site evaluations for analyzing the industrial potential of local properties; (3) management consulting for small minority businesses; and (4) assistance in organizing and conducting market surveys.

As a service in industrial financing, the TIC assists in organizing foundations for local industrial development by: (1) raising funds for such foundations; (2) establishing procedures for economic development and policies for local development corporations; (3) selling industrial revenue bonds; (4) establishing finance programs for rural industry; (5) assisting local packaging for small minority owned business; and (6) developing of secondary sources of funds for purchasing loan paper of small minority businesses.

The TIC also assists in research and special activities such as state comprehensive industrial development plans, community plant location profile programs, community analysis reports, special industries studies, research on trends in Texas industrial economic development, and surveys of minority owned business in Texas.

Industrial prospective services are provided by the TIC. These include prospect development, screening, and dissemination; out-of-state prospect tours; in-state prospect tours; industrial suspect lists, and special suspect lists. Industrial expansion services of the TIC include: (1) assistance in organizing and conducting an expansion program for existing industry, (2) beginning start up industrial training programs, (3) assistance in organizing and conducting foreign trade missions, (4) on-seminar missions, and (5) international trade leads bulletin.

Awards and internships encourage economic development in the state. Some of these are: (1) the governor's industrial expansion award, (2) the citizen's aid award, and (3) the industrial development internship program. TIC also has combined programs of instruction and consultation, and makes available growth industry and advance in industrial development seminars, special consulting services, and professional consulting services.[21]

The Texas Industrial Commission is given as an example of government activity to promote economic development. Texas has been rather successful in combining public and private efforts to attract industry, such as the LBJ Space Center and military bases with their sizeable payrolls. In 1965 Texas was second only to California in the amount of payroll disbursements for military and civilian salaries related to defense payrolls. The sum, $1.2 billion, represented 4.8 percent of total personal income in the state of Texas.[22]

DEVELOPMENT OBSTACLES

While the Texas economy accomplished a great deal in the post-World War II period, it also had failings. In 1970, for example, the poverty rate in Texas was 18.8 percent of its population, and 48.6 percent in the Lower Rio Grande survey region. The comparable rate for the United States was 13 percent, so Texas, with 5 percent of the nation's population, accounted for approximately 10 percent of the country's poor.[23] Furthermore, there were approximately 2.5 million poor in Texas in 1971, and the incidence of poverty was higher for each level of education than in the rest of the country. In the United States as a whole, only 19 percent of the persons who had an elementary school education were poor as compared with 42 percent in Texas. Among college graduates, 3.5 percent were poor in Texas while the national figure was 2 percent.

The incidence of poverty in the state was much higher for Mexican-Americans (35.5%) and blacks (38.6%) than it was for Anglos (10.4%). While blacks and Mexican-Americans accounted for 30 percent of the population in 1971, they made up 60 percent of the poor.[24] Almost one-fourth of the poor (24.2%) but only 9.2 percent of the total population lived in over-crowded housing in Texas. Table 2-7 presents the incidence of poverty by school years completed for the population twenty-five years of age and over in Texas and the United States. It should be noted that the one year difference from 1970 to 1971 gives Texas an advantage in the comparison.

While unemployment for Texas in 1971 was 3.2 percent, that for the state's Blacks was 5.2 and for Mexican-Americans 6.2. This indicates the need to absorb into the economy an increasing number of individuals from these two minority groups. The infant death rate has been declining in Texas; however, as previously indicated, the decline has been slower than that of the whole United States. In 1968, the Texas rate was 22.4 percent while that for the nation was 21.7 percent. In 1973 the comparable figures were 19.2 and 17.7 percent.

In terms of health in 1972, Texas ranked among the top four states in the incidence of two major communicable diseases. With only 5.5 percent of the nation's population, Texas reported 27 percent of all diphtheria cases in the United States, 14 percent of all poliomyelitis cases, 26 percent of all leprosy cases, 5 percent of all measles cases, and 6 percent of all pertussis.[25] Despite the considerable efforts that have been made to improve them, health and nutrition problems, particularly among migrant workers, remain. In reference to a study made in Hidalgo County in July 1970, Dr. Raymond M. Wheeler, an internist from Charlotte, North Carolina testifying before the Senate Subcommittee on Migratory Labor on July 20, said:

High blood pressure, diabetes, urinary tract infections, anemia, tuberculosis, gall bladder and intestinal disorders, eye and skin diseases were frequent findings among the adults . . . . Almost without exception, intestinal parasites are found in stool specimens examined. Most of the children had chronic skin infections, chronically infected inner ears with resulting partial deafness occurring in an amazing number of the smaller children. We saw rickets of a sort thought to be nearly abolished in this country and every form of vitamin deficiency known to us that could be identified by clinical examination was reported.[26]

TABLE 2-7

INCIDENCE OF POVERTY BY EDUCATION FOR TEXAS AND THE U. S.
(In percents)

Educational Groups	U. S., 1970	Texas, 1971
8th grade or less	19.2	42.9
Part High School	11.7	26.9
High School Graduate	5.6	10.9
Part College	4.5	6.3
College Graduate	4.0	3.5

Sources: "Texas Household Survey, May 1971." Department of Commerce, Bureau of the Census; *Current Population Reports*, Series No. 77, p. 60. Texas Office of Economic Opportunity. *Poverty in Texas*, Austin, Texas, 1971, pp. III-1-III-14.

By 1970, educational levels in Texas lagged behind those of the United States in terms of school years completed. In spite of progress, 9.3 percent of Texans in 1970 had less than five years of education compared with 5.5 percent in the rest of the United States. During the same year, 47.4 percent of Texans had four or more years of high school, or other formal training, while the United States figure was 52.3 percent.

These negative aspects, in view of the fine achievement of the Texas economy in the post-World War II period, indicate that a great deal remains to be done. The degree of economic progress yet to be realized can be noted in per capita income: compared with other states in the union, Texas ranked thirty-fourth in 1950 and thirty-first in 1975.[27] While this indicates considerable advances, it also reveals that there is much room for improvement.

SUMMARY

The evolution of the Texas economy, particularly between 1950-70, has been marked by several major developments and trends. With the coming of the great importance of oil and gas, Texas resource bases has assumed unprecedented value. The rise of manufacturing and the decline of agriculture has brought about a higher standard of living. Pronounced population increases provided labor in the rapidly expanding industrial sector. Population in Texas became increasingly clustered in Standard Metropolitan Statistical Areas of over 100,000 people. While gains have been registered in per capita income, Texas' was still only 95 percent of the national average by 1975. Major shifts in origins of income in Texas have been marked by an increase in the importance of wages and salaries and a decline of proprietor income. During the post-World War II period, the Texas economy increasingly resembled that of the nation. Educationally, Texans lag behing the other Americans in terms of average years completed. The health of the Texas population remains a problem in the state, and Texas has a higher rate of infant deaths than do the other states. The incidence of dangerous diseases also occurs more frequently in Texas than in the rest of the United States. State and local governments have generally been positive factors in the state's economic development. Specifically, the Texas Industrial Commission has made a major, positive contribution to the development of the Texas economy.

NOTES

1. Charles H. Ball, *Texas Real Estate* (Houston: Gulf Publishing Company, 1969), p. 1.

2. *Texas Almanac* (Dallas: The Dallas Morning News, 1940), pp. 229-235.

3. Ralph W. Steen, *Twentieth-Century Texas* (Austin: Steck Company Publishers, 1942), pp. 83-85.

4. For an excellent, thorough coverage of Texas resources through the early 1940s see: *Texas Looks Ahead: The Resources of Texas*

vol. 1, (Austin: University of Texas Board of Regents, 1944), pp. 1-365.

5. *Texas Almanac*, op. cit., pp. 90-239.

6. Wilburn E. Benton, *Texas: Its Government and Politics*, 3d ed. (Inglewood Cliffs, N. J., 1966), pp. 24-29.

7. The reader should keep in mind the distorting effects of having one base which is considerably larger than the other.

8. Most of the data on personal income in Texas, by Leonard C. Bower, was obtained from *Business Review* (Federal Reserve Bank of Dallas, May 1971). The article was reprinted in *Texas Resources and Industries*, Bureau of Business Research, The University of Texas at Austin, Austin, Texas, pp. 47-52.

9. Much of the information dealing with population came from Benjamin S. Bradshaw and L. Dudley Poston, "Texas Population in 1970," *Texas Business Review*, Federal Reserve Bank of Dallas, XLV, no. 5 (May, 1971).

10. Information for this section comes from Kenneth Wieand, "Wage Differentials per Rural-to-Urban Movement," *Business Review*, The Federal Reserve Bank of Dallas, April, 1971. The article is reprinted in *Texas Reserves and Industries*, Bureau of Business Research, The University of Texas at Austin, Austin, Texas, 1971, pp. 43-46.

11. For a brief evaluation of the pluses and minuses of industrialization in Texas, see: Stanley Walker, *Texas*, (New York: The Viking Press, 1961), pp. 153-166.

12. For a more detailed analysis of the role of education on poverty in the state of Texas, see *Poverty In Texas* (Austin: Texas Office of Economic Opportunity, May 1974), Chapter 5.

13. U. S. Department of Health, Education, and Welfare. Office of the Assistant Secretary, *Delivery of Health Services for the Poor* (Washington: Government Printing Office, 1967).

14. Texas Public Welfare, *Annual Reports*, 1968, 1969, 1970, and 1976.

15. For a summary of Texas resources and conservation effort, see: Harry Hansen (ed.), *Texas, A Guide to the Lonestar State*, rev. ed. (New York: Hastings House Publishers, 1969), pp. 15-29.

16. Much of the information dealing with minerals in the state is taken from W. L. Fisher, *Texas in the Seventies: Mineral Resources and Industries*, Bureau of Business Research, The University of Texas at Austin, Austin, Texas, 1971, pp. 219-223.

17. *Texas Almanac* (Dallas: The Dallas Morning News, 1976),

p. 122.

18. Robert Orton, "Climatology at Work in Texas," *Texas Business Review* XLI, no. 8 (August, 1967). Also, *Texas Almanac*, 1974-1975, p. 445.

19. For a summary coverage of Texas regulation of economic activities, see: Clifton McClesky, *The Government and Politics of Texas*, 2d ed. (Boston: Little, Brown & Company, 1966), pp. 398-462.

20. There are other governmental units that have played prominent roles in the economic development of Texas. Because of the general nature of this essay and the fact that some of these activities will be covered in essays in this collection, the writer did not comment on their contributions.

21. This summary of information on TIC activities was obtained from Edwin F. G. Latta, *Texas Industrial Commission Programs and Services*, January, 1973, pp. 1-33.

22. Stanley A. Arbingast and Dennis Richardson, "Military Payrolls and the Texas Economy," *Texas Business Review*, XLI, no. 3 (March 1967).

23. *News Release* (Austin: Texas Office of Economic Opportunity, August 3, 1972); *Poverty In Texas*, May, 1974, p. 198.

24. Ray Marshall, Foreword, *Poverty In Texas* (Austin: Texas Office of Economic Opportunity, June, 1972; also May, 1974, p. 198.

25. *Poverty In Texas* (Austin: Texas Office of Economic Opportunity, 1972), pp. IX-7; also 1974, p. 12 and pp. 157-158.

26. Hearings before the Subcommittee on Migratory Labor, a Committee on Labor and Public Welfare, United States Senate, Ninety-first Congress, July 20, 1970, part 8-A.

27. *Statistical Abstract of the United States* (Washington: U. S. Department of Commerce, 1973), p. 326; also 1976, p. 714.

THREE

NATURAL RESOURCES IN TEXAS
Jared E. Hazleton

Natural resources have shaped not only the economic development of Texas but also its social and political development. In the nineteenth century, the economy of Texas was based largely on the exploitation of the state's abundant land resources. Conscious public policies were adopted to promote settlement on state-owned land. The open range gave rise to the longhorn cattle industry which, under the unrelenting pressure of the westward movement of settlers, gave way to the development of farming and ranching. Thus, Texas was born as an agricultural state dominated by rural interests and values.

The turn of the century witnessed the development of a new resource orientation for the state. The discovery of oil at Spindletop marked the beginning of the petroleum industry in Texas. Mineral resource exploitation soon led to the establishment of processing industries as petrochemical manufacturing took root. While agriculture continued to play an important role in the state's economy, marked by increasing output and the development of food processing industries, the former dominance of this sector gradually gave way to the mining industry.

By mid-century, Texas was no longer a rural state—and nearly 60 percent of the population was classified as urban. By 1970 the figure had risen to 80 percent. Reflecting in part the increasing urbanization of the state, Texans in recent years have become concerned not only with the efficient exploitation of the state's natural resources but also with the conservation of these resources and protection of environmental quality. Thus, much of the public discussion about resources today centers on problems of controlling land use, preventing air and water pollution, and expanding recreational facilities. In addition, there is a renewed concern today with water scarcity. The energy crisis of 1973 turned attention back to the petroleum industry with concern focused on the impact of declining domestic oil and gas reserves, the development of alternative sources of energy, and the future of the state's refining and petrochemical industries.

Some important natural resource concepts will be presented here, followed by sections describing the physical features of Texas and the state's renewable and non-renewable resources, concluding with a brief discussion of major natural resource policy issues in Texas.

NATURAL RESOURCE CONCEPTS

Economists have developed a number of useful concepts which help improve our understanding of natural resources and the role they play in the economy. Natural resource development and protection of environmental quality may be viewed as a materials balance problem for the entire economy.[1] A simplified diagram which depicts the general relations between the economy and the natural environment is shown in Figure 3-1.

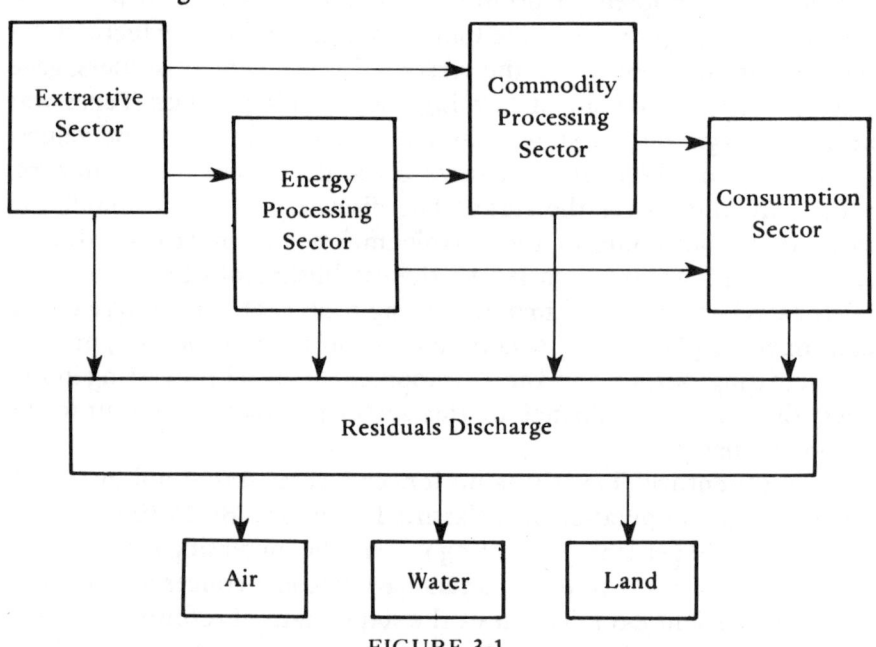

FIGURE 3-1

THE ECONOMY AS A MATERIALS BALANCE SYSTEM

Our economy may be thought of as a throughput process: we extract ores, fossil fuels, nutrients, and other materials from the environment; we process these into energy and commodities which are then "consumed" by the economy; in so doing, we produce negative outputs of pollutants, that is, by-products of production and consumption with negative values; we dispose of these wastes in pollutable reservoirs in the natural environment, in what Kenneth Boulding has termed "negative mines."[2]

One advantage of viewing the economy in this way is to stress that there is no such thing as "final consumption"—think of the piles of junk cars that litter the countryside. When we speak of consumption of certain commodities, we are actually referring to the consumption of services rendered by them. Their material substance remains in existence either to be reused or to be disposed of in the natural environment. The total tonnage of materials extracted for use by an economy, if we assume no foreign trade or capital accumulation, would be approximately equal to that of waste products generated by the economy in the long run.

While this analysis may be thought to be unduly academic, its implications for natural resource development and conservation are clear. First, production of goods and services in a growing economy requires increasing amounts of raw materials which are subject to varying degrees of depletion. Thus, one important public policy concern is with the exhaustion of natural resources. Second, production and consumption of goods and services inevitably result in the production of wastes which must be discharged into the natural environment. The disposal of these wastes into the air, the water, and the land often causes environmental degradation. This process gives rise to the second public policy concern over deterioration in the quality of the environment.

Definition of Natural Resources

Classical economics treated resources as a single entity for analysis, subsumed under the term land. This led to the identification of resources with substances, or tangible things. Later analysis resulted in the development of a functional concept of resources, stressing that the word resources does not refer to a thing or substance but to a function which a thing or substance may perform.[3] The function is to attain a given end, the satisfaction of man's wants.

This semantic advancement has several important implications.

Resources should be defined in terms of known technology. For example, mineral deposits which are unknown, or which are inaccessible, or which cannot be processed and used with known technology and given current costs, are not in this sense resources. An equally important implication is that resources should be defined in relation to the needs of man. This leads to the conclusion that pollution, the deterioration in the quality of a resource, should be defined and analyzed in the context of its effect in impairing the serviceability or usefulness of that resource to man.

Resources are generally classified as either being renewable or nonrenewable. Nonrenewable resources are those whose stock or supply is fixed by geological considerations. For example, there is a finite amount of coal in the earth. When this resource is depleted, it is gone forever, never to be available for use again. Renewable resources, on the other hand, are not considered fixed in amount. They include soil, water, and air—all of which have the capacity to regenerate their serviceability. One can harvest the flow of services of renewable resources indefinitely, provided care is taken not to exceed the maximum sustainable yield, that is, the long-run regenerative capacity of the resource. Thus, renewable resources are seen to be less subject to finite limits. While it is true that the stock of soil, water, and air available to man is as limited as the amount of coal, oil, and copper, the services capable of being rendered by the latter are fixed.

The traditional dichotomy, however, is not entirely satisfactory. Some nonrenewable resources are in fact renewable at least in part through recycling and reuse. Further, the services capable of being rendered by nonrenewable resources are affected both by technology and development. By the same token, the serviceability of renewable resources can be greatly restricted or enhanced by man's actions. If the regenerative capacity of a renewable resource is exceeded, the resource may become degraded or endangered. Soil made infertile through excessive use does not regenerate in and of its own accord. Overharvesting of fish and animal populations may render them extinct. On the other hand, terracing of sloping farmland may increase soil productivity and selected breeding of plants and animals may improve both the quantity and the quality of the annual yield.

Thus, the distinction between nonrenewable and renewable resources is much less useful than first believed. In fact, the degree of renewability of a resource depends in large measure on the actions taken by man. However, the distinction has been very important in setting priorities for man's concern.

Concern Over Nonrenewable Resources

Traditional concern over resource sufficiency focused attention on the stock of nonrenewable resources. The economic literature of the nineteenth century is replete with dire predictions of impending resource scarcity in such vital raw materials as coal. Around the turn of the century The Conservation Movement of the United States emphasized the need to conserve natural resource stocks for the use of future generations. Even as recently as 1952, the President's Materials Policy Commission (the Paley Commission) expressed concern over diminishing supplies of "evident, cheap, and accessible" resources.

It would be expected that increasing scarcity of nonrenewable resources would result in a secular increase in their price. However, economic studies reveal that the relative unit costs of extractive and agricultural goods have remained constant, while those of minerals have fallen over the past century.[4] Analysis shows that in those instances in which resource scarcity has developed, the inevitable result has been an increase in price which in turn has stimulated the discovery or development of alternative resources, not only equal in economic quality but often superior to those replaced.

Close examination of the likely existing reserves of the major raw materials reveals no evidence of developing shortage over the remaining years of this century.[5] In those few instances in which the short run outlook is for shortage, given the existing price structure and state of technology, there is good reason to believe that in the long run, changes in price will encourage the development of new sources of supply or the substitution of alternative materials for most uses. Thus, the market provides a built-in mechanism for dealing with natural resource scarcity in the form of sociotechnical change which is brought into force by an increase in the price of a raw material. It is sociotechnical change then, that helps maintain resource sufficiency.

Concern Over Renewable Resources

Even if one accepts the probability that the world will not face serious resource depletion over the remaining years of this century, it should be recognized that the price system is not completely infallible. While the market system works to ensure the continued availability of nonrenewable resources, it may fail to prevent the impairment of the quality of renewable resources.

Residual wastes as noted previously are an inherent part of the economy of a modern state. If they cannot be recycled, they must be discharged into the air, the land, or the water. These, together with the living organisms which they house, constitute the renewable resources. They are interrelated in a manner that has caused them to be considered as a single entity called the biocycle. All living things draw their sustenance from air, water, and soil in various combinations and make their home within one or more of these aspects of nature. They form the environment for the living creatures within them.

Population growth and increasing urbanization and affluence have led to a greater and more concentrated volume of residual waste discharge into the environment. The transformation of technology which has supported economic growth since the end of the second World War has significantly increased the damage done by the discharge of residual wastes into the natural environment.[6] It is not surprising that we are today witnessing a repetition of the pessimistic resource forecasts of the last century, only with concern shifted from the nonrenewable to the renewable resources. The increasing volume and more harmful nature of residual waste discharges have resulted in our exceeding the regenerative capacity of many of our renewable resources and a deterioration in the quality of the environment.

The deterioration of a renewable resource may give rise to changes in its price and stimulate corrective action. We might expect, for example, that an increase in the price of water will make us take more effective efforts to conserve our water supplies. However, one cannot be complacent about sole reliance on market forces to take care of the allocation of renewable resources. For unlike the nonrenewable resources, the market functions less efficiently in providing for the sufficiency of renewable resources.

The basic distinction between renewable and nonrenewable resources is that the latter are almost always vested with property rights, while many of the former are "free goods" in the sense that they are common property resources. As Garrett Hardin has pointed out, common property resources are inevitably overused, since there exists no incentive for the individual to practice efficient use.[7] Another way of explaining the failure of markets to efficiently allocate renewable resources is to emphasize that the overuse of these resources imposes costs on society rather than on the firm or individual.[8] Thus, the market frequently fails to effectively allocate renewable resources creating the necessity for public policy to deal with problems of pollution and other forms of environmental degradation.

TEXAS: A LAND OF CONTRASTS[9]

The evolution and development of the resource base and public policies toward natural resources in Texas illustrate many of the concepts discussed above. Texas is richly endowed with both renewable and nonrenewable resources. This endowment is closely related to the physical diversity of the state.

Texas has a total area of 267,339 square miles, which amounts to about 7 percent of the total water and land area of the United States. A land of contrasts, the state includes twenty-three million acres of forests, 6,300 square miles of lakes and streams, over ninety mountain peaks above 1 mile in height, and 3,359 miles of shoreline along its 375-mile Texas Gulf Coast. In geological terms, Texas forms the intersection for four major physiographic subdivisions of North America: the Gulf Coastal Forested Plains, the Great Western Lower Plains, the Great Western High Plains, and the Rocky Mountain Range.

The wide variation in Texas geography and climate make concise descriptions difficult. The state is generally divided into eighteen major physiographic regions, ten principal climatic and vegetation areas, and fourteen soil subdivisions. The more important features are shown in Figure 3-2 and all are described below in terms of the four principal land regions of the state.

The Coastal Plains

The Coastal Plains stretch southeastward from the Sabine River to the Rio Grande, extending inland from the Gulf of Mexico to the Balcones Escarpment. The latter feature is a geological fault running from a point on the Rio Grande near Del Rio to Travis County in the center of the state where it breaks into severals fingers extending all the way to the Red River on the Oklahoma border. The Balcones Fault divides the state roughly into a lowlands and uplands area. Below the fault, the surface is generally composed of deposits of soil brought down from above. Above the fault, the surface is characteristically eroded.

The eastern portion of the Coastal Plains contains the *Piney Woods*, a picturesque area of sixteen million acres extending from the eastern boundary of the state inland for 75 to 125 miles and running from the Red River on the north to within 25 miles of the Gulf Coast on the south. This region receives from forty to sixty inches of rain yearly and contains most of the state's large commercial timber production.

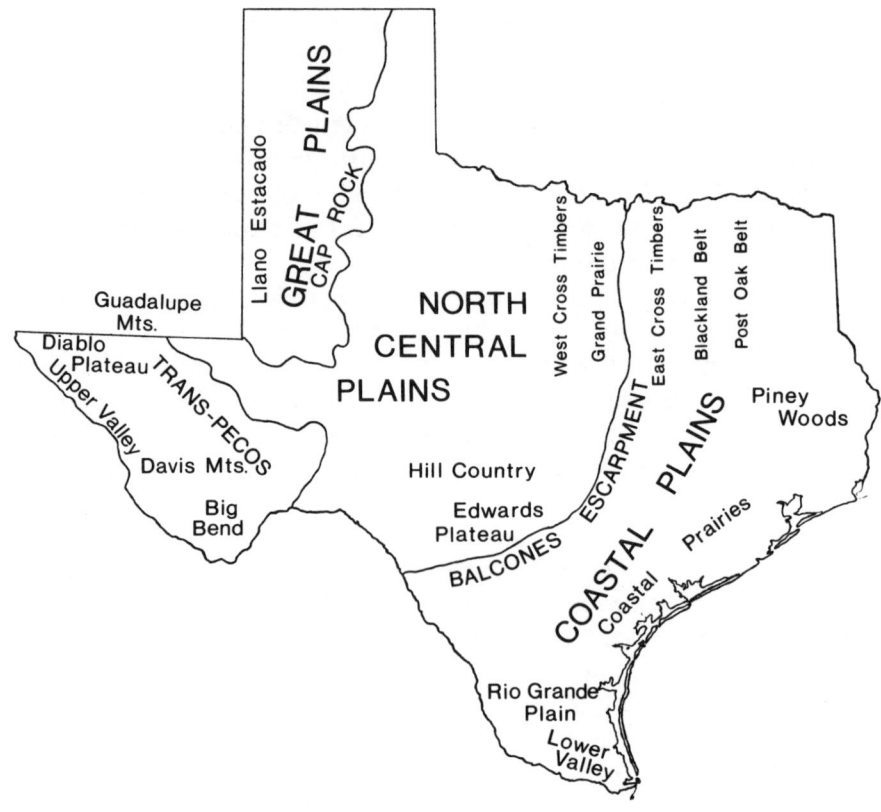

FIGURE 3-2
PHYSIOGRAPHIC REGIONS OF TEXAS

While pine is the principal timber, hardwoods, including various oaks, elm, hickory, magnolia, sweet and black gum, and tupelo, also abound. The area is scattered with native and improved grasslands. This region was the scene of the largest oil field discovery made in Texas when the East Texas Field (Rusk County) was discovered in 1930. Iron ore is mined from open pits in Cass, Morris, and Nacogdoches Counties. Deposits of a variety of clays, lignite, and other minerals in this area also offer potential for development.

Bordering the Pine Belt on the west is the *Post Oak Belt*, a narrow strip containing nearly seven million acres. Vegetation in this area consists of scattered stands of post oak and black jack oak with tall bunch grass in the uplands. Yaupon and other underbrush are prevalent in other places. The Post Oak Belt also contains lignite, commercial clays and other minerals.

The *Blackland Belt* extends all the way from the Rio Grande to the Red River, bordering the Balcones Fault and varying in width from fifteen to seventy miles. The eastern half is covered with a heavy growth of grass, while the more arid western half is covered with short grass, brush, and small timber. The soil is heavy alluvial and the grass grown in this area supports a thriving cattle industry. Rice, cotton, and truck crops are also grown in the region. The many underground salt domes of the coast contain rich deposits of petroleum and sulphur.

The *Texas Coastline* consists of a series of narrow sandbars, or barrier islands, enclosing shallow lagoons. The largest is Padre Island, site of the 133,918-acre Padre Island National Seashore. Other large coastal islands include Galveston, Matagorda, and St. Joseph. The coast includes twenty-eight manmade ports, all dredged from silt-ladened harbors. The coast attracts millions of recreationists from within and outside the state each year.

The southern portion of the coastal prairies consists of the fertile *Lower Rio Grande Valley*. The subtropical climate of this area and its deep alluvial soils combine to make it one of the nation's most intensively cultivated fruit and truck farming regions.

The southwestern portion of the Gulf Coastal Plains is a wedge-shaped area of approximately twenty million acres, the *Rio Grande Plain*, which gently slopes from San Antonio to the Rio Grande and the Gulf Coast. Part of the area is prairie, but much of it is covered with sub-tropical dryland vegetation including small trees, shrubs, cacti, weeds, and grasses. While there is some dryland farming in the region and some irrigated farming from wells and streams, the major industry is cattle, sheep, and goat ranching.

The North Central Plains

The North Central Plains form a portion of the lower level of the Great Western Plains which extend northward to the Canadian border. In Texas, they stretch from the Red River on the north to the Colorado River on the south, and from the Blackland Belt on the east to the Cap Rock Escarpment on the west.

The *West Texas Rolling Prairies* constitute approximately the western two-thirds of the North Central Plains, and cover an area of twenty-six million acres. These plains rise in altitude from about seven hundred fifty feet on the east to twenty-five hundred feet above sea level on the west at the base of the Cap Rock Escarpment. Average annual rainfall in this region varies from about thirty inches in the east to twenty inches in the west. The area is largely devoted to cattle ranching and farming, with vegetation evenly divided between mesquite woodland and prairie grasses.

Near the eastern edge of the North Central Plains is the *Grand Prairie*, an area of approximately six million acres extending south from the Red River to the Colorado River. It is underlain with limestone and is usually treeless except along the river bottoms. The area is adapted to growing primarily livestock and staple cotton.

The *East and West Cross Timbers* describes an area of about 3.5 million acres situated over the top of the Grand Prairie and extending down to border it on both sides. The two southward extensions are connected by a narrow strip along the Red River. The native vegetation in this area is mainly post oak and black jack oak trees and a few other hardwoods.

The Great Plains

The Great Plains reach westward from the North Central Plains into New Mexico. They constitute the southern part of the series of treeless plains that extend northward through the western United States and Canada.

Stretching over the largest level plain of its kind in the United States, the High Plains cover an area of nearly twenty million acres. Although flat in appearance, the area actually gradually rises from about twenty-seven hundred feet above sea level on the east to an altitude of more than four thousand feet in spots along the New Mexico border. The portion of the High Plains which lies along the New Mexico border is known as the *Llano Estacado* or *Staked Plains*. The level topography and porosity of the soil restrict drainage from the area. The relatively light precipitation which averages about eighteen inches a year flows into numerous shallow playas, small intermittent lakes. Only about 10 percent of the annual precipitation drains into the large Ogallala aquifer which underlies most of the region.

The famous *Texas Panhandle* makes up a major part of the area. The region is divided from lower rolling plains of West Texas by the Cap Rock Escarpment, a striking physical feature similar to the Balcones Escarpment, but caused by erosion rather than by geological faulting. The northern portion of the region is primarily an area of wheat and grain sorghum farming, while the southern part produces grain sorghum and cotton. Cotton farming in the area around Lubbock is irrigated from wells drawing on the Ogallala aquifer. This region has become the center of the cattle feeding industry in Texas. It also is a major oil and gas producer.

The *Edwards Plateau* lies between the Rio Grande and the Colorado River, being bordered on the southeast by the Balcones Escarpment and on the north by the Pecos River. The area is thought to be a southern and eastern extension of the High Plains. It ranges in altitude from about seven hundred fifty feet at its southern and eastern boundaries to twenty-seven hundred feet in places. Its twenty-four million acres include shallow soils overlaying limestone into which streams have cut many valleys and canyons. Large herds of cattle, goats, and sheep feed on mesquite shrubs and various grasses that cover the plateau.

A varied region of hills and streams lies east of the Edwards Plateau. The *Hill Country* is the name commonly given to the area of hills and spring-fed streams along the edge of the Balcones Escarpment, and it is a major recreational center for Texans. The *Burnet-Llano Basin* lies at the junction of the Colorado and Llano rivers. Earlier this was known as the Central Mineral Region because of the evidence there of large mineral deposits. The *Highland Lakes* describes a series of impoundments on the Colorado River running from Llano to Austin. Some of the world's oldest rocks are found at the surface in this area making it the most interesting geological area in Texas.

Trans-Pecos Texas

The westernmost part of Texas consists of an eighteen million acre triangular-shaped region, Trans-Pecos Texas, running west of the Pecos River and bordered on the north by New Mexico and on the south by the Republic of Mexico. It includes high, partly dry plains that are crossed by spurs of the Rocky Mountains.

The eastern third of the Trans-Pecos lies in the valley of the Pecos River and on the Stockton Plateau at the eastern base of the Davis Mountains. A land of rolling to rough topography and scant rainfall, it was exclusively devoted to ranching until two decades ago when irrigation of cotton, alfalfa, and other crops was begun following the discovery of large quantities of ground water.

Highest of the Trans-Pecos Mountains is the *Guadalupe Range* which extends southward into Texas from New Mexico, coming to an abrupt end about twenty miles south of the boundary line where are situated Guadalupe Peak (8,751 feet), the highest mountain in

Texas, and El Capitan (8,078 feet). The Diablo or basin is the name given an area lying just west of the Guadalupe Mountains and extending westward to the Hueco Mountains near El Paso. Since it has no drainage outlet to the sea, the runoff from the small amount of rain that falls on its surface drains into a series of salt lakes that lie just west of the Guadalupe Mountains.

In the central part of the Trans-Pecos stand the *Davis Mountains*. The highest peak in this range is Mount Livermore (8,382 feet), but a number of mountains of more than 7,000 feet in height are found. These mountains intercept the moisture-bearing winds and consequently receive more precipitation than elsewhere in the Trans-Pecos. As a result they are greener in growth of grass and forest trees than the other Trans-Pecos mountains.

South of the Davis Mountains lies the *Big Bend* country, named for the great southward swing of the Rio Grande forming the southern border of Texas. It is a rough country containing a variety of geological features, from spectacular mountains to desert. Its principal mountains, the Chisos, rise to an elevation of 7,835 feet. Along the Rio Grande are the beautiful Santa Elena, Mariscal, and Boquillas canyons which reach depths of nearly 2,000 feet.

The *Upper Rio Grande Valley* is a narrow strip of irrigated land which extends more than seventy-five miles down river from El Paso. The chief product of the valley is long staple cotton.

THE RENEWABLE RESOURCES

The physical diversity of Texas and its great size provided the state with what appeared to early settlers as an almost inexhaustible supply of renewable resources, including soil, water, and forests. The economic history of the state in the nineteenth century is largely a story of the progressive exploitation of these resources. However, it was not long before Texans learned from experience that renewable resources can be destroyed through unwise use. This recognition gave rise to significant efforts in resource conservation in the twentieth century.

Land

When the Republic of Texas came into existence in 1836, it had abundant natural resources, foremost of which was over two hundred sixteen million acres of unappropriated public domain. These land resources had scarcely been touched by man, for less than fifty thousand people resided here, mostly clustered in a few settlements near the upper Gulf Coast. When Texas was annexed into the United States in 1845, Texas retained its public lands in return for assuming responsibility for the $10 million debt of the Republic. In 1850, Texas ceded sixty-seven million acres of land to the United States and received in return $10 million to pay off its debt.

Excluding the cessation of land to the United States, Texas since 1836 has disposed of about one hundred forty-nine million acres of public land. The bulk of this was disposed of between 1836 and the time of the 1876 Constitution. Thomas Lloyd Miller provides a succinct description of the disposition of these lands:

She (Texas) gave nearly 40,000,000 acres to settlers; granted nearly 10,000,000 acres to Texas soldiers and their survivors; gave 32,000,000 acres to railroads, and another 5,000,000 acres for other internal improvements; sold for cash 4,500,000 acres; exchanged 3,000,000 acres for a magnificent red-granite capitol building; and reserved 52,000,000 acres for education. Another 3,000,000 acres still possessed by Texas comprise river beds, channels, lakes, and submerged areas. [10]

This account reveals that the public lands of Texas were distributed to achieve three major objectives: (1) encourage settlement; (2) develop social overhead capital, largely for improvement of transportation; and (3) provide support for public education. Of these objectives, settlement appears to have been given first priority, as Miller wrote:

If there was any one central theme in the Texas land policy, it was the desire to place the land in the possession of actual settlers rather than to permit corporations, and speculators to obtain them. [11]

The rich soils of Texas and the attractive terms on which land became available played a major role in attracting early settlers to the state, particularly to the eastern portion where rich soil was coupled with abundant water. The development of the windmill extended the area of cultivation to the prairies in the latter part of the nineteenth century and to the High Plains in the twentieth century.

The value of soil as a renewable resource has always been closely tied to the availability of water, as is reflected in the land use pattern in Texas today. A recent conservation needs inventory compiled by state and federal agencies gives the following breakdown of land use in Texas: cropland, 35.6 million acres; pasture, 14.1 million acres; range, 85.6 million acres; forest, 22.7 million acres; other land, including non-inventoried lands, 10.0 million acres.[12]

Thus, cropland accounts for only about one-fifth of the land use in the state. Of this area, about one-fourth is irrigated and accounts for more than half of the total crop value in Texas. Sixty percent of this irrigation is on the High Plains. The remainder is accounted for by rice irrigation in southeast Texas and irrigation of fruits and vegetables in the Lower Rio Grande Valley and Winter Garden districts of South Texas. The major portion of the non-irrigated agriculture in Texas is in the eastern half of the state, where annual rainfall is sufficient for the most part to support dryland farming.

The largest single use for land in the state is the millions of acres that are devoted to providing grazing for domestic and wild animals, watersheds for streams, and sites for recreation.

While range is one of the state's most valuable renewable resources, experience has shown that overuse or poor management of this resource can destroy its value. Overgrazing of publicly owned lands is perhaps the most frequently cited example of the problem of resource market failure. The problem of the commons, as it has come to be known, stems from the fact that the market system fails to provide for the efficient allocation of common property resources. In Texas, if the open range had not given way to the inroads of settlers, it probably would have been destroyed through unregulated use.

The greatest soil conservation problem in the state, however, resulted from a different type of failure of the market economy. In the high price era of the 1920s, Texas farmers who had done so well in cattle raising during World War I switched their efforts to dryland farming of wheat on the prairie. A risky business at best, dryland farming required little in the way of investment, and even though yields were low when compared with agriculture in more humid areas, wheat could be a profitable crop in years of average or better rainfall.

However, the stress upon the land from dryland farming was quite different from grazing. The prairies, with their natural cover of short buffalo grass, could withstand the periodic droughts that befell the area. When rain came, the prairies bloomed, and in the absence of rain, the thick-matted buffalo grass served to conserve moisture and hold the soil together until the cycle again turned to moisture. Wheat farming removed the protective cover of the buffalo grass and broke the soil. The collapse of wheat prices in the late 1920s gave rise to both economic and ecological disaster. As farmers left the submarginal lands uncultivated, they became vulnerable to the winds that swept the prairie. The result was the great dust bowl of the 1930s. The productivity of millions of acres of farmland was impaired, and millions of tons of topsoil were removed through erosion.

The incentives provided by the market, and the inevitable short-range emphasis of economic activity, thus led to overutilization of the soil. Its regenerative capacity was overwhelmed by the forces of wind and water erosion. To correct this situation, the government stepped in, and preservation of the soil from erosion and prevention of overuse became a matter of both state and national concern. The submarginal dust bowl project lands purchased by the federal government under the Bankhead-Jones Act of forty years ago are today administed by the federal government. In Texas, these lands include the Caddo National Grasslands, 17,729 acres located in Fannin County, and the Cross Timbers National Grasslands, 20,343 acres located in Wise and Montgomery counties. In addition, the U. S. Department of Agriculture provides technical assistance on soil, water, and related resources to locally organized soil and water conservation districts. There have been created in Texas 188 of these districts covering nearly all of the lands in the state.

Texas Forest Resources

The forest areas of Texas, including some secondary woodland and forest areas, are estimated to total 23.4 million acres, about half of which is of commercial value.[13] The principal forest and woodland regions are: pine-hardwood, 11.3 million acres; post oak, 3.6 million acres; East and West Cross Timbers, 2.2 million acres; cedar brakes, 4.6 million acres; mountain forests, 0.3 million acres; coastal forests, 0.6 million acres; and miscellaneous, 0.8 million acres.

The most important forest area of the state, producing nearly all of the commercial timber, is the East Texas pine-hardwood region known as the Piney Woods. It extends over forty-three counties. In 1971, the estimated standing value of marketable timber in this region was over one billion dollars.

Forests, like other renewable resources, are capable of providing a more or less permanent stream of annual yields. These sustained yields, however, may be threatened by overutilization. Before the 1930s, the evidence indicates that Texas forests were being overutilized, threatening the state with deforestation. Fortunately, increased public awareness of the need for conservation brought about public and private cooperation to reduce forest fires, increase tree planting, and foster natural regrowth of timber. Thus, it is now estimated that annual tree growth in the principal forest area of East Texas exceeds the yearly harvest by 25 percent.

Today's major public policy issue concerning forest lands relates not strictly to their conservation but to the problem of striking a balance between commercial and recreational use of these areas. The continuing debate over the preservation of the Big Thicket area in East Texas reflects the complexity of this issue. In particular, the value of these lands as wilderness can be easily threatened by commercial exploitation. On the other hand, there are many examples of compatible multiple use of forest areas for commercial timber harvesting and recreation. In East Texas, there are four National Forests in which multiple-use is fostered: Angelina (154,537 acres); Davy Crockett (161,748 acres); Sabine (184,767 acres); Sam Houston (158,411 acres).

Water

Texas receives on the average a little over 366 million acre-feet of precipitation annually. Rainfall distribution across the state is quite uneven, however. Annual precipitation averages approximately forty-five inches in the eastern portion of the state, falling to about twelve inches in the extreme western portion. As a rough approximation, average annual precipitation decreases by about one inch for each ten miles as one travels from east to west across the state.

In addition to wide geographic variation, rainfall also varies greatly from year to year. Over the period 1882 to 1970, average rainfall ranged from a high of 48.62 inches in 1941 to a low of only 14.30 inches in 1917. Major droughts hit Texas in 1909-10, 1916-17, 1933-34, and 1959-60.

Water availability has strongly influenced the settlement pattern in the state. Early settlements concentrated along rivers, which constituted major transportation routes. The eastern portion of Texas which afforded sufficient rainfall for farming was settled first. With the advent of the windmill, cultivation moved to the prairies in the latter part of the nineteenth century and to the High Plains in the twentieth century.

The vital nature of water in the prairies of West Texas was reflected in the enactment of a new system of water rights by the Texas Legislature in 1889. The riparian system in use at the time under the common law had been the legal basis for the use of water not only in Texas but throughout the United States. As settlement moved west, it was discovered that the riparian doctrine was not well suited to the arid and semiarid conditions of the western plains.

The basic premise of the riparian doctrine of water rights is that the owner of land abutting the stream has the right to take water for use on his land. All owners whose lands border on a stream are given equal rights to riparian use, which is generally restricted to being "reasonable" in the sense of not impairing the rights of other riparian users. In the case of conflict, determination of what constitutes reasonable use is generally left to the courts. Riparian rights need not be exercised to be maintained.

The riparian system presented numerous difficulties in the dry lands of Texas, particularly to those seeking to use water for irrigation.[14] Under one doctrine, no substantial diversion of water from a stream is permissible, precluding irrigation. A broader interpretation would permit irrigation but would confine it to riparian land, that is, land in one ownership abutting the stream. In the humid lands of the eastern United States and England, the riparian system had worked reasonably well, principally because the supply of water in these regions far exceeded the demand. The practical limitations of the system in the more arid regions stemmed from the fact that some of the best agricultural land could not be irrigated (non-riparian land), and considerable uncertainty existed for the potential irrigator as to whether his use of water would be found reasonable if challenged in court.

The prior appropriation system is based on the concept that a water right is acquired by use. Further, those users who are first-in-time are given preference over those users who arrive later. Use of water in this system is limited to specific quantities withdrawn under specified conditions. A water right which is not exercised may be forfeited. Under this system, water could be diverted for irrigation of lands distant from the stream. The first-in-time, first-in-right principle had a stabilizing influence which encouraged farmers to make the expenditure required for construction of canals and preparation of land for irrigation. Further encouragement came from the fact that a water right, once granted, was legally secure.

The Irrigation Act of 1889 which established the prior appropriation system of water rights in Texas thus had tremendous significance for the development of irrigation in the state. The legislation did not, however, repeal the riparian doctrine; thus, Texas is one of nine western states having a dual system of water rights.

Recently, Texans have become increasingly concerned over the quantity and quality of groundwater supplies in the state. Groundwater comes under the riparian doctrine in the sense that the owner of the overlying land has the right to withdraw water from the aquifer. Thus, underground aquifers represent a form of common property resource which is important in supporting irrigated agriculture, as well as being the source of municipal and industrial water supplies. Competitive exploitation of these resources leads to their overutilization and to impairment of water quality.

The most serious area of state concern over groundwater is in the High Plains, where annual withdrawals from the Ogallala aquifer to supply irrigation needs are in excess of the annual replenishment of the aquifer from precipitation with the result that the future of the entire region is threatened. A similar but as of yet less serious problem exists with the Edwards underground aquifer, where water is being pumped to supply the municipal requirements of San Antonio and other cities as well as to meet agricultural and industrial needs. The problem is made more complex in this region because urban expansion into the recharge zone may pose a threat to the quality of the water. Along the Gulf Coast, concern is being voiced over salt water intrusion into fresh water aquifers in the Baytown, Texas City, and Galveston areas and over land-subsidence due to groundwater pumping in the Baytown-Pasadena and Houston Ship Channel areas.

The Texas Legislature did pass the Underground Water Conservation District Act of 1949, which provided for the establishment of Underground Water Districts to help conserve underground water supplies. Unfortunately, the voluntary nature of these Districts has limited their usefulness. Thus, the problems posed by the unregulated use of underground aquifers remains unaddressed by public policy in Texas today.

The geographical concentration of water in Texas has given emphasis to measures to fully utilize this scarce resource. One of the major natural resource developments in the state during the past fifty years has been the construction of a large number of reservoirs to improve water conservation and increase water supplies. The construction of reservoirs has been dramatic. In 1913, Texas had eight reservoirs with a combined storage capacity of about 359,000 acre-feet. By 1930, the number of reservoirs had increased fourfold to thirty-two and the total storage capacity had risen to over 1.2 million acre-feet. By 1950, the number of reservoirs had again doubled, rising to sixty-six having over 9.6 million acre-feet of storage capacity. In October 1974, there were 160 reservoirs in Texas existing or under construction, with over 29 million acre-feet of conservation storage capacity.[15]

The construction of reservoirs serves many interests. Farmers are attracted by the prevention of flooding and the availability of water for irrigation. Municipalities also benefit from the control of storm waters and from the provision of water supply. In a few instances, reservoirs in Texas have been used to supply hydroelectric power and small impoundments are used as cooling ponds for steam-generated electric plants. Recreationists find in the lakes new resources for swimming, fishing, and other water-oriented pursuits. These interests have provided powerful political support for water resource development. The supplier of these services, for the most part, has been the U. S. Government, in particular, the Army Corps of Engineers.

Development of surface water impoundments is not without its critics, however. One basis for objection arises from the controversy surrounding the efficacy of dams and other flood control structures in preventing flood damage. Critics have pointed out that despite the millions of dollars spent by the federal government on dams since 1936, the average annual flood losses have increased dramatically during this period. The increase in damages arises because of construction of dwellings and other types of buildings on the flood plain.

In 1968, Congress sought to provide an alternative to flood control structures by passage of the National Flood Insurance Act. This legislation sought to induce municipalities and other local governments to adopt regulations restricting development of riverine and coastal areas subject to risks of flooding by making available federally subsidized flood insurance to existing owners of residential and small business buildings in communities having federally approved regulations.

The Texas Legislature has enacted enabling legislation which authorizes local governments to participate in this program and has designated the Texas Water Development Board as the coordinating agency. However, the Legislature has not conferred any authority upon the Board or any other state agency either to regulate flood plain land uses directly or to do so indirectly by imposing standards upon local governments. Sixty-six Texas cities and towns have adopted flood plain management controls and are currently seeking federal approval.

Another source of concern, particularly in Texas, has been that construction of upstream impoundments will unduly restrict the fresh water inflow to coastal bays and estuaries, with the result that their salinity levels will rise. While it is difficult to estimate fresh water requirements, it is generally recognized that increases in salinity levels can adversely affect the natural life in these coastal waters.

A third source of concern over the development of large dams relates to the loss of valuable natural waterways and the destruction of wildlife habitat. There are those who value the aesthetic quality of natural streams and who believe that the construction of large reservoirs offers a poor substitute for the beauty of the meandering river.

During the 1950s, the Texas Water Conservation Association and other interested parties began pressing for the adoption of a coordinated statewide approach to the development of water resources. In part, this interest developed out of recognition of the fact that the water resources of Texas were largely concentrated in the eastern half of the state, while the western half had insufficient water resources to meet present and future needs. Water was viewed as a facilitating resource, indispensible to the development of an area. Substantial interest in comprehensive water resource development came from the West Texas Plains area where it was realized that the underground aquifer would not be able to continue to support the existing pace of irrigation. These interests urged that water resources of the state be viewed in their entirety and developed as widely as possible in accordance with a comprehensive plan rather than on a project-by-project basis.

Comprehensive planning of water resources development on a state-wide basis became official state policy with the enactment of the Water Planning Act of 1957 by the Texas Legislature. Responsibility for this function was assigned to the Texas Board of Water Engineers, and later to the Texas Water Development Board. A constitutional amendment was passed authorizing $200 million in bonds to support water development. With legislative action, the amount could be doubled. This legislation was unique in entering the state into the area of financing major water development projects, a province formerly left almost entirely to the Federal Government.

The Texas Water Development Board, after years of planning and numerous public hearings across the state, in 1968 adopted the Texas Water Plan. The most controversial part of the Texas Water Plan was the concept of interbasin transfers which it embraced. Among these numerous proposed transfers, two were of gigantic proportions. Each would traverse the entire width of Texas from east to west. One would be located in North Texas, the major purpose of which would be the replacement of the declining Ogallala aquifer as the basis for extensive irrigation on the High Plains. To obtain enough water, it would be necessary, according to the plan, to import water from the Mississippi River. The other would be on the coastal plain and would bring surplus water from East Texas south and west to the coast where it would be used to meet agricultural and municipal water supply needs.

Implementation of the Texas Water Plan received a setback in 1969, when Texas voters refused to authorize issuance of state water bonds to an additional extent of 3.5 billion dollars, the amount needed to finance the first phases of the plan. The total construction costs of the plan were estimated to be nearly nine billion dollars. The major objections to the plan were its huge costs and the possible environmental damages that might result from massive interbasin transfers. The defeat of the bond proposal did not, of course, eliminate the need to plan for the future water needs of the state. The comprehensive planning process continues, and the Texas Water Development Board continues to coordinate water resources development in the state.*

THE NONRENEWABLE RESOURCES

The discovery and development of the state's nonrenewable resources has characterized the economic growth of Texas in this century. The economic impact of the development of Texas mineral resources has not been limited to the value of the raw materials produced, but has been magnified by the long list of enterprises spawned to service the state's mining industry and process its output into finished products.

In 1974, the U. S. Bureau of Mines reported that the value of mineral production in Texas exceeded $13.8 billion, placing it first among states for the thirty-eighth consecutive year. The value of petroleum, natural gas, and natural gas liquids produced amounted to $13.1 billion or over 95 percent of the state total. Texas leads the nation in the production of crude petroleum, natural gas liquids, Frasch and recovered sulphur, natural graphite, and magnesium metal and is second to Louisiana in the production of natural gas.

It now appears as if the mineral fuel industry in Texas has reached its peak and the state's future production of oil and gas is likely to decline, both absolutely and relatively. Since 1950, the production

---

*The Texas Water Development Board, Water Quality Board, and Water Rights Commission have been consolidated into the Texas Department of Water Resources.

of nonfuel minerals in Texas has risen at a faster rate than that for fuel minerals. While the nonfuel minerals will continue to experience a relative increase in importance, it is unlikely that they will become as significant in terms of the value of output and economic importance to the state as the oil and gas industry has been for the past fifty years. It is also clear that in the remaining years of this century, the oil and gas industry will continue to dominate mining activities in Texas. Concern is now focused on conserving these scarce mineral fuel resources and ensuring that the decline in production will not deprive the associated processing industries of their raw materials.

Mineral Fuels

Petroleum was discovered in Texas as early as 1866, and scattered efforts to discover and produce oil continued in the following years. It was not until 1894 that the drilling of a water well for the City of Corsicana led to the discovery of a major oil deposit, in what subsequently became known as the Powell Field, and the establishment of the state's first refinery.

It was on 10 January 1901, however, that the Texas petroleum industry came of age when Spindletop, the most famous well in the world, blew in with an explosion that was said to have been heard for miles around and a jet of oil and mud hundreds of feet high. Spindletop was discovered by Anthony Lucas, a former captain in the Austrian Navy. The well was spectacular but short-lived. In 1900, Texas oil production had been 836,000 barrels. By 1901, it had risen to over 4 million barrels and in 1902, Spindletop alone produced over 17.4 million barrels, accounting for 94 percent of the state's production. In a pattern that was to be repeated periodically, the large increase in supply resulting from this discovery led to a rapid decline in price, with oil selling at one point for as little as three cents a barrel.

Spindletop was significant in that it broke the monopolistic hold on oil production held by Rockefeller and the Standard Oil Trust and permitted the entry of a number of new interests into the industry. The well demonstrated that major oil deposits could be found with the salt dome formations which dotted the Texas and Louisiana Gulf Coast and which, in many instances, were visible from the surface. It stimulated a large investment in oil exploration in Texas and surrounding states.

The next three decades saw the discovery of major new fields in the Texas Panhandle, East Texas, and the Gulf Coast. However, the culmination came in October 1930 when "Dad" Joiner, an aging wildcatter, prospecting in an area of the widow Daisy Bradford's farm in Rusk County that had been explored and abandoned by the geologists of the larger petroleum companies, brought in the granddaddy of them all, the East Texas Field. This discovery was such a bonanza that it brought a glut on an already distressed market suffering from the effects of the Depression. The combination of the vast new supply and the depressed state of demand led to pressure for the state to regulate production and stabilize prices. The response was quick in coming, as a system of prorationing was introduced, thus bringing to an end the free market for oil.

In subsequent years, numerous additional major petroleum discoveries were made in Texas. The most significant of these was the discovery of the West Texas Field in Scurry County in 1948.

Since its inception, the Texas petroleum industry has discovered an estimated fifty billion barrels of recoverable crude oil and about 275 trillion cubic feet of natural gas. Of this discovered amount, however, an estimated 80 percent of the oil and 75 percent of the natural gas have already been produced and consumed. Texas oil has contributed about 37 percent, Texas natural gas nearly 40 percent, and Texas natural gas liquids about 46 percent of the total amount of these commodities produced in the entire history of the United States.[16]

The development of oil and gas production in Texas has been accompanied by concurrent development of service and processing industries. Texas refines about 85 percent of its crude oil production. The importance of the oil and gas related industries to the state's economy can be seen from the fact that in 1974, employment in these industries totaled 247,359, of which only 60,094 was accounted for by individuals engaged in the actual production of petroleum, natural gas, and natural gas liquids. Oil and gas field services gave employment to 53,584 persons; processing, including the manufacture of carbon black, paving and roofing materials, and other products as well as petroleum refining, provided 40,626 jobs; pipeline transportation and distribution of oil and gas gave employment to 26,537 individuals; and petroleum and gas marketing provided 66,168 jobs.

In addition to the direct benefit provided by oil and gas production, processing, transporting, and marketing, the Texas economy also receives substantial indirect benefits from the industry. Analysis of data developed by the U. S. Department of Commerce and included in an input-output model of the structure of the national economy for 1967 indicates, for example, the contribution of oil refining to production in other industries. Excluding petroleum and natural gas, a one dollar increase in oil refining is estimated to generate thirty-nine cents worth of output in the industrial chemicals, iron and steel foundries, motor freight transport and warehousing, water transportation, pipeline transportation, utilities, wholesale trade, banking, real estate, and other service industries. In addition, minor industries together, no one of which requires even one cent of output per dollar of oil refining, produce another twenty-seven cents of output per dollar of oil refining output.[17]

The oil and gas industry in Texas has been affected significantly by public policies at both the state and federal levels. Federal tax incentives for exploration and development, including the percentage depletion allowance and the provision for expensing of allowable drilling costs, have encouraged investment in the industry. The Federal Power Commission, largely at the instigation of the Supreme Court, has established price regulation over natural gas. The most far reaching controls, however, have come at the state level where a comprehensive system for controlling production in the industry was developed.

The necessity for regulating oil production resulted mainly from the fact that the legal system of land tenure in the United States leads to fragmented ownership of the property rights to oil deposits, while the physical nature of the deposits gives them some of the attributes of common property resources. Competitive exploitation of deposits often results in inefficient production and waste in the sense of a reduction in the percentage of the deposit eventually recovered.

In the United States, ownership of land traditionally has been in the hands of thousands of individuals, with the average holding being relatively small. This was particularly true in East Texas where public policy had encouraged the settlement of small farmers. Under the American law, unlike that of many countries, the landowner also owns the subsoil minerals underneath his property.

Oil is found in pools or reservoirs deep beneath the ground. The dimensions of the deposit seldom if ever conform to the pattern of ownership of the overlying lands. Oil pumped from a deposit to the surface may have originated anywhere within the pool. Further, technical factors of production make the total amount of oil recoverable from a given deposit a function of the rate and pattern of pumping.

At an early date in the petroleum industry's history, the Supreme Court held that a landowner was entitled to the oil and gas he could capture on his own land, regardless of origin. Thus, once a sizeable deposit was found, it became advantageous for each landowner in the area to drill wells as rapidly as possible in an attempt to capture as much of the oil as possible from the deposit before his neighbor could do the same. The rush to production created not only overproduction and physical waste of the resource, but also led to distressed markets and falling prices.

Texas, which accounted for about 40 percent of the nation's petroleum output at the time of the discovery of the famous East Texas Field, was particularly hard hit by the boom and bust nature of oil production. Following the East Texas Field, Governor Sterling had to call the National Guard and establish martial law to prevent chaos in the area. In a 1932 special session, the Texas Legislature authorized the Texas Railroad Commission to establish a system under which oil production in the state would be limited to estimated market demand.

Under this system of prorationing, the Railroad Commission, a three member elected body, would estimate monthly market demand for the state's oil and allocate the allowable production to the oil wells in the state. First, the Commission allocates production to the so-called "stripper" wells, that is, wells which are in the last stages of production and cannot yield more than twenty barrels a day. Next, it allocates production to the East Texas Field, which is given preferential treatment in order to maintain reservoir pressure in this field where some 19,000 wells have been drilled, and to newly discovered fields which are given a privileged position during their first two years of operation. The remaining production is then divided between every well in the state so that each can be operated for only a certain number of days each month.

Prorationing to market demand actually began in January 1938. It effectively terminated in March 1972 when the Commission set the allowable at 100 percent, a level which effectively has been maintained ever since and which, given the current shortage of petroleum, appears likely to be permanent. During the 411 months in which prorationing held sway, wide open production was permitted in only fifteen. The effect of the system was not only to prevent waste, but also to control prices, since waste was defined as production in excess of market demand, the latter being computed at the established market price. The system was highly significant in the early years, but as demand expanded and new sources of petroleum came to supply these new demands, the system became obsolete long before it became academic. Robert M. Lockwood has written:

The relative decline of the share of Texas oil in the national and international supply and the slower growth and eventual decline of the surplus productive capacity in Texas were accompanied by a progressive localization of the influence of the Railroad Commission . . . Even with a drastic change in price conditions or import policies—and neither appears likely—the Texas Railroad Commission probably will never again need to curtail output from fields in the state merely because of insufficient markets.[18]

Texas is estimated to possess about 35 percent of the proven liquid hydrocarbon reserves of the United States (including natural gas). The level of reserves, however, has been falling as production has been exceeding annual additions to reserves. One knowledgeable observer has warned that if future production of petroleum and natural gas continues with the trend established since 1972, and if new reserves are added at the rate experienced in recent years, measured reserves of Texas crude oil will be depleted in a decade, and proven reserves of Texas natural gas will be depleted by the early 1990s.[19]

This dismal forecast is borne out by recent trends in production and reserves. During the past five years, there has been an average annual decline in oil production of 4.6 percent and in natural gas production of 4.1 percent in the state. Even more telling are the declines in proven reserves—with a recent annual average reduction of 6.0 percent in oil reserves and 7.0 percent in natural gas reserves in Texas.

In the period since 1920, an average of about 860 million barrels of recoverable oil have been found each year; during this same period, production and consumption of crude oil has averaged about 710 million barrels per year. Average figures, however, do not reflect the current situation. In the heyday of discovery, from 1925 to 1944, average annual reserve additions amounted to 1.5 million barrels; during the period from 1945 to 1953, this average fell to about a billion barrels a year, roughly equivalent to average annual production during that period. Beginning in 1954 and continuing through 1963, a rapid decline in average annual reserve additions occurred, dropping to only 350 million barrels, roughly one-third of then-existing production rates. From the early sixties to the present, a period during which oil production climbed to a record 1.3 billion barrels in 1973, average annual reserve additions amounted to a mere 60 million barrels.

The trends in natural gas reserves, reserve addition, and production are comparable, though not quite as critical as those trends for crude oil. Since 1920, Texas has added natural gas reserves at an annual average rate of about 4 trillion cubic feet. In the early years, 1920 to 1954, the average annual rate of addition was about 4.8 trillion cubic feet. Beginning in 1955, a steady decline in the volume of natural gas discovered occurred, interrupted only by substantive additions in 1963. During this later period, additions averaged 2.8 trillion cubic feet annually. Over the past six years, the average rate has dropped to 1.4 trillion cubic feet per year, about one-sixth of the average rate of production.

The combination of increasing production rates and decreasing discovery and reserve addition rates is reflected dramatically in reserve-life statistics (the ratio of annual production to proven reserves). In the case of crude oil, the decline began in 1961, twelve years preceding inevitable production declines, and has persisted to date. In the case of natural gas, the decline in reserve life began twenty-five years ago and has persisted to the present, but not as steeply as reserve life decline in oil.

Of course, the future of oil and gas production in the state may be substantially extended by: (1) conversion of indicated and inferred reserves into proven reserves; (2) enhanced recovery techniques which increase recovery from known oil in place; and (3) possible new discoveries of oil and gas which expand the resource base. The possible magnitudes of expansion in proven reserves from each of these sources is described below.

Indicated reserves (recoveries from known reservoirs in excess of proved or measured reserves) and *inferred reserves* (probable additions to known fields through extensions, revisions, and new plays) of Texas crude oil amount to about ten billion barrels. It may be reasonably expected that these reserves, about equal to proven reserves, can be developed as proven reserves and become available for production. Reserves of Texas natural gas, classed in the indicated and inferred category, are estimated to amount to about eighty trillion cubic feet, roughly ten trillion cubic feet in excess of proven natural gas reserves.

Out of the approximately 300 billion barrels of oil that have been found in place in the United States, about 150 billion barrels have been found in Texas. Oil recovered or classed as recoverable from this base, through existing economical recovery techniques, is about 50 billion barrels (40 billion of which have already been produced).

The remaining 100 billion barrels obviously represents a major potential source of additions to recovery. Techniques are available to recover a significant percentage of this oil, but at costs substantially higher than existing oil prices. A recent analysis published by the National Petroleum Council concluded that at a price of twenty-five dollars a barrel (in 1976 dollars), an estimated 9 billion barrels of additional Texas crude could be recovered between now and the year 2000 through *enhanced recovery techniques*. Under these assumptions, approximately 80 billion barrels of oil a year could be produced in 1980, and up to 570 million barrels in 1995. Thereafter, production through enhanced recovery techniques would decline to about 540 million barrels in 2000.

In summary, of the 150 billion barrels of oil discovered in place in Texas, forty billion barrels have already been produced. About 10 billion barrels remain as proved reserves, about 10 million barrels exist as indicated and inferred reserves, and approximately 9 billion barrels constitute a relatively near term target for enhanced recovery techniques.

Clearly, one of the most important elements in the future of Texas as an oil and gas producing state is how much oil and gas remain to be discovered. Published estimates of undiscovered oil and gas resources vary widely, due to differing assumptions and methods utilized in assessing an unknown quantity. A review of eight estimates made since 1960 show United States resources (onshore and offshore) varying from 67 to 450 billion barrels of crude oil and 361 to 2,100 trillion cubic feet of natural gas. Based on this data, inferred undiscovered reserves for Texas range from as little as 5 billion barrels of oil and 65 trillion cubic feet of gas to as much as 30 billion barrels of oil and 400 trillion cubic feet of gas.

As the burgeoning demand for energy subject oil and gas to increasing pressures, importation of oil is likely to increase. A major concern in Texas is the development of a superport in the deep water of the Gulf of Mexico to facilitate the importation of crude petroleum needed to make up the deficit in domestic supply and maintain output in Texas refineries and petrochemical plants.

Industry spokesmen are calling for additional incentives to promote the exploration for new deposits of oil and gas. They are particularly critical of the regulation of natural gas prices by the Federal Power Commission. In the meantime, emphasis is being given to methods to obtain more efficient recovery of oil from existing deposits. Secondary recovery techniques, such as waterflooding, are increasingly being resorted to.

One issue which has long been of concern to the petroleum industry is the desirability of compulsory unitization of oil fields. It can be shown that in a technical sense, more oil can be recovered from a given deposit when it is managed as a unit than when it is exploited by a number of parties in an uncoordinated fashion. However, legislation calling for compulsory unitization has always met with opposition from those producers, particularly small ones, who fear that their interests will not be fully protected under such a system.

As the energy crisis brings home the likelihood of a decline in Texas oil and gas production, attention is being shifted to the state reserves of coal and lignite. Prior to the large scale development of oil and gas, bituminous coal, including channel coal, was a major energy source in Texas. From 1895 through 1943, Texas mines produced more than twenty-four million tons of coal. Much of the bituminous coal occurs in North Central Texas, with deposits also being found in South Texas and in the Trans-Pecos region.

Of greater interest today are the large deposits of lignite, a low grade coal, which is found in two narrow belts transversing the Texas Gulf Coastal Plain from near Laredo to the Arkansas and Louisiana borders.[20] Potential statewide resources at depths of less than 200 feet or available to conventional surface mining are estimated at 10.4 billion short tons. To this is added deep-basin lignite, a huge potential resource at depths of 200 to 5,000 feet below the surface, available through in situ recovery methods. More than 100 billion tons have been mapped, equivalent on a BTU basis to 277 billion barrels of oil.

As with coal, lignite production was significant in the state prior to 1930, when abundant oil and gas reserves became available. Today, lignite is an attractive source of fuel for electric power generation and may in time come to replace natural gas in this capacity. Twenty-six mine mouth electric power plants utilizing lignite are planned to come on line in Texas over the next decade.

Nonfuel Minerals[21]

In addition to its abundant petroleum resources, Texas also possesses many other minerals which are either economically important today or which offer potential for future development. In 1974, nonfuel mineral output in Texas was valued at more than $753 million.

The leading nonfuel mineral in terms of the value of output is cement. Thirteen companies operate eighteen cement plants in twelve Texas counties. The total output in 1974 amounted to about eight million short tons with a value of $211 million. Many plants utilize cretaceous limestone and shales or clays as raw materials for portland cement. Such materials occur widely in the Blacklands, Grand Prairie, Edwards Plateau, and Trans-Pecos areas of Texas. Iron oxide, also required as an input of cement, is available from the iron ore deposits of East Texas and from smelter slag. Gypsum, which is added to cement as a retarder, is found chiefly in North Central Texas, Central Texas, and the Trans-Pecos regions. Along the Gulf Coast, cement producers use large amounts of oyster shells as a source of calcium carbonate. On the Texas High Plains, a cement plant near Amarillo uses impure caliche as the chief raw material.

Texas has been a leading producer of sulphur for over fifty years. The sulphur industry in the United States was born about the time of the Spindletop discovery and in the same area, when Herman Frasch developed a hot water process for extracting sulphur from salt dome deposits. The Frasch process proved to be immensely successful, and Texas shortly became the world's leading producer of elemental sulphur.[22] Frasch sulphur still is produced along the Texas Gulf Coast, but recently, the Frasch process has been used to mine sulphur from sulphur-bearing non-salt dome formations in Culberson, Pecos, and Tom Green counties in the Trans-Pecos region. Total known reserves in this region have been estimated at 100 million long tons at prices of $35 per long ton. An additional 100 million long tons of undiscovered reserves are thought to exist in the region.[23] Following World War II, sulphur recovery from sour natural gas became significant and Texas also assumed the lead in this field. Followed closely by Louisiana, Texas leads the nation in the production of Frasch sulphur and in the output of recovered sulphur from sour natural gas. In 1972, Texas produced nearly 3.8 million long tons of Frasch sulphur with an estimated value of $65 million dollars, representing 51.5 percent of the nation's total output. Recovered sulphur production amounted to 852,000 long tons, having a total value of $11.2 million, and accounting for over one-third of the nation's production.

Texas is among the leading producers of crushed stone, mostly limestone and dolomite. In 1974, production totaled 63.3 million short tons, with a total value of $102 million.

Sand and gravel are among the most extensively utilized resources in Texas. In 1974, production amounted to 40.5 million short tons, having a value of about $86.2 million.

The salt resources of Texas are virtually inexhaustible. Enormous deposits occur in the subsurface Permian Basin of West Texas and in the salt domes of the Gulf Coastal Plains. Salt is also found in the salt lakes of the High Plains, Trans-Pecos area, and along some of the bays and lagoons of the South Texas Gulf Coast. Texas is one of the leading salt-producing states. Most of the salt is produced as brines from wells drilled into underground deposits and is used as a basic raw material in the chemical industries. Production in 1974 was 11.2 million short tons with a total value of $49.3 million.

Limestone is burned to produce lime (calcium oxide) at several plants in Texas. Along the Gulf Coast, where suitable limestone deposits are not found, shell dredged from shallow bays is utilized in lime manufacture. In 1974, output totaled 1.8 million short tons, with a value of $29.5 million.

Texas possesses abundant and various ceramic and nonceramic clays and is one of the nation's leading producers of clay products. In 1974, Texas output of clays totaled 5.4 million tons with a value of $13.6 million.

Talc is produced in the Allamore area of Hudspeth County in the Trans-Pecos region. In 1974, production amounted to 233 million short tons with a value of over $1.4 million.

In addition to the above materials, Texas also produced in 1974 small quantities of gemstone, pumicite, asphalt, graphite, iron ore, helium, magnesium chloride, magnesium compounds, mercury, sodium sulphate, dimension stone, and uranium.

NATURAL RESOURCE POLICY ISSUES IN TEXAS

The development of the renewable and nonrenewable resources of Texas has been affected significantly by public policies at both the federal and state level. Today the state faces a number of policy issues with respect to its natural resources. Some issues are old, having been the subject of much discussion and concern in the past. Others are strikingly new, the product of the rapid urbanization of Texas and the new attitudes toward preservation of environmental quality.

The most pressing public policy issue regarding renewable resources is an old concern, the problem of developing water resources. The defeat of the bond proposal dealing with financing the Texas Water Plan did not resolve the issue of the future water resource development in the state. The rapidly depleting supplies of groundwater in the

Texas High Plains makes the issue of dominant importance, since it is clear that unless new supplies of water for this area can be found, irrigated agriculture on the scale presently existing in this region will become a thing of the past by the end of the century. Given the importance of irrigation to the economy of the High Plains, loss of revenue from this source would create substantial problems for the region and the state.

If it appears unlikely that Texas can rely on importation of water from outside the state to provide for its water needs, then the future of water development in the state will revolve around two central issues: the geographical allocation of water within the state and the functional allocation of water to competing uses. Geographical allocation of water essentially involves transporting the surplus waters of East Texas south and west to augment the supplies of the more arid regions of the state. The issue is likely to become the subject of much controversy. The definition of "surplus" waters is largely a matter of judgment in which available supplies have to be measured against anticipated demands. Regions may resist the export of their surplus waters to their neighbors, on the principle that in the future these waters may be needed to support economic growth and development in their home region. Also, the environmental effects and large costs of massive trans-shipment schemes ensure that they will become major political issues.

The allocation of water among competing uses poses another problem for Texas. The demand for water in the state, particularly in different areas, inevitably will press upon the available supplies. Growing demands for municipal and industrial water may conflict with the allocation of water to irrigation. The amount of water which needs to be allocated to supporting fresh water inflow to the state's bays and estuaries must be determined and a source of supply found.

Given the difficulties of developing new sources of water for the state, the conservation and wise use of the existing water supplies becomes a matter of high priority. It would appear that the prime area for concern is the establishment of some type of system to protect and allocate the groundwater supplies of the state. Unregulated use of these common property resources will likely result in their impairment or destruction.

Water resource development is closely related to land use. This represents the second major area of concern in Texas with respect to renewable resources. Traditionally, the states have abdicated their responsibility for controlling land use to municipalities, where land use controls have been largely limited to zoning, building codes, and subdivision regulations. Today, a host of new issues, many associated with the problems of a highly urbanized society, are creating pressures for the establishment of a land use policy at the state level. Numerous states have already responded to these pressures by instituting major land resource management systems.[24]

Major land resource management problems include those related to urbanization, the location of key facilities, and the preservation of critical environments. Urban growth, which has characterized Texas in the past two decades, has caused a redistribution of people within the state and created new land use concerns. Such growth often results in the decay of the central city core, urban sprawl, leapfrog development, and environmental problems associated with congestion and the related difficulties of waste discharge. The concept of key facilities relates directly to the man-made environment. For example, the location of airports, regional waste treatment plants, power plants, and highways frequently poses serious land resource management issues which are difficult to resolve under the existing structure of state government. Finally, there is the concern over destruction or degradation of critical environments, defined in terms of major ecosystems such as forests, bays and estuaries, and beach shorefront areas. In Texas, the preservation of some portion of the Big Thicket, the protection of Gulf Coast bays and estuaries, and the control of development along lakes and rivers represent major environmental issues concerned with land use.

Problems of land use also characterize the major concern in Texas regarding nonrenewable resources; in particular, the energy resources. The construction of a superport, for example, may pose such problems as destruction or impairment of the marine environment, and pollution of beach areas and wetlands from oil spills. As energy demands grow, it is likely that increasing use will be made of the uranium and lignite reserves in Texas. Exploitation of these resources, however, involves strip mining, with its accompanying problems of waste disposal and reclamation.

One of the most important areas of public policy relating to continuance of Texas' dominant role in oil and gas production is the passage of legislation providing for unitized management of oil and gas reservoirs. Unitization is particularly important for adoption of enhancement techniques to expand recovery from known deposits.

Beginning with Oklahoma in 1945, nineteen states have enacted involuntary unitization statutes. Texas, alone among the major producing states, has failed to enact such legislation. Involuntary unitization laws are now so widely accepted that the Interstate Oil Compact Commission includes the necessary provisions in its model oil and gas conservation statute which it recommends to all states. There can be no doubt that the Texas economy would benefit in both the short and the long run from enactment of an involuntary unitization statute for oil and gas.

The major organizational issue relating to natural resources in Texas is the problem created by the host of agencies, boards, and commissions which share responsibility for the state's natural resources.[25] Because responsibility for various aspects of natural resources is now parceled out to seven independent agencies, thirteen special boards and commissions, and hundreds of special districts, coordination of policy efforts is frequently left to administration imagination. Although it can be pointed out that some coordinative mechanisms have been developed in the area of natural resources, the structure of government in Texas makes much more difficult the task of coordination and comprehensive planning.

Lack of coordination is more serious when dealing with natural resources than with many other areas of state concern because the environmental media—air, water, and land—are closely interrelated. Recently, state governments have tended to reorganize their pollution control efforts into a single agency. Forty states, for example, now combine air and water pollution abatement programs. During 1971-72, the latest year for which data are available, eleven states conducted a major reorganization of their pollution control agencies.[26]

Other natural resource related functions also offer good opportunities for coordinated and comprehensive planning. The planning of major public investments in water supply and flood control needs to be closely related to recreation planning. Decisions on the leasing of submerged coastal land for minerals exploration should be coordinated with fish and wildlife management programs and policies. The construction of reservoirs on the state's major drainage systems needs to reflect consideration of the impact of reduced water inflows on estuarine water quality. The planning of major public investments, such as power plants, regional sewage treatment plants, and airports, should be considered in conjunction with planning for environmental quality control.

In recognition of these types of needs, over half of the states have taken action to consolidate their major natural resource related functions in a single department. The reorganization of state government to reflect the interrelated nature of natural resource issues presents perhaps the greatest challenge to natural resource management in Texas.

NOTES

1. See Robert U. Ayres and Allen V. Kneese, "Production, Consumption, and Externalities," *American Economic Review*, June 1960, p. 285.

2. Kenneth Boulding, *Economics As A Science* (New York: McGraw-Hill Book Company, 1970), p. 42.

3. See Erich W. Zimmermann, *World Resources and Industries*, rev. ed., (New York: Harper and Brothers, 1951).

4. Harold J. Barnett and Chandler Morse, *Scarcity and Growth* (Baltimore: The Johns Hopkins Press for Resources for the Future, Inc., 1963).

5. Hans H. Landsberg, *Natural Resources for U. S. Growth—A Look Ahead to the Year 2000* (Baltimore: The Johns Hopkins Press for Resources for the Future, Inc., 1964), p. 13.

6. See Barry Commoner, *The Closing Circle* (New York: Alfred A. Knopf, 1971).

7. Garrett Hardin, "The Tragedy of the Commons," *Science*, December 13, 1968, pp. 1243-48.

8. See Ralph Turvey, "Side Effects of Resource Use," in Henry Jarrett, ed., *Environmental Quality in a Growing Economy* (Baltimore: The Johns Hopkins Press for Resources for the Future, Inc., 1966), pp. 3-14.

9. This section draws extensively on the excellent descriptions of the physical features and geology of Texas contained in the *Texas Almanac and State Industrial Guide, 1976-1977* (Dallas: A. H. Bellow Corporation, 1976), hereinafter cited as *Texas Almanac*.

10. Thomas Lloyd Miller, *The Public Lands of Texas, 1519-1970* (Norman, Oklahoma: University of Oklahoma Press, 1971), p. XII.

11. Ibid., p. 94.

12. *Texas Almanac*, op. cit., p. 90.

13. Ibid., p. 94.

14. See Corwin Johnson, "Historical Perspectives," in *Texas Land*

Use, Report Number 1 (Austin: The Interagency Council on Natural Resources and the Environment, 1973), p. 8.

15. *Texas Almanac,* op. cit., p. 119.

16. Statement made by Dr. W. L. Fisher, Director, Bureau of Economic Geology, The University of Texas at Austin in "Texas Oil and Gas: Past and Future Trends in Production, Reserves, and Resources," mimeographed, March 1977.

17. Lorna Monti, "How Oil Supports Prosperity in Texas," *Texas Business Review,* January 1977, pp. 1-3.

18. Robert M. Lockwood, "The Energy Economy: The Death of Prorationing," *Texas Business Review,* December 1971, p. 167.

19. These figures, and those pertaining to oil and gas production and reserves in subsequent discussions below, are taken from Fisher, op. cit..

20. W. R. Kaiser, "Texas Lignite: Near-Surface and Deep-Basin Resources," *Report of Investigation Number 79,* Bureau of Economic Geology, The University of Texas at Austin, Austin, Texas, 1974.

21. This section draws on the information on non-petroleum minerals in Texas prepared by the Bureau of Economic Geology at The University of Texas at Austin, and published in the *Texas Almanac,* op. cit., pp. 423-30.

22. Jared Hazleton, *The Economics of the Sulphur Industry* (Baltimore: The Johns Hopkins Press for Resources for the Future, Inc., 1970).

23. J. B. Zimmerman and Eugene Thomas, "Sulfur in West Texas: Its Geology and Economics," *Geological Circular Number 69.2,* Bureau of Economic Geology, The University of Texas at Austin, Austin, Texas, April 1969.

24. For a comprehensive discussion of these approaches to land resource management, see Jared Hazleton, in *Texas Land Use, Report No. 6* (Austin: The Interagency Council on Natural Resources and the Environment, 1973).

25. Jared Hazleton, *The Impact of the Texas Constitution on Natural Resources* (Houston: Institute for Urban Studies, University of Houston, 1973).

26. R. Deane Conrad, "Water and Air Pollution," in the Natural Resources Section, *The Book of States* (1972-1973), p. 465.

FOUR

TEXAS-THE ENERGY ECONOMY*
Allen Commander · Mary C. Schiflett
John V. Zuckerman

In recent years, Texas has been producing about 40 percent of the oil and gas for the United States, or about 25 percent of all fossil fuel energy produced in the entire nation. Texas also has about 26 percent of the nation's refining capacity. In April 1977, an addition to a large refinery near Houston created one of the largest—if not the largest—multiple-product oil refining complexes in the world. This unit will refine 640,000 barrels per calendar day. Texas contributes a major proportion of the nation's petrochemicals, with approximately 43 percent of the carbon black, 54 percent of propylene, 67 percent of methanol, and 87 percent of butadiene being produced in the state.

Texas not only plays a significant role in the manufacture of petroleum-based products, but because of its supply of petroleum and natural gas, a large industrial base has grown up in the state. As a result, Texas is the largest consumer of energy in the nation by a wide margin, exceeding the consumption of the next nearest state California, by over 30 percent. All of this allows us to regard Texas as having

---

*This essay is an adaptation and condensation of the monograph, Texas Energy: Flows, Forecasts and Policy Implications, *published in September 1974 by The Energy Institute, The University of Houston, Houston, Texas. Mrs. Schiflett is Director of Publications of The Energy Institute, and during the time this essay was written, Drs. Commander and Zuckerman were Director and Deputy Director, respectively.*

a true energy economy.

The availability of energy has led to the location in Texas of large basic metals and processing facilities. Because of the vast size and climatic character of the state, it is the nation's largest supplier of ten separate food and fiber commodities, and is a major exporter of agricultural products.[1] Given the reliance of agricultural production on chemical fertilizers, pesticides, herbicides, etc., that are petroleum derivatives, Texas energy production assumes an even greater importance in the economy of the state.

Two out of every seven non-farm jobs in Texas are directly related to the petroleum resources of the state. While Texans expend massive amounts of energy to heat and cool their homes and move their vehicles, it is notable that industry is the largest single consumer of energy in the state.

Since fossil fuel energy dominates the state's presence, it is important to examine the implications of possible economic consequences of environmental changes which could alter the oil and gas supply of Texas. This essay provides the results of a research study of Texas energy supply and demand flows and forecasts, and examines the impact on the state of a projected diminishing of relative supplies of energy over the next ten years. Alternatives for the future of Texas are reviewed, based on the premise that the Texas economy must be optimized no matter what outside constraints are present to diminish present and future supplies of petroleum and natural gas.

ENERGY FLOWS AND FORECASTS

During the last months of 1973, a study of Texas energy flows was conducted under the auspices of The Energy Institute at the University of Houston, including a historical survey of energy flows in the state for the years 1960 and 1970, and several projections for 1980 and 1985.[2] The projection for 1980 is based on the growth of demand as predicted by the historical trends for 1960-70. Two projections for 1985 are included. One is based on the assumption that demand will continue at about the present rate of growth, and a second projection is based on the assumption that there will be some switching of fuel from gas or oil to coal, some conservation measures, as well as more efficient utilization of the fuel available.

In making the flow study, Texas information was collected in such a way that it may be compared with national information collected by the Joint Committee on Atomic Energy of the United States

Congress, and disseminated in a report of the Committee.[3] The unit of energy most convenient for the Texas flow studies was that used in the national study, the equivalent of a million barrels of oil a day, expressed by MBL/DOE. All energy values utilized herein have been converted to this unit by first calculating the equivalents of different fuel amounts in British thermal units (BTUs) and then re-converting to the amount of oil which would produce the equivalent energy.[4] For example, the number of tons of coal burned for a particular use has been converted into the number of barrels of oil needed to obtain the same amount of heat.

TEXAS ENERGY FLOWS—1960

The following discussion may be aided by frequent references to the tables presented in this essay.

Oil. As is indicated in Table 4-1, the total oil supply in Texas in 1960 consisted of oil from domestic sources and from imports. Even in 1960, a significant amount of oil was imported from other states into Texas. On the other hand, a major amount of Texas oil was sent into other states. The largest share of this Texas oil was used by automobiles, planes, trains, and other modes of transportation. A small amount was used for residential and commercial end uses, such as for heating and cooling single dwellings, apartment houses, offices, and shopping centers. Industry used a larger amount for boiler fuel in petroleum refining, and chemicals. The use of oil for non-energy uses, such as feedstock in the manufacture of chemical fertilizers, plastics, and synthetic rubber, accounted for approximately the same amount. No scaleable amount of oil was used in the production of electrical energy in Texas in 1960.

Coal. In 1960, the total Texas production of coal was very small and little was imported. Of the total supply, about half went for industrial use, and the other half went into non-energy uses. No measurable amount of coal was used in Texas for heating purposes.

Gas. Texas natural gas production was high and only a trace of gas was imported from other states. Electrical energy was being produced almost entirely from natural gas. A somewhat smaller amount was used for residential and commercial heating. The largest single use of gas went to the industrial sector, which underscores that in Texas, gas has been the primary industrial energy provider. Finally, a very small amount of gas was used in transportation, as energy to operate pipe lines.

Hydroelectric. The supply of hydroelectric energy in Texas in 1960 was insignificant. Texas had no production of energy from nuclear, geothermal, nor other sources of energy in 1960.

In 1960, the total input into electrical energy generation consisted of gas and hydroelectric power. Table 4-2 analyzes the conversion of energy. The total amount of electrical energy turned into useful industrial and into residential and commercial use was only about one-quarter of the amount used in generating the electricity. Such losses were normal in 1960, and are not unusual even today. In Texas, no measurable amount of electricity was utilized in the transportation sector.

During 1960 in Texas, the least efficient user of energy was the transportation section. About 75 percent of the total energy supplied was lost or wasted and the remaining 25 percent was converted to useful work in moving automobiles, trucks, trains, aircraft, and ships. This rather low efficiency shows the penalty that Texans have been paying for their mobility. By comparison, the industrial sector looks good: almost 70 percent was effectively utilized, and about 30 percent was lost. These are the percentages for the industrial energy

TABLE 4-1

SUPPLY OF ENERGY IN TEXAS*

	Flows			Forecasts	
	1960	1970	1980	Base 1985	Variation 1985
Nuclear			0.03	0.5	0.5
Hydro-Electric	0.002	0.002	0.002	0.002	0.002
Imported Gas	0.05	0.3	1.5	1.7	0.8
Domestic (Texas) Gas	2.5	4.0	3.1	2.7	2.7
Coal	0.02	0.02	0.2	0.2	1.4
Imported Oil	0.5	0.7	1.7	2.3	1.7
Domestic (Texas) Oil	3.0	4.2	3.2	3.0	3.0
Total	6.072	9.222	9.732	10.402	10.102

*All flow figures in this and the succeeding tables are MBL/DOE. See Note 4.

Source: *Texas Energy*, Energy Institute, The University of Houston, 1974.

TABLE 4-2

CONVERSION OF ENERGY IN TEXAS

	Flows			Forecasts	
	1960	1970	1980	Base 1985	Variation 1985
Electrical Power Generation	0.2	0.5	1.1	1.7	1.6
Interstate Exports: Gas	1.5	2.3	1.7	1.4	1.4
In-State Use: Gas	0.8	1.5	2.5	2.8	2.0
Interstate Exports: Oil	2.9	3.6	2.7	2.6	2.6
In-State Use Oil	0.6	1.3	1.7	2.0	1.7

Source: *Texas Energy*, Energy Institute, The University of Houston, 1974.

supplied in the form of electrical energy, gas, coal, and oil in Texas presented in Table 4-3.

The residential and commercial sector took a little more than half of its input from gas and the rest of its energy came from oil and electrical energy. The efficiency of use was again better than in the transportation sector, with nearly 70 percent utilized while about 30 percent was lost.

TEXAS ENERGY FLOWS-1970

During the ten years between 1960 and 1970, a massive expansion in the use of oil and gas occurred in Texas. Oil utilization increased more in Texas than in the rest of the United States, and the use of natural gas in the state increased at an even higher rate. The early stages of the move to a greater use of electricity can also be seen, for electrical energy output more than doubled during the 1960s. Natural gas use in industry also doubled. There was no significant change in coal use in Texas from 1960 to 1970. The overall efficiency of conversion was about the same as in the earlier decade, for the lost energy was nearly at the same level as the used energy.

TEXAS ENERGY FLOW FORECASTS—1980

The basic commitments of the nation for the energy use pattern in 1980 have already begun. It is true that the response to the Arab oil embargo in late 1973 has shown that the nation can make significant reductions in demand through the conservation of energy. On the other hand, the Census Bureau has projected the population will continue to increase for at least forty-five more years. The basic requirements for energy consumption between now and 1980 will be largely determined by decisions which have already been made.

Information for projections has been derived from publications by state agencies such as the Railroad Commission of Texas, industrial sources such as the U. S. Bureau of Mines and the Federal Power Commission. The patterns of energy production and consumption for 1980 are reasonably well-established. A large part of the electrical capacity that can be functioning commercially by 1980 has already been ordered, but this increase will not go very far in helping to solve the state's energy problems. No significant growth in hydroelectric power is expected by that time.

There are no nuclear power plants currently operating in Texas, and there can be none operating by 1980 which are not already past the drawing board and federal agency approval stages. Taking this into consideration, nuclear power can be assumed to be the fuel for approximately 3 percent of electric power generation by utilities in 1980.

The assumptions for coal are that Texas lignite will be used for mine-mouth electric power generation by both industry and public utilities in 1980, and that small amounts of coking coal will continue to be imported.

All of this simply shows that Texas energy in 1980 will still be derived primarily from oil and gas. At the present time, Texas wells are operating at full capacity, and new major domestic discoveries have not been made within the Texas borders. The largest recent United States discoveries have been made on the Alaskan North Slope while reserves are believed to lie along the off-shore Continental shelf. Even if this oil were destined to be piped to Texas, it takes several years lead time before oil can flow to the refineries. Furthermore, concern for the environment may delay the production even more. Extensive offshore leasing has begun only recently. Realistically, large amounts of energy from some new source or by some improved technology simply cannot be counted on by 1980.

Conservation, increased efficiency, and less waste have already demonstrated that certain measures can be taken voluntarily or mandatorily to extend the supply of energy. The factors of the market place have also entered, and it is not likely that fuel prices will ever be as low as in the past. Even with conservation and foreseen price increases, though, the projected demand predicted for the future exceeds the projected supply. If present trends continue, projected consumption of natural gas and oil in Texas will also require decreasing exports to the rest of the nation, or increasing imports from the other producing states or from foreign sources. Neither of these alternatives is satisfactory. Most natural gas exported from Texas, for example, is done so under long term contracts which are not apt to be terminated easily. The foreign supply of oil can be abruptly cut off by edicts of embargo, as was recently demonstrated by the Arab nations.

Like all Americans, Texans continue to commit themselves to an increasing number of automobiles as well as to an ever greater use of energy in all parts of their lives. In fact, the only thing which seems certain for the future is that if the growth of demand continues as projected, then the requirements for imports of both oil and gas either from other states or from outside the country will be increased markedly in Texas during the 1970s.

The specific assumptions which have been made with respect to the supply forecast of Texas oil and natural gas are:

—The Texas proportion of the mainland United States' total production of oil and natural gas will remain static

—Production in Texas will decline. In 1970, Texas produced 4.2 million barrels of oil a day; in 1980 it is expected to produce only 3.2 million barrels, and in 1985, 3 million barrels.

—The recent trends of success in United States oil drilling activities are assumed to remain at the present rate

—Low real prices for domestic oil and natural gas are also assumed to continue

—Efforts to improve the quality of the environment will continue

Based on these premises concerning the supply, the demand forecast for Texas for 1980 includes the following assumptions:

—No significant improvement will occur in the end use efficiencies

—The use of the automobile will continue at the present growth trend

—Environmental quality objectives will generally remain as they are at present

—Domestic trade relationships between Texas and other states will

remain the same in 1980 as at present
- —Population growth in Texas will be 1.5 percent a year
- —Per capita energy growth will be 2.1 percent a year
- —Industrial output growth between 1970-80 will be 41 percent
- —Fuel mix will remain the same as in 1970 in the residential, commercial, industrial, and transportation sectors
- —Chemical feedstocks will change from 12 percent use of oil as a base to 50 percent use of oil as a base in 1980
- —Electric power generation by fluid fossil fuels will be about 50 percent oil and 50 percent natural gas[5]

TEXAS ENERGY FLOW FORECASTS—1985—BASE FORECAST

Oil and gas production in Texas is expected to drop by 1985 unless major changes are made in exploration patterns and major new reserves are discovered. The pattern of use in Texas will continue to show growth. The assumption was made that, because of long-term contractual and regulatory obligations, a constant proportion of Texas' production of natural gas and oil will continue to be exported. The data in the four tables indicate that the supply of natural gas and oil available for consumption within Texas will become smaller, year by year.

TEXAS ENERGY FLOW FORECASTS—1985—VARIATION

The possible shortages and increasing prices of energy sources indicate possible major changes in the trends of energy production and consumption. Recent experience demonstrated the potential for adjustment in energy consumption by all sectors, particularly the residential and commercial and transportation sectors. The 1985 variation indicates the long-term effects of such adjustments. Let us assume that decreased availability and high prices of oil and natural gas result in an increased demand for coal in the electric power and industrial sectors. With a direct curtailment of approximately 10 percent in consumption by the residential and commercial sector and a 23 percent decrease in the transportation sector, the 1985 picture would be considerably different.

The 1985 energy flows make several assumptions: (1) all new electric power and large industrial boilers built in the period 1970-85 were to be coal-fired, (2) moderate conservation measures could decrease oil and natural gas use in the residential and commercial sector by 10 percent, and, (3) changes are made in automobiles to increase the average miles per gallon of passenger automobiles from the present 13 mpg to 17 mpg with widespread use of small automobiles averaging 20 mpg. The overall savings in net energy use would be only about 4 percent, but the savings in oil and natural gas consumption would be about 20 percent to 30 percent, respectively.

INTERPRETATION OF TRENDS

The four tables also provide trend information. In Table 4-1, the figures for domestic and imported oil and natural gas are given separately to show the major increase required to support the projected demand from 1980-85. If the imported oil or gas is not available, then the amount of energy which can be supplied to meet Texas' demand will fall short of demand by 1985. It also must be remembered that many of the existing natural gas and oil contracts are for twenty to thirty years' duration, so the supply cannot be diverted as the Texas demand increases.

Tables 4-1 and 4-2 show that electricity is a form of power which will grow markedly in the late 1970s, and then even more rapidly between 1980-85. On the other hand, coal is not shown to increase in use between 1980-85 for the base forecast. An alternate variation for 1985 shows coal increasing between 1980-85 with the exploitation of lignite resulting in a large change for this variable.

Also, Table 4-3 indicates the end uses by the various sectors of the Texas economy. All of the end uses show growth over the time span of 1960 to 1985. Industrial activity in Texas increases markedly, particularly from 1970-85. The growth in residential and commercial use also reflects the growth in population.

Finally, Table 4-4 provides information on efficiency. It is clear that no significant improvement in consumption efficiency is forecasted by 1985.

WHAT CHANGES ARE AHEAD?

From the data just presented, a critical time frame begins to emerge, bracketing the problems and solutions as being for the short, the intermediate, and the long term.

The short term is now. The two most effective measures for helping to solve immediate energy shortages are conservation and increased efficiency. Car pooling, installing proper insulation to increase heating and cooling efficiency in all homes and buildings, recycling whenever possible for some additional use, and utilization of all by-products in processing and refining procedures—all of these add up to be the greatest relief for the energy problem in the shortest time. The total savings through such measures can be very large and should be considered the best source of energy available immediately.

For the intermediate term—probably for the next five years at least—conservation and increased efficiency will continue to be paramount, but there also will be time to refine these two methods of saving energy by planning, rearranging of priorities, and increased research. Impact studies can be done to determine where energy shortages will

TABLE 4-3

ENERGY UTILIZATION IN TEXAS

	Flows			Forecasts	
	1960	1970	1980	Base 1985	Variation 1985
Residential & Commercial Heating & Cooling	0.2	0.4	0.6	0.7	0.6
Industrial Heating & Cooling Processing	0.7	1.4	2.1	2.4	2.4
Non-Energy*	0.2	0.6	1.0	1.2	1.2
Transportation	0.4	0.6	0.8	1.0	0.8

*Production of chemicals, fertilizer, butadiene, etc.

Source: *Texas Energy*, Energy Institute, The University of Houston, 1974.

TABLE 4-4

ENERGY EFFICIENCY IN TEXAS

	Flows			Forecasts	
	1960	1970	1980	Base 1985	Variation 1985
Lost Energy	0.7	1.4	2.1	2.6	2.5
Used Energy	0.7	1.4	2.1	2.6	2.4

Source: *Texas Energy*, Energy Institute, The University of Houston, 1974.

have the greatest and the least effect on the overall economy. National, regional, state, and local planning can be done to ease fuel shortages and misallocations so that one group does not suffer disproportionately. Shifts in energy choices can be made which will lead to a better utilization of all the fuels, but especially those in short supply or with declining reserves. Supplemental aid can be granted to those who, through no fault of their own, must undergo hardship because of shortages and cost increases. Studies should be made so that, should an energy crisis such as the one of the winter of 1977 reoccur, the governmental bodies will be ready to handle alternative choices with knowledge and assurance.

The third time frame is long range, and a whole spectrum of problems will need to be addressed. There is no doubt that short term and intermediate solutions to the problems caused by energy shortages can be achieved through conservation, whether it is voluntary or by mandatory allocation. A long-term program based on limiting usage, however, would be contrary to the American tradition of free choice. A climate of cooperation must be achieved among the governing bodies, the educational and research institutions, and the industrial and business sectors. For the long-range future, the economy of the United States and Texas can best be served not only by continuing the conservation and efficient use of all natural resources but also by improving technology in the energy field, by developing new energy sources, and by passing legislation which will guarantee the success of these goals.

Effective energy conservation in Texas and the nation can also mean that in both the short and long run there will be more raw materials available for Texas' important petrochemical industry. Rather than wasting gas and oil in inefficient heating and cooling systems or wasteful powering of transportation systems, these resources can be utilized for making fertilizers, chemical products, feedstocks, pharmaceuticals, and plastics.

OIL AND GAS

Currently, Texas leads the nation in oil and gas production and in refinery capacity. In addition, a large part of the economic wealth of Texas is based on the petrochemical industry. Facing a future of dwindling petroleum resources, Texas could move from being a net energy exporter to being a net energy importer. There are two viewpoints of such a shift: that it spells the end of the booming Texas economy, or that it does not matter where raw materials originate if Texas can protect its position as a petroleum processing and marketing center.

The first opinion is a realistic one if the policy makers in Texas fail to meet the challenge to set some new goals and to establish policies for researching them. It is equally true, however, that increased imported raw materials will not be flowing into Texas unless plans are made now. Texas has the modern petrochemical processing plants, the giant refineries, and the trained scientists and technicians—all of which are essential to the development and expansion of the economy. Up until now, Texas has not sought to import natural resources on any large scale; but if Texas can increase its imports to balance its gradual decline in oil and gas reserves, then a large sector of the state economy will remain stable. The decision of 1977 to build a deep-water mono-buoy terminal (or superport) off Texas shores is one important factor. Favorable laws and mutually beneficial contracts also will help secure for Texas a steady flow of materials to supply its production lines.

Texas flows and forecasts indicate that there will be some necessary changes in how Texans live, perhaps in the way many will earn their living, and in some of the state's laws and regulations.

It is ironic that had Texas not been so well-endowed with oil and gas, or had the energy flows begun to dwindle even ten or fifteen years ago, the national energy shortage would not have seemed to be so threatening to the Texas economy. Prior to World War II, the Texas oil fields were a source of stories about those who "struck it rich." While the state did benefit from this exploration in a number of ways, only a few Texans made their livelihood in the petroleum industry. As oil began to be joined by natural gas as a recognized valuable natural resource, the Texas economy changed. It entered a period of rapid development into what can only be described as an energy economy.

To make this distinction more clear, two statements repeated recently by national energy spokesmen should be considered: first, that transportation is the greatest user of energy, and it is therefore the hardest hit by any shortage in petroleum; and second, there is a shortage of energy materials in most states. Neither statement holds true for Texas. It is energy-consuming industries, not transportation, which account for the largest single block of energy demands in Texas. There is presently no shortage of energy materials in Texas, but the large surplus may be effectively wiped out by long-standing contractual agreements and by geographic imbalances.

Crude Oil Production. In 1980, Texas will have had a 12 percentage point decrease in its proportion of the crude oil production in the United States. This amounts to a million barrel per day decrease. By 1985, Texas' share of the crude production will have decreased an additional percentage point. Unless alternative outside sources of crude oil are assured, the adverse impact on the state's industrial and agricultural economy will be very heavy.

Although the fiscal impact on the state was softened somewhat by the increases in the price of oil, the public sense of confusion which accompanies the new energy shortage economy was reflected both in consumer and financial markets. Nationally, sales of large cars plummeted. Motor home retailers in some cases were forced into bankruptcy. Fears of gasoline shortages and weekend restrictions on gasoline sales began to affect motel chains and the outlying recreational areas such as state and national parks. Investments in the more recently developed large private parks and playgrounds became shaky. Many job layoffs in the airline, automobile, hotel, and other travel-related fields were charged to the energy problems. But the impact does not stop there. A cutback in petroleum production not only creates problems in that industry, but also affects steel, aluminum, chemicals, forging, transportation, agricultural production, and construction—often with dire effects for the whole economy. Any major shift in a major resource industry creates not arithmetic, but geometric, impact on all the tangent industries and businesses. The significance for Texas in oil is shown by its having the largest currently active land reserves of oil in the nation, and forty big refineries which process about one-fourth of all the crude oil for the entire country.

In the Western Hemisphere, Alaska is the only state in the nation which can possibly equal the reserve supply of oil in Texas, and production activity on Alaska's North Slope is only beginning. There are also no large refineries available nearby, so the oil must move long distances by pipeline or tanker to the market. Finally, if the construction of the Alaskan pipelines were already completed, the North Slope could furnish only about the same amount of oil per day as the nation lost through the Arab embargo.

Still more oil will have to be recovered by drilling wells offshore, and by recovering through secondary and tertiary methods the oil left in the existing fields. Both of these sources make Texas the best prospect for domestic oil in the near future.

Natural Gas. Since many of the conditions for oil exploration also exist for natural gas exploration in Texas, it is not surprising that a similar forecast is made. By 1980, Texas will experience a decrease of about eight points in its percentage share of the United States natural gas production. By 1985, because of decreases in production in other parts of the country, there will be a seven point increase in the percentage supplied by Texas, but with a net volume decrease in total production.

There could be no better example of the need for careful legislative action than what has happened to natural gas in Texas. Long regarded as a nuisance to oil drilling, and therefore flared at the wellhead to eliminate it, natural gas has only gradually become recognized for its enormous spectrum of uses. As its use for heating in Texas and in other gas producing states increased, natural gas became known as a clean, efficient fuel. It was sought as a substitute for coal and other fuels in other regions. Homes and industries throughout the nation welcomed the clean, inexpensive fuel, and long-term contracts were quickly drawn up and signed.

In 1954, the Supreme Court ruled in the *Phillips* decision that the 1938 law authorizing federal regulation of gas prices in interstate pipelines extended to the control of gas prices at the wellhead. Subsequent Federal Power Commission rulings in the late 1960s added uncertainty to production in the industry by creating the so-called "sanctity of contract issue." A price approved by the Federal Power Commission could not be guaranteed for the lifetime of contracts governing natural gas sales. For many years, gold and natural gas were the only commodities with a regulated fixed value in the United States which is far below the world market price.

Within only a few years of the natural gas wellhead price regulation, two other factors developed. First, the technological advances in the chemical industry caused many new and old companies to develop or expand into petrochemical manufacturing and to locate along the Texas Gulf Coast. Second, natural gas became necessary as a feedstock at the same time it was becoming more and more desirable as a fuel. For many Texas industries, it served both as a feedstock and fuel. All of this was accomplished with the price of natural gas held at an artificially low level. Soon the reserves were dropping in relation to production; yet, there was no real push to allow the market place to restructure gas prices. The low price of gas meant that gas exploration eventually failed to keep up with gas demand. State and national policy-makers and the industrial decision-makers have learned from the example of natural gas, so laws and regulations for future use of all natural resources hopefully will be drawn more wisely. This would result in efficient production for present users and efficient allocation of future supplies.

The estimated reserves of natural gas in the United States which can be produced cheaply are much smaller than crude oil supplies. It is essential that alternative sources of fuel be provided to substitute for natural gas. This will allow natural gas to make its main contribution to the Texas economy as petrochemical feedstock, and perhaps allow some other fuel which is not so versatile to be used for boilers, heating and air conditioning, and power generation.

A BALANCED ENERGY ECONOMY FOR TEXAS

The following brief suggestions map the major considerations which state and national policy-makers must face to insure a balanced energy picture for Texas.

Conservation. The greatest immediate relief for the energy problems is in conservation. A program to achieve conservation in buildings and appliances could seek to establish standards for reduced lighting. Furthermore, it could serve to label the efficiency of major energy-consuming appliances, to stimulate the reinsulation of homes to increase thermal efficiency, and to encourage the adoption of more energy-conscious building codes. Also, specific measurable auto efficiency goals could be established for every year through 1980. Methods to shift people and freight to more efficient modes of transit would save energy. Mass transit systems in Texas have been steadily declining. The public systems frequently operate at a loss, and many privately-owned companies are disappearing through sales to or takeovers by governments. To give some relief to the mass transit companies, perhaps some tax rebate on fuel could be granted.

Measurable efficiency goals ought to be established for each of the six or seven major energy-consuming industries. For example, a standard for the use of lighting in night advertising ought to be established and gradually raised each year until such time as adequate energy is available again. A national conservation ethic could be created through media advertising and through distribution in elementary and secondary schools of energy conservation kits.

The use of energy in the utilities in Texas gives another high-use area where more efficiency would serve to benefit the Texas economy. Multiple energy industrial centers could be developed that would combine generation of electricity with the production of industrial steam. New approaches would permit the realization of high combustion efficiencies within existing furnaces as well as new designs. The use of off-peak electrical power, methods to recapture waste heat for production uses, and the use of municipal solid wastes as utility boiler fuel should all be studied. The effects of altering the existing rate structure of utilities, such as the practice of regressive utility rates which rewards greater use of energy, need to be examined in the light of current energy conditions.

Regulatory Commission. At present, the authority for regulation of energy production is a task which has traditionally been handled by the Texas Railroad Commission. Energy is important enough to warrant its own separate regulatory body.

An Energy Commission could have the duty of regulating the developing sources of energy such as coal, geothermal, wind, solar, and the continuing search for natural gas and oil. It could have regulatory authority over the carriers of energy from the point of production to the end use distributor. The Commission could supervise the land use in Texas on the basis of statewide considerations so that such activities as strip mining landfills, coal-fired electric generators and nuclear power station locations are planned from the beginning for ecological restoration. This agency could be given the power to require prior approval of industrial fuel uses, perhaps even to require new plants to plan from the beginning on alternative sources of energy.

Such an Energy commission logically could be included in the present structure for regulating bidding on state-owned lands for exploration and production of natural resources. The statutes regulating such bidding ought to require variable royalty bidding methods, and continue to require the authority in new state leases to accept royalties in-kind on all leases. Also, there could be some guideline on unitization, perhaps making it mandatory on state-owned lands, and rule of majority consent at 75 percent for privately-owned wells. There could be legislation spelling out the clear authority of the Energy Commission to allocate the end use of natural gas and other natural resources within the state. Such authority could then be exercised evenly in like situations throughout the state.

A Utility Commission was established in September 1976 to govern the end uses of energy and to establish the rate regulations for all utilities in the state. Appeals from rates not only for natural gas but also from electrical and telephone rates set by cities are handled by this commission, just as are done in other states. This action further necessitates the establishment of an Energy Commission.

Furthermore, there should be some agency designated as a clearing house for all land use considerations to which the proposed Energy Commission, the Utility Commission, the General Land Office, the Air Control Board, and the Water Quality Board could turn for guidelines. If expanded land use regulations are needed, then the determination could be made as to which of these agencies, if any, should act as the primary promulgator of such regulations. This agency ought to be structured so as to expedite the prior approval necessary for new energy production sites. Appropriate application procedures could be developed so that an applicant would deal only with this commission and the commission itself would seek interagency review and approval of the application.

Taxation. From the Gulf Coast petrochemical industry to the agricultural and ranching activities of the Panhandle, the Texas economy is integrally related to energy supply. While the entire Texas economy is affected in many ways by the energy industry, perhaps the most significant impact is on the Texas tax structure. A large percentage of the total Texas tax dollar is derived from oil and the gas industry. Texas has avoided levying the general business and income taxes which have been enacted by most other states because of the income received from taxing the oil and gas industry. By using the market value of these products as the determinative tax base, Texas will benefit from price increases even in a period of declining production. A careful study should be conducted, however, to determine at what point the total tax income from these oil and gas taxes will begin to decline.

While higher prices for fuels and increased demand will mean some additional incentive for exploration, there is also a strong belief that no one should profit excessively from such efforts. Legislators should carefully determine that an amended energy tax structure is fair and equitable to the industry and provides an equitable return to the people of Texas for the depletion of their state's natural resources. There exist, for example, large producers of energy such as coal who pay no direct taxes for the production and depletion of Texas resources.

Both tax incentives and disincentives must be carefully weighed by the Legislature to achieve the proper balance for Texas. The Texas Legislative Budget Board should be given the resources necessary to conduct a study to define as precisely as possible the present and future interrelationship of the Texas energy industries, the state budget, and tax income for the state.

Other items deserving careful review include the write-offs for intangible drilling and development costs, differential allowances for exploration of various products in various locations, and special allowances for low grade or marginal resource yield. Finally, there should be ample incentives to attract independent explorers and producers. In short, in a time of decreasing supply and increasing exploration and demand, a unified reasoned analysis should be made of the entire tax structure.

Technological Research and Development. For years, advancing technology has aimed to make jobs easier and safer or to make products quicker and more efficient. Now, there must be technological goals set toward less waste and increased energy efficiency. Conserving present energy sources and developing new alternatives must be given the highest technological priority.

Solar energy has been used on a limited scale for water heating, space heating, and air conditioning in other countries and experimentally in the United States. However, the sun offers an unlimited source of power, if only the technology can be economically developed. At the University of Houston, scientists are developing a central tower concept solar collector for electrical power generation. A technological assessment of the potential for large and small scale solar energy conversion for Texas has been completed at the University of Houston. Also, work is ongoing to develop advanced low cost solar collectors that will be compatible with absorption units for residential and commercial air conditioning. In Austin, a different approach to solar collection is being proposed by scientists at the University of Texas. The collectors are being designed to fly as space stations, transmitting energy to the earth via microwave-radio or laser beams.

Another source of energy which has not been thoroughly considered is geothermal reservoirs which could, in time, provide a good percentage of Texas' energy needs.

Improvements in the technology for liquefaction and gasification of lignite in Texas are being investigated by the chemical engineering departments of both the University of Houston and the University of Texas at Austin. Wind, one of man's earliest sources of power, is being looked upon as a possibility. Tests have been run recently by several of the major offshore drilling companies to see if small windmills are suitable for recharging the batteries that power some of the equipment on the unmanned production platforms. One estimate predicts that windmills may be used for power on about half of the twenty-eight hundred platforms in the Gulf of Mexico. Also within the past eighteen months, some companies have been installing tiny solar power devices on several hundred of the smaller drilling platforms offshore. Improved efficiency and lower costs in providing massive electricity from a variety of sources—such as from solid wastes—are also other possibilities for the future. While some high voltage lines do travel hundreds of miles at the present time, technology still has not solved the loss factor in long distance electrical energy conversion, so it is basically still an uneconomical fuel other than on a short-term or emergency basis.

Money for technological development and for research in the energy field has already been pledged by the federal government. Much of the announced $10 billion for a five-year energy research and development program has already been specifically designated for coal and nuclear research and development. It is also anticipated that private industry will continue to invest larger amounts of capital in expanded research and development programs. Various state governments will have to augment the federal program with additional funds. If Texas hopes to continue to play an important role in supplying energy to the nation in the future, it should begin now to draft the legislation necessary to encourage public and private investment in extensive programs of energy research.

Long-Range Planning. A long-range planning mechanism needs to be developed to serve both the Executive and Legislative branches of Texas government. Texas should financially support those engineering and economic system analyses which study the impact on the economy of various conversions and limitations of production. Data gathering and analyses on resource inventories, economic supply and demand, alternative sources of energy, and price and policy oriented research studies should be funded by the state.

Texas needs to prepare for the eventuality of becoming a net energy importer. Increased conservation efforts should be geared to delay this shift, if possible, but Texas should protect its supply factor for its continued economic growth and stability. So far, the state's wealth has been enhanced by its natural resources; its wealth will be assured if Texas can maintain a leading position as the supplier of the end products.

NOTES

1. Texas Department of Agriculture information furnished to the office of Lieutenant Governor William P. Hobby, Austin, Texas.

2. The authors are indebted to Dr. Russell G. Thompson, Professor of Quantitative Management Science, College of Business Administration, University of Houston and Director of the Texas Energy Supply and Demand Analysis Project, and his Research Assistants, Drs. Rodrigo J. Lievano and Robert R. Hill, for the information on energy flows and forecasts reported herein. The authors retain the responsibility for interpretation of the data and conclusions drawn therefrom. The authors acknowledge the contributions of Dr. Michael T. Johnson, Professor of Law and Associate Dean, Bates College of Law and Robert Shults, Research Assistant to the legislative and policy portion of this chapter.

3. The Energy Institute of the University of Houston, and the Center for Strategic and International Studies at Georgetown University, Washington, D. C., have reprinted this report as: *Understanding the National Energy Dilemma*. The report may be obtained from the Center for Strategic and International Studies, 1800 K Street, N. W., Georgetown University, Washington, D. C., 20006.

4. One 42-gallon barrel of oil = 5.62 million BTUs
   One cubic foot of natural gas = 1,032 BTUs
   One kilowatt hour of electricity = 3,423 BTUs
   One short ton of lignite = 15 million BTUs
   One short ton of coal = 25 million BTUs

A British thermal unit (BTU) is the amount of energy needed to raise one pound of water by one Fahrenheit degree.

5. These items were taken from Dr. Russell G. Thompson, et al, "Texas Energy Statistics and Forecasts," 1974, and are reprinted in *Texas Energy: Flows, Forecasts and Policy Implications*.

FIVE

HUMAN RESOURCE DEVELOPMENT IN TEXAS

Antonio Furino • William S. Franklin

Human resource development is a special issue for a number of reasons. First, human labor is the only resource that develops itself in order to increase its own productivity, its value to employers, and the income it is able to earn. Second, people invest in themselves for reasons other than economic gain. Investments in education and health, for instance, make workers more productive and better able to compete in the labor market, but they also yield significant noneconomic returns. Third, human resources perform a dual role in the economy, in that they are both producers and consumers of goods and services. A worker who becomes more productive as the result of training not only produces more for his employer, but is also able to buy more of the products of the economy. Thus we are interested in human resources both as contributors to production and as consumers of what is produced, and often we evaluate people's contributions to the economy by looking at their ability to earn and consume as much as we do their ability to produce.

Our efforts at human resource development include education, training, retraining and rehabilitation, labor market information and mobility, health care, and supportive services such as child care for the children of working parents. Of this host of programs, however, education and training are the two areas that serve more people than the others, and to which more resources are devoted. Accordingly, we give our attention in this chapter principally to education and training in Texas. We begin with a discussion of the "traditional" programs that were in place prior to 1960, after which we consider the manpower programs that comprised a substantial part of the "War on Poverty" in the 1960s. We then summarize the programs that exist to aid the disadvantaged that make up so much of our manpower policy in the 1970s, and conclude with a discussion of problems and public policy implications.

TRADITIONAL PROGRAMS OF EDUCATION AND TRAINING

There are four major areas in which public policy has been directed toward the development of human resources for generations—public vocational education, apprenticeship, college and university education, and vocational rehabilitation. Since these are our oldest formal efforts at developing our labor resources, we begin by describing them before considering the newer programs of the last two decades.

Vocational Education

Public vocational education serves more people than any other formal program of skill training in Texas. More than 900,000 high school students and adults participated in vocational education programs in 1975. Yet serious doubts remain as to whether the public schools are doing the job they need to do in order to ensure that their graduates will be employable in a modern industrial economy.

Public support for vocational education in the United States began in 1917 with the passage of the Smith-Hughes Vocational Education Act. Augmented by the George-Barden Act of 1946, the Smith-Hughes Act provided federal matching funds for state-sponsored programs in vocational agriculture, homemaking, and trades and industry. The early concentration of vocational programs was probably a response to the skill requirements of the United States economy, but the changing occupational skill mix led to criticism of vocational education on the grounds that schools had failed to adapt their subject offering to the needs of the labor market. For example, as late as 1957, two-thirds of all enrollments in vocational programs in Texas were in agriculture and homemaking—the first providing training for a declining industry, and the second offering little hope of gainful employment at all.[1] Further, little conscious effort was being made to serve disadvantaged youth—the group least likely to go on to college, and hence the most in need of skill training for employment.

Dissatisfaction with vocational education, together with increased public awareness of the problems of structural unemployment and poverty, led to the passage of the Vocational Education Act of 1963.

Designed to upgrade the quality of vocational education and expand its offerings, the 1963 act apparently led to substantial increases in training for office occupations, but otherwise failed to change the structure of vocational education. This failure prompted Congress to pass the Vocational Education Amendments of 1968, which assured funding specifically for programs deemed especially worthwhile—postsecondary and cooperative programs, training for expanding occupations, and programs to train the disadvantaged and handicapped.[2]

The results of the 1968 amendments, while not spectacular, indicate a trend toward the provision of vocational training for truly marketable skills. As Table 5-1 indicates, the greatest growth in enrollments in vocational education in Texas has occurred in technical, health, occupational home economics, and special programs (usually for vocational counseling and orientation). Distribution and office training programs have also grown at a more rapid rate than total enrollments, and there has been an encouraging growth of participation by the disadvantaged. While agriculture and homemaking still account for slightly more than half of all vocational enrollments, the

TABLE 5-1

ENROLLMENTS IN VOCATIONAL EDUCATION PROGRAMS IN TEXAS, FY 1971-1975

	FY 1971	Percent of total FY 1971	FY 1975	Percent of total FY 1975	Percent Change from FY 1971
Total	608,252	100	912,236	100	50
Secondary	327,684	53.9	460,064	50.4	40.4
Post Secondary	41,912	6.9	93,481	10.2	123.0
Adult	238,656	39.2	358,691	39.3	50.3
Agriculture	146,988	24.2	143,976	15.8	-2.0
Distribution	39,707	6.5	72,669	8.0	83.0
Health	13,880	2.3	33,539	3.7	141.6
Consumer & Homemaking	229,357	37.7	330,547	36.2	44.1
Occupational Preparation	10,361	1.7	23,725	2.6	129.0
Office	42,112	6.9	69,902	7.7	66.0
Technical	7,862	1.3	40,559	4.4	415.9
Trades & Industry	95,135	15.6	132,316	14.5	39.1
Special Programs	22,009	3.6	65,003	7.1	195.3
Disadvantaged	56,183	9.2	134,316	14.7	139.1

Source: Texas Education Agency, Department of Occupational Education and Technology, *Annual Vocational Education Reports*, FY 1971-1975.

relative importance of those two categories is shrinking over time.

As promising as these developments are, it is necessary to assess the efforts of vocational education in meeting the actual demands of the labor market. On that score, the picture is less bright. As recently as 1971, the Texas State Advisory Council for Technical-Vocational Education estimated that only 15 percent of high school students were prepared with specific job skills.[3] And projections of supply and demand for workers in various occupational categories point out some serious imbalances between the kinds of skills demanded by employers and those being supplied in vocational education programs (see Table 5-2). In 1980, according to the Texas Education Agency, vocational education will supply only about one-third of the workers needed to fill vacancies in distributive occupations, about one-half of those in trades and industry, one-fourth of the office workers, and two-thirds of the workers needed in health occupations—this while supplying

TABLE 5-2

PROJECTED LABOR DEMAND AND SUPPLY
FROM PUBLIC VOCATIONAL EDUCATION AND
OTHER TRAINING PROGRAMS, 1980

Occupational Category	Total Employment 1975	Projected Additional Manpower Requirements	Projected Labor Supply	
			Output from Public Vocational Education	Output from Other Training Programs
Agriculture	223,490	1,912	7,056	316
Distribution	778,253	44,996	15,026	685
Health	164,520	17,296	11,177	3,478
Home Economics (outside home)	78,922	8,088	6,146	158
Office	895,011	76,880	19,260	19,025
Technical	56,221	3,265	2,243	3,689
Trades & Industry	1,213,729	59,485	31,787	25,349
Totals	3,410,146	211,922	92,695	52,700

Source: Texas Education Agency, *Texas State Plan for Vocational Education, Fiscal Year 1976*, Tables 1A, 1B.

nearly four times as many workers as will be required in agriculture and continuing to train more than 300,000 students in what for many are non-salable homemaking skills.

The data cited here indicate that the situation is somewhat more bleak than it really is. Obviously, even if there is little market demand for homemakers, the fact remains that homemaking is, or will be, the vocation of many students; certainly a strong case can be made for preparing those students for their lives' work, however nonremunerative it may be. Some of the apparent oversupply of workers in agricultural occupations is probably due to confusion over whether to include certain agricultural jobs under agriculture or other occupational groupings. Further, in small school districts it is common for agriculture and homemaking programs to teach some skills that are usually taught in separate programs in larger schools. Too, there are other training programs besides vocational education supplying skilled workers for the job market; it is perhaps too much to expect vocational education to do the entire job. Finally, large numbers of students for whom vocational programs are available do not participate in them, preferring instead to enroll in general or college preparatory programs. While this reluctance to enroll in vocational classes undoubtedly stems from many students' perception of vocational education as a "dumping ground" for the schools' disciplinary problems, one may still sympathize with educators whose offers of training are ignored by the majority of students. Still, even though the trends noted earlier seem to point in the right direction, there remains room for concern over the degree to which public educational institutions are meeting the skill demands of the labor market.

Apprenticeship

The oldest form of formal vocational training in Texas, and perhaps in the world, is apprenticeship. Dating from at least the Middle Ages, apprenticeship combines hands-on training on the job with related classroom instruction after work. Ideally, an apprentice is exposed to all phases of a craft during the three-to-five-year period of indenture, so that he is a truly well-rounded craftsman when he graduates into journeyman status. While in practice many apprentices are not given the broad range of instruction they are supposed to receive, recent research has shown that, on balance, the average apprentice is more broadly trained than other workers in his craft, and thus enjoys more regular employment and faster promotions than his informally trained counterpart.[4]

Numerically, apprenticeship is one of the least important forms of human resource development. Though some 425 occupations are considered apprenticeable, only about 291,000 apprentices were active in 1974 throughout the United States,[5] of whom 13,389 were in

Texas.[6] Moreover, the majority of apprentices are found in relatively few trades. Union construction almost always account for around 60 percent of all apprentices; and as Table 5-3 indicates, nearly four-fifths of Texan apprentices were construction workers.

Table 5-3 also demonstrates the role apprenticeships have played in lowering the barriers to minority entry into the skilled trades. One-sixth of all United States apprentices—and nearly one-fourth of those in Texas—are minority-group members; by comparison, only 2.2 percent of all apprentices were minorities in 1960.[7] While strenuous efforts have been required to remove discriminatory obstacles to minority training and employment in some crafts, it is clear that apprenticeship is presently functioning as an effective conduit for minority youth seeking to enter the skilled trades.

TABLE 5-3

COMPOSITION OF APPRENTICESHIP ENROLLMENTS
IN TEXAS AND UNITED STATES, BY MINORITY STATUS
AND CONSTRUCTION TRADES, 1974

	Total Apprentices	Minority Apprentices (Percent of Total)	Construction Apprentices (Percent of Total)	Minority Construction Apprentices (Percent of Total)
Texas	13,389	3,168 (23.7%)	10,487 (78%)	2,413 (23%)
United States	291,049	45,808 (15.8%)	182,018 (63%)	31,299 (17%)

Source: Bureau of Apprenticeship and Training (SNAPS data).

Given the strong points of apprenticeship alluded to above, the apparent increase in the importance of apprenticeship is a welcome development. Over the years, the percentage of construction workers with apprenticeship backgrounds has increased; further apprenticeship programs are being implemented in some construction unions which have not had a long tradition of apprenticeship, as well as in the nonunion sector.[8] Still, apprenticeship seems destined to furnish a relatively minor part of all skill training. One reason for this is due to the nature of apprenticeship: since most training takes place on the job, there can be only as many apprentices in training as there are jobs on which they can be trained. But more important, until nonunion employers increase their modest efforts, and unless additional sectors (such as health care and government employment) are opened to apprenticeship, apprenticeship will remain a form of training that is notable more for the quality of its trainees than for their quantity.

Higher Education

One of the most important sources of training in Texas is college and university education. In the fall of 1973, there were 531,939 persons enrolled in Texas colleges and universities, up from 409,438 in the fall of 1968.[9] While not all of these half-million students were pursuing academic degrees leading to or increasing their employability, it is safe to assume that most of them were interested in preparation for work as well as the joy of academic enlightenment.

Public institutions of higher education enrolled 85.6 percent of college students in Texas in 1973, compared with 81.9 percent in 1969. Thus not only did enrollments increase by nearly 30 percent over this four-year period, but nearly all of the increase was in public institutions. A significant part of the trend in enrollments could be found in the newer state colleges and universities: 75,000 students, or nearly 15 percent of all enrollments, were in public institutions founded since 1960. In particular, almost half of all students in public community colleges were attending institutions that did not exist fifteen years before. These enrollment trends clearly demonstrate both the increased importance of higher education, and an increased commitment to providing college training for groups that previously would not have had the opportunity to attend college.

Vocational Rehabilitation

The Texas Rehabilitation Commission offers a variety of services to persons who are blind, deaf, or physically disabled, in order to allow them to function more effectively in society and in the labor market.[10] Among the services provided by TRC are evaluation of work potential, counseling and guidance, interpreter services for the deaf, medical treatment, prosthetic devices, training for employment, placement, tools and licenses, and supplies and stocks of materials for the disabled who wish to start their own businesses.

Vocational rehabilitation appears to be highly successful at increasing the employability of its clients. In fiscal year 1976, more than 133,000 persons were assisted by TRC, including 23,318 who were "successfully rehabilitated." These clients raised their incomes an average of $4,000 per year, at a cost per case of only $1,063. The gains to society were even greater: nearly four thousand of those placed in jobs were able to move off the welfare rolls, at a savings of over $2 million in public assistance payments.

THE MANPOWER REVOLUTION OF THE 1960s

Apart from the programs of vocational education, vocational rehabilitation, apprenticeship, and college and university education discussed [here] there were only two significant efforts made to develop human resources in the United States before 1960. The GI Bill of Rights allowed for payment of training costs and some living expenses to veterans, and millions of veterans took advantage of the GI Bill to finish high school, attend college, or enroll in other training programs. The National Defense Education Act of 1958—largely a reaction to Sputnik and the fear that Soviet science and technology would outstrip the United States—was aimed at improving scientific and technical education in American universities. Beginning in the early 1960s, laws and programs intended specifically at developing human resources were developed; collectively they have come to be known as "manpower programs."

The Manpower Development and Training Act of 1962

uring the 1950s the problem of persistent and rising unemployment and the increased awareness of poverty in the United States led labor market analysts to conclude that some effort should be made to improve workers' employability and earning power. Some observers were especially concerned that the rising education and skill levels required in industry had rendered formerly productive employees useless to employers—that the problem, in other words, was one of "structural unemployment," which could best be solved by programs to retain household heads for meaningful jobs.

Acting on this assumption, Congress passed the Manpower Development and Training Act (MDTA) in 1962, providing institutional (classroom) and on-job training for unemployed family heads. Almost as soon as those manpower programs went into effect, however, the economy began to expand, and, aided by tax cuts in 1962 and 1964, was soon employing workers whose skills had formerly been viewed as obsolete. It then became obvious that the real employment problems were those suffered by youth, the uneducated and inexperienced, and nonwhite citizens. Accordingly, MDTA was liberalized and expanded to admit more youth, pay more generous training allowances to discourage drop outs, and to emphasize serving the disadvantaged.

The Economic Opportunity Act of 1964

President Johnson's "War on Poverty" was fought with many weap-

The Manpower Revolution of the 1960s

ons, but chief among them was the Economic Opportunity Act (EOA) of 1964. Administered by the Office of Economic Opportunity (OEO), EOA and its several amendments added a number of new programs to serve the poor and disadvantaged; while these are often included under the rubric of manpower programs, the only one that accomplished much in the way of skill training was the Job Corps. It was felt that some youths lived in environments that were so bad that they had to be relocated if any real training and upgrading was to occur. Thus, Job Corps trainees were taken away from home and placed in training centers for remedial education, medical and dental care, and occupational training.

There were several other programs included under EOA. The Neighborhood Youth Corps (NYC) was designed to combine work experience with enough income support to induce disadvantaged youth to stay in school or return to school. Operation Mainstream provided employment in rural beautification projects to older workers in rural areas. In the New Careers program, the disadvantaged were employed in subprofessional and paraprofessional jobs, in the misplaced hope that they would be able to make the transition later into permanent professional employment.

Perhaps the most controversial of OEO's programs were the Community Action Programs (CAPs). Based on the premise that existing agencies and programs such as apprenticeship, vocational education, and the Employment Service had largely failed to serve the disadvantaged, the CAPs were established by local Community Action Agencies (CAAs), and were funded directly by OEO, bypassing state, county and city officials in the process. While many of the CAPs' efforts were worthwhile—as, for example, Operation Headstart—the fact that the CAAs acted as advocates for the disadvantaged displaced local power structures and probably contributed to later demands for decentralization of manpower programs.

The Public Employment Program

During the 1960s many attempts were made to convince Congress of the desirability of creating jobs in the public sector for those who were willing to work but could not find jobs. The concept of government as the employer of last resort never advanced beyond the suggestion stage, however, and it was not until 1971, in the midst of a recession, that Congress passed even a modified job creation program. This Public Employment Program (PEP) made federal funds available to state and local governments to allow them to maintain employment (instead of laying off workers due to the shortfall of local tax revenues) or to hire additional workers for worthwhile local projects. Nationally the PEP program was successful in hiring over a million workers (although it is difficult to say how many of them would have been hired anyway), but it did not serve the disadvantaged very effectively and provided little training.

Evaluation of Manpower Programs

The above summary of efforts made during the 1960s toward training the unemployed and the disadvantaged is even too brief to cover all the programs that were implemented, much less to discuss the major problems in detail.[11] The lessons from the programs of the sixties, however, are becoming fairly clear. For one thing, special efforts must be made, over and above normal education and training activities, to train and employ the disadvantaged. Second, if we hope to employ the disadvantaged, a prerequisite is an expanding economy with low unemployment rates; most employers were unwilling to provide on-job training to the disadvantaged until the late 1960s, when the supply of mainstream workers had already been employed. Third, it is possible to train and employ disadvantaged workers in a cost-efficient manner; in spite of assertions to the contrary by numerous critics, the evidence is that most of the manpower programs for which the necessary data are available produced benefits for their clients that outweighed program costs.[12] Fourth, the proliferation of programs to serve the disadvantaged pointed up the desirability of implementing comprehensive programs tailored to serve the specific needs of target groups, rather than forcing clients to search for programs that they could fit into. Finally, the experiences of the sixties underscored the wisdom of planning and implementing programs at the local level in response to local needs, rather than forcing local areas to accept the imposition of programs conceived and planned in Washington. The efforts to put these lessons into practice form the core of our present manpower policy, and are discussed in the next section.

HUMAN RESOURCES DEVELOPMENT IN THE 1970s

The 1970s are characterized by a new generation of manpower strategies promoting the involvement of state and local governments and placing unprecedented emphasis upon comprehensive services within individual programs. Decentralized decision-making, if effectively used, allows improved control over many factors affecting local labor markets. Once comprehensive planning becomes a reality, manpower policy truly becomes a major tool for human resources development.

The act that represents the culmination of the changes from the philosophy and strategy prevailing in the sixties is the Comprehensive Employment and Training Act (CETA) signed into law in December 1973.[13] CETA, designed to provide "job training and employment opportunities for economically disadvantaged, unemployed, and underemployed persons" to enable them to secure self-sustaining, unsubsidized employment, inherits most of its elements from previous programs. The emphasis on training the disadvantaged began with MDTA, and made up important parts of EOA programs. The need to coordinate the efforts of the numerous manpower programs gave rise to two pre-CETA programs. The idea of grouping several different programs into one had been partially achieved after 1967 by the Concentrated Employment Programs (CEP) in order to develop a capability to respond to individual client needs with a variety of programs. The coordination of state and area planning efforts, inter-agency relationships, and state autonomy had been attempted by the Cooperative Area Manpower Planning System (CAMPS), initiated in 1967, almost at the same time as the CEP programs. Even the concept of transferring the responsibility of decision making from the national offices of the Department of Labor to local officials had been already written into law under EOA. What is new under CETA is that all of those concepts and approaches are written into one act. The CETA mechanism, if effectively operated, could avoid proliferation of efforts, competition among sponsors for similar manpower programs, and overlapping program approaches. Also, as a consequence of transferring decision making to the local level, federal, state, and local resources are being directed toward the development of timely and accurate labor market information to assist local decision makers.

CETA has seven titles. Title I provides funds for local prime sponsors (defined below) for the provision of comprehensive manpower services.

Title II provides funding for public service jobs in areas of greater than 6.5 percent unemployment.

Title III provides for federal programs for youth, ex-offenders, migrant workers, American Indians, and persons having difficulties with the English language.

Title IV re-establishes the Job Corps, again under Federal direction.

Title V establishes the National Commission for Manpower Policy, a nonpartisan advisory group working with the Secretary of Labor.

Title VI, added in 1974, authorizes funding for emergency public employment programs (similar to the PEP program).

Title VII contains specific requirements for all programs, such as nondiscrimination.

The basic concepts incorporated in the seven titles of CETA address four strategic areas of human resources development. First, local government officials, who are more directly accountable to those being affected by the quality and the efficiency of manpower programs, now have major responsibilities in the design and implementation of the programs. As mentioned earlier, the decentralization of the programs offers a real opportunity for truly comprehensive planning. Problems of human resources development are multifaceted and involve the totality of human behavior and aspirations. Therefore, approaches to their solution must involve economic, social, cultural, and institutional considerations as well as a fiscal policy cognizant of trade-offs among regional economic sectors.

Second, CETA concentrates federal funding into block grants to the chief state and local elected officials so that regional programs can be coordinated and funds utilized more economically.

Third, the categorical nature of the manpower programs of the sixties has been pártially abandoned under CETA. Certain categorical programs, such as the Job Corps, remain under federal supervision; but under Titles I, II, and VI, the decision on the mix of programs is left to local elected officials, so that program categories may be more flexible and varied in response to local needs. This third area is essential to human resources development since social systems are dynamic systems and corrective actions to problems must be responsive to different and changing socio-economic environments.

Fourth, the responsibility and accountability of making decisions increase the awareness of and the need for reliable information. Consequently, more public funds are likely to be devoted to produce adequate and timely regional data. This in itself is a most significant development benefiting local public and private sectors.

Funding under CETA

At this point, it may be helpful to outline the major components of the CETA approach and review its progress in Texas. The focus of the CETA approach is the local prime sponsor, defined as a state, a city, or a county with a population of at least 100,000, or a combination of units of government called consortia in which at least one member jurisdiction has a population of 100,000 or more. The persons directly responsible for making decisions on allocating funds are the elected officials in each of these political jurisdictions. The responsibility of the prime sponsors is complete: it includes determination of local needs, program design, decisions to provide programs directly or through contracts with other agencies, and the responsibility for program monitoring and evaluation. Funds are allocated among prime sponsors according to formulas that take into consideration the number of unemployed persons, the proportion of low income families in the area, and the employment and training funds received during the previous budget period. States receiving grants under Titles I, II, and VI of the 1973 Act have a complex function in the CETA approach. They are responsible for operating programs in those areas within the state that do not qualify as prime sponsors, and they are expected to coordinate and evaluate all the programs being implemented in the state. Additionally, grants are given under Title I to governors for vocational training services in prime sponsor jurisdictions and for coordination and special state-wide manpower services. The federal role under CETA is limited to establishing national objectives, reviewing and approving plans, and evaluating program performance.

Since planning for human resources development at the local level implies an understanding of how labor markets operate and how they affect and are affected by regional economic development, data on the labor force and on employment and unemployment are now being collected for all counties; information systems using demographic, occupation, and industry statistics are being implemented in most states. Firms in the private sector are becoming heavy users of these data for marketing, industry studies, and forecasting.[14]

CETA Operations in Texas

Funding. Figure 5-1 shows the total federal and state funds spent in Texas for manpower and related services during 1976. Tables 5-4 through 5-6 present in greater detail the allocation of funds under the Comprehensive Employment and Training Act.

Of the $200 million allocated to Texas in 1976 (a 17 percent increase over 1975), $84.5 million went under Title I to prime sponsors for a comprehensive array of services to the disadvantaged, unemployed, and underemployed.[15] Also, under Title I, $7.7 million went

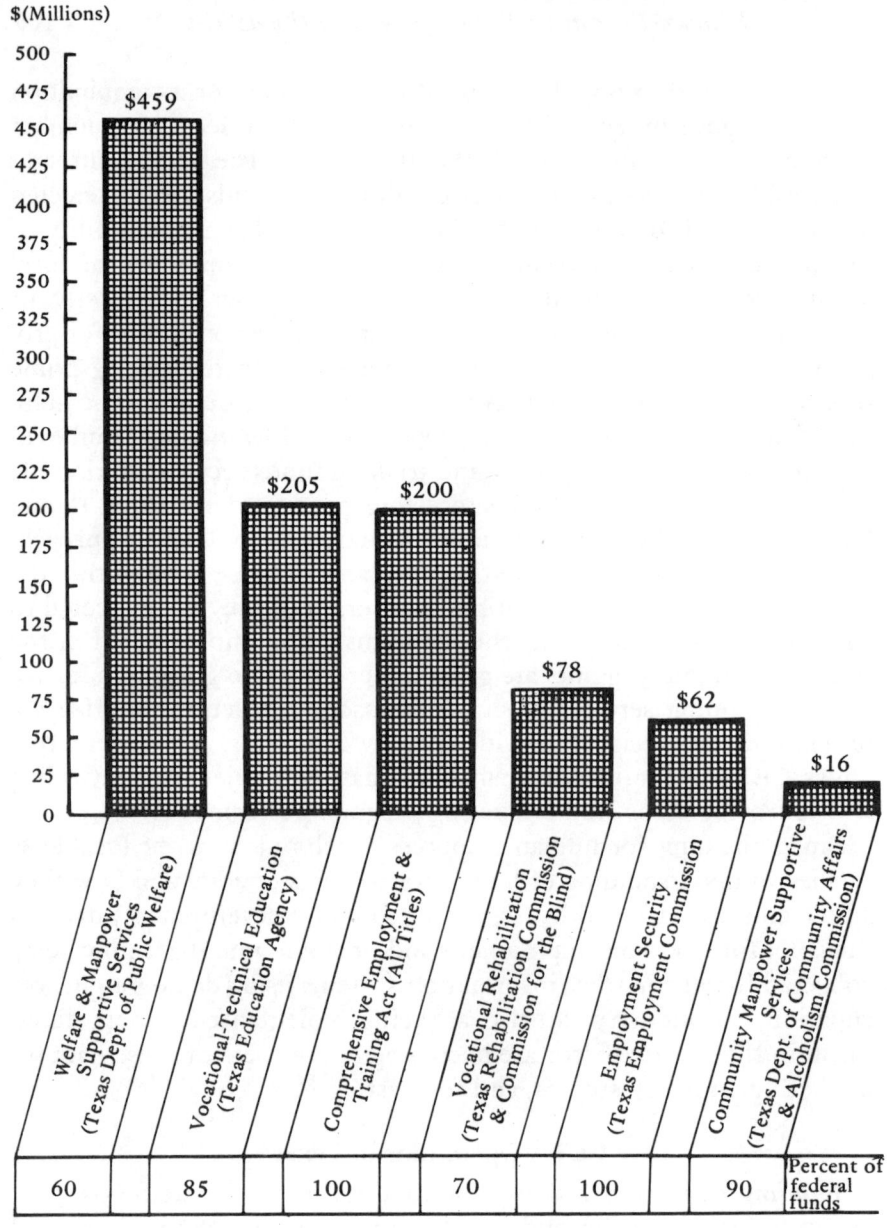

FIGURE 5-1
1976 FEDERAL AND STATE FUNDS
FOR MANPOWER & RELATED SERVICES

Source: *1976 Annual Manpower Report to the Governor.* Prepared by Texas State Manpower Services Council

to the state to support its coordinating and advisory function and to provide supplemental vocational education services to prime sponsor areas. All Title II monies ($10.4 million) were allocated to prime sponsors in areas having 6.5 percent or greater unemployment rates to provide public service employment to the unemployed. Additionally, Title VI monies (almost $43 million) were distributed among prime sponsors for emergency public service employment.

In summary, $137.9 million (approximately 70 percent) of the $200.9 million of CETA funds went directly to prime sponsors. Of the remaining $62 million, $26 million were earmarked for summer youth programs and the balance was divided among the contractors of Indian and migrant programs and three Job Corps Centers.

The $200 million of CETA funds are only approximately 20 percent of total federal and state expenditures in Texas for manpower

TABLE 5-4

CETA FUNDING FLOW AND STRUCTURE IN TEXAS
FY 1976: $200 MILLION

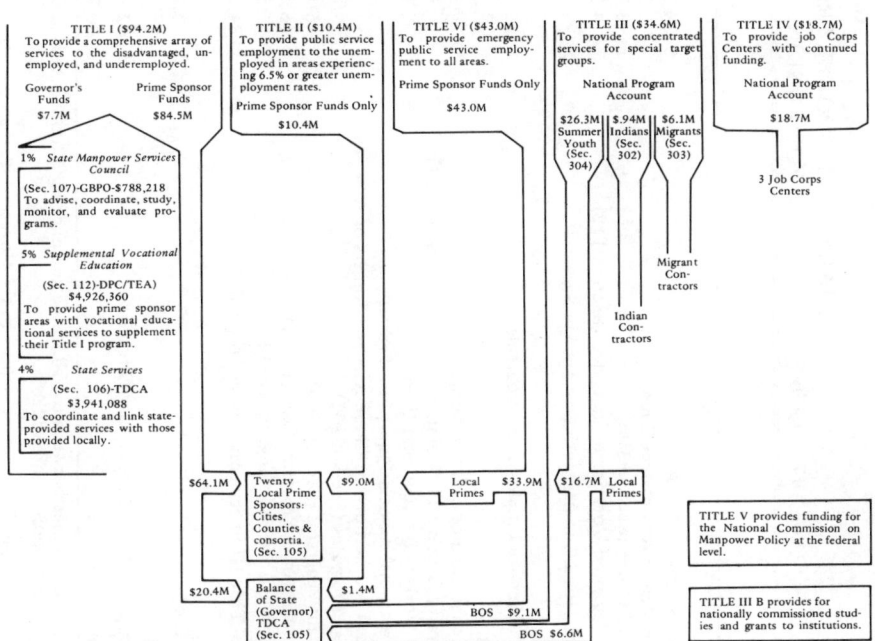

Source: 1976 Annual Manpower Report to the Governor. Prepared by the Texas State Manpower Services Council (forthcoming).

TABLE 5-5

SUMMARY OF MANPOWER PROGRAMS FUNDED UNDER CETA
FOR FY 1975, 1976 STATE TOTALS FOR FUNDING LEVELS, FUNDS EXPENDED AND PERSONS SERVED

	Total Allocation 1976	Total Allocation 1975	Total Expended* 1976	Total Persons Served 1976
Title I				
Prime Sponsor's Total	$ 84,540,560		$ 95,751,000	116,630
State Manpower Services Council	788,218		491,237	100
State Services (Section 106)	3,941,088		4,370,001	22,075
Supplemental Vocational Education (Section 112)	4,926,360		2,345,775	12,863
Total Title I Comprehensive Manpower Services	$ 94,196,226	$ 79,857,451	$105,303,788	151,568
Title II				
Public Service Employment Programs	$ 10,443,686	$ 12,280,134	$ 18,006,391	11,899
Title III				
National Alliance of Businessmen (NAB)	$ 379,475			31,625
Minority Group Skill Training (Apprenticeship Outreach)	577,788			1,220
Iron Workers International Union	182,000			90
International Association of Fire Fighters	21,640			84
United Brotherhood of Carpenters and Joiners of America	86,351			450
Indian Programs (Section 302)	940,659	752,128		INA
Migrant Programs (Section 303)	6,100,000	6,415,000		INA
Summer Youth Program (Section 304)	26,307,515	26,730,803		INA
English as a Second Language (ESL)	537,200			4,002
Total Title III Special Manpower Programs	$ 34,595,428	$ 33,897,931		37,471
Title IV				
Job Corps	$ 18,700,700	$ 19,429,000	$ 24,253,060	4,476
Title VI				
Emergency Public Employment Programs	$ 42,991,915	$ 25,598,875	$ 54,193,144	20,275
State Totals All Titles	$200,927,955	$171,054,391	$201,756,383	225,689

*Note: The difference between the allocated and expended funds is due to the carryover of allocated funds from 1975 to 1976 that were not expended in 1975. INA information not available.

Source: 1976 Annual Manpower Report to the Governor. Prepared by the Texas State Manpower Services Council

TABLE 5-6

FUNDING TO TEXAS PRIME SPONSORS, 1974-1975 FUNDS

Prime Sponsor	Title I	Title II	Title III Summer Youth	Title VI	Prime Sponsor Total
Alamo Area Consortium	$ 9,073,529	$ 1,398,136	$ 3,153,517	$ 2,380,955	$ 16,006,137
Balance of State (TDCA)	19,764,330	1,550,618	9,316,994	8,820,187	37,055,476
Cameron County	1,279,208	906,090	437,403	1,043,553	3,666,254
Capital Area Consortium	2,714,336	---	946,040	490,627	4,151,003
Central Texas Consortium	1,065,261	---	292,332	189,260	1,546,853
Coastal Bend Manpower Consortium	3,244,543	720,063	1,089,116	810,795	5,824,295
Dallas (City)	4,282,470	89,286	1,538,754	957,998	6,868,508
Dallas (County)	1,628,910	---	339,502	539,353	2,507,765
El Paso City & County Consortium	2,557,378	1,171,913	762,255	1,249,758	5,389,980
Fort Worth Consortium	2,580,702	355,604	565,715	856,842	4,284,982
Galveston County	1,281,960	---	611,349	199,472	2,092,781
Harris County	1,458,450	---	386,620	921,084	2,766,154
Hidalgo-Willacy Consortium	2,100,458	1,537,438	710,190	1,426,493	5,774,579
Houston (City)	8,829,900	2,149,897	2,969,651	2,202,085	15,829,833
North Texas Consortium	1,423,220	---	593,906	192,046	2,209,172
Panhandle Manpower Consortium	1,771,352	---	627,443	307,364	2,664,803
Region XI Consortium	1,821,699	119,121	690,110	384,938	3,015,868
South East Texas Consortium	2,121,677	930,330	451,755	970,912	4,474,674
Tarrant County	688,410	---	164,541	363,568	1,018,668
Webb County	1,333,710	977,007	833,770	824,596	3,907,213
Bowie County*	896,400	363,755	249,840	466,989	1,948,258
Title Totals	$71,917,903	$12,269,258	$26,730,803	$25,598,875	$133,003,256

*Bowie County is in consortium with Miller and Little River Counties in Arkansas.

Source: *1975 Annual Manpower Report to the Governor*, p. 58.

and related services during 1976, but the focus on comprehensive planning, coordination, and local decision making makes them the most important leverage at the regional level to promote activities in the public and private sectors toward the efficient development and use of human resources.

There are twenty prime sponsors in Texas[16] (see Figure 5-2a). Six of them are consortia whose jurisdictions are coterminous with the Texas Planning Regions (see Figure 5-2b).[17] Thirteen others are individual jurisdictions (such as counties or cities); the last is the "balance of the State" (areas that did not qualify as prime sponsors), for which the governor is directly responsible.

Tables 5-7 and 5-8 offer a brief socio-economic and demographic profile of the state planning regions. Seventeen of the planning regions have a higher proportion of urban population than the state, and only four of them have a higher per capita income than Texas.

Table 5-7 presents information on Texas labor markets as of April 1973 and 1974. The tables offer an interesting comparative view of regional differences within the state but should not be used, for example, to evaluate the severity of unemployment in any one area since later figures (Table 5-10) would indicate much higher unemployment rates.

Four planning regions, Alamo (major urban labor market—San Antonio), Capital Area (major urban labor market—Austin), Gulf Coast (major urban labor market—Houston), and North Central Texas (major urban labor market—Dallas-Fort Worth) were host to 57 percent of the people living in Texas in 1974 (Table 5-8). The number of persons in the labor force has increased throughout the state. Increases in the labor force may be caused either by net increases in the population (more births than deaths in the region or more inmigration than outmigration) or by greater labor force participation rates (more people who have found a job or are actively looking for one) relative to the total population. The Alamo planning region has the lowest labor force participation rate (37 percent) than the other largest labor markets (Capital Area—42 percent, Gulf Coast—45 percent, North Central Texas—44 percent) and lower than the state (42 percent). In Table 5-8 several characteristics of the population throw further light into the physiognomy of the labor markets. For example, in the Alamo region the urban environment is combined with a higher minority population, a higher population in the 16-21 age group, and a lower number of persons aged 22-44 (the prime income earning period in

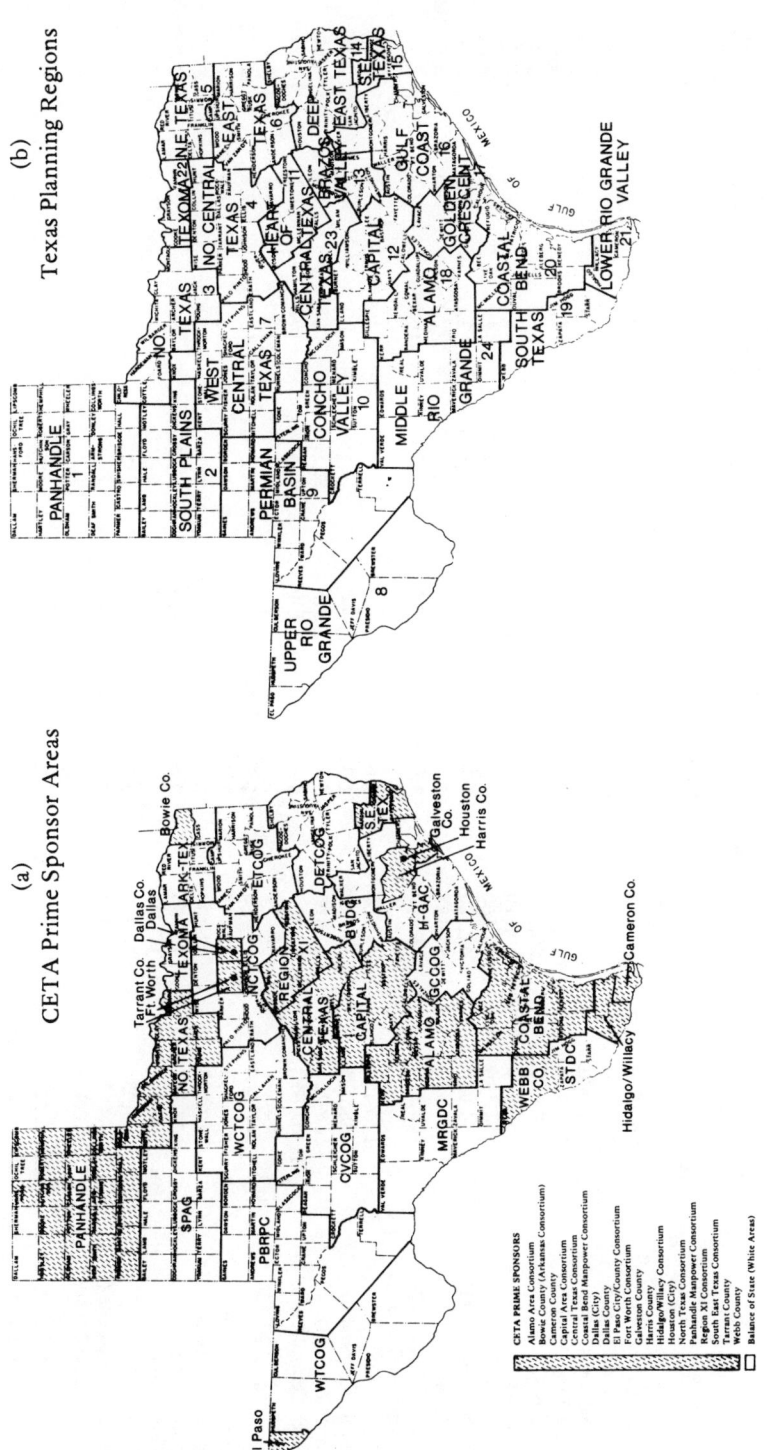

FIGURE 5-2

THE GEOGRAPHY OF MANPOWER PLANNING IN TEXAS

Source: *1975 Annual Manpower Report to the Governor.* Prepared by Texas State Manpower Services Council.

TABLE 5-7

TEXAS LABOR MARKET STATISTICS BY STATE PLANNING REGION 1973-1974

State Planning Region (No.)	Labor Force			Unemployment			Percent Unemployed	
	April 1973	April 1974	Percent Change	April 1973	April 1974	Percent Change	April 1973	April 1974
Alamo (18)	394,265	400,690	1.6	12,220	15,865	29.8	3.1	4.0
Brazos Valley (13)	60,330	62,285	3.2	1,155	1,150	-0.4	1.9	1.8
Capital Area (12)	223,120	226,435	1.5	4,655	4,645	-0.2	2.1	2.1
Central Texas (23)	72,060	75,495	4.8	1,830	1,695	-7.4	2.5	2.2
Coastal Bend (20)	162,150	163,430	0.8	7,580	7,250	-4.4	4.7	4.4
Concho Valley (10)	48,600	50,410	3.7	1,110	1,020	-8.1	2.3	2.0
Deep East Texas (14)	85,630	86,170	0.6	3,715	2,840	-23.6	4.3	3.3
East Texas (6)	191,690	195,160	1.8	6,345	6,165	-2.8	3.3	3.2
Golden Crescent (17)	64,050	64,920	1.4	1,620	1,680	3.7	2.5	2.6
Gulf Coast (16)	1,087,550	1,152,185	5.9	43,450	40,375	-7.1	4.0	3.5
Heart of Texas (11)	102,520	104,365	1.8	3,015	3,535	16.9	2.9	3.4
Lower Rio Grande Valley (21)	126,480	135,160	6.9	9,810	11,410	16.3	7.8	8.4
Middle Rio Grande (24)	38,015	38,510	1.3	3,440	3,215	-6.5	9.0	8.3
North Texas (3)	88,280	90,905	3.0	2,155	2,190	1.6	2.4	2.4
North Central Texas (4)	1,169,810	1,216,760	4.0	29,350	32,560	10.9	2.5	2.7
North East Texas (5)	86,190	86,690	0.6	3,445	3,875	12.5	4.0	4.5
Panhandle (1)	144,560	147,720	2.2	4,100	3,540	-13.7	2.8	2.4
Permian Basin (9)	117,255	121,745	3.8	2,280	2,310	1.3	1.9	1.9
South East Texas (15)	140,300	143,400	2.2	9,200	7,100	-22.8	6.6	5.0
South Plains (2)	142,325	148,395	4.3	3,400	3,285	-3.4	2.4	2.2
South Texas (19)	34,245	35,600	4.0	5,260	5,500	4.6	15.4	15.4
Texoma (22)	55,350	57,230	3.4	1,970	2,150	9.1	3.6	3.8
Upper Rio Grande (8)	149,520	150,445	0.6	8,215	8,130	-1.0	5.5	5.4
West Central Texas (7)	120,465	123,250	2.3	2,725	2,545	-6.6	2.3	2.1
Texas Total	4,904,760	5,077,355	3.5	172,045	174,030	1.2	3.5	3.4

Source: Texas Employment Commission. From *1975 Annual Manpower Report to the Governor.* Prepared by Texas State Manpower Services Council.

TABLE 5-7 (Continued)

TEXAS LABOR MARKET STATISTICS BY STATE PLANNING REGION 1973-1974

State Planning Region (No.)	Wage and Salary Employment							Total Employment			Total Wage & Salary Employment		
	Manufacturing			Nonmanufacturing									
	April 1973	April 1974	Percent Change	April 1973	April 1974	Percent Change	April 1973	April 1974	Percent Change	April 1973	April 1974	Percent Change
Alamo (18)	40,755	39,945	2.0	284,860	289,460	1.6	382,045	384,825	0.7	329,765	333,275	1.1
Brazos Valley (13)	5,565	5,725	1.1	32,945	34,485	4.7	59,175	61,135	3.3	38,510	40,110	4.2
Capital Area (12)	18,025	18,790	4.2	161,880	165,095	2.0	218,465	221,790	1.5	179,905	183,885	2.2
Central Texas (23)	7,845	8,175	4.2	42,325	45,115	6.6	70,230	73,800	5.1	51,195	54,360	6.2
Coastal Bend (20)	13,720	13,650	0.5	106,530	108,570	1.9	154,570	156,180	1.0	120,500	122,480	1.6
Concho Valley (10)	4,430	4,950	11.7	18,170	19,160	5.4	47,490	49,390	4.0	29,700	31,460	5.9
Deep East Texas (14)	20,909	20,425	1.7	18,170	19,160	5.4	81,915	83,330	1.7	58,100	59,135	1.8
East Texas (6)	40,080	40,275	0.5	90,385	93,155	3.1	185,345	188,995	2.0	130,940	133,895	2.3
Golden Crescent (17)	10,200	9,655	5.3	30,595	32,095	4.9	62,430	63,240	1.3	40,795	41,750	2.3
Gulf Coast (16)	170,450	182,700	7.2	801,275	837,850	4.6	1,044,100	1,111,900	6.5	971,725	1,020,550	5.0
Heart of Texas (11)	17,585	17,525	0.3	56,825	57,930	1.9	99,505	100,830	1.3	74,410	75,455	1.4
Lower Rio Grande Valley (21)	13,400	14,835	10.7	70,045	75,657	8.0	116,670	123,750	6.1	83,445	90,510	8.5
Middle Rio Grande (24)	485	525	8.2	4,730	4,940	4.4	34,575	35,295	2.1	20,820	21,620	3.8
North Texas (3)	8,980	9,960	10.9	44,340	47,110	6.2	86,125	88,715	3.0	61,560	63,630	3.4
North Central Texas (4)	245,620	252,990	3.0	812,860	846,140	4.1	1,140,460	1,184,200	3.8	1,060,480	1,101,190	3.8
North East Texas (5)	16,405	15,370	6.3	81,500	83,780	2.8	82,745	82,815	0.1	64,395	64,450	0.1
Panhandle (1)	13,780	14,205	3.1	63,640	65,545	3.0	140,460	143,980	2.5	91,910	93,410	1.6
Permian Basin (9)	8,600	8,565	0.4	81,500	83,780	2.8	114,975	119,435	3.9	91,100	94,730	4.0
South East Texas (15)	39,700	41,250	3.9	78,000	81,950	5.1	131,100	136,300	4.0	117,700	123,200	4.7
South Plains (2)							138,925	145,110	4.5	97,190	103,045	6.0
South Texas (19)	1,500	1,575	5.0	21,225	21,475	1.2	28,985	30,100	3.8	23,930	24,460	2.2
Texoma (22)	15,150	16,100	6.3	26,490	27,190	2.6	53,380	55,080	3.2	41,640	43,290	4.0
Upper Rio Grande (8)	28,350	30,100	6.1	100,005	99,560	0.4	141,305	142,315	0.7	129,855	132,595	2.1
West Central Texas (7)	13,995	14,800	5.8	60,855	59,725	1.9	117,740	120,705	2.5	78,040	80,515	3.2
Texas Totals	764,900	795,975	4.1	3,148,220	3,256,925	3.5	4,732,715	4,903,205	3.6	3,987,610	4,133,000	3.6

Source: Texas Employment Commission. From 1975 *Annual Manpower Report to the Governor*. Prepared by Texas State Manpower Services Council.

TABLE 5-8

DEMOGRAPHIC CHARACTERISTICS OF TEXAS PLANNING REGIONS, 1970, 1974

Region	Total Population				Population Characteristics, 1970 Percent of Regional Totals							
	1974 (1000)	Percent of State	Percent of Change 1970-74	1970 (1000)	Blacks %*	Mexican Americans %*	Rural %*	Urban %*	Age Groups			
									16-21 %*	22-44 %*	45-64 %*	65& Over %*
Alamo	1,094.9	9.1	8.8	1,006.5	6.1	43.3	12.8	87.2	12.2	27.6	18.4	8.7
Brazos Valley	142.9	1.2	10.3	129.5	24.5	8.1	43.0	57.0	14.7	24.3	19.7	13.6
Capital Area	533.9	4.4	19.5	446.6	12.2	16.1	25.1	74.9	15.2	28.6	18.4	10.1
Central Texas	252.7	2.1	22.6	206.1	10.9	8.7	26.5	73.5	17.7	29.4	16.4	10.0
Coastal Bend	447.5	3.7	6.4	420.4	3.6	47.0	18.7	81.3	12.1	27.9	18.3	7.0
Concho Valley	115.4	1.0	4.6	110.3	3.3	21.3	32.0	68.0	10.9	26.0	21.6	12.6
Deep East Texas	268.3	2.2	24.3	215.8	24.3	1.8	63.6	36.4	11.5	24.2	21.3	13.6
East Texas	471.3	3.9	8.1	436.1	23.3	1.3	50.2	49.8	10.1	25.0	23.1	13.9
Golden Crescent	143.8	1.2	.9	142.4	9.1	26.1	44.9	55.1	10.0	24.5	21.2	11.9
Gulf Coast	2,543.9	21.1	10.4	2,305.1	19.6	10.8	13.2	86.8	10.5	31.7	18.4	6.5
Heart of Texas	236.8	2.0	4.0	227.6	17.8	6.5	34.9	65.1	11.1	23.6	23.6	15.3
Lower Rio Grande Valley	402.0	3.3	19.1	337.5	0.3	77.8	25.5	74.5	12.2	25.9	16.5	8.1
Middle Rio Grande	104.6	.9	10.7	94.5	1.0	67.9	28.2	71.8	11.5	24.4	17.0	8.4
North Texas	210.1	1.7	-1.1	212.5	6.1	4.8	21.7	78.3	11.4	26.3	21.6	13.4
North Central Texas	2,749.7	22.8	4.3	2,636.4	13.4	5.8	9.2	90.8	10.5	31.4	18.7	8.2
North East Texas	211.0	1.8	4.4	202.3	19.7	0.8	51.6	48.4	9.2	29.7	23.3	14.7
Panhandle	333.5	2.8	1.0	330.3	3.4	9.3	28.7	71.3	10.5	28.1	20.9	9.0
Permian Basin	296.2	2.5	-2.6	304.3	5.2	18.9	21.4	78.6	10.2	29.7	19.8	6.1
South East Texas	311.5	2.6	-9.9	345.9	20.7	3.9	17.0	83.0	10.8	28.1	20.9	8.1
South Plains	342.5	2.8	4.5	327.7	6.5	20.3	29.5	70.5	12.8	27.9	18.3	8.0
South Texas	108.0	.9	8.4	99.6	0.3	88.3	19.7	70.3	11.3	25.9	16.2	8.3
Texoma	125.3	1.0	-3.2	129.4	7.6	1.7	38.3	61.7	9.9	25.4	22.3	14.4
Upper Rio Grande	430.7	3.6	13.6	379.3	2.7	56.9	6.8	93.2	12.8	29.5	15.6	5.9
West Central Texas	290.5	2.4	3.7	280.1	4.4	9.8	34.5	65.5	10.6	24.2	22.9	15.3
State Total**	12,049.9	100.0	7.6	11,196.7	12.5	18.4	20.3	79.7	11.3	28.9	19.1	8.9

* Percent within individual planning regions.   **Totals may not be exact due to rounding.

Source: 1970 U. S. Census of Population.

an individual work life). This indicates a vulnerability to high unemployment and a need for training and economic development so that young people would not need to migrate outside the region to find jobs. It is interesting to note that the incidence of unemployment is not always correlated by increases in population since an area with job opportunities may attract population from other regions that is qualified to fill the available positions. Yet, as will be seen in more detail later, increases in employment may be occurring contemporaneously to increases in unemployment if the skill mix of the population does not fit the demand for workers.

Table 5-9 shows the difference in economic opportunities in the various regions more clearly. For example, North Central Texas and Gulf Coast planning regions contribute approximately 25 percent of the state total personal income and 23 and 21 percent in population respectively. By contrast, San Antonio, with 9 percent of Texans within its boundaries, shares only 8 percent of the state's personal income payments.

Clients Served under CETA. As Table 5-5 indicates, over 225,000 persons were served in some way by CETA-sponsored programs. Of that number, slightly more than half were enrolled in the various programs under Title I prime sponsors; in all, some two-thirds of all CETA clinets were Title I enrollees. About 32,000 persons were employed in public service employment programs under Titles II and VI, while a like number were employed and given on-job training by members of the National Alliance of Businessmen. Job Corps and English as a Second Language accounted for almost half of the other CETA trainees. (It should be noted that data on enrollees in one of the largest programs, the Summer Youth Program, were not available for comparison with other CETA programs.)

A large proportion of the persons served by CETA are economically disadvantaged.[18] In Texas, of those receiving services under Title I, 85.3 percent were in the economically disadvantaged category, compared with 77.3 percent for the nation as a whole; 59.4 percent of Title II participants were disadvantaged, compared to 48.3 percent nationwide; and 46.0 percent of Title VI beneficiaries were in that same group, compared with 43.6 percent for the nation. More people served by CETA in Texas under Titles I, II, and VI had less high school or post high school education than comparable groups in the United States.[19] The observation brings to light an important problem in human resources development for the state of Texas—the

TABLE 5-9

SOCIO-ECONOMIC CHARACTERISTICS OF TEXAS BY PLANNING REGIONS

Region	1974 Personal Income by Place of Residence (1)			Per Capita Income 1974		Persons Below Poverty in 1969 (2)	
	$1000	Percent of State	Percent Change 74/70	$	Rank	No.	Percent
Alamo	4,960,579	8.3	45.4	4,531	10	203,201	21.0
Brazos Valley	517,656	.9	43.6	3,623	20	37,368	30.8
Capital Area	2,299,833	3.9	55.6	4,308	14	89,689	21.4
Coastal Bend	1,787,704	3.0	35.6	3,995	19	107,707	26.1
Concho Valley	520,521	.9	38.7	4,511	11	23,041	21.5
Deep East Texas	987,534	1.7	50.3	3,681	21	57,575	27.6
East Texas	2,006,512	3.4	48.4	4,257	15	96,033	22.5
Golden Crescent	611,016	1.0	45.2	4,249	16	37,949	26.9
Gulf Coast	14,792,919	24.8	58.4	5,815	1	309,252	13.6
Heart of Texas	1,032,103	1.7	37.8	4,359	13	53,137	23.3
Lower Rio Grande Valley	1,195,260	2.0	63.2	2,973	24	162,812	48.5
Middle Rio Grande	328,827	.6	47.8	3,144	22	39,935	42.9
North Texas	1,033,069	1.7	37.7	4,917	6	34,742	17.2
North Central Texas	14,901,055	25.0	43.5	5,677	2	305,911	11.8
North East Texas	863,919	1.4	40.5	4,094	18	45,016	22.6
Panhandle	1,885,041	3.2	31.6	5,652	3	47,563	14.6
Permian Basin	1,509,886	2.5	41.0	5,098	5	48,519	16.1
South East Texas	1,723,457	2.9	43.6	5,533	4	51,398	15.0
South Plains	1,605,970	2.7	32.3	4,688	7	72,671	22.9
South Texas	311,903	.5	43.7	3,073	23	46,549	47.3
Texoma	587,397	2.0	36.7	4,688	8	20,786	16.5
Upper Rio Grande	1,827,424	3.1	52.8	4,243	17	81,874	22.1
West Central Texas	1,279,417	2.1	38.6	4,404	12	58,269	20.8
State Totals**	59,716,794	100.0	47.4	4,956		2,046,593	18.7

**Totals may not be exact due to rounding.
Source: (1) U. S. Dept. of Commerce, Bureau of Economic Analysis. (2) U. S. Census of Population.

existence of a large pool of people who are unequipped to successfully compete in the job market. Lacking the opportunity of contributing to the production processes taking place in their region, they do not share in the blessings of economic growth and, therefore, often become a social cost rather than a "resource" for their community. The continuing phenomenon of untrained persons unsuccessfully seeking work while jobs requiring relatively high skill endowments remain unfilled is a persistent indication that our approach to human resource development has so far been inadequate. The causes of unemployment and poverty and suggestions for their alleviation form the concluding sections of this chapter.

PROBLEMS OF UNEMPLOYMENT AND POVERTY

An important test of a society's success in developing its human resources is the extent to which its people are able, through their contributions to the production of goods and services for the society, to earn incomes sufficient to afford them a decent standard of living.

In this respect the Texas economy, overall one of the most prosperous of all the states, can hardly be said to function as it should. As recently as 1970, Texas ranked second among the states in the number of poor people living within its borders. More than two million people, or nearly one-fifth of the population, lived under conditions officially categorized as below the poverty line; the 18.8 percent incidence of poverty in Texas was the twelfth highest rate among all the states.[20] The principal characteristics of the Texas poverty population were:

Age. More than half of the poor were either under the age of fifteen or over sixty-five. The incidence of poverty was highest (34.4 percent) in the over-sixty-five age group; the second highest incidence, 22.5 percent, was found for the under-fifteen group.

Race or ethnicity. Minority groups had the highest incidence of poverty in Texas. Whereas blacks comprised only about 12 percent, and Mexican-Americans about 19 percent of the state's population, the two groups made up 25 and 36 percent, respectively, of all poor Texans. Put another way, about 39 percent of blacks and 36 percent of Mexican-Americans—but only about 10 percent of Anglos—lived in poverty.

Female-headed households. Although only about one Texas family in nine was headed by a female, female-headed households made up nearly half of all poor households in Texas. The incidence of poverty among male-headed households was only 13 percent, compared to 44 percent for female-headed households.

Education. Lack of education contributed heavily to problems of poverty. Sixty percent of the poor in Texas had less than a ninth grade education; another 22 percent were high school dropouts. Thus the 52 percent of Texans without high school diplomas comprised 81 percent of the poverty population.

Unemployment and underemployment. The poor in Texas had a higher unemployment rate—8.7 percent—than the 3.6 percent rate for the labor force as a whole. Even that high rate, however, underestimates the extent of unemployment among the poor, since there were nearly twice as many poor adults out of the labor force as in it. Finally, among the poor who were in the labor force, nearly one-third were working less than full-time, while over half were working full-time, but for sub-poverty wages.

Geography. Almost one-fourth of all rural residents were poor, compared with 17 percent of urban dwellers. Since 80 percent of the population lived in urban areas, though, most of the poverty population lived in urban areas as well. Minorities made up nearly two-thirds of the urban poor, while Anglos comprised just over half of the rural poor. The poorest areas of the state were in the Rio Grande Valley and in East Texas; generally, the Houston-Beaumont, Dallas-Fort Worth, and West Texas areas had the lowest incidence of poverty.

Given these dimensions of poverty in Texas, what can we say about the efficacy of our system of human resource development? To what extent has the poverty problem been caused by changing economic conditions, and to what extent by failure of public and private institutions to respond to change and to prepare people to compete in the labor market? Are the critics of manpower policy correct in saying that manpower programs have had no appreciable impact on the problems of unemployment and poverty? And what should we reasonably expect the role of human resource development to be in alleviating these conditions?

THE CHANGING DEMANDS OF THE LABOR MARKET

Fortunately, the pace of economic growth in Texas has been more rapid and less subject to cyclical change than the United States economy as a whole. This growth has not been uniform for all sectors, however, particularly in its implications for the labor force. Declines in employment in agriculture and personal services—two generally low-skill sectors—were more than offset by growth of employment opportunities in the higher-skill sectors. These structural changes in the labor market have effectively left many poorly educated and unskilled workers useless in a modern economy.

Tables 5-10 and 5-11 present a brief summary of employment trends in Texas and in the nation as a whole during the past three decades. Table 5-11, showing the industrial composition of employment, testifies to the remarkable effort made in the state to catch up with the national economy. The distributions of employed persons in the two geographic areas were quite different in 1940; these differences had almost disappeared by 1970. The changes, of somewhat lesser size,

TABLE 5-10

EMPLOYMENT AND UNEMPLOYMENT IN SELECTED TEXAS LABOR MARKETS, JULY 1975-1976

	Percent Change in employment		Unemployment rate July 1976
	Nonag.	Mfg.	
Abilene	1	-2	4.1
Amarillo	4	24	3.5
Austin	4	13	4.7
Beaumont-Port Arthur-Orange	7	-2	7.2
Brownsville-Harlingen-San Benito	6	4	10.5
Corpus Christi	1	1	6.1
Dallas-Fort Worth	2	3	5.1
El Paso	4	2	10.3
Galveston-Texas City	**	2	7.3
Houston	3	1	5.9
Laredo	11	20	12.1
Longview	3	2	6.7
Lubbock	**	8	4.0
McAllen-Pharr-Edinburg	5	16	11.5
Midland	2	**	3.7
Odessa	**	**	4.1
San Angelo	2	7	4.4
San Antonio	2	11	7.9
Sherman-Denison	7	11	9.4
Texarkana	2	-6	8.4
Tyler	3	6	4.9
Waco	3	6	5.2
Wichita Falls	2	2	4.2
Total Texas	3	4	5.7

**Change is less than one half of one percent.
Source: *Texas Business Review*, September 1976, page 201.

are reflected in the occupational distribution of Texans during the same thirty years. As one would expect, the greatest changes occurred

TABLE 5-11

PERCENT DISTRIBUTION OF EMPLOYED PERSONS BY INDUSTRY FOR TEXAS AND THE UNITED STATES, 1940 TO 1970

Industry	1940	1950	1960	1970	Change in Percent 1940-1970
TEXAS: Total employed	100.0	100.0	100.0	100.0	
Agriculture, forestry, fisheries	30.4	16.2	8.8	4.4	- 26.0
Mining	2.9	3.3	3.0	2.4	- 0.5
Construction	5.3	8.6	7.6	7.0	+ 1.7
Manufacturing, durable	3.8	5.7	7.5	9.7	+ 5.9
Manufacturing, nondurable	6.1	7.7	8.7	7.7	+ 1.6
Transportation, communications, and other utilities	6.6	8.2	7.4	6.5	- 0.1
Wholesale and retail trade	18.1	21.4	21.2	20.9	+ 2.8
Finance, insurance, and real estate	2.7	3.2	4.2	4.9	+ 2.2
Business and repair services	2.1	2.6	2.7	3.2	+ 1.1
Personal services	11.1	8.3	8.0	5.4	- 5.7
Entertainment and recreation	.8	.9	.7	.7	- 0.1
Professional and related services	6.4	7.9	11.4	15.8	+ 9.4
Public administration	2.4	4.3	4.7	5.2	+ 2.8
Industry not reported	1.3	1.7	4.1	6.2	
U.S.: Total employed	100.0	100.0	100.0	100.0	
Agriculture, forestry, fisheries	18.9	12.4	6.7	3.5	- 15.4
Mining	2.0	1.6	1.0	.8	- 1.2
Construction	4.6	6.1	5.9	5.5	+ 0.9
Manufacturing, durable	11.4	13.7	15.2	14.4	+ 3.0
Manufacturing, nondurable	12.2	12.3	11.9	10.0	- 2.2
Transportation, communications, and other utilities	6.9	7.9	6.9	6.3	- 0.6
Wholesale and retail trade	16.6	18.7	18.2	18.9	+ 2.3
Finance, insurance, and real estate	3.3	3.4	4.2	4.7	+ 1.4
Business and repair services	1.9	2.3	2.5	2.9	+ 1.0
Personal services	8.7	6.1	6.0	4.3	- 4.4
Entertainment and recreation	.9	.9	.8	.8	- 0.1
Professional and related services	7.5	8.5	11.9	16.5	+ 9.0
Public administration	3.1	4.5	4.8	5.2	+ 2.1
Industry not reported	2.0	1.6	4.0	6.2	

Sources: U. S. Bureau of Census, *Census of Population: 1950, Characteristics of the Population*, Vol. 2, Part 43, Texas, Table 31; U. S. Bureau of Census, *Census of Population: 1970, General Social and Economic Characteristics, Texas*, Final Report PC(1)-C45, Table 47; U. S. Bureau of Census, *Census of Population: 1960 General Social & Economic Characteristics, U. S. Summary*, Final Report, PC(1)-1C, Table 92; U. S. Bureau of Census, *Census of Population: 1970 General Social & Economic Characteristics, U. S. Summary*, Final Report PC(1)-C1, Table 82. From: *Texas Business Review*, Sept. 1973, p. 208.

The Changing Demands of the Labor Market

from less desirable and unskilled occupations (farmers, blue collar workers) to the more prestigious ones (white collar workers, professionals). However, this upgrading by-passed large sectors of the population who were unskilled or possessed the less desirable and less remunerative skills.

Table 5-12 gives further insights into the changes just described. Three large ethnic groups of Texans have all followed the national trends, but with remarkable differences among them. While the gains

TABLE 5-12

PERCENT OF EMPLOYED PERSONS IN TEXAS IN MAJOR OCCUPATIONAL CATEGORIES AND CHANGE IN PERCENT, 1950-1970, BY SEX AND ETHNICITY

	Anglo				Mexican American				Black			
Occupation	1950	1960	1970	Change 1950-1970	1950	1960	1970	Change 1950-1970	1950	1960	1970	Change 1950-1970
MALES	100.0	100.0	99.9		100.1	100.1	100.1		100.1	100.0	100.0	
Total white collar	36.1	40.9	46.5	+10.4	12.7	15.9	24.7	+12.0	7.2	9.0	15.1	+ 7.9
Professionals	8.2	11.5	16.1	+ 7.9	1.7	3.1	6.9	+ 5.2	2.7	3.2	4.6	+ 1.9
Managers	13.8	14.5	14.0	+ 0.2	4.4	4.6	6.2	+ 1.8	2.1	1.9	2.7	+ 0.6
Sales and clerical	14.1	14.9	16.4	+ 2.3	6.6	8.2	11.6	+ 5.0	2.4	3.9	7.8	+ 5.4
Total blue collar	41.8	41.6	42.7	+ 0.9	47.6	53.5	57.0	+ 9.4	51.4	53.7	63.3	+11.9
Craftsmen	20.2	20.5	22.4	+ 2.2	12.4	15.9	21.5	+ 9.1	6.1	8.0	15.1	+ 9.0
Operatives	16.6	16.9	15.9	- 0.7	16.4	21.8	23.2	+ 6.8	16.9	21.2	28.8	+11.9
Laborers	5.0	4.2	4.4	- 0.6	18.8	15.8	12.3	- 6.5	28.4	24.5	19.4	- 9.0
Total farm workers	17.3	9.3	5.3	-12.0	32.0	18.8	8.9	-23.1	22.1	10.1	4.3	-17.8
Farmers	13.1	7.1	3.7	- 9.4	5.2	2.6	1.1	- 4.1	11.3	3.0	.6	-10.7
Farm laborers	4.2	2.2	1.6	- 2.6	26.8	16.2	7.8	-19.0	10.8	7.1	3.7	- 7.1
Total service workers	3.6	3.8	5.4	+ 1.8	6.7	7.6	9.5	+ 2.8	18.0	19.5	17.3	- 0.7
Service	3.5	3.8	5.3	+ 1.8	6.5	7.4	9.4	+ 2.9	16.9	18.6	16.7	- 0.2
Private household	0.1	0.04	.1	0.0	0.2	0.2	0.1	- 0.1	1.1	0.9	0.6	- 0.5
Not reported	1.2	4.4	*		1.1	4.3	*		1.4	7.7	*	
Absolute total**	1590	1753	1941		222	278	400		233	237	259	
FEMALES	100.0	99.8	100.0		100.1	100.0	100.0		100.0	100.1	100.0	
Total white collar	66.6	67.4	73.1	+ 6.5	31.6	33.3	46.4	+14.8	10.7	12.1	25.9	+15.2
Professionals	14.7	15.6	18.0	+ 3.3	3.8	5.3	- 8.9	+ 5.1	6.0	7.3	10.3	+ 4.3
Managers	6.6	5.6	5.0	- 1.6	4.3	2.8	2.8	- 1.5	1.9	1.3	1.4	- 0.5
Sales and clerical	45.3	46.2	50.1	+ 4.8	23.5	25.2	34.7	+11.2	2.8	3.5	14.2	+11.4
Total blue collar	11.7	9.5	10.4	- 1.3	24.1	22.5	22.0	- 2.1	8.5	7.7	15.1	+ 6.6
Craftsmen	1.4	1.1	1.9	0.5	1.2	1.0	2.2	+ 1.0	0.3	0.4	1.2	+ 0.9 !
Operatives	9.9	8.1	7.7	- 2.2	21.5	20.3	18.2	- 3.3	7.2	6.5	12.2	+ 5.0
Laborers	0.4	0.3	0.8	+ 0.4	1.4	1.2	1.6	+ 0.2	1.0	0.8	1.7	+ 0.7
Total farm workers	3.5	1.5	0.6	- 2.9	8.5	5.9	2.0	- 6.5	5.3	1.7	0.7	- 4.6
Farmers	1.0	0.7	0.3	- 0.7	0.4	0.2	0.1	- 0.3	1.1	0.3	0.1	- 1.0
Farm laborers	2.5	0.8	0.3	- 2.2	8.1	5.7	1.9	- 6.2	4.2	1.4	0.6	- 3.6
Total service workers	16.3	16.1	15.9	0.4	33.5	32.2	29.6	- 3.9	74.2	71.8	58.3	-15.9
Service	13.2	12.8	14.3	+ 1.1	14.8	16.1	22.5	+ 7.7	22.5	25.0	32.4	+ 9.9
Private household	3.1	3.3	1.6	- 1.5	18.7	16.1	7.1	-11.6	51.7	46.8	25.9	-25.8
Not reported	1.9	5.3	*		2.4	6.1	*		1.3	6.8	*	
Absolute total**	5.31	782	1107		58	104	200		130	166	216	

* In 1970 persons not reporting their occupation were allocated to a major group on the basis of other information by the U. S. Bureau of Census.
** Totals are given in thousands. Columns do not add to 100 percent because of rounding errors.

Source: U. S. Bureau of Census, *U. S. Census of Population: 1950 Special Report, Persons of Spanish Surname*, Final Report P.E. No. 3C, Table 6; U. S. Bureau of Census, *U. S. Census of Population: 1960 Special Reports, Persons of Spanish Surname*, Final Report PC(2)-4B, Table 6; U. S. Bureau of Census, *U. S. Census of Population: 1950 Characteristics of Population*, Vol. 1, Part 43, Texas, Table 28a; U. S. Bureau of Census, *U. S. Census of Population: 1960 General Social and Economic Characteristics, Texas*. Final Report PC(1)-C45, Table 58; U. S. Bureau of Census, *U. S. Census of Population: 1970 General Social and Economic Characteristics*, Final Report PC(1)-C45, Table 54. From: *Texas Business Review*, March 1974, p. 60.

of the Anglo group were mainly in the various white collar occupations, Mexican-Americans and blacks moved into the blue collar jobs left open by the Anglos and left in large numbers the menial farm activities once representing their only job options.

SHORTCOMINGS OF PROGRAMS TO AID THE DISADVANTAGED

It is all very well to argue that structural changes in the labor market have caused hardships for large numbers of workers, but we have implemented a great number of programs to attack this problem. Should not the problem be disappearing as a result of all our efforts?

The answer appears to be "no," and the principal reason is that the programs offered simply do not have the resources to reach enough people or to serve with enough intensity the groups they do reach. We have already shown the extreme shortfall in the number of workers supplied by vocational education for most job categories, and vocational education reaches more people than any other program. And only some 15 percent of those served by vocational education are disadvantaged.

The newer manpower programs, on the other hand, serve a clientele that is probably about 75 percent disadvantaged, but the number of the disadvantaged being served is less than 10 percent of the total in the state. And many of those who are enrolled in CETA programs are not engaged in the kind of training that will ultimately lead to improved job skills, increased productivity, and higher incomes. To be fair, we must add that the CETA programs have not had an easy time; no sooner was CETA implemented in 1974 than the economy plunged into a depression that it has still not entirely escaped. Since it is almost axiomatic that a *sine qua non* for programs to assist the disadvantaged is an expanding economy with tight labor markets, it would be unrealistic to expect CETA to have done much to alleviate unemployment.

Other Problems of Poverty

In spite of our predisposition in favor of greater commitment to education and training for human resource development, there are aspects of the poverty problem that require other measures entirely—or, at least, a liberal admixture of policies to supplement education and training. Among these, the most important are the welfare problem, rural poverty, and the persistence of discrimination.

The Problem of Dependence. Since more than half of all Texans living in poverty were either too young or too old to be gainfully employed, it is unrealistic to expect education and training programs to do very much good for these groups, at least in the short run. Of course, since lack of education is one of the principal factors accompanying the poverty problem, children of school age must be encouraged at all costs to stay in school, and be given instruction and work skills training during their sojourns in the educational system. But until these children enter the labor market with salable skills, there is probably no way to elevate their incomes above the poverty level except through income transfer programs.

We would make the same case, though less categorically, for older workers. Many senior citizens are still able to work and should be encouraged to do so; still, erosion of health and job skills makes it impracticable to employ the majority of older workers. Some success in employing older workers, however, has been achieved by the Mainstream and Green Thumb programs in the 1960s. A more immediate means of improving the economic status of the elderly would be to extend the benefits of existing programs to the elderly poor: in 1970, only about 53 percent of poor persons in Texas over sixty-five years of age were receiving Old Age Assistance.

A similar set of circumstances applies to many female-headed households. As mentioned previously, almost half of such households receive less than the poverty level of income, principally because many women—especially minority and poorly-educated women—are able to earn so little, even if they can find jobs, that their families cannot escape from poverty. It is these women and their offspring who are the legitimate targets of the AFDC program (Aid to Families with Dependent Children) or "welfare." Unfortunately, only 36 percent of poor children under eighteen in Texas were receiving AFDC payments in 1970, and those payments are woefully inadequate. The average four member AFDC family in Texas receives $140 a month—far less than the poverty level of income.[21] Defenders of this low-payment policy claim that it encourages people to go to work, rather than to rely on welfare, and it certainly does. Large numbers of teenagers drop out of school to take low-paying, dead end jobs to augment their meager AFDC payments, thereby consigning themselves to lifetimes of low-paying jobs and dependency on welfare to support their children.

To end this vicious cycle, programs must be directed toward AFDC parents who can reasonably be reeducated and retrained for salable job skills. For the rest, Texans must simply reconcile themselves to the fact that the only way for welfare children to escape being welfare parents in the future is for the state to support them in a fashion such that they are not forced to take dead end jobs, while foregoing the schooling that is their only conceivable ticket out of the cycle of poverty.

Rural Poverty.[22] More than one-fourth of Texas' poor live in rural areas, but, contrary to popular belief, most do not live on farms. The problem of rural poverty has numerous causes: relatively poor education; lack of industrial development in rural areas to absorb the rural work force leaving agricultural employment; discrimination against minority rural residents; special problemss of migrant farm workers; and lack of manpower training programs for rural residents.

Rural school districts tend to be small and relatively poor, and therefore are largely unable to offer skill training for a variety of occupations; all too often, agriculture and home economics are the only vocational programs available to rural high school students. Moreover, the area vocational schools in Texas, especially postsecondary schools, are located almost exclusively in urban areas; most rural residents have little access to these facilities.[23] Rural students and workers, then, who have difficulty finding farm employment, are not readily able to obtain training for other marketable skills. Poorly educated and relatively untrained, many migrate to urban areas, where they are least able to complete in the labor market, and where they either fail to find employment at all or take poor jobs.

An important facet of the problem of rural poverty in Texas is the plight of the state's 375,000 migrant farm workers. These workers often face even more severe problems than other rural residents, not least of which are low pay and poor working and living conditions. The necessity to follow the crops prevents many migrant children from attending school, and the fact that around 95 percent of migrants are minority group members leads to problems of discrimination. The migrants' transient lives have served to impede the progress of unionization, which has also been opposed by growers and, frequently, public officials. Too, farm workers are usually not protected by unemployment insurance, workmen's compensation, and the Fair Labor Standards Act or state legislation setting minimum wages and working conditions. And although most migrant and seasonal farm worker households are eligible for a wide range of social services, only 52 percent receive assistance from social service agencies.[24]

Clearly, the movement of labor-intensive industry into rural areas could have a major impact on the problem of rural poverty, if firms moving to rural areas would hire rural residents. To encourage such hiring, "start-up" training to endow rural workers with job skills demanded by industry has been attempted, with some success, in a number of states. Increased productivity results in higher incomes for rural workers, and the influx of industry brings more money into rural areas for other rural businesses. Higher incomes and expanding tax bases would lead to more revenues for rural schools, which would in turn enable the schools to offer better skill training for rural residents. Finally, the increased likelihood of earning decent incomes would undoubtedly slow the exodus of rural workers to urban areas, thereby lessening the pressures of the poor on urban labor markets.

Industrialization alone, however, is an incomplete remedy for the problems of rural poverty. In rural areas that are not developing, special efforts need to be made to counsel workers about the availability of employment and training programs elsewhere, and to provide training and subsidized or public employment for rural residents who are unable or unwilling to relocate. Operation Mainstream is an example of such an employment program for older rural workers. Manpower planners and programmers need to become aware of the special needs of rural workers, and sufficient manpower funds must be earmarked under CETA to enable effective programs to be implemented in rural areas. Finally, protective legislation that applies to virtually all other workers should be extended to farm employees.

Undocumented Workers. One problem of increasing seriousness in many areas, but especially in the Southwest, is the existence of some six to eight million "undocumented workers"—aliens working in the United States without having received official permission to do so. These workers are attracted here by wages that, though low by American standards, are high relative to those in Mexico and other low-wage countries. While they undoubtedly take some jobs that American citizens are unwilling to fill, it is difficult to avoid making the assumption that they also displace many other citizens and contribute to the generally low levels of wages and living standards in areas such as the Rio Grande Valley. It is perhaps superfluous to point out that undocumented workers have virtually no recourse against unfair or illegal treatment by employers, landlords, or civil authorities.

The problem of illegal aliens will not be solved until the countries from which these workers emigrate have developed economically enough to be able to offer higher wages and better standards of living for their people. A number of suggestions have been made, however, for dealing with the problem as it exists in the United States. These proposals include deportation of all illegal aliens, strict penalties against employers of undocumented workers, resumption of the *bracero* program, amnesty for aliens already illegally in the United States, and stricter patrolling of the border. Still, until very recently, this issue has received little attention from public policy makers. Early steps taken by the Carter administration indicate that the problem is finally at least being taken seriously at the national level.

Race and Sex Discrimination. Much of the problem of poverty in Texas stems from unequal opportunity for education, training, employment, and advancement for members of minority groups and for women. Though legislation such as the Civil Rights Act of 1964, court actions, and changing public opinion have brought pressure on employers, unions, schools, and other institutions to end most overt discrimination against women and minorities, much inequality remains as the perpetuated results of past discrimination. Women still earn only about 60 percent as much as men, and nonwhites only about 60 percent as much as whites. Earning less income, these groups are able to give their children fewer opportunities to advance themselves (for example, minorities living in low-income, segregated neighborhoods send their children to poorer schools); hence the cycle of poverty tends to be renewed every generation.

Race or sex discrimination in wages is illegal under the Civil Rights Act, and is susceptible to litigation by aggrieved parties. One difficulty in proving discrimination, however, has been the practice by some employers of assigning different job descriptions to men and women, with different rates of pay, even though their tasks are virtually identical.

Even more intractable has been the difficulty with which minorities and women have penetrated (or failed to penetrate) many of the higher-paying, higher-status occupations. Texas has been particularly slow in rectifying the problems of occupational discrimination. For example, in the early 1970s, Houston ranked forty-third out of forty-five surveyed cities in the occupational status of black women,[25] and either forty-fifth or forty-sixth out of forty-six other cities in a survey of minority participation in numerous occupations.[26]

Human resources development programs should aid significantly in breaking down barriers to meaningful employment for women and minorities. We have already remarked on the relatively high percentage of those groups served by manpower programs (though not by the Public Employment Program), and there has been an encouraging increase in the number of disadvantaged persons served by vocational education programs. Unfortunately, manpower programs have not had much impact to date on employment patterns in many high-status occupations, and the number of clients served by those programs has been fairly small, in any case.

There are two efforts aimed specifically at increasing minority and female participation in better-paying jobs that deserve special mention. One, the Apprenticeship Outreach Program, has been operating in the larger cities in Texas for several years. Modeled on successful outreach programs in other cities, and operated by the local Building and Construction Trades Councils, AOP is designed to recruit and prepare minority youths for application and admission to construction apprenticeship programs. Though no rigorous appraisals of the workings of the Texas programs have been made, records of the Bureau of Apprenticeship and Training indicate that some 2,300 youths, nearly all minorities, have been placed in construction apprenticeships by AOP since the late 1960s.

The other program, the Minority Women Employment Program (MWEP), is an outreach program intended to place qualified minority women in managerial, technical, and professional jobs. Begun in 1972 in Atlanta, and extended into Houston in 1973, MWEP now operates as well in Dallas, New Orleans, Tulsa-Oklahoma City, Cincinnati-Dayton, and Los Angeles. Its experience in Houston, where it succeeded in its first two years in placing some seventy-five minority women in higher-paying jobs that they previously had been unable to acquire, and with favorable benefit-cost ratios, indicates that such programs can be effective in substantially increasing the productivity and earning power of victims of discrimination.[27] Obviously, however, MWEP or programs like it would have to be many times larger in order to have much overall impact in the employment patterns of black and Mexican-American females.

CONCLUSION

We have endeavored to summarize, in a comparatively short space, the major public efforts being made toward the development of human resources in Texas, and to outline some of the major problems that remain to be solved. Past experiences with traditional programs such as vocational education and apprenticeship led to a widespread belief that additional measures were needed to assist the disadvantaged, while the profusion of programs developed in the 1960s to serve the disadvantaged demonstrated the need for a more rationalized and better coordinated public policy. The present manpower planning and delivery system emphasizes local initiative, expertise, and responsibility. Such a system is highly logical on its face; whether local officials are equal to the task remains to be seen. Even if CETA programs are ultimately successful, other problems persist. The lack of equal opportunities for women and minority groups, the decay of central cities as well as many rural areas, and the need to support those who are too old, young, or sick to support themselves are pathologies that are not likely to be solved by education and training.

There is one significant matter that we wish to comment on before closing, and that is the importance of the private sector in the development of human resources. The existence of a multitude of formal, public programs may obscure the fact that most practical training takes place informally, on job sites—and that five jobs out of six are found in the private sector. Thus an important task of education and training for employment is to develop in trainees those characteristics most highly valued by employers, such as pride in doing quality work, responsibility, dependability, and appreciation of employers' needs and aims.[28] Manpower development is worker-oriented in that it aspires to increase people's earning power and standard of living. That aspiration will be realized, however, only if training and education programs are also employer-oriented, stressing the development of traits that lead to increased productivity. It is crucial that all concerned understand that what is at stake is not a mechanism for redistributing income from employers to employees, but rather a means of increasing production, earning power, and profits, while reducing the dependency of some citizens on private charity or on tax-supported income transfer programs. The greater the extent to which productivity and employability can be enhanced, the greater the benefits will be for workers, employers, and to society as a whole.

NOTES

1. Texas Education Agency, Department of Occupational Education and Technology, *Annual Vocational Education Report*, 1957.

2. For a fuller discussion of developments in public vocational education, see Sar A. Levitan, Garth L. Mangum, and Ray Marshall,

Human Resources and Labor Markets, 2nd ed. (New York: Harper and Row, 1976), Chapter 11.

3. Texas Urban Development Commission, *Urban Texas: Policies for the Future*, November 1971.

4. Ray Marshall, Robert W. Glover, and William S. Franklin, *Training and Entry into Union Construction*, Manpower Research Monograph No. 39, U. S. Department of Labor, Manpower Administration, 1975.

5. U. S. Department of Labor, Employment and Training Administration, Bureau of Apprenticeship and Training, *Apprenticeship: Past and Present*, p. 18.

6. Bureau of Apprenticeship and Training (SNAPS) data).

7. U. S. Department of Labor, Office of Information, News Release No. 73-206 (May 27, 1973).

8. Marshall et al, loc. cit.

9. Data in this section came from *Statistical Supplement to the Annual Report of the Coordinating Board, Texas College and University System*, Fiscal Year 1974.

10. Data in this section are taken from Texas Rehabilitation Commission, *1976 Report to the Governor*.

11. For excellent discussions of the manpower programs of the sixties, see Garth L. Mangum, *The Emergence of Manpower Policy* (New York: Holt, Rinehart and Winston, Inc., 1969); on the PEP program, see Sar A. Levitan and Robert Taggart, *Emergency Employment Act: The PEP Generation* (Salt Lake City: Olympus Publishing Company, 1974).

12. See Charles R. Perry, Bernard E. Anderson, et al, *The Impact of Government Manpower Programs*, Manpower & Human Resources Studies, No. 4, (Industrial Research Unit, the Wharton School, University of Pennsylvania, 1975).

13. The Act is presented in its entirety in the 1973 *Manpower Report of the President*, pp. 193-242. A progress report on CETA implementation appears in the 1975 *Manpower Report of the President*, pp. 79-104. The first evaluation of planning and delivering manpower services under the new Act can be found in the *Employment and Training Report of the President*, submitted to Congress in 1976, pp. 87-114.

14. For an annotated list of available data sources, see Antonio Furino and Henry Cisneros, *Planning Human Resources Development at the Local Level* (Center for Studies in Business, Economics, and

Human Resources of The University of Texas at San Antonio, 1974), pp. 271-302.

15. An underemployed person is one who is working part-time and seeking full-time work or is working full-time but whose salary in relation to family size is below the officially determined poverty level (presently $5,500 of yearly income for a four-person family).

16. Bowie County at the northeast Texas boundary with Arkansas forms with Arkansas County an interstate consortium under the Arkansas state program.

17. The Texas Planning Regions are multi-county areas designated by the governor. State planning regions were delineated in 1968 as a framework for the coordination of functional planning and as a guide to federal and state agencies in the delivery of services. They are reviewed bi-annually by the governor. Presently, there are twenty-four such planning regions. Their boundaries are shown in Figure 5-2.

18. An economically disadvantaged person is defined as a member of a family that receives cash welfare payments or whose annual income in relation to family size that does not exceed the poverty level determined in accordance with criteria established by the Office of Management and Budget.

19. More specifically, in 1975, 26 percent of those assisted under CETA in Texas were high school graduates, compared with 29 percent in the United States. For Title II and III, the figures were 41 percent and 44 percent, respectively. A larger difference exists in post-high school graduates (participating in Texas and United States CETA programs): 6 and 10 percent for Title I, 20 and 31 percent for Title II, 19 and 30 percent for Title VI, respectively.

20. The data on poverty in this section are taken from Texas Department of Community Affairs, Office of Economic Opportunity, *Poverty in Texas*, 1974.

21. "Texas Skimps on Aid to Poor, Saves Money; But Some Call It Cruel," *The Wall Street Journal*, 10 November 1976.

22. Much of the information in this section is taken from Ray Marshall, *Rural Workers and Rural Labor Markets*, (The University of Texas at Austin, Center for the Study of Human Resources, 1973) Chapter VII.

23. Texas Education Agency, Texas State *Plan for Vocational Education*, Fiscal Year 1976, p. 128.

24. See "Migrant and Seasonal Farm Workers in Texas," *Report of the Governor's Office of Migrant Affairs*, July 1976.

25. Barbara R. Bergman and Jerolyn R. Lyle, "The Occupational Standing of Negroes by Areas and Industries," *Journal of Human Resources*, Fall 1971, pp. 414-15.

26. Vernon Briggs, "Black Employment in Houston," in *Negro Employment in the South*, vol. II, The University of Texas at Austin, Center for the Study of Human Resources, February 1973.

27. Robert W. Glover, Gloria Gutierrez Rowland, and Paula S. Webre, *The Minority Women Employment Project: A Demonstration Program to Facilitate Entry of Minority Women into Managerial, Professional, and Technical Occupations*, (The University of Texas at Austin, Center for the Study of Human Resources, June 1975).

28. Advisory Council for Technical-Vocational Education in Texas, *Qualities Employers Like and Dislike in Job Applicants*, 1975.

SIX

ORGANIZED LABOR IN TEXAS
Robert W. Glover · Allan G. King

This essay presents a general survey of the role, status, and future of unionism in the state of Texas. Because considerable confusion and controversy frequently surround discussions of unions in the state, it is useful before proceeding further to review the role that unions play in America's industrialized economy.

THE ROLE OF UNIONS IN AN INDUSTRIAL SOCIETY

However unions are viewed, philosophically or theoretically, it is a fact that largely because of the characteristics of labor markets in modern economies, labor organizations are a universal phenomenon in an industrial society. Unions, in one form or another, exist in every nation and in almost every industry.

Generally speaking, unions function in economic, political, and social roles in an industrialized society. The relative emphasis placed on these functions varies with the political, social, cultural, historical, and economic context of the particular place and time. While unions themselves are an almost universal phenomenon, the functions they perform may vary considerably.

In many countries the unions play an important political role, providing the leadership for labor parties, and regularly providing their candidates with a line on the ballot. Indeed, the United States is unique in that it is virtually the only industrialized country in which the labor movement is not aligned with a particular political party, and for the most part, confines its political activities to pressure politics, and to bread and butter unionism.[1]

Political activity on the part of unions is well accepted. In representative forms of government, each segment of society has a right to have its views made known and presented to the rest of the body politic. To the extent that people in their role as workers have interests that are distinguished from interests of other groups in the society, most would agree that workers should have the right to band together to promote the policies they favor. The manner in which unions attempt to have their interests represented varies among countries, and even within the same country at different points in time. Since the time of Gompers, the United States labor movement has maintained a loose alliance with the Democratic Party, preferring to reward their friends and punish their enemies in electoral politics, and to apply political pressure through active lobbies at the federal, state, and local levels. The right of unions to engage in political activity is no longer seriously questioned in the United States, nor are their goals regarded as subversive or inherently detrimental to the society.

In terms of its social objectives, the labor movement has usually presented itself as the advocate for all laboring persons and it has been in the vanguard of those campaigning for progressive social policies such as the eight-hour day, free universal public education, minimum wage legislation, workmen's compensation, child labor laws, and the abolition of imprisonment for debt. Reflecting its pragmatic concern for the well-being of workers, the American labor movement has not been bound by a blind adherence to any ideology in its social programs, so along with those progressive policies previously noted, unions have advocated restrictions on immigration, specific tariffs and import quotas, and limitations on the production and sale of goods by convict labor.

Labor's advocacy role on issues of social policy is generally unquestioned. Policies advocated by labor can only be implemented through the actions of government and they thus require the consent of substantial numbers of non-unionists. In order to accomplish its political and social objectives, it follows that labor must extend its influence well beyond the limits of general membership by convincing the general public of the justice or sense of its position.

In contrast to labor's conduct in the political and social realms are the economic actions of unions. Contrary to merely relying on persuasion to achieve its goals, as in the socio-political arena, direct action is often used by organized labor in pursuit of its economic ends. In the economic sphere, success does not require that labor gain consensus among the general populace, but only that it have the strength to influence the actions of an employer or a group of employers. No longer must labor's position be ratified by the majority of the populace. Now, it needs only be acceded to by its economic opponents. It has been in their economic role that the activities of unions have been most controversial and where some public factions have sought to limit their power.

The relationship between worker and employer is often conceived of in purely market terms, the worker supplying labor to the employer for an agreed upon wage determined by the law of supply and demand. According to theories of the competitive market, the forces of supply and demand prevail, making all economic agents who engage in market transactions helpless to affect the terms of the exchange, and leaving them only to decide the quantity of the commodity they will buy or sell. When this view of markets is applied to the particular case of the labor market, it suggests that labor's wage should also be beyond the influence of any single participant in the market, and for a group of workers to join together to alter wages is to have one collective of individuals gain something for themselves at the expense of others who play the game fairly. However, before this principle is accepted uncritically, one must consider the unique characteristics of labor markets which distinguish them from other markets.

Perhaps the most distinctive feature of the labor market derives from the fact that, unlike other commodities, an individual's labor cannot be employed separately from his person. While an individual may be indifferent as to the personalities of those who hire his car, or the location of the ranch where his livestock will be raised, he is likely to have strong feelings about the conditions under which he works. The motivation which governs the purchase and sale of a person's property may be entirely monetary and so may be reasonably analyzed by considering this kind of action as a purely economic phenomenon. On the other hand, a person's decision about where and at what wage the individual works is complex, with pecuniary factors being only one of several relevant considerations.

Because an individual's labor cannot be separated from one's person, a worker may be very slow or reluctant to change jobs in response to higher wages offered by other employers. Because of family attachments, community ties, and friendships formed at work, the typical employee may willingly forgo supplying his labor to employers who offer substantially higher earnings. In market terms, this means that supply only sluggishly responds to higher wages. Moreover, supply pressures on wages are likely to be felt only in the long run, largely through the process of *new* entrants to the labor market and those with little attachments to particular firms distributing themselves among alternative employers.

Just as workers may refuse to move in response to higher paying jobs, employers may be willing to pay their experienced workers wages substantially above what they could obtain on the market from other employers. This situation arises from another distinctive feature of labor markets: as workers gain experience with a particular firm and progress up the ladder, their value to the firm increases. Very likely they have mastered certain processes or techniques that are peculiar to the production processes of their employer. For example, even standard machines are often modified for use in a particular plant and each machine has its quirks that a worker learns only with experience.

As a result, a worker's productivity or value to his present employer, and his wage, may be higher than it would be were he to work for another employer. This divergence between what a worker is worth to his current employer and the wage he could receive elsewhere acts to partially insulate the wage setting process, as it relates to the experienced employee, from the competition of the external labor market. The wage of this worker may have to rise considerably before the employer begins to regard workers outside the firm as possible substitutes for current employees. From the perspective of the experienced employee, outside wages would need to rise substantially before he would consider seeking work elsewhere. Accordingly, there is a considerable differential between the wage below which an employee will quit his work and look elsewhere for employment, and above which the employer will find it unprofitable to retain him. Where in this range the actual wage will lie is a question only distantly governed by market forces in the short run.

The underlying consideration which leads us to this conclusion is the important role of the firm in training its work force. Interviews with firm managers and workers reveal that, for the most part, work-related skills are primarily acquired on the job. Much of this training occurs informally, through close association with other workers, in a kind of socialization process. It is important, therefore, that workers be promoted through the firm in a manner that exposes them to more advanced skills and, at the same time, takes advantage of the skills these workers have already acquired.

Essential to the successful functioning of the training process is the cooperation of the work force. Since workers play such an important role in communicating their skills to other workers, a work environment must be created that is conducive to this activity. Most importantly, a worker must be made to feel that he is not putting himself out of a job by sharing his knowledge with others rather than trying to monopolize his skill. A feeling of job security is essential to both employer and employee.

To this end, formal and informal procedures usually develop in the work place regarding the way in which individuals are promoted, laid off, assigned to jobs, and disciplined. It is the worker's knowledge of these rules, his belief that they will be adhered to, and his confidence that unfair rules or improper application can be contested in grievance hearings that provides workers with security they desire and creates an internal labor market in firms where training activities are important.

Viewing the labor market this way provides a much different picture of the way in which jobs are allocated and workers are rewarded. Rather than a market in which homogeneous goods are exchanged between buyers and sellers, with the seller of each good indifferent to the use to which it is put, provided the sale is at the going price, the model of the labor market sketched above recognizes skill differentiation in the labor force. Within each firm there is a great array of decisions to be made regarding the compensation and employment of labor, many of which are guided only loosely by the external labor market. Labor-management negotiation provides one vehicle to resolve these issues. Since the work environment cannot be made to vary from individual to individual but is, in effect, a collective good, it can be reasonably argued that work rules be established through collective negotiations. In this light, labor unions are seen not as an aberration, or a force which impedes a market from arriving at its natural solution, but rather as an aid to the functioning of a system that receives only limited direction from a market that broadly limits the discretion exercised by firms and workers but fails to establish the details and inner workings of the system.

In this context, the emotional anti-union sentiment, voiced in Texas' churches, media, and schools, while in tune with the general tone of the history of organized labor in Texas, seems inappropriate.

A GLIMPSE AT TEXAS UNION HISTORY

The Texas labor movement is heir to a colorful history of struggle since April 1838, when printers in Houston formed the earliest known bona fide labor union, the Texas Typographical Association, and successfully struck for a 25 percent wage increase six months later.[2] One of the most important strikes in American labor history, the Great Southwest Strike of the Knights of Labor against Jay Gould's railway system, was initiated on Texas soil in 1886. The failure of this strike was a major factor in the downfall of the Knights of Labor.[3]

The difficulty of labor's struggle in Texas is perhaps most vividly illustrated by events surrounding the construction of the State Capitol Building during the 1880s. In response to the contractor's proposal to train prison laborers as stonemasons on the project and to undertake other measures perceived as undesirable, the International Association of Granite Cutters boycotted work on the famous domed structure. When the contractor attempted to circumvent the boycott by importing sixty-two stonemasons from Scotland in clear violation of the Alien Contract Law of 1885, the Granite Cutters took the case to court and won. However, the victory was an empty one because the assessed fines against the contractor were subsequently reduced from $64,000 to $8,000 by President Benjamin Harrison in a special order a week before he left office.[4]

A more recent indicator of the anti-union climate is Texas' "Right to Work" law, initially passed in 1947. In 1977, only nineteen other states have joined Texas in enacting such a law. In addition, the Texas Union Security Act of 1951 declared union shop provisions to be in a restraint of trade. Beginning in 1961, a move was made to amend the state constitution to include a right to work provision, but such efforts have died in committee. Although the impact of right to work laws is probably more symbolic than real, the laws do prohibit agency shop agreements (between willing employers and employees), whereby employees are not required to join unions but are required to pay an amount of money to the union—usually equivalent to union dues—for performing functions as their agent in collective bargaining activities. According to federal law, unions have a duty to fairly represent workers in their bargaining unit, regardless of union membership status. Union officials point out that right to work laws are misnamed because they do not guarantee anyone the right to work. Rather they effectively permit individuals to take advantage of union representation without paying for it, thereby undermining union security.

Despite obstacles, however, the labor movement in Texas has grown slowly and steadily. The Texas State Federation of Labor, formed in

1900 with a total membership of 8,475, was able to claim a membership of 42,000 in 1919.[5]

Historical data on union membership in Texas are sketchy at best. For periods prior to 1964, the best data have been published by the National Bureau of Economic Research, which collected information on union membership by state for the years 1939 and 1953. The data, which refer to dues-paying members, were derived from unions' financial reports, convention credential committee reports on voting representation, and correspondence with individual unions.

Table 6-1 shows a comparison of the absolute and relative growth of unions in Texas and the United States from 1939 to 1972. Texas union growth has not been exceptional when compared with growth of the labor force and growth of unionism in the nation. Since 1939, the incidence of unionism in the Texas labor force has consistently remained about half that of the United States labor force. According to available data, Texas has ranked among the ten least unionized states in the nation for more than three decades. Texas is also less unionized than any of the states which border it.

It should be noted that the comparison between the incidence of unionism in Texas and of unionism in other areas of the nation may overstate the extent to which Texans are less prone to join unions. One reason for this is that such a comparison does not take account of differences in industrial structure between Texas and the rest of the nation. That is, it may be that Texas is less unionized merely because the Texas industrial mix contains larger than average portions of traditionally nonunion industry.

It is well known that unions tend to be concentrated in certain industries, although it is less clear why these industries are highly organized. Some economists have pointed to the degree of product market concentration in these industries, or average plant size as being important factors. Regardless of the particular explanation one prefers, the historical relationship between unions and firms in particular industries is well established.

The extent to which differences in industrial structure account for the difference in the incidence of unions in Texas as compared to the nation could be tested if appropriate data were available. However, the data collected and published by the U. S. Bureau of Labor Statistics are inadequate for these purposes. One study considering the issue for the entire South was performed using data specially gathered in 1953. Leo Troy, the author of the study, concluded that industrial structure was a significant factor accounting for the relatively small incidence of union membership across the South.[6] A study of Texas today would likely reach the same conclusion: industrial structure accounts for some of the low incidence of unionism in the state. By implication, as Texas continues to industrialize and come closer to the national industrial pattern, the incidence of unionism in Texas will increase.

In 1954, Frederic Meyers attributed much of union growth in Texas over the period 1933 to 1953 to industrial growth in the state. He observed that union growth was strongly associated with Texas growth industries over the period, that is, transportation equipment, paper, primary metals and chemicals. He pointed out that collective bargaining came to such industries even in areas without any union tradition, including rural areas with large industrial facilities.[7]

Why then has the incidence of unionism failed to more closely approach the national average as Texas has continued to industrialize since the mid-1950s? First, union membership in traditionally union industries such as construction, printing, trucking, and apparel has

TABLE 6-1

UNION MEMBERSHIP DATA
TEXAS AND ALL STATES: SELECTED YEARS

	Texas		All States	
Year	Membership in Thousands	Membership as a Percentage of Employees in Nonagricultural Establishments	Membership in Thousands	Membership as a Percentage of Employees in Nonagricultural Establishments
1939	110.5	10.3	6,518	21.3
1953	374.8	16.8	16,217	32.3
1964	394.0	14.1	17,188	29.5
1966	419.0	13.5	18,301	28.6
1968	474.0	13.9	19,297	28.4
1970	523.0	14.4	19,757	28.0
1972	525.0	13.5	19,789	27.2

Source: Data for 1939 and 1953 taken from Leo Troy, *Distribution of Union Membership Among the States 1939 and 1953*, New York: National Bureau of Economic Research, Occasional Paper 56, 1957. Data for other years taken from U. S. Bureau of Labor Statistics, *Directory of National Unions and International Labor Unions*, 1970, 1968, 1966, and 1964 editions, Washington, D.C.: U. S. Government Printing Office and the January 1976 supplement to *Directory of National Unions and Employee Associations, 1973*. Washington, D.C.: U. S. Government Printing Office.

been low in Texas. This was true in 1977 as it was when Meyers observed it in 1954. Union growth has continued to be slow in such occupations that form the backbone of union membership in other states. Second, much of the recent growth in Texas industries has been in new fields spawned by technology, such as computers and semiconductors that have not yet developed a strong union tradition.

PATTERNS OF UNIONIZATION IN TEXAS

The pattern of unionization in Texas differs from the national pattern in at least one respect: industries which have represented the core of American unionism—printing, apparel, construction, and transportation—are not well unionized in Texas. On the other hand, some industries and areas of Texas are strongly unionized. For example, in the telephone and telegraph industry, unionization nears 100 percent.

Historically, unionism in the state has been most concentrated in the Houston-Beaumont area. Partly, this is because Houston is a port area and transportation hub. In such cities, unionization seems literally "to spread from the docks" (as in San Francisco and Seattle). Another contributing factor is that Houston-Beaumont is a highly industrialized urban complex, and unions seem to thrive better in such places than in smaller towns and rural areas.

Data in Table 6-2 show Texas membership statistics for all unions which reported to the U. S. Bureau of Labor Statistics in both 1968 and 1970, the only years for which this type of data was available.

Although these data constitute the most reliable information on union membership in the state, they have several limitations. First, they represent only part of the Texas total because several dozen unions failed to report membership data by state. Second, they represent only two years. Third, membership is defined as dues-paying members of unions, including retired members. Fourth, although the data are reported by national unions, U. S. Bureau of Labor Statistics officials acknowledge that some unions merely estimate rather than make precise counts by state. Fifth, membership figures for each union reflect two separate characteristics: the size of the industry or craft from which the union traditionally draws its membership, and the strength of the union in the state. Consequently, a union may have a large membership even though it is not aggressive in organizing, because there is a large concentration of its traditional membership base in Texas, or because it thoroughly organizes a smaller number of potential members, or through some combination of these circumstances. Care must be exercised in interpreting membership or growth figures as measures of union "strength."

Of all unions reporting, the largest in Texas was the Communications Workers of America, with 31,618 members in 1970, followed closely by the International Association of Machinists, which reported 29,364 members. Other large unions in Texas included the International Brotherhood of Teamsters (25,601), the United Automobile Workers (25,055), the American Federation of Government Employees (25,511), and the Oil, Chemical, and Atomic Workers (24,960). Of all of these unions, Texas membership accounted for less than 5 percent of national membership except in the Oil, Chemical, and Atomic Workers in which almost one out of every six members resided in Texas.

Table 6-2 shows changes in union membership in Texas between 1968 and 1970. During this period, membership in all reporting unions increased by 8.8 percent. Of the fifty-five unions for which membership data are available for both years, twenty-eight, or slightly over one-half, had gains of more than 8 percent. At the other end of the spectrum, eighteen unions lost members during this period.

Large unions which ranked toward the top in membership growth include the Teamsters (17.9 percent), the Meat Cutters (23.7 percent), and the Communications Workers (13.4 percent). Unions that have declined in membership between 1968 and 1970 include large unions such as the Machinists (-1.2 percent) and the Automobile Workers (-4.3 percent), as well as smaller unions such as the Transport Service Employees (-23.3 percent) and the Upholsterers (-8.8 percent).

In reviewing the data it is difficult to generalize about those factors which distinguish unions that gained members from unions that lost members. The rapid growth of the service sector suggests that those unions which organize service workers in the private sector are likely to grow rapidly. However, the evidence is mixed: some service sector unions such as the Retail, Wholesale, and Department Store Union (81 percent), and Hotel and Restaurant Employees Union (43 percent) are among the fastest growing on the list, while other service sector unions such as the Guards' Union (28 percent), and the Transport Service Employees (23 percent) rank near the bottom of the list. While unions of service employees may have grown substantially as a group between 1968 and 1970, the growth was not evenly distributed among all unions. Of greatest significance are gains made by the unions active among public employees. The Service Employees International Union, beginning from a small base, nearly doubled its

TABLE 6-2

MEMBERSHIP IN REPORTING UNIONS IN TEXAS, 1968 & 1970

Ranking	Union	Reported Membership 1968	Reported Membership 1970	Change in Reported Membership 1968-1970 No.	%
1	Roofers (RDWW)	115	772	657	571.3
2	Service Employees (SEIU)	108	305	197	182.4
3	Shoe Workers; United (USW)	241	523	282	117.0
4	Mailers (IMU-Ind.)	144	300	156	108.3
5	Retail, Wholesale, and Department Store Union (RWDSU)	1,107	2,000	893	80.7
6	Air Line Pilots (ALPA)	2,513	4,149	1,636	65.1
7	State, County, & Municipal	4,340	7,112	2,772	63.9
8	Rubber Workers (URW)	2,036	2,987	951	46.7
9	Hotel & Restaurant Employees (HREU)	632	907	275	43.5
10	Quarantine Inspectors (FPQI-Ind.)	50	70	20	40.0
11	Potters (IBOP)	238	298	60	25.2
12	Meat Cutters (MCBW)	9.075	11,223	2,148	23.7
13	Government Employees (AFGE)	20,821	25,511	4,690	22.5
14	Railway & Airline Supervisors (RASA)	147	180	33	22.4
15	Brewery Workers (BFCSD)	2,039	2,473	434	21.3
16	Lithographers & Photoengravers (LPIU)	782	940	158	20.6
17	Boilermakers (BBF)	7,444	8,832	1,388	18.6
18	Teamsters (IBT-Ind.)	21,723	25,601	3,878	17.9
19	Bakery Workers (BCW) Merger in 1969				
	Bakery Workers; Am. (ABCW)	2,155			
	Bak. & Confect. Workers (BCW-Ind.)	167			
		2,322	2,729	407	17.5
20	Horseshoers (UJH)	12	14	2	16.7
21	Elevator Constructors (IUEC)	589	684	95	16.1
22	Garment Workers; Ladies (ILGWU)	404	465	61	15.1
23	Pulp & Sulphite Workers (PSPMW)	3,086	3,518	432	14.0
24	Communications Workers (CWA)	27,885	31,618	3,733	13.4
25	Airline Dispatchers (ALDA)	15	17	2	13.3
26	Painters (PAT)	5,935	6,678	743	12.5
27	Electrical Workers (IBEW)	19,405	21,745	2,336	12.0
28	Guard Workers; Plant (PGW-Ind.)	685	756	71	10.4
29	Letter Carriers (NALC)	10,037	10,787	750	7.5

TABLE 6-2 (Cont'd)

MEMBERSHIP IN REPORTING UNIONS IN TEXAS, 1968 & 1970

Ranking	Union	Reported Membership		Change in Reported Membership 1968-1970	
		1968	1970	No.	%
30	ASCS County Office (ASCS-Ind.)	1,341	1,428	87	6.5
31	Brick & Clay Workers (UBCW)	559	594	35	6.3
32	Aluminum Workers (AWU)	870	900	30	3.4
33	Die Sinkers (DSC-Ind.)	33	34	1	3.0
34	Flight Engineers (FEIA)	183	187	4	2.19
35	Papermakers & Paperworkers (UPP)	2,169	2,216	47	2.17
36	Carpenters (CJA)	23,905	24,330	425	1.8
37	Marine Engineers (MEBA)	609	618	9	1.5
38	Maintenance of Way Employees (BMWE)	5,984	5,972	-42	-0.7
39	Machinists (IAM)	29,711	29,364	-347	-1.2
40	Railway Clerks (BRASX)	11,321	11,155	-166	-1.5
41	Laborers (LIUNA)	12,491	12,190	-301	-2.4
42	Messengers (SDM)*	154	150	-4	-2.6
43	Woodworkers (IWA)	477	462	-15	-3.1
44	Plumbers (PPF)	16,931	16,316	-615	-3.6
45	Auto Workers (UAW-Ind.)	26,176	25,055	-1,121	-4.3
46	Electrical Workers	4,080	3,900	-180	-4.4
47	Laundry & Dry Cleaning Union (LDC)	158	147	-11	-7.0
48	Upholsterers (UIU)	980	894	-86	-8.8
49	Railway Carmen (BRC)	4,591	4,091	-500	-10.9
50	Typgraphical Union (ITU)	4,169	3,670	-499	-12.0
51	Baseball Players (BPA-Ind.)	45	39	-6	-13.3
52	Pattern Makers (PML)	34	29	-5	-14.7
53	Post Office & General Service Maintenance Employees (POSM)*	617	485	-132	-21.4
54	Transport Service Employees (UTSE)	60	46	-14	-23.3
55	Guards Union (GUA-Ind.)	245	176	-69	-28.2
TOTALS, ALL UNIONS		291,823	313,608		8.8

*The Special Delivery Messengers and the Post Office & General Service Maintenance Employees merged with three other unions to form the American Postal Workers Union in 1971.

Source: U. S. Bureau of Labor Statistics.

membership in the three year period. The American Federation of State, County, and Municipal Employees (AFSCME), which had 4,340 members in the state in 1968, generated a 64 percent increase in its membership by 1970. Perhaps most impressive is the increase in membership in the American Federation of Government Employees. This union gained over forty-six hundred members in the two year period, recording the largest absolute gain of any union in the state, and increased its membership by 22 percent. Such growth among public sector unions in Texas indicates that public employee unions will play a larger role in the Texas labor movement of the future. However, there are some obstacles to this development which are discussed in the next section.

PUBLIC EMPLOYEE UNIONISM: HAMPERED BY TEXAS LAW[8]

Unions of public employees are presently the fastest growing segment of organized labor. Throughout the country, these unions have been organizing aggressively and taking a more militant stance in their collective negotiations. The result has been a rapid increase in the incidence of strikes in this sector. With a large pool of unorganized workers remaining, unions of public employees may be the force which revives organized labor from the doldrums it entered subsequent to the merger of the AFL with the CIO in 1955. In addition, public employee organizations may be the door through which unions enter the rapidly expanding service sector of the economy, providing the link which would at last break organzied labor's historical identification with blue-collar, industrial workers and signal the beginning of a new era for labor.

Although organizing activity among public employees has been occurring at a rapid pace in the rest of the country for several years, the pace in Texas has been picking up only recently. Undoubtedly this contrast reflects the legal and political climate in the state, which in itself may be indicative of the attitudes prevailing among the population. In any event, there can be little doubt that the Manford Act (1947) which banned collective bargaining in the public sector has inhibited the unionization of public employees in Texas.

The Manford Act, while permitting workers to join unions, prohibited unions claiming the right to strike from representing its members in the grievance procedures. Although the Texas legislature granted collective bargaining rights to police and firefighters by special exception in 1973, the realization of these rights was made contingent upon voter approval in local option elections. Insufficient time has passed to permit a determination of the relative ease with which organizations representing these public servants will be able to negotiate with their employers; however, the "contingent recognition" provision will, in all likelihood, significantly postpone the granting of bargaining rights to the uniformed services.

There appear to be several motives which explain the reluctance of the Texas legislature to extend collective bargaining rights to public sector employees. Perhaps most important is the general public's fear of the costs and inconvenience posed by strikes in the public sector. While strikes are no doubt costly, alternative means of determining conditions of employment have their costs as well. Moreover, the extension of bargaining rights need not result in more frequent strikes. Many contracts affecting employees call for fact-finding and mediation procedures to resolve impasses. Binding arbitration, whereby each party agrees in advance to accept the decision of the arbitrator, is another method by which strikes could be averted and yet permit public employees to bargain over wages, hours, and other conditions of employment. Thus collective bargaining need not be the first step toward public strikes. It should be added that the outright prohibition of collective bargaining has not resulted in the elimination of public employee strikes in Texas. Helburn reports that between 1966 and 1970 fifteen work stoppages occurred among local public employees in Texas. While this is far less than Texas' proportionate share of the 1,400 stoppages which occurred among public employees nationwide during the same period, it has not been immune to strikes by public employees. Many strikes have accompanied the initiation of new bargaining relationships in states and municipalities, as inexperienced negotiators received heavy doses of on-the-job training. After peaking in this initial period, the incidence of strikes typically decreases over time.

Despite the relaxation of the ban on collective bargaining for the uniformed services, the majority of Texas public employees are unlikely to see a major change in their relations with their employers. As a result, a principal means by which groups of public employees endeavor to improve their lot is political activity. By lobbying state and local governments, these groups have enjoyed a measure of success, at least as indicated by the rate at which new members have joined their ranks. One of the fastest growing organizations of public employees is the Texas Public Employees Association (TPEA), which grew from 25,000 in 1970 to 40,000 in 1977, an increase of 60 percent. Identifying itself as an employee association rather than a labor union, TPEA represents state employees engaged in nonteaching activities before the state legislature on issues of interest to them, including higher pay and improved benefits. Partly in response to pressures from its membership, TPEA in 1974 began to move toward protecting members' rights on the job through assisting workers in grievance procedures.

TPEA has been criticized for accepting supervisors into its ranks. Opponents of TPEA contend that this organizational arrangement precludes the effective presentation of its members' grievances, for it is possible that the individual filing the grievance and the person against whom it is filed may both be members of the Association. Perhaps the 15,000 new members are persuaded otherwise or perhaps they simply lack effective alternatives under present legal constraints. Whatever the reason, TPEA was undeniably the chief organization representing nonteaching state employees in Texas in 1977.

At the local level, the legal environment has become somewhat less restrictive during the past decade and modest gains have been made in organizing workers. The principal organizations involved have been the American Federation of State, County, and Municipal Employees (AFSCME), the Texas State Teachers' Association, the Texas Classroom Teachers' Association, the International Association of Fire Fighters, and a group of three police associations.

One significant change that has occurred is the recourse to public referendum granted to the policemen and firemen. This provision enables these employee groups to call for a public referendum on the acceptance of their demands should they fail to come to agreement with the administrative body. Helburn expresses the opinion that during the 1960-70 period public referenda provided the uniformed services with increased wages and reduced hours in many instances. The recourse to public referendum granted these workers does not appear to be affected by the recent change in state law aimed at them.

Since 1967, the Texas Education Code has granted consultation rights to organizations of public school teachers. Although specific consultation agreements vary among school districts, there are some which provide for the teachers' organization to name one member of a three-member board to aid in dispute settlement. The board is usually empowered to mediate between teachers and either the district supervisor or school board when an impasse is reached. Should these efforts fail, the board may make recommendations.

A third concession made to public employees has been the extension of the "checkoff" to organizations of municipal workers in larger cities (over 10,000 in population) and employees of larger counties (over 20,000). The checkoff requires an employer to deduct union dues and assessments from an employee's paycheck (with his permission) and remit these payments to the union. In effect, the employer becomes the union's collection agent. Although the employer may charge the union a fee for this service, most unions regard the checkoff as indispensable. Rather than relying on its members to pay their dues in person at the union office, or remember to send them by mail, the checkoff provides the union with a reliable flow of income with which to meet its expenses.

From surveying these comparatively recent developments, it may appear that organized labor has made significant strides in the public sector. While there can be no doubt that some progress has been made, Texas unions have far to go. As significant as the extension of bargaining rights to the uniformed services is, the provisional nature of these rights is equally noteworthy. While public employee organization and bargaining are occurring at a furious pace elsewhere in the country, change in Texas is barely discernible. While the potential is vast, if present performance is any indicator of the future of public sector unionism in Texas, the unions will continue to face great obstacles in their drive for increased membership.

Another key to the future of union organization in Texas is the Mexican labor force. Largely nonunion and employed in many disagreeable work situations, this population provides a fertile field for union organizers. Mexicans in many companies across the state have begun to assert themselves in strikes and picket lines to gain collective bargaining rights, for example, strikes against Economy Furniture in Austin, Longhorn Machine Works at Kyle, and La Casita Farms and Farah in South Texas.

ORGANIZING CHICANOS: LABOR ORGANIZATION IN A LABOR SURPLUS ECONOMY

Any discussion of the labor-organizing efforts by agricultural workers and the largely Mexican labor force in the border towns of Texas must acknowledge the pervasive influence of the Mexican border on these labor markets.[9] The large daily influx of Mexican workers into

Texas provides a supply of workers who compete for work with those American workers who can least afford this competition—the low skilled, poorly educated workers.

Perhaps more than the absence of federal labor relations law, the availability of foreign workers has forestalled the unionization of agricultural workers. Those who are union members or union organizers can be readily dismissed by employers who can attract ample supplies of foreign workers at prevailing wage levels. To foreign workers the lowest wages paid to domestic workers are likely to be several times what they can earn in Mexico. Although the foreign workers and the citizens they displace may share the same ethnic background, economic necessity more than overcomes whatever kinship may exist between American and Mexican workers.

This observation is borne out by the events that occurred during the recent strike at the Farah Manufacturing Company in El Paso. While several unfair labor practice charges were processed through the machinery of the National Labor Relations Board, and law suits were filed in the courts, the Farah plant remained in operation, replacing the striking workers with both domestic and foreign workers. The ease with which workers can be replaced in an economy that has a large reservoir of unskilled labor on which to draw has been an important influence shaping labor relations in industries along the Texas border.

Throughout the history of organized labor, the strike has been its greatest weapon. The dramatic strikes that occurred on the railroads in the late 1800s and the confrontations that accompanied the organization of the automobile and steel industries during the late 1930s and the early 1940s are legendary. In essence, the strike is a concerted withdrawal of labor for purposes of bringing economic pressure to bear on the employer. The success of a strike is likely to vary directly with the effectiveness with which the union can shut off the supply of labor. The most violent and controversial strikes have occurred over the issue of union recognition, the most fundamental aspect of union-management relations.

The nature of the labor markets along the Texas border have virtually eliminated the strike as a viable union weapon. High rates of unemployment for domestic workers and the easy entry of foreign workers make it futile to merely attempt to reduce the supply of workers by means of a strike. Consequently, these unions have resorted to other tactics in an effort to gain recognition.

The consumer boycott has been a principal weapon in the effort to organize the agricultural workers and the employees of Farah Manufacturing. While most unions favor action aimed at the labor market since it is most direct, the labor surplus economy created along the border precludes effective action in that sphere and has thus forced these workers to enlist the aid of the consumer. The aim of the boycotts is to significantly reduce the demand for the product the employer produces and so reduce his profits. The success of the consumer boycott in bringing Farah to the bargaining table in 1974 demonstrates the effectiveness of this weapon.

The details of the tactics employed by the Farah workers differ from those employed by the agricultural workers. Since the Farah workers are under the jursidiction of the Taft-Hartley Act, they are bound by the limitation set out in the Act. Although they may publicly call for a boycott of Farah products, they cannot urge consumers to boycott those retailers who carry Farah goods as only one of a number of products.

On the other hand, the agricultural workers are outside the jurisdiction of the Taft-Hartley Act and are not bound by its proscription against the secondary boycott. As a result, it is common to find the farm workers' boycott is waged not only against particular types of grapes and lettuce, but at particular food chains as well. Broadening the boycottt has the effect of putting pressure on the growers directly, by affecting their profits, and indirectly, by affecting the profits of their customers. However, such secondary boycotts may adversely affect union employees of customer chain stores and thus result in some friction within the labor movement.

The United Farm Workers' Organizing Committee (later the United Farm Workers) was chartered by the AFL-CIO to organize farm workers. Shortly after its formation, it was seriously challenged by the Teamsters in California, a union not affiliated with the AFL-CIO. Jurisdiction disputes led to years of farm labor strife marked by occasional violence in California. The United Farm Workers accused the Teamsters of raiding their jurisdictions and gaining employer recognition by signing "sweetheart contracts" with the growers. The Teamsters countered that they were merely following food-processing work (which they had traditionally organized) from the shed to the fields in response to technological change. Hope for resolution of the long-standing dispute surfaced again on 10 March 1977 with announcement of an agreement between the two unions, whereby the Teamsters were allotted sole jurisdiction over cannery workers and the United Farm Workers obtained sole jurisdiction in the fields.

In terms of the substantive nature of the agreements each union has negotiated, they differ principally in the Teamsters' retention of the "labor contracting" system, whereby a grower can subcontract the hiring responsibility to a crew foreman who recruits and pays wages to the workers. The Farm Workers believe the system has led to much abuse and has instead instituted the traditional hiring hall, which has drawn charges of corruption from the Teamsters. In terms of the wages and hours each union has negotiated, a comparison of contracts shows little difference between the unions. However, an important dimension of the union struggle is the Farm Workers' claim that rather than simply building a union, they are trying to mold a movement by and for Mexican workers under the direction of Caesar Chavez. There can be no doubt that this population is severely disadvantaged and, except in a few localities, without any significant political strength. If the progress of black Americans during the past decade can be taken as a lesson, it seems evident that both political and economic cohesion are necessary for the progress of the Mexican population.

PROSPECTS FOR FUTURE UNION GROWTH

Predictions about the proliferation of unionism are risky, largely because the data from the past are so sketchy and forecasting future events is a very uncertain science. Some general comments can be made, however.

The spread of unionism is in part a response to industrial growth. Since Texas is enjoying a faster rate of industrialization than the nation as a whole, it is natural to assume that it will increasingly become a target for union organization. Further, the incidence of unionism traditionally has been much greater among large establishments (employing 250 people or more) than among smaller organizations.[10] Thus, as industry becomes more concentrated in Texas, it is reasonable to expect union organizing to show greater success. Likewise, the rise of agribusiness in Texas may induce unionization of certain types of farmwork.

While the industries that comprise the core of American unionism remain remarkably nonunion in Texas, there are indications that the Texas pattern may change in at least one traditionally unionized industry—apparel. The success in early 1974 of the boycott and strike against Farah has given hope to union organizers that the rest of the

Texas apparel industry can soon be organized.

The success of unionism among the public employees will hinge largely on elimination of the Texas statute prohibiting collective bargaining by public employees. Several signs point to the eventual demise of this provision, which is unique among all state laws in the nation. In 1973, the sixty-third Texas legislature passed an exception allowing municipal firemen and policemen to bargain collectively at local option. Admittedly a small and tenuous exception, the new law does signal a change in direction. Several new developments looming on the horizon may change the Texas law completely. Such developments include the very real possibility of federal legislation establishing collective bargaining rights for public employees on a national basis. Whatever the outcome of these particular developments, the Texas legal stance prohibiting public employee bargaining will be increasingly called under question.

Part of the future of the labor movement is tied to its stance toward Chicano workers in the state. Comprising 14.8 percent of the state's work force in 1970, Chicano workers offer significant potential for union organization. However, before meaningful progress can be made by these workers, particularly in South Texas, some attention needs to be paid to remedying the problems caused by border crossers from Mexico.

In summary, the potential for the growth of unionism among the Texas labor force exists, and there is some cause for optimism on the part of union officials. However, considering the history of anti-union sentiment in Texas, none of these union advances will come without determined effort on the part of the Texas labor movement itself.

NOTES

1. "Bread and butter" unionism or "business unionism" as contrasted with "reform unionism" or "revolutionary unionism" is concerned predominantly with improvement of wages, hours, and working conditions.

2. James V. Reece, "The Worker in Texas," 1821-1876 (Ph.D. dissertation, University of Texas, 1964), pp. 233-34.

3. See Ruth A. Allen, *The Great Southwest Strike* (Austin: University of Texas publication, 1942).

4. Ruth Allen, *Chapters in the History of Organized Labor in Texas* (Austin: University of Texas publication, 1941), pp. 44-88.

5. Ibid., pp. 121 and 152.

6. Leo Troy, "The Growth of Union Membership in the South, 1939-1952," *Southern Economic Journal*, 24, no. 4 (April 1958), pp. 407-20.

7. Frederic Meyers, "The Growth of Collective Bargaining in Texas—A Newly Industrialized Area," *Proceedings of the Seventh Annual Meeting of the Industrial Relations Research Association*, December 28-30, 1954, Detroit Michican, pp. 286-97.

8. See I. B. Helburn, *Public Employer-Employee Relations in Texas: Contemporary and Emerging Developments* (Austin: Institute of Public Affairs, University of Texas at Austin, Public Affairs Series No. 84, 1970).

9. For an excellent discussion of U. S. border policy and its effects on the Chicano population, see Vernon M. Briggs, Jr., *The Mexico-United States Border: Public Policy and Chicano Economic Welfare* (Austin: Bureau of Business Research, The University of Texas, Studies in Human Resource Development, No. 2, 1974).

10. This point was similarily made by Meyers, op. cit.

SEVEN

MANUFACTURING IN TEXAS
Stanley A. Arbingast

Since frontier times Texans have been extractors. Some plowed and planted large acreages of land and harvested crops and some pastured livestock. Some cut trees. Others dug deep for solid minerals such as stone, and later many others dug much deeper for hydrocarbons, primarily oil and gas. And then, by and large, they shipped out the goods they had extracted and they returned to the earth for more.

The extractive days are far from done; they never will be. But today, industries that depend on materials extracted from the earth—forestry, fishing, mining, and agriculture—use almost as many machines as workers, and thousands of workers who were employed in extractive occupations are now busy with fabricating goods in manufacturing plants and moving those goods to the consumer, rather than with producing raw materials.

Texas manufacturing began with the processing of local raw materials such as trees, farm and ranch commodities, and local clays. Sawmills were numerous in the pine forests of East Texas. Mills to grind wheat, corn, and other cereal grains were well distributed throughout the farming areas. Cotton gins and cottonseed-oil processing facilities were constructed to take care of cotton, the most widely produced field crop. Slaughtering plants to convert animals on the hoof to meat for the table were established. Food processing ranked first in manufacturing employment during the Texas colonial period, and it was second only to nonelectrical machinery in April 1977.

Later, the discovery of petroleum and natural gas in large quantities provided a strong basis for the development along the coast of one of the largest refining and petrochemical complexes found anywhere in the world. Investment in these industries totals many billions of dollars and expansion is still proceeding at an impressive pace, even though mineral resources are not renewable. These two industries, refinement of petroleum and manufacture of petrochemicals, account for a very large share of the total value added by manufacture in the state. Moreover, gas, petroleum, and lignite are the major sources of energy needed for operation of factories.

Texas resources for manufacture are not confined to those produced by farms, ranches, forests, and mines, but in a sense also include location, climate, and topography. Location midway between both coasts on the west south central fringe of the nation with access to the shipping lanes of the warm Gulf, open to transportation the year around, and to the major inland waterway networks of the country, is a marketing advantage *par excellence*.

The mild climate of the state is also an asset. Warmth prevailing throughout most of the year has been a boon to the construction industry, not only extending the building season several months, but making feasible the construction of lightweight economical structures for factories where there is little need for heavy weatherproofing. Variation in climate contributes to the growth of a wide variety of crops, ranging from those of the temperate zone (wheat and grain sorghum) to those of the subtropics (citrus, rice, and sugar cane). The long growing season makes it possible for farmers to be flexible in their cropping procedures; some are able to grow three and even four crops a year on the same plot of ground. Rapid growth of trees in the forested areas gives the lumber industry of Texas an advantage over the lumber industry operating in colder areas.

The vast expanse of Texas' level-to-gently-rolling landscape has been advantageous to manufacturing development. Most of the land gently slopes in the direction of the Gulf. Thus the problem of transporting petroleum from the far-flung hinterlands to the refineries and chemical plants on tidewater is eased; no intervening ranges of mountains or high hills impede movement of hydrocarbons by pipeline. The level forest lands of East Texas facilitate logging at low cost. The flat terrain has encouraged farmers to make extensive use of automated equipment, enabling them to produce more crops on larger acreages.

People are the most important of all resources, serving as extractors, managers, manufacturers, transporters, and as servicers of machines. In fact, it is human imagination acting upon resources that gives rise to manufacturing and to improvements in techniques of servicing the needs of the population. The imagination may be that of the manufacturer, who designs and fashions a useful or attractive product, or it may be that of the consumer, who wants something he has never had or not had enough of. It takes people to be the entrepreneurs and to do the manufacturing and transporting, and raw materials and capital to finance buildings, machines, and other equipment.

Manufacturing growth in Texas has been especially rapid during the past three decades. A study of gains in manufacturing jobs shows that employment has been increasing faster in Texas than in the nation. In 1973 Texas ranked eighth among the states in value added by manufacture. Although this high ranking owes much to the huge investment and to the efficiency of operation of the state's refining and petrochemical industries, increases in value added and employment in other segments of manufacture in the state are impressive.

Texas' manufacturing growth stems to a considerable degree from the favorable conditions present. Abundant mineral raw materials located in close proximity to each other and the availability of power were perhaps the most important growth factors. Almost as significant was the large pool of labor available to manufacturers of apparel, electrical machinery, and transportation equipment. The region's own foods, and construction materials, have been a drawing card for market-oriented industries; in turn, expansion in the total income received by factory workers stimulated demand for manufactured goods.

Specialization is to be expected in a state having as much territory as Texas, and specializations have developed in some areas. Examples of specialization include refining and petrochemicals in coastal cities, food processing in the Lower Rio Grande Valley, and apparel, transportation equipment, and electrical machinery in the North Central region.

Most Texans live east of Fort Worth and San Antonio in the better-watered sections of the state where manufacturing is concentrated. During the last few years, many factories have been established in West Texas and along the Rio Grande in areas where few manufacturing plants existed in 1950; the available labor supply was the primary factor when plant sites were decided upon. There is also a pronounced trend for new factories to be built in communities with populations of five thousand to forty-five thousand, although most new plants continue to locate in or near the largest of the standard metropolitan statistical areas.

Diversity in types of manufacture and in output of end products has accompanied the manufacturing growth that has characterized the last twenty-five years. Every major manufacturing category is represented in Texas. Products range from industrial chemicals to sophisticated electronic equipment and medical instruments. An analysis of each major type of manufacture represented follows:

Food and Kindred Products. Predictably, food processing in Texas has shown steady growth; this industry keeps pace with the expansion of population. It is market-oriented as well as resource-oriented.

The segment of food processing that has shown the fastest growth is meat packing. The trend to decentralize beef processing away from the old traditional locations is well illustrated in Texas, where several large new plants have been built, particularly in the Amarillo-Lubbock area where grain sorghum is used in huge feed lots to fatten cattle for slaughter. Processing of poultry and fish is also important, the former primarily in East Texas, south and east of Austin, and San Antonio. Port cities are centers of fish processing.

Plants that manufacture food from cereal grains are distributed over the eastern and coastal sections of the state and in the irrigated areas of West Texas. These grains include wheat, oats, barley, rice, and grain sorghum. Production of feed for livestock is concentrated in and near areas where cattle and poultry are most numerous.

Climate has a pronounced influence on the market for beverages. Per capita consumption is high in Texas because the weather is generally warm. Breweries are located in San Antonio, Shiner, Houston, Galveston, Longview, and Fort Worth. Several of these are large and comparatively new. Soft drinks are bottled in many communities, plants being most numerous in areas of dense population. There are only two small wineries, one of which makes wine from citrus fruit rather than grapes.

Cottonseed oil mills tend to locate in or near areas where the most cotton is grown. (Lubbock is home to some of the world's largest mills.) Processing into margarine, cooking oil, and salad dressing takes place for the most part in the area between Dallas-Fort Worth and the Oklahoma border.

Location of fruit and vegetable processing sites is strongly influenced by proximity to raw materials. Hidalgo and Cameron counties in the Lower Rio Grande Valley have the greatest concentration of such factories, but they are also found in East Texas (for example, Campbell Soup in Paris).

Dairies and bakeries are market-oriented and are found in and near the large cities. Houston and the Dallas-Fort Worth area have large bakeries producing hard goods (cookies, snacks, and crackers). Production of refrigerated and frozen dough is a specialty of North Central Texas, particularly Dallas, a major distribution center for many types of food products.

Preparation of various types of Mexican foods is important. As might be expected, most of these factories are in San Antonio and El Paso. Sales of these products have increased substantially in recent years as their popularity has increased.

Some Texas food-processing plants are dependent on raw materials imported from other countries. Examples are factories that process raw cane sugar, roast coffee, blend tea, or prepare spices for market. These plants are most numerous in tidewater areas: Houston is one of the nation's largest coffee-importing and/or roasting centers.

Textile Mill Products. Texas does not rank high in the production of fabrics, but it is the number one state in production of cotton, wool, mohair, and the chemical intermediates from which synthetic fibers are spun. Ironically, all of these compete for the market. Yet employment in the manufacture of textiles has been declining because many cotton-weaving mills have become obsolete, ceasing to operate. One new mill has been built at Littlefield, and two mills, each closed for a time, have reopened after extensive modification. Japanese, German, and Dutch companies have shown interest in investing in Texas mills.

Apparel. This labor-intensive category of manufacture is one of the state's most expansive. It employed approximately seventy-three thousand persons in early 1977. Major specialties are military wear, western wear, men's and boys' furnishings and trousers, uniforms, and women's dresses and undergarments. The attraction of Texas for garment manufacture is well illustrated by the fact that one well-known firm, Levi Strauss and Company, has twenty-one large plants in sixteen Texas cities, with three or more plants in two of the cities. Other firms operating in Texas include Willamson-Dickie, H. D. Lee, Farah, Haggar, Mann, and Blue Bell.

Most of the Texas apparel industry is concentrated in Dallas-Fort Worth and surrounding area. El Paso and San Antonio are also large centers for employment. Smaller cities, particularly those in West Texas and along the Rio Grande, have been very successful during the past five years in attracting garment plants because of the available supply of labor and because operating costs are generally low. The majority of the nation's cutting and sewing plants employ less than fifty workers; most small cities can supply such labor with ease.

Manufacture of leather and leather products is not classed as a major employer in Texas, but output is increasing. Demand for western boots has contributed to the need for more workers. Other products include men's and women's belts and saddles.

To be economically viable, apparel-manufacturing establishments must maintain high productivity, a difficult objective to attain in an industry whose products compete for the market on the basis of quality more than on price. Fortunately, most Texas apparel plants are fairly new, and they are somewhat more efficient than many older plants located elsewhere. Furthermore, a high proportion of Texas garment factories are geared to produce western-style clothing and sportswear for which there is great demand.

Lumber and Wood Products. Virtually all large factories using wood as the major raw material are located in the pine woods of East Texas. Output includes lumber, plywood, veneer, window/door frames and other mill work, flooring materials, boxes and crates, wooden pallets and skids, and handles for brooms, brushes, and mops. A fast-growing segment of this industry is the manufacture of mobile homes and other prefabricated structures, the market for which has been particularly dynamic. Texas ranks second in the nation in mobile home manufacture. Many mobile homes and prefabs are used as second homes in recreational and vacation areas, because of their low cost, and have become popular as homes for young marrieds and retirees. Suburban areas near major cities are major markets for mobile homes, and demand continues to be high.

The lumber and wood industry is probably one of the most responsive to fluctuations of the economy. When business is good, the industry booms. The long-range outlook is for steady growth.

Paper and Allied Products. Leading products of this industry are bleached and unbleached pulp, newsprint, paper and paperboard, container board, kraft linerboard, and magazine stock. All plants manufacturing these products are located in or nearby the pine forests. On the other hand, paper products are manufactured primarily in or near the largest market centers. The outlook for this industry is optimistic for several reasons: population is expanding; per capita consumption is increasing; the introduction of tree farming on a large scale in East Texas almost guarantees availability of raw materials; and trees are a renewable resource, local conditions favoring tree farming.

Furniture and Fixtures. Mattresses, church and school furniture, cabinets, and household furnishings are specialties of this segment of manufacture in Texas. Most of the mattress factories are located in the old cotton-growing area of Central Texas. Most of the large furniture factories are located in the same area, perhaps because its population is generally more dense and the largest markets are nearby.

Printing and Allied Products. Newspapers account for approximately one-third of the employment in this industry, and commercial printing, lithography, and printing trade services employ the other two thirds. Dallas-Fort Worth, Houston, San Antonio, and Austin are the major centers. Austin is important because the many state government reports are printed there and it is the headquarters of over two hundred trade associations. Technology is improving the productivity of this industry at a time when public demand for printed products is at an all-time high.

Chemicals and Allied Products. This is a materials-oriented industry, and one of the largest chemical manufacturing complexes in the world has developed along the Texas and Louisiana coasts. Hydrocarbons (petroleum and gas) are the major raw materials, and they have been in abundant supply. Other important coastal resources available for chemical manufacture include salt, sulfur, and limestone (oyster shell). All three of these are found close to petroleum and gas, so assembly costs of raw materials are low, and there is a substantial saving in transportation costs from mine and well to plant. Not all chemical plants are located along the coast. There are several large installations inland, primarily in Ector, Hutchinson, Gray, Moore, Howard, and Harrison counties.

Chemical manufacture accounts for a high proportion of value added in Texas. Plants are highly automated and highly efficient. Investment per worker is high. Total expenditure for plants amounts to billions of dollars, and impressive sums are still being spent for new facilities and equipment. (Almost a billion dollars was designated for expansion in this industry during the first nine months of 1974.)

Some economists have forecast that investment in facilities for chemical manufacture at the national level in this decade will be greater than the gross investment in plants now standing. This bold forecast may seem unreasonably optimistic, but investment in Texas chemical plants in 1950 was negligible when compared with that of 1977. At any rate, it is safe to say that the amount of money spent in Texas for expansion during the next few years will be enormous.

Petroleum Refining and Related Industries. Petroleum refining, like chemical manufacture, is materials-oriented. Most of the large plants are along the Gulf Coast, where production from local sources of raw material supply is high, where petroleum pipelines from the interior focus on the port cities, and where it is cheapest to process crude oil brought in from foreign sources by tanker. Refineries located in the interior of the state near the oil fields tend to have less productive capacity than those located along the coast.

It is increasingly difficult to draw a line separating petroleum refining from chemical processing. Texas refineries are producing greatly expanded amounts of end products, which include many types of chemicals as well as gasoline and jet engine fuel. Integration of the two industries is likely to become even more pronounced in the future. The end product of a refinery is often the raw material for a chemical plant located nearby. Materials move from one plant to another by a network of pipelines so intricate that the Houston area is dubbed the "spaghetti bowl."

Closely associated with refinery and chemical plant production is the manufacture of synthetic rubber, an industry that mushroomed during World War II. Texas has some of the largest synthetic rubber manufacturing plants in the world, and demand for the output of these plants will continue to rise.

Two large factories that manufacture tires from Texas-produced rubber are located at Tyler and Waco. Other factories producing rubber products for local markets have concentrated in Dallas-Fort Worth and Houston.

Stone, Shell, Clay, Glass, and Concrete Products. Cement, wallboard and other gypsum products, fiberglass, insulation materials, brick, tile, sewer pipe, ceramics, and glass containers are the chief products of this category of manufacture in Texas. Approximately thirty-seven thousand workers were employed in this industry in 1977. Some segments of the industry are materials-oriented (clay products), while others such as glass containers are strongly market-oriented. Most concrete, wallboard, and cement plants are located in or near large city markets, even though they must depend on bringing some raw materials from considerable distances. PPG Industries recently built the world's largest float glass plant at Wichita Falls, and officials of Certain-teed Products built a large fiberglass factory in the same city. Proximity to deposits of sand and the availability of natural gas caused Wichita Falls to be chosen for the plant sites.

Primary Metals. This industry, which employed approximately thirty-eight thousand Texans in 1977, can be expected to expand capacity rapidly. Iron and steel, magnesium, aluminum, antimony, lead, copper, tin, cadmium, and zinc are processed in Texas smelters and metal refineries.

Low cost power derived from burning natural gas has been an attractive factor for smelters. Since natural gas supplies have become scarcer and thus more expensive, aluminum processors are now turning to lignite as a power source. The Rockdale Smelter of Alcoa, the world's largest, is powered by lignite. The same company completed a smelter near Palestine in 1976 which, also using lignite for power, is expected to surpass the Rockdale facility in size.

Output from the Texas primary metals plants is used to manufacture construction materials, containers, pipe for the oil industry, tubing, wire, and many other products. Demand continues to accelerate, and the potential for expansion is encouraging.

Fabricated Metals. Almost seventy-nine thousand Texans were working to produce fabricated metals products in 1977. Typical of these products were cans, drums, barrels, kegs, pails, tools, and other hardware, plumbing fixture fittings, heating and air conditioning equipment, boilers, and fabricated structural metal. Fabricated structural metal accounts for about 40 percent of the employment. Most plants are concentrated in and around the largest cities because of market orientation. Many factories that produce metal cans are located near breweries, and fruit/vegetable canning and preserving facilities. Long-range prospects for this segment of manufacture are considered bright.

Nonelectrical Machinery. Oil field machinery, for which Houston is the world's chief production center, and construction-related machinery are the two major products of this industry in Texas. Other sizeable segments produce pumps and compressors, computing equipment, general industrial machinery, service industry machines, and refrigeration equipment.

According to the Texas Employment Commission, almost one hundred ten thousand Texans were employed in making nonelectrical machinery in 1977. The number of workers can be expected to increase substantially, especially in the manufacture of computing equipment and oil field machinery. Many new challenges shaped up for the manufacturers of oil field machinery during the late sixties and early seventies because there was more drilling offshore and deeper drilling onshore, as well as because of the peculiar requirements of equipment needed for exploration and drilling on the North Slope. Expertise developed during the past decades by Texas manufacturers of machines needed by the oil and gas industries helped to meet the challenges. Optimism pervades the outlook for this fast-growing category of Texas manufacture.

Electrical and Electronic Machinery. Leading products of this fast-growing Texas industry are transformers, switchgear, fuses, motors, generators, controls, electric fans, appliances, heaters, navigational aids, search and detection apparatus, military electronic equipment, transistors, and integrated circuits. Demand in the mid-seventies for electronic equipment for the military establishment is not dynamic, but market demand for the other products, especially for transistors and integrated circuits, continues to accelerate.

The Dallas-Fort Worth area has been the hub of this industry and continues to be so, but it is a labor-intensive industry and many smaller centers have developed in other areas of the state. A significant economic characteristic is that the industry is footloose; it can locate almost anywhere if workers and research personnel are available. Its end products are typically low in bulk and high in value; therefore the availability of raw materials and of rail and water transportation is not essential (as it is in the chemical industry).

Texas has developed momentum in the electrical and electronic machinery industry, which is highly dependent on technology and on expenditures for research and development. Its role is expanding in automation, pollution control, communication, and education. No Texas slowdown is in sight for the immediate future. However, trends toward internationalization of the industry may cause the rate of growth in Texas and in the United States to slow by 1990.

Transportation Equipment. The Southwest Aerospace Manufacturing Belt begins at Wichita, Kansas, and extends southward through Oklahoma and North Texas to San Antonio. Specialization in aerospace equipment began during World War II because inland location away from vulnerable coasts was desirable and because the labor force was sufficient to support the industry. Employment has fluctuated greatly since the end of that conflict, because output was primarily focused on the needs of the Department of Defense. Little emphasis was placed on end products needed by the commercial and private sectors of the market. In the mid-seventies, however, after a slump in employment caused by the cessation of hostilities in Viet Nam, and after more emphasis was given to markets in the private sector, employment began to stabilize. Major aerospace products in Texas include helicopters, military aircraft, small planes for business, agricultural, and recreational use, and manufactured parts including hydraulic equipment, airconditioning and heating installations, and interior furnishings such as seats and galleys. The San Antonio SMSA and nearby Kerrville are the chief centers for production of business aircraft and for modification and remodeling of planes. The Dallas-Fort Worth SMSA is the major focus for production of helicopters and military aircraft. One Japanese company, Mitsubishi Aircraft International, assembles executive turbo planes at San Angelo.

One important segment of the aerospace industry in Texas is the manufacture of guided-missile and space-vehicle propulsion units. These are manufactured in Dallas, Fort Worth, Karnack, San Antonio, and McGregor.

Production and assembly of automobiles and automotive equipment is important, especially at Arlington, where General Motors assembles cars. Intercity transit and motor coaches are produced by Eagle International at Brownsville. Hobbs Trailers builds trailers and truck bodies at Fort Worth, as do several other companies located around the state, that is, at Longview and Lufkin. Much trailer and truck body production is slanted toward manufacture for the special needs of the market in Texas and the Southwest. Examples of such needs are equipment designed to haul cotton, oil and gas pipe, lumber and pulpwood, livestock, vegetables, and grain. The manufacture of travel trailers and campers is expanding rapidly; many of the plants that produce these are located in small communities where a stable labor force is assured.

Shipbuilding and repairing is increasingly active in Texas because of expansion of offshore drilling and expansion in the production of petroleum and gas from the ocean floor. Drilling platforms and vessels designed to meet the unique needs of the offshore industry are in demand. Houston, Galveston, Beaumont-Port Arthur-Orange, and Corpus Christi are the chief centers. Manufacture of pleasure boats became important after World War II. The largest of these plants is located in Austin and Plano.

Instruments. The manufacture of instruments and related products has continued to outdistance all other Texas industries in the rate of employment growth, although the total number of workers, about seventeen thousand, is relatively small when compared with other categories of Texas manufacture. This industry, like the electrical machinery industry, is mobile, although market orientation has considerable attraction for plants. Most plants are located in or near cities with a population of at least ten thousand.

Typical products are devices used in controlling and monitoring factory processes and pollution—such as instruments to control and measure temperatures. Sophisticated monitoring devices and other goods needed by the health care services are also produced, along with many other products, including watches and clocks. This industry seems to have established a solid base for growth in Texas, and it will continue to grow somewhat faster than other industries.

Several economic and social factors will contribute to the continued rapid growth of manufacturing in Texas. Population is increasing at a faster rate than in most other states. The pull of the Sun Belt is strong. The labor supply is attractive because of its size and productivity. The state is still endowed with the raw materials and energy resources that modern industry needs (although mineral resources are not renewable and new large discoveries are unlikely). Location on the warm Gulf midway between the east and west coasts is an asset for economical distribution and marketing. Texas has plenty of room for expansion of its cities and its industries. There should be little pessimism in the short-run outlook.

EIGHT

THE AGRICULTURAL ECONOMY OF TEXAS
Thomas J. Stanly

Agriculture is a basic industry in the state of Texas, and has enjoyed this position since the first settlement. In view of increasing world demand for food and fiber, the comparative advantage provided by the vast natural and renewable resources of the state in production of agricultural products places Texas in an enviable position in the United States and the world.

IMPORTANCE TO THE STATE

Historically, this agricultural potential encouraged United States Presidents Tyler and Jackson to urge annexation of the Texas territory during 1844-46.[1] England specifically had its eye on Texas as an unlimited source of raw cotton for its textile mills. Americans were pouring into this territory in search of more productive and less expensive land during this period with farming or "cattle raising" as their primary objective. As recently as the first decade of the 1900s, more than one-half the income of the state was produced from cultivated land and grass.

Subsequent diversification of industry has not reduced the importance of agriculture to the economy of the state. Growth in agriculture income and productivity per unit has been continuous.[2] The rapid industrialization that has taken place throughout the state in the mid-twentieth century has complemented this growth in agriculture. Population increase stemming from expanded industry has provided closer markets for all types of agricultural products. This expanded domestic market supplemented what was initially a large export trade that was begun primarily with cotton. Livestock products, grain sorghum, peanuts, fruit and vegetables were among the many other crops that were to follow cotton in significant production.

A complementary effect of agriculture to other industry has been the availability of a large labor force that was displaced by the mechanization of agriculture. As the cotton industry moved from the hills of East Texas and the central portion of the state to the plains region in the west from 1920 to 1950, the majority of these rural East Texans found employment in the expanding industrial complexes of Houston, Dallas-Fort Worth, and other industrialized areas. In fact, the availability of labor has been a positive factor in the choice of location for many manufacturing industries coming to the state of Texas. Historians have noted that the 1920 census marked the first time that less than half the people in the state lived on a farm.[3]

Service industries supporting agriculture are a significant part of the total industrial production of the state. The fertilizer industry is a primary example. In addition to supplying an international market, it has supplied increased requirements for Texas farmers. The amount of chemically formulated fertilizer used in Texas has more than quadrupled, increasing from 553,535 tons in 1950 to 2,492,490 tons as reported in 1976.[4] The presence of the raw material from the state's mining industry is one of several instances where Texas has the advantage over other geographic areas in the complementary relationship of its industries.

The structure of the agricultural industry has changed with the pendulum swinging from the domination of crops to livestock and livestock products. Considering the diversity of land resources in Texas, change of relative product demand could result in a swing back to a dominance of crop production. The combination of the wide range in climate, growing season, topography, and adaptability of soil types makes such a shift possible with a minimum loss in advantage of production.

The present domination of livestock as the major source of farm income to the state is relatively new. Contrary to the traditional image of Texas projected to the outsider as being singularly "cow country," cotton production did not yield its crown to livestock until 1938. Grain sorghum has since taken over as the crop with the largest acreage despite Texas' number one rank in the United States in cotton production. Beginning with the 1920s, while East Texas was losing its cotton industry due to the boll weevil, West Texas was gaining in cotton production.[5] Cotton's reduction in rank as the primary source of agricultural income to farmers in Texas to third behind livestock and grain sorghum reflects the growth of the latter two rather than a decline in cotton.[6] The vacuum left by the abandoned cotton fields of the eastern area of the state has been filled with highly fertilized deep-rooted coastal bermuda meadows and improved pastures seeded to other adapted forage plants. Thick field stands of shortleaf or loblolly pine and plantations of these species, hybrid, and slash pine occupy the remainder of this former crop land.

AGRIBUSINESS ORGANIZATION

The expansion of grain sorghum production complemented by wheat production in North Texas has contributed to further restructuring of agriculture in Texas, that is, the feedlot. Large scale feedlots in the northern plains have been the most spectacular development in Texas agriculture in the twentieth century. Availability of grain sorghum with a ready source of stocker calves, climatic advantages, relative freedom from pollution, and other supporting requirements have succeeded in making Texas the leading state in cattle on feed. The momentum of this example of vertical integration of the livestock industry may be documented by comparing the number of cattle in the state marketed from feedlots in 1963 (869,000) to 1975 (3,067,000).[7] This shows an average increase close to twenty percent a year over the 1963 base. Computer technology combined with automation has altered the feedlot economy of scale upward to the extent that this pattern of mass production appears to be fixed. Several feedlots exceed a capacity of 50,000 head.

Another case of integration of agricultural industry in the state is the production of broiler chickens, located principally in eastern and southeastern portions of the state. Processors began vertical integration toward the end of the 1950s and early sixties.[8] Presently all significant commercial broiler production is accomplished by integrated firms. These businessmen usually own the chicken from the parent flock producing the broiler eggs to the delivery of the dressed bird to the retail market. The farmer contracts as a grower, being paid for use of facilities and labor.

Escalating demands for investment capital per production unit have to a great extent been responsible for the trend of increase in both vertical and horizontal expansion of scope of farm businesses. Growth in farmer-owned cooperatives, one of the major changes in Texas agriculture since World War II, has enabled small farmers to integrate their businesses.[9] While the dominant type of business organization for Texas farms is the single proprietorship, partnerships and corporations are becoming more common with increased capital investment requirements.

Part-time farming is expanding. Motivation for this activity varies from a means of supplementing family income to a means of a young man's gradual entry into farming with limited capital. Other part-time farmers will fit in the categories of hobby or tax shelter farmers. Although trends indicate that more will be produced on fewer farms, part-time farming appears fixed as a significant sector in Texas agriculture.

Texas usually ranks among the top three states in total agriculture cash income.[10] In 1975, it ranked third behind California and Iowa. Agriculture's total cash receipts in Texas of $5,933,000,000 in 1975 represented 6.6 percent of the United States total. During the same year Texas led in cash receipts from three of the nation's top twenty-five commodities—cattle, cotton lint, and grain sorghum.

About 30 percent of the state's labor force is employed in the complex of agribusiness. This includes both farm workers and those in off-farm agribusiness employment. The off-farm sector is increasing due to greater specialization on farms resulting in removing many traditional farm activities to service industries.

TRENDS IN TEXAS AGRICULTURE

During the period from 1963 to 1976 total acreage in Texas farms decreased 4.8 percent. This decrease does not appear negative in view of a slightly larger national decline.[11] Meanwhile, productivity per unit continued to increase at a rate proportionately greater than that of retirement of land from farms and ranches, resulting in a net increase in agricultural production in the state.

Comparable data indicate that from the mid-twentieth century, agriculture as an industry in the state has shown greater relative strength than in the nation as a whole. National trends show a decrease in number of farms accompanied by an increase in acres per farm. Farms in Texas are following the same pattern. The rate of decrease in number of farms in Texas has not been as great as the average for the other states.[12] This sustained relative strength of agriculture is against a backdrop of other industry in the state expanding at a more rapid rate than the national average.

Increase in land values, buildings, and improvements in the state during the period 1960-76, reflects confidence in expanding agricultural industry.[13] Per acre value of farm land in Texas from 1960 to 1976 increased more than the consumer price index during the same period. This indicates a solid trend toward a real increase in land value. The increase in value per farm may be accounted for not only by an increase in land value, but also an increase in size per farm and equipment capitalization.

The need for more efficient machinery in production has resulted in changes in the labor force required in Texas agriculture. Fewer people are required to operate the farms. This has been accompanied by an elevation in the educational level of the farm laborer and owner. Educational institutions at secondary and college levels offering curricula in agriculture are more numerous in the state than ever. Adult education of farmers by the Cooperative Extension Service and other public services have played important roles in raising this standard of capability.

Machinery has become a major component of capital investment for the Texas farmer. Repair and operating costs of machinery have brought about growth in businesses serving the mechanical needs of the industry.

Texas farm population has followed the United States trend of rapid reduction during the mid-twentieth century. The 1950s showed a farm population decrease of 38 percent compared to 42 percent in the decade of the sixties.[14]

The Crop Reporting Board reported the average hourly wage for farm workers in the year 1976 as $2.77. In the same year farm laborers numbered ninety-three thousand. It is estimated by the Texas Department of Agriculture that four out of every ten persons in the state owe their jobs directly or indirectly to agriculture and agribusiness.[15] Farm operators have decreased in number but not as rapidly as in the nation as a whole. These facts, coupled with a near doubling of farm output per man-hour, reflect changes brought about by increased mechanization within the industry.

AGRICULTURAL RESOURCES

Resources most important to agricultural production are labor, land, and water, and each of these varies in its influence on agriculture. Texas is richly endowed in agricultural resources. In 1976 Texas provided 13 percent of the total United States farm land. The relative

Labor

The population in Texas is growing at a greater rate than that of the nation. This growth rate, due largely to employment opportunities, is favorable to agriculture. In addition to providing labor for the industry, the local demand for agricultural products is expanded. The vegetable and fruits sectors of agriculture are dependent on a great deal of hand labor, despite increasing availability of machinery used in harvesting. The major agricultural industries such as livestock, cotton, and grain sorghums lend themselves to minimum labor input by virtue of adaptation to use of automated systems and maximum capacity production equipment.

Trends in farm labor show higher wages for skilled employees. In recent years more farm laborers are living off the farm. There has been an increase of year round employment for hired labor though the total labor required has decreased. Fringe benefits for employees have been expanded.

These changes have been influenced to a large degree by the farmers having been forced to compete with other industries for the available labor supply. Government labor and civil policy changes have contributed to these reforms.

Assuming that agricultural policy of the federal government continues to move in the direction of fewer restrictions in production, competitive marketing, and reduction in price supports, it is anticipated that continued input of complex production equipment will make opportunity for highly skilled employees on farms competitive in terms of income with comparable skills in other sectors of industry. Until the scale of production units adjusts to the higher capitalization requirements of this specialized equipment, the demand for custom agricultural services will grow.

Land

The farm and ranch land of Texas totals 141.8 million acres.[16] Eighty-eight million of these acres are considered arable. Crops occupy 40 million acres, and an additional 15 million acres are planted to adapted or introduced forage crops and classified as pasture. Farmers and ranchers have captured an increasing share of the recreation revenue in the state by promoting multiple usage of their pasture, rangelands, and water reservoirs. Forest products from rangeland and farms are a supplementary source of income to the Texas farmer.

The 1970 Texas Soil and Water Conservation Needs Committee shows over eighty-five million acres of rangeland used primarily by domestic livestock.[17] This same land is the home of wildlife such as deer, turkey, javelina, antelope, quail, dove, and prairie chickens.

Acres used for crops have shown a gradual recession. Pasture lands have increased. Urban uses of land are expanding, paralleling the movement of rural people to cities and population growth of the state. This urban buildup is slowly making inroads on forest and rangelands.

Land: Resource Areas of Texas, designates and describes the sixteen divisions of the state based on similarity of soils, topography, climate, and vegetation. This division and description of soils is excerpted in the following information.[18]

Coast Marsh. 500,000 acres; elevation—sea level to a few feet; frost-free period 270-300 days; annual rainfall 40-55 inches. These are low, wet, and marshy areas. Soils may be described as dark, poorly drained, sandy loam and clays and light, neutral sands.

Coast Prairie. 9,000,000 acres; elevation—sea level to 250 feet; frost-free period 240-300 days; annual rainfall 28-56 inches. The Coast Prairie is nearly level with slow surface drainage.

East Texas Timberlands. 16,000,000 acres; elevation—200 feet to 700 feet; frost-free period 235-265 days; annual rainfall 49-56 inches. Nearly level to gently undulating forested area, generally well dissected and locally hilly with slow to rapid surface drainage.

Claypan Area. 6,900,000 acres; elevation—200 to 400 feet; frost-free period 235-280 days; annual rainfall 30-45 inches. Nearly level to gently rolling, moderately dissected woodlands—savannah to brush area with moderate surface drainage.

Rio Grande Plain. 20,500,000 acres; elevation—sea level to 1,000 feet; frost-free period 260-340 days; annual rainfall 18-30 inches. Nearly level to rolling, slightly to moderately dissected brush plains with slow to rapid surface drainage.

Blackland Prairie. 13,000,000 acres; elevation—250-700 feet; frost-free period 230-280 days; annual rainfall 30-45 inches. The blacklands are nearly level to rolling, well-dissected prairies, with moderate to rapid surface drainage. Flood plains are slowly drained; some areas are wooded.

East Cross Timbers. 1,000,000 acres; elevation—500-700 feet; frost-free period 230-250 days; annual rainfall approximately 35 inches.

Gently rolling, moderately dissected, narrow strip of scrub oak woodlands, with moderate to rapid surface drainage.

Grand Prairie. 7,000,000 acres; elevation—600-1,100 feet; frost-free period 230-240 days; annual rainfall 30-35 inches. Undulating to hilly, deeply incised prairies, moderate to rapid surface drainage.

West Cross Timbers. 2,000,000 acres; elevation—900-1,500 feet; frost-free period 230-240 days; annual rainfall 28-32 inches. Undulating to gently rolling, well dissected scrub oak woodland area, with rapid surface drainage.

North Central Prairie. 6,000,000 acres; elevation—900-1,400 feet; frost-free period 225-240 days; annual rainfall 25-30 inches. Undulating prairies and nearly level valleys with slow to rapid surface drainage, interspersed with rapidly drained sandstone and shaley ridges and hills with scrub oak and mesquite vegetation.

Central Basin. 1,500,000 acres; elevation—1,000-1,800 feet; frost-free period 220-230 days; annual rainfall 25-30 inches. The Central Basin is rolling to hilly and stony, scrub oak and brush cover the area, with moderate to rapid surface drainage.

Edwards Plateau. 24,000,000 acres; elevation—1,200-3,000 feet; frost-free period 220-260 days, annual rainfall 12-32 inches. Deeply dissected, rapidly drained, brush and grass covered, stony plain with broad, flat to undulating divides; hilly, broken and very stony adjacent to the incised, less sloping stream valleys.

Rolling Plains. 24,000,000 acres; elevation—1,000-3,000 feet; frost-free period 185-235 days; annual rainfall 18-28 inches. Broad, nearly level to rolling, grass and brush covered plains with moderate to rapid surface drainage and entrenched well-drained stream valleys.

High Plains. 19,000,000 acres; elevation—3,000-4,000 feet; frost-free period 180-220 days; annual rainfall 14-21 inches. The High Plains are nearly level, practically undissected, high tableland with slow-to-moderate surface drainage and many small, shallow lakes or playas.

Bottomlands. 2,000,000 acres. The flood plains of major importance for dry land and irrigated agriculture are along the lower Red, Trinity, Brazos, Colorado rivers, and the upper and lower Rio Grande.

Trans-Pecos. 18,000,000 acres; elevation-1,500-8,751 feet; frost-free period 220-245 days; annual rainfall 8-18 inches (mostly less than twelve inches). Mountain ranges and rough rock lands, intermixed with flat basins and plateaus. Rapid drainage in the mountains, slow in the basins, and absent in the bottoms; high evaporation.

Water

Water in Texas, as it is worldwide, is a vital element to virtually all production processes—particularly agricultural production. Withdrawal, flow, and on-site uses of water are increasing each year. Expanded industrialization, population, and recreational activity determine the rate of water use. In terms of withdrawal uses, irrigation is by a wide margin the greatest user of fresh water. Increased world demand for United States food and fiber will create added pressure on the state's fresh water supply as farmers react to this stimulus.

Average annual rainfall in East Texas at the Louisiana border is fifty-six inches compared to eight inches at El Paso in the west end of the state, according to the *General Soil Map of Texas* prepared by Texas A&M University Department of Agricultural Communications.[19]

The annual average runoff in Texas is thirty-nine million acre-feet. Reservoirs in the state have a total acreage of 1.3 million. Construction of an additional sixty reservoirs is under consideration. According to the above source, 75 percent of the water used for domestic, industrial, and irrigation purposes comes from ground water. Ground water is being depleted at a faster rate than it is being replaced by precipitation in many areas. Consequently, it may be concluded that developing additional surface water and redistribution to areas of high demand for water are major problems.

In recent years the state has engaged in negotiations for water supplies outside its borders. These efforts are directed toward long range supplementation. Existing regional interests and the capital investment required for the movement of water over great distance places this possibility in the future when demand becomes greater and supply is smaller. Additionally, thought and some developmental planning have been directed at moving water from East Texas where approximately three-fourths of the state's runoff occurs to the western part of the state where water is the greatest restriction to agricultural and industrial development.

PRINCIPAL FARM AND RANCH PRODUCTS

The wide range of growing seasons, soil and resource areas, and rainfall offers some sections of Texas advantages in the production of almost any principal product grown in the United States.

Livestock and Livestock Products

Texas ranked second to Iowa in cash receipts from livestock and its products with an income of $3,061 million in 1975. It was first in several of the particular livestock products. Livestock contributes approximately 52 percent of the state's cash receipts from agriculture. Beef cattle account for more than 70 percent of the livestock income. The number of cattle rose sharply in the 1960s and the trend continues. Cattle outnumber people in the state. Other significant livestock enterprises in the state are dairying, sheep, hogs, poultry, and goats. Though not indicated as a significant source of income in the United States Department of Agriculture's annual statistical report on farm income, horses have made a spectacular comeback primarily for pleasure use.

Beef Cattle. The beef cattle industry by legend and fact is the lead-agricultural enterprise in the state. Together with other livestock production, it uses 75 percent of the land in farms and ranches. The state ranked first in the nation in 1975 for cattle and calves, totaling $15,600 million.[20]

The dominance of cattle in Texas is evident from several perspectives. First, as one moves about the state, cattle are seen everywhere. They are found grazing as range and woods cattle from the Sabine River bottoms and piney woods of the east to the semi-arid plains and hills of the west—from the brackish marshes of the coastal prairies in the south to the High Plains of the Panhandle. In between are cattle grown in a wide range of conditions varying from the most excellent to minimum levels of management. Complementing this widespread cow-calf production are the feedlots of the Plains area which are filled with feeder calves from Texas and other states. In 1975 Texas reported inshipments of approximately 2.4 million head.[21]

The influence of cattle raising as a way of life has always been a factor in shaping the image of the Texan inside and outside the borders of the state. Language, dress, architecture, and recreation are just a few of the characteristics of the people that reflect the influence of cattle on society. Even with the state's rapid urbanization, a Texan's status is most readily comprehended when described in head of cattle and acres of land.

The trail of cattle to this position of social and economic influence on the state is marked with legendary and real milestones of travail and triumph. After an erratic history, cattle prices bottomed in the 1930s. Many ranches changed hands. Great herds were decimated by sales, disease, drouth, and poor management. From this low, the 1940s saw renewed vigor in the Texas cattle industry. Eradication of the tick, a flushed demand resulting from the World War II speed-up of the economy, and a rising standard of living launched the industry on a road to prosperity which it still enjoys in moderate cycles.

Texas commands an international position of leadership in cattle production. Its ranches have exported more than their share of breeding stock for developing beef herds around the world. Stock from famous herds such as the Hudgins Brahmans of Hungerford and King Ranch's Santa Gertrudis of Kingsville have not only provided a foundation for these breeds in the United States, but have been exported in large numbers to all parts of the world. These breeds and others developed from Brahman crosses have been used extensively in crossing on European breeds to develop the first generation (F-1) cross that has been so profitable to cattlemen. The hybrid vigor of these offspring has revolutionized the industry. Their ability to outgain straight bred cattle under ranch conditions has caused many ranchers to redirect their breeding programs.

Livestock expositions in the state have set world standards in quality and attendance. The Houston Livestock Show and Rodeo has become one of the truly great shows in the world. The Southwestern Exposition and Fat Stock Show in Fort Worth has enjoyed major status for years. The San Antonio Livestock Exposition and Rodeo has gained international recognition along with several other established shows in the state. These serve as an international show window for some of the outstanding herds in the United States.

Market facilities, primarily the regional auctions, are growing in number and volume. The expansion of slaughtering and meat processing facilities equals or is exceeding the pace of growth of cattle numbers.

The commercial feedlots, located primarily in the Panhandle, have continued in the long range to grow in size, number, and volume. These provide a growing demand for calves produced in that and other sections of the state. One key to success of these installations has been the achievement of economy of scale permitting use of all automated equipment available to the operator. In 1975, 257 feedlots were reported with a capacity of one thousand or more head. The capacity of 68 of these lots exceeded sixteen thousand head.[22]

In addition to the complementary effect of commercial cattle feeding to the production of grain sorghum, this enterprise has stimulated the production and wintering of quality feeder calves in other sections of the state. Availability in adequate numbers and quality is the prime consideration in their purchase. Given this advantage of location in addition to the state's existing national adaptation to cattle production, the number of feeder calves produced has increased.

An intermediate segment of this chain of integration evolved from the feeding of cattle in feedlots has been the carrying of feeder calves on winter pastures in the more temperate zones of the state. Recently, gains have been made in successfully grazing these calves on winter pastures of oats, rye grass, and other cool season forage crops in the eastern and central regions of the state. These calves compare favorably in feedlot performance with those wintered on wheat and oats in the Great Plains.

Dairying. Dairy products accounted for a $304 million income for Texas dairymen in 1975.[23] This industry is second to cattle and calves as a source of income from livestock. In 1975 Texas ranked ninth among the states in production of dairy products. The majority of dairies are located near the large population centers in the eastern and central areas of the state. The trend is toward larger dairies, and dwindling labor supply has forced the dairymen to automation. Consequently, increased capital investment has raised the average dairy in size from thirty-five cows in 1963 to eighty-three in 1972, a trend which continues.[24] This expense has forced a reduction in number of dairies in the last two decades. However, increased production per cow coupled with higher prices has caused the cash farm income from dairy products to increase significantly.

American Milk Producers, Incorporated, a large farmer-owned milk marketing cooperative, is the largest marketer of dairy products in the state. Principal dairy products manufactured in the state are creamery butter, American cheddar cheese, cottage cheese, and unsweetened condensed skimmed milk.

Considering the degree of inelasticity of demand for milk, the future milk production in the state should be influenced by the rate of population growth and external competition. In recent years, however, costs of production have increased at a faster rate than milk prices. This cost together with higher prices received for dairy cattle used in production of F-1 females for beef cattle herds has caused some dairymen to consider seriously the question of going out of business. Many of the older dairymen who owned their land have sold out, taking advantage of capital gains on the appreciation of the price of their land and cattle. In the long run, with most of the milk being marketed under federal milk marketing orders, a more favorable cost-price ratio should prevail. The discontinued dairies could then be replaced by dairies large enough to attain the optimum economy of scale.

Despite occasional imbalance of cost and price in the dairy business, it remains one of the most prosperous of Texas farm enterprises in terms of return on capital invested. The prospect of a relatively high rate of population growth in the state should insure the industry's future prosperity.

Hogs. Texas is a deficit pork producing state, providing less than 30 percent of its own consumption. It ranks sixteenth among the states in swine production. Growth has been sporadic but has continued to increase at a remarkable rate. Texas Crop and Livestock Reporting Service shows an increase in hogs marketed during the span of 1965-75 from 198 million pounds to 286 million pounds.[25]. This rate of increase has been reasonably consistent through earlier years.

The availability of feed grain in the Panhandle has generated interest in fattening hogs. There has been a steady increase in finishing facilities built in that area. As in the case of beef cattle, the eastern and northeastern sections of the state have responded in increased production of feeder pigs. Several successful feeder pig sales have been promoted in East Texas. Farm units producing these pigs vary in scale from small part-time operations of just a few sows to a completely automated system housing several hundred sows. A number of producers have successfully integrated feeding with feeder pig production. The opportunity is great for Texas to expand swine production. However, tradition weighs heavily in the small farmer's selection of enterprises. Therefore, a faster rate of expansion will likely depend on the introduction of sufficient capital to set up more large scale integrated facilities.

Sheep and Wool. Early explorers, with Anglo-American settlers, introduced sheep to Texas, which with approximately 20 percent of the nation's sheep, has a long record of ranking first in the United States. In the last decade, competition for grazing land and losses from predatory animals have caused reductions that approach 25 percent of the herd.

Most of the sheep are produced in the central and southwest sections of the state with the Edwards Plateau having the largest concentration. San Angelo serves as a center for sheep and wool marketing. The combined cash receipts from wool, lambs, and sheep were $72 million in 1975.[26] Sale of sheep and lambs provides most of this income. Most outshipments of sheep and lambs go to Colorado.

Goats and Mohair. Two types of goats make up the industry for the state. Texas Angora goats produce a major portion of the world's supply of mohair. Production for the last three years has averaged above fifteen million pounds. Spanish goats are of lesser economic importance but do produce some income from sales of breeding stock and for slaughter. Their foraging habits of brush eating are often used in brush control by producers of other livestock.

Poultry and Eggs. Poultry and egg production statistics show the state ranking seventh in 1975 in the production of broilers, fourth in production of turkeys, and ninth in egg production.[27] Total income from this commodity grouping in the same year was $340 million. Broilers and eggs contribute approximately 5 percent of the average yearly income of Texas farmers.[28] Egg and broiler production have shown steady increases in recent years.

This industry has capitalized on technology to gain stability in competition. Integration has provided better business practices. Adequate financing resulting from large firms has enabled these producers to sustain periodic low prices. However, erratic prices and costs joined by cyclical overproduction plague poultry producers. Industry organizations, particularly among the broiler growers, have made efforts to control production internally.

Broiler production, the largest component of poultry income, is concentrated in East and South Central Texas. Nacogdoches, Gonzales, and Shelby counties lead in broiler production.[29] This concentration of the industry promotes efficiency in production and marketing. Each of the above counties has several processing plants averaging a capacity of six thousand birds per hour.[30] Feed mills, hatcheries, and other service facilities are necessarily located in these areas. This permits a reduction of transportation costs which are significant in the broiler industry. Labor and services are specialized to the extent that great efficiency is gained. A large volume of credit is required for this industry, and credit sources in these areas are staffed with people who specialize in these loans. Feed conversion ratio, volume, and quality control are the major factors determining profits in the broiler industry.

Commercial egg production has shown steady increase in the state. The growth of this segment of the industry, assuming normal competition, will be geared to the state's continued population growth. Residents consume most of the eggs produced in the state. Egg production is more widespread in the state than that of broilers, but the heaviest concentrations are still in East and South Central Texas. General distribution relates to the large population centers of the state. The slim profit margin in recent years has discouraged new investment in egg production. Prices received for eggs continue to be erratic.

Turkey production is located principally in the southern portion of the Blacklands. Bell, Hill, and McLennan counties lead the state in that order. The number of turkeys produced has declined. Prices received have shown little advancement in the last few years. The future of turkey production in the state is tied closely to the market for broilers. To an extent, the same external factors affect both. The relative price of beef is most significant. Price of feed and feed conversion ratio are also significant factors in the determination of returns from the enterprise. Continued efforts to break the tradition of serving turkey only on holidays will provide opportunity for greater returns to the growers.

Principal Crops

Crops have competed on a near equal basis with livestock products in terms of agricultural value to the state. Cash receipts do not reflect this in that a large portion of the grain is fed directly to farm livestock. Approximately half of the total value comes from two crops— sorghum grains and cotton. Rice and wheat are other grain crops of major importance in the state. Other feed grains, oilseed crops, vegetables, fruits, and nuts are significant producers of agricultural income along with numerous other specialty crops.

Labor is the primary restriction to increased crop production. However, upward scaling of size of farms has provided capital for use of labor saving machinery. Land is available for expansion of crop production, and improvement of irrigation technology has made more tillable land available and has increased yields on land presently under cultivation.

Cotton. Cotton is basic to industry in Texas. As a raw material which generates more income and business off the farm than for those who grow it, cotton is indeed a good industrial citizen. The agribusiness effect of the 1975 cotton crop grown in the state, using a multiplier of 3.5, accounted for $2,019 million of business.[31]

Texas has been the leading cotton producing state since 1880, a position it now holds by a comfortable margin. The shift in the 1920s of cotton production from the east to the west—beyond boll weevil territory—was the saving of the industry in Texas. This shift was characterized by larger farm units which justified mechanization and adoption of better cultivation practices.

Cotton is grown on an economically significant scale in 72 percent of the counties in the state with lesser production in 20 percent of the others. However, the greatest concentration of production is in the High Plains, Lower Valley and the Blacklands districts.

On the domestic and world markets, cotton has recently faced competition from synthetic fibers. Vigorous promotion by the American Cotton Council and other cotton organizations has met this challenge to the extent that the aggregate demand for cotton remains strong. Devaluation of United States currency, which stimulates exports, has contributed to sustaining the use of cotton abroad. The increasing practice of the farmer contracting cotton to the buyer before or during production serves as a price stabilizing force, reducing risk.

Texas produced 2.4 million bales of cotton in 1975 which yielded $506 million for lint cotton plus $76 million for cottonseed for a total crop value of $583 million. Much of the cotton is exported. The state accounts for nearly 25 percent of all United States cotton export.[32] This approaches 50 percent the value of the crop excluding seed.

The variety of business generated by cotton in the state has a wide magnitude. However, most of the lint that is not exported is shipped to textile mills in other states. For a complexity of reasons, yarn and textile mills have not kept pace in the state with the remainder of the industry. It is reported that a number of these mills in the state are considering expansion with new mills being contemplated.

Grain Sorghum. Grain sorghum is the most extensively grown crop in the state. It yields the greatest cash return while occupying the largest acreage planted to any single crop. From a grain first grown by Indians on the Comanche and Brazos reserves, to West and Northwest Texas farmers' work stock feed, grain sorghum has recently made its most spectacular contribution to the economy as the determining factor in the relocation of the United States cattle feeding industry to Texas, which contributes nearly half of the nation's total grain sorghum production.

Grain sorghum is the primary feed crop in the state. Virtually all of it is shipped from the farm on which it is grown to commercial feedlots. Texas exceeds all other states in the export of grain sorghum. Return to farmers in 1975 for the sale of the grain was $748 million.[33] The cash farm income to farmers increased in excess of 75 percent in the decade of 1960, and this rate of increase continues. Development of successful hybrids contributed significantly to the long-range increase in production per acre.

Grain sorghum production has its heaviest concentration in the High Plains where more than half the crop is produced. The remainder of the production is distributed throughout the state except in the extreme eastern and western sections. Grain sorghum has largely replaced corn in the Blacklands.[34] The Lower Valley and Coastal Bend districts have significant production. Irrigation is used to produce approximately one-third of the crop, particularly in the Northern High Plains. If present trends of increased exports continue, more grain sorghum will be grown in Central and South Texas.

Milo, as the grain is commonly referred to in the feeding industry, is becoming more acceptable as an ingredient in feed mixed for swine, poultry, and other animals as well as for cattle. Digestibility is being improved by mechanical processes. The relative price advantage as compared to corn has hastened its acceptance as a substitute. It is generally agreed by nutritionists that sorghum grain has 95 percent of the feed value of corn.

Cultivation and harvesting are adapted to the use of large scale farm equipment. The topography of the areas where the grain is grown lends itself to the use of maximum sized equipment. Farm labor demand is minimum. There is a growing trend toward contracting to a buyer all or a portion of the crop before planting or harvest. More of the production operations involved are being done by custom operators.

Vigorous promotion by commodity groups has resulted in expanded domestic use of grain sorghum. Increased meat consumption resulting from higher living standards in foreign nations should strengthen demand for the grain. Presently, foreign investment in American feedlots should stimulate domestic demand for grain sorghum. The comparative advantage of Texas should insure continued leadership in the production of this feed grain.

Rice. Rice is produced on a significant scale in about twenty counties in the Upper Coastal district of Texas. It yielded $224 million to farmers of the state in 1975.[35] Texas exchanges rank of leadership in rice production in the United States with the states of Louisiana, Arkansas, and California. The 1975 rice crop was produced on 548,000 harvested acres. Rice is the fourth ranking crop in value in the state. The rice milling industry is located in the Houston area.

Rice growing lends itself to mechanization and large scale cultivation practices. Much of the planting, fertilization, and weed and insect control are done by aerial applicators. Irrigators and drying-storage facilities are often owned cooperatively by farmers. Much of the cultivation and harvesting is done by custom operators. There may be some truth to the old rice country jest that all a good rice farmer needs to make a crop is a telephone to call the custom operators and a comfortable rocking chair.

Texas farmers grow both long and medium grain rice with long grain being in the majority. The state produces more than its proportionate share of long grain rice which has been in increased demand in recent years. Approximately 60 percent of United States rice crop is exported. Texas furnishes one-fourth of this amount. Therefore, future production will depend to a great extent on factors outside the state and United States. The devaluation of the dollar in the last decade stimulated export demand for rice, along with other food and feed grains. However, subsequent worldwide overproduction of rice has softened the export demand.

Wheat. Wheat is important to the agriculture of Texas as food, a feed grain, and as winter pasture for cattle. Both hard and soft wheat are grown. The value of the Texas wheat crop sold for the years 1969, 1970, and 1971 averaged over $63 million.[36] Its susceptibility to drouth accounts somewhat for a high degree of fluctuation of acres harvested from year to year.

Though the majority of the state's wheat is used in the milling industry, increased amounts are being used in feeds. Wintering calves for the feedlot industry has created a greater demand for wheat acreage to be used for winter grazing. Historically, concentrated wheat production has shifted from the North Central to Northwest Texas Panhandle regions. Slightly less than one-fourth of the crop is irrigated. It is produced for grain or grazing in varying acreages throughout the state.

Oilseed Crops. Production of oilseed crops in Texas reflects the general worldwide increase in demand for vegetable oils. Total production is increasing though shifts in acreage are occurring within the group. Recent years have shown increases in soybean production with decreases in others.

Cottonseed production was valued at $81 million in 1975 making it the most important oil crop. As with some of the other oil crops, by-products of processing such as meal and hulls are used as a source of nutrients in livestock feed. Acreage production of cottonseed is not flexible as is the case of most other oil crops, being entirely dependent on acreage of cotton for lint.

Texas was third among states in peanut production with 307,000 acres planted in 1975.[37] Of this total, 123,100 acres were irrigated. Most of this irrigation of peanuts is in South Texas. However, the heaviest concentration of peanut production is on the southeastern fringe of the Cross Timbers Crop Reporting District in and north of Comanche County. There are other pockets of peanut production primarily further east. The Spanish peanut, grown primarily for oil and processed edible peanut products, dominates other varieties grown in the state.

The soybean is the oilseed that perhaps has the greatest potential in the state. Recent price increases spurred by worldwide feed and food protein shortages have resulted in increased soybean acreage. To date the majority of production has been the upper coastal, the southern sector of the Northern High Plains, and the northern East Texas districts. The wide adaptation of soybeans combined with irrigation potential in the state places Texas in a position to increase its acreage if the relative price of soybeans remains high.

Flaxseed, guar, and castorbeans are other significant oil crops in the state.

Vegetable Crops. Texas truck farmers harvested 178,730 acres in 1975. This yielded a product value of $224 million. Texas ranks fifth among the states in harvested acreage of fresh vegetables.[38] The most significant production of truck crops in the state is onions, carrots, potatoes, cabbage, watermelons, and spinach. Most of the vegetable crops produced in the state are marketed fresh.

Agricultural Specialties

Significant agricultural income is generated from farm enterprises that do not fit the classifications of crops or livestock. Major agricultural specialties are timber, greenhouse and nursery products, horses, fish farming, and recreation.[39]

Timber. Texas farmers received $30.4 million from the sale of forest products in 1975. This share represents more than 20 percent of the income received from the total sale of forest products. Most of this farm income is supplementary to other enterprises. In many cases, it is growth from farms that have retired crop land to timber farming. The majority of this production is in the eastern portion of the state.

Greenhouse and Nursery Products. Nationwide increases in fuel and transportation costs have stimulated production of ornamental, potting, and bedding plants within the state. The Texas Crop and Livestock Reporting Service reported the 1975 value of these products at $39 million.

Horses. The horse has returned to Texas as a recreational animal rather than one kept on farms and ranches for work. Presently two-thirds of the horse population in the state is owned by people other than farmers and ranchers. Texas ranks first in number of horses.

Fish Farming. Fish farming has become a significant source of farm income, particularly in the eastern and southeastern sections of the state where there is an ample supply of water. Though most of this production is channel catfish, there is a mounting interest in domestic production of shrimp, crayfish, baitfish, trout, and exotic species of fish. The catfish industry began about 1960. The Texas Almanac reports that the industry has stabilized at 5,000 acres producing a crop valued at more than $8 million. Texas is one of the leading states in fish production. Market organization appears to be the major hurdle confronting this growing industry.

Recreation. The Texas farmer has added recreation to his sources of income. Farm reservoirs and woodlands provide places for swimming, fishing, skiing, hunting, hiking, and horseback riding. Many farmers are developing facilities that will attract people with leisure time. Cash receipts from recreation paid to farmers exceed $40 million. Hunting leases and related activities generate over half of this amount.

IRRIGATION AGRICULTURE

Farm land under irrigation in Texas has increased more than eight times since 1940. More than eight million acres are presently irrigated. The source of most of this is ground water.

Increase in irrigation is due primarily to two reasons. First, yields are significantly increased. Mechanical and agronomic technologies have made additional capital investment required for irrigation profitable. Increased land and labor costs have also been factors requiring higher yields per production unit. Secondly, much of the row crop agriculture has moved from the heavier rainfall eastern section of the state to the productive but drier west.

The major irrigated farming areas are the Rio Grande Plain and the High Plains. Nearly half of the grain sorghum acreage is irrigated. Irrigation is used in production of over half the cotton. Twenty-five percent of the wheat and peanuts planted in the state are irrigated. Irrigation is required for all rice production though located in a humid section of the state.

Economic returns do not generally warrant irrigation for livestock production. However, irrigation of grain crops for grazing, silage, and green-chop is becoming more common in the dairy industry.

The present rate of underground withdrawal points to a water shortage. This would result in a restriction or decrease of agricultural production if additional sources of water are not developed.

FINANCES
Income

Texas farmers' cash receipts were approximately $5.9 billion in 1975. Using the cumulative commodity group multiplier of 2.6, this generates in excess of $15 billion of agribusiness.[40] Total net farm income for proprietors was $954 million in 1975. Government payments to agriculture in the same year accounted for $96,349 million in income to the state's farmers. This is less than the national average per farmer. Texas farmers, like those in the rest of the nation, are experiencing the pinch between gross returns and expenses. During 1975 farmers showed an increase in gross farm income but a lower realized net income.

Investment

The value of Texas farmland and buildings in 1974 was $34.26 billion. Total value of real estate is increasing at an average rate per year of 6 percent. Growth of value of other assets approach the farm real estate percentage rate. Though these escalating values are due partly to recent decreases in dollar value, the real increase is significant. Increased farm size and escalating land prices primarily account for this rise. In recent years the debt of farmers in the state has amounted to approximately 15 percent of the value of their assets.

Credit

The equity position of Texas farmers is favorable. Total money owed by farmers is increasing annually but the percent of borrowed capital in relation to total assets is expanding at a relatively slower rate.

In today's agriculture when technical change is paramount to economic survival, capital input with subsequent efficient financial management is perhaps the sector of agriculture with the greatest potential for increasing revenue. Technical changes require investment capital particularly in an industry where substitution of machinery for labor is escalating at such a rapid rate. Examples of this in Texas have been the aforementioned cattle feedlots and the integrated broiler industry. A secondary but wider spread force creating demand for more investment capital is the necessity of greater returns per production unit. This accounts for more money being spent on higher quality breeding stock, irrigation equipment, and other capital goods that will increase the efficiency of resource use.

The major sources of farm real estate credit are individuals, the Federal Land Bank, and life insurance companies. Each of these has in excess of $500 million on long-term real estate loans. Commercial banks and the Farmers Home Administration also provide credit for farm real estate loans.

Principal lenders of capital to farmers for non-real estate expenditures are private individuals, businesses, commercial banks, and the Production Credit Association. A smaller volume of short-term loans is made by the Farmers Home Administration and Federal Intermediate Credit Bank.

Farm Taxes

Real estate taxes on farms, subject to adjustment by change in appraised value or tax rates, have shown an overall increase in total revenue through the years. In 1971, total revenue for the state was $124.6 million, more than four times the amount in 1930.[41] The tax paid in 1973 per acre of farm land in Texas was $1.07. Taxes levied on farm real estate in 1976 were in excess of $188 million.

OFF-FARM SECTOR OF AGRICULTURE

Texas agriculture is the single largest multiplier of income in the state with over $10 billion annually added to the economy from agriculture and related business. Texas has over fifteen hundred manufacturing plants for processing food and kindred products.[42] More than one million Texans are employed in these phases of agribusiness which include handling, storage, processing, and distribution of farm products. Supplying agricultural inputs represents another major sector of agribusiness. Land, buildings, machinery, vehicles, and other capital investments in off-the-farm agriculture represent a vital part of the Texas economy. Many small towns exist because of service to the agricultural industry. Thirty percent of the business activity in Dallas, one of the state's largest cities, is generated by agriculture, and virtually all of the larger and intermediate sized cities share some degree of this dependency.[43]

The cattle industry may be used as an example of how production of one commodity activates other sectors of the economy. Cattle ranchers are users of feed, veterinary services and supplies, fertilizers, seed, building materials, chemicals, transportation, farm machinery, automotive equipment, petroleum products, and many other supplies and services in producing beef. Beyond production, there are 167 state inspected livestock auction markets through which the majority of the state's cattle are initially sold.

Texas has a total of 530 slaughter plants—more than in any other state.[44] The state ranks first in the slaughter of cattle, second in calves, third in sheep and goats, and eleventh in slaughter of hogs. The services provided by the plants range from the sale of dressed carcasses to preparation of processed meat products that go directly into retail trade. Government inspectors are involved in each of these steps. Transportation is in constant demand from hauling cattle to the auction barn to delivering the edible products to consumer outlets. Refrigerated storage is required in each step. Commission agents are involved at several levels of marketing beef products.

Partial or total financing of these transactions is done on borrowed capital. Some observers have said that the average cow is sold eight times before it gets to the consumer, perhaps an exaggerated figure, but it does point up the demand for capital. The evolvement of the feedlots which started out feeding cattle on a cost plus contract for owners, has recently commanded huge sums of outside investment capital. More of these establishments are investing in a portion of the cattle on their lots as insurance against price changes and unoccupied capacity.

When focused on the broad spectrum of this example of the business activity generated by cattle production, it is evident that the economic effect of this and other agricultural commodities is far reaching. However, it is recognized that some commodities generate more added value income than others. Promotional organizations from the local to state level are constantly active in enticing new manufacturers that use the state's agricultural raw materials.

Another major example of business generated by agricultural production is the cotton industry. Numerous cotton gins are scattered over the state. Cotton compresses and shipping facilities are required for the exportation of most of this cotton. The limited number of textile mills in the state point up a situation where there is need of expanding manufacturing of cotton products.

Grain sorghum is somewhat unique in its having been largely responsible for the development of two other levels of agricultural production—fattening livestock, and expanded slaughter facilities.

EXPORT AGRICULTURE

The American farmer can commercially produce food and fiber crops that lend themselves to labor saving technologies cheaper than any other nation in the world. On this basis, it may be assumed that worldwide demand for United States agricultural exports will continue. Presently, exportation of food and fiber is the major area of expansion in United States foreign trade, accounting for a more favorable balance of trade.

Texas presently plays a major role in the exportation of farm products, ranking with Illinois and Iowa as the top three states in total value of export sales. The income to Texas from these sales was $1,262.7 million in 1976.[45] The state ranks first in exports of cotton and grain sorghum. Other major exports are hides, tallow and lard, and meat products. Texas exports more beef cattle than any other state.

The economy of Texas, though comparatively well balanced, is heavily dependent on the complex of agribusiness. Trends do not indicate a change in this relationship. The natural advantages represented by the availability of vast renewable natural resources provide a base for continuing the major contribution of agriculture to the business activity of the state.

Financial and governmental leadership show evidence of recognition that production of raw agricultural products represents a major sector of the state's economy. Though the significance of the rural farmer's vote has waned with population shifts and redistricting of political subdivisions, the influence of agricultural interests supplemented by that of supporting businesses has remained a potent influence in the government of the state.

Major restrictions are not foreseen that would cause competition between expansion of the industrial sector and a viable agricultural industry. The complementary relationship holds promise of enhancing the standard of living for residents of the state. Stability of the industry is accented by the adaptability of many unique geographic areas to shifting agricultural production. This capability provides insurance against loss of any particular commodity group.

Business organization in agriculture is rapidly moving in the direction of big business. Corporate farming, integrated organizations, and large scale family farms are evolving to cope with the demand of increased capitalization. Part-time and specialty farming are expanding proportionately with total agriculture in their capacity of serving specific individual needs.

There is evidence that the state could capitalize on more processing and manufacturing facilities that utilize raw agricultural products. Recent growth in value added by agribusiness and increased fuel costs indicate that time will see this relocation from less productive regions. Texas has established a desirable industrial climate that should augment the shift in this sector of the economy.

Texas' dominance in production of so many major commodity groups may be explained in part by the sheer number of acres in production. However, comparative yield studies with other product areas in the United States show that efficiency of production is competitive.

Change in the relative importance of various agricultural commodities will be influenced primarily by external factors of demand and price. Favorable comparative advantage of the state in the production of such a variety of crops insures more than a proportionate share of future production that may result from shifts in domestic and world demand.

NOTES

1. Louis Wortham, *A History of Texas*, IV, 135.
2. *Texas Almanac and State Insustrial Guide, 1976-1977*, p. 391.
3. Ralph W. Steen and Francis Donecker, *Texas: Our Heritage*, p. 165.
4. *Annual Report Commercial Fertilizer, July 1, 1975 to June 30, 1976*, Agricultural Experiment Station Miscellaneous Publication 1279, p. 192.
5. Faculty and Staff, University of Texas, *Texas Looks Ahead*, I, p. 36.
6. *1975 Cash Receipts From the Sale of Texas Farm Commodities,*

Texas Crop and Livestock Reporting Service Bulletin 138, p. 6.

7. *1975 Texas Livestock Statistics*, Texas Crop and Livestock Reporting Service Bulletin 135, p.4.

8. Cecil Jones, interview, 5 November 1976.

9. *Texas Almanac and State Industrial Guide, 1976-1977*, p. 391.

10. *1975 Cash Receipts From the Sale of Texas Farm Commodities*, p. 31.

11. *1975 Texas Field Crop Statistics*, Texas Crop and Livestock Reporting Service Bulletin 136, p. 10.

12. Ibid., p. 10.

13. United States Bureau of the Census, *Statistical Abstract of the United States, 1976*, p. 640.

14. "Human Resources." *Texas Food and Fiber Facts*, no page numbers.

15. *What Texas Agriculture Means to You*, Texas Department of Agriculture, no page numbers.

16. Ibid., no page numbers.

17. *Conservation Needs Inventory, Texas, 1970*, United States Soil Conservation Service, p. 165.

18. Curtis L. Godfrey, Clarence R. Carter, and Gordon S. McKee, *Land: Resource Areas of Texas*, Agricultural Experiment Station Bulletin 1070, pp. 4-24.

19. *General Soil Map*, Department of Agricultural Communications, Miscellaneous Publication 1034, Part II, no page numbers.

20. *1975 Texas Livestock Statistics*, Texas Crop and Livestock Reporting Service Bulletin 134, p. 58.

21. Ibid., p. 15.

22. Ibid., p. 4.

23. *1975 Texas Dairy Statistics*, Texas Crop and Livestock Reporting Service Bulletin 134, p. 5.

24. Ibid., p. 3.

25. *1975 Texas Livestock Statistics*, p. 5.

26. Ibid., pp. 7-8.

27. *1975 Texas Poultry Statistics*, Texas Crop and Livestock Reporting Service Bulletin 97, p. 16.

28. *1975 Cash Receipts From the Sale of Texas Farm Commodities*, p. 6.

29. *1975 Texas Poultry Statistics*, p. 8.

30. Don Perkins, interview, 14 December 1975.

31. James W. Graves, *Effects of 1966 Cotton Adjustments in*

Texas, Agricultural Experiment Station Miscellaneous Publication 842, p. 2.

32. *What Texas Agriculture Means to You*, Texas Department of Agriculture, no page numbers.

33. *1975 Texas Field Crop Statistics*, Texas Crop and Livestock Reporting Service Bulletin 136, p. 8.

34. Ibid., pp. 12, 60.

35. Ibid., p. 4.

36. *1975 Small Grains Statistics*, Texas Crop and Livestock Reporting Service Bulletin 138, p. 6.

37. *1975 Texas Field Crop Statistics*, Texas Crop and Livestock Reporting Service Bulletin 137, p. 88.

38. *1975 Texas Vegetable Statistics*, Texas Crop and Livestock Reporting Service Bulletin 133, p. 42.

39. "Agricultural Specialties," *Texas Food and Fiber Facts*, Texas A&M University, no page numbers.

40. "Texas Agriculture," *Texas Food and Fiber Facts*, Texas A&M University, no page numbers.

41. "Financing Agriculture," *Texas Food and Fiber Facts*, Texas A&M University, no page numbers.

42. *What Texas Agriculture Means to You*, Texas Department of Agriculture, no page numbers.

43. L. S. Pope, address to Nacogdoches Farm and Ranch Club, 6 December 1973.

44. *1975 Texas Livestock Statistics*, p. 12.

45. *What Texas Agriculture Means to You*, Texas Department of Agriculture, no page numbers.

NINE

THE FINANCIAL SYSTEM OF TEXAS
Vernon E. Sweeney, Jr.

A study of the Texas economy must include a description and analysis of the major entities which make up the financial system of the state of Texas. The important parts of the state's financial system considered in this section are commercial banking, savings and loan associations, finance companies, the securities industry, consumer credit unions, and some of the lending activities of insurance companies. A brief history of the development of these institutions and some current issues are provided. Ultimately the question of the adequacy of the financial system to foster and promote growth and well-being of commercial and consumer interests in the state constitutes the major thrust of this essay.

With few exceptions, other comparable regional studies within political subdivisions of the United States complain of insufficient data, and I do not differ. In this study, some data were not strictly appropriate for analysis of financial activity within the boundaries of the state of Texas and adjustment of the data are necessary.

In order to assess the financial system of Texas, it is necessary to describe some of the characteristics of the Texas economy. It is important to determine whether the Texas economy is predominately rural or urban, agricultural or industrial, composed of small or large businesses in order to evaluate the requirements of a financial system which supports the state's economy.

Recent estimates by the staff of the Dallas Federal Reserve Bank indicate that the urban areas of the District have shown rapid increases in population since 1950. Population in the Standard Metropolitan

Statistical Areas (SMSA) of the District grew from 3.8 million in 1950 to 8.9 million persons in 1970.[1] The data indicate a trend toward concentration of the state's economic and financial activity in urban areas. These population changes have come from the diminution of the rural and agricultural sector which characterized the Texas economy in earlier times.

In 1940 about 30 percent of the Texas labor force was employed in agriculture, and by 1970 less than 8 percent were classified as agricultural employees.[2] During the same period, manufacturing employment increased from 10 percent to about 16 percent of the Texas labor force.[3]

Further indication of transition of the Texas economy from an agrarian and small business orientation to an urban and industrialized one is shown in the trend and composition of personal income generated within the state. Economic growth and development at the national level is measured in terms of gross national product—the money value of goods and services produced for final demand in one income period, usually a calendar year. There are no regular statistics generated for states or regions comparable to gross national product. Since total output in money terms reflects total income, personal income data, which are available for states, may be used as a proxy for changes in the level of a state's economic activity. Also, changes in the sources of personal income for a state may reflect changes in the structure of that state's economic activity. If the structure of the economy changes over time then the nature of the financial system might be expected to change also.

In 1940 wages and salaries accounted for 56 percent of personal income in the state of Texas. By 1959 wages and salaries were 63.8 percent of personal income, and by 1968 the figure was 66.8 percent. In 1940 farm income was 12.2 percent of personal income, but by 1959 that figure had fallen to 5.3 percent and to 3.1 percent by 1968. Non-farm proprietor's income (small business) also declined during the period. In 1940 non-farm proprietors generated 14.2 percent of personal income in the state of Texas; that percentage fell to 10.5 percent in 1959 and stood at 7.4 percent in 1969.[4]

Changes in the major sources of personal income for the state of Texas were similar to changes experienced by many other states as the process of industrialization continued to displace other modes of production. As stated in *Business Review*, "relative to the total, small businesses and farms operated by proprietors and self-employed workers were becoming less important as sources of income."[5]

In place of agriculture and small businesses, large corporations based on capital intensive technologies, which require increasing amounts of money capital for their initiation and sustenance, began to characterize the Texas economy.

NATURE AND FUNCTION OF THE TEXAS FINANCIAL SYSTEM

Commercial Banks in Texas

In Texas as in other states, commercial banking is the single most important agent providing credit and financial services to businesses and households. Total assets of Texas banks as of the beginning of 1975 were greater than $50 billion compared to savings and loan association assets of about $13.56 billion, total assets in Texas credit unions of $2.7 billion, and finance companies of $1.3 billion.[6] Because of the relative size of commercial banks, and because they provide a broad range of functions to the public as opposed to more specialized financial services afforded by non-bank financial institutions, commercial banks stand paramount in the Texas financial system.

Another indication of the relative size of commercial banking compared with other financial intermediaries is gained from the Federal Reserve Board's Flow of Funds Accounts. It will be shown that the Texas financial system generally reflects the national financial system so that inferences about the relative size of Texas intermediaries can be approximated from national data. During the first half of 1973, commercial banks supplied about $87 billion to the nation's private credit market. During the same time period, savings institutions supplied $49.2 billion, insurance and pension funds provided $21.6 billion, and $14.8 billion from other financial sources.[7] Thus, commercial banks supplied more credit funds to the private national economy than the total of all other credit sources. The importance of the commercial banks to the Texas economy is certainly of a similar proportional magnitude. The Federal Bank at Dallas estimates that all Texas banks supplied about $7.1 billion of business in 1972.

Table 9-1 shows the total assets of financial intermediaries for the United States in 1950, 1960, and 1970. The data show that the position of the commercial banks has declined since 1950 but remains by far the largest in terms of assets.

Commercial banks exhibit other characteristics setting them apart from other non-bank financial institutions and from other businesses.

Commercial banks accept demand deposits (checking accounts) and loan these funds to the general public and to business. As banks loan to individuals and firms, they create demand deposit money and the total amount of demand deposits created through these loans by the banking system is greater than the initial deposit by a multiple. The multiplier depends upon a policy variable determined by the central bank—the Federal Reserve System. No other industry has the power to create money and the power of the commercial banks to do so requires regulation. Regulation of the banking system and the central bank's periodic adjustment of the supply of money and credit is outside the scope of this work but should be noted at the onset.

The banking industry in Texas has demonstrated rapid growth since 1950. Total deposits in the state have increased fourfold since 1950 and the number of banks has increased by a third. Two categories of commercial banks exist in Texas as in other states. The State Department of Banking overseas state banks and the Comptroller of the Currency issues charters for national banks. In 1975 total deposits in state banks were $13.758 billion and nationally chartered banks held $28.772 billion in deposits.[8] State banking laws prohibit branch banks (except for facilities of a parent bank on some military bases)

TABLE 9-1

TOTAL ASSETS OF FINANCIAL INTERMEDIARIES
UNITED STATES, 1950-1970
(Billions of dollars, percent distribution and growth rates)

Intermediary	1950		1960		1970	
Commercial Banks	$149.9	54.1%	$230.9	41.0%	$516.9	40.9%
Savings and loan Associations	16.9	6.1	71.5	12.7	176.2	13.9
Mutual savings banks	22.4	8.1	40.6	7.2	79.0	6.2
Credit unions	0.9	0.3	5.0	0.9	15.4	1.2
Life insurance companies	62.6	22.6	115.9	20.6	200.5	15.9
Private pension funds	6.7	2.4	38.2	6.8	110.8	8.7
State and local government pension funds	5.0	1.8	19.6	3.5	58.0	4.6
Finance companies	9.3	3.4	24.1	4.3	60.4	4.8
Open-end investment companies	3.3	1.2	17.0	3.0	47.6	3.8
TOTALS	$277.0	100.0%	$562.8	100.0%	$1,264.8	100.0%

Source: Board of Governors of the Federal Reserve System, Flow of Funds Account.

and the industry has accomodated increased demand for banking services by creating new banks. The number of banking establishments in Texas has grown from 891 in 1950 to 1,313 in 1975.[9] Texas ranks fourth in the magnitude of bank deposits and first in the number of banking establishments compared to the other fifty states.[10]

As Texas has become industrialized, the financial system of the state has taken on many of the characteristics of the national financial system. The growth curves of commercial bank deposits for the state and nation reflect this similarity as shown in Figure 9-1. Table 9-2 shows the 20 largest commercial banks in Texas as of 30 September 1975.

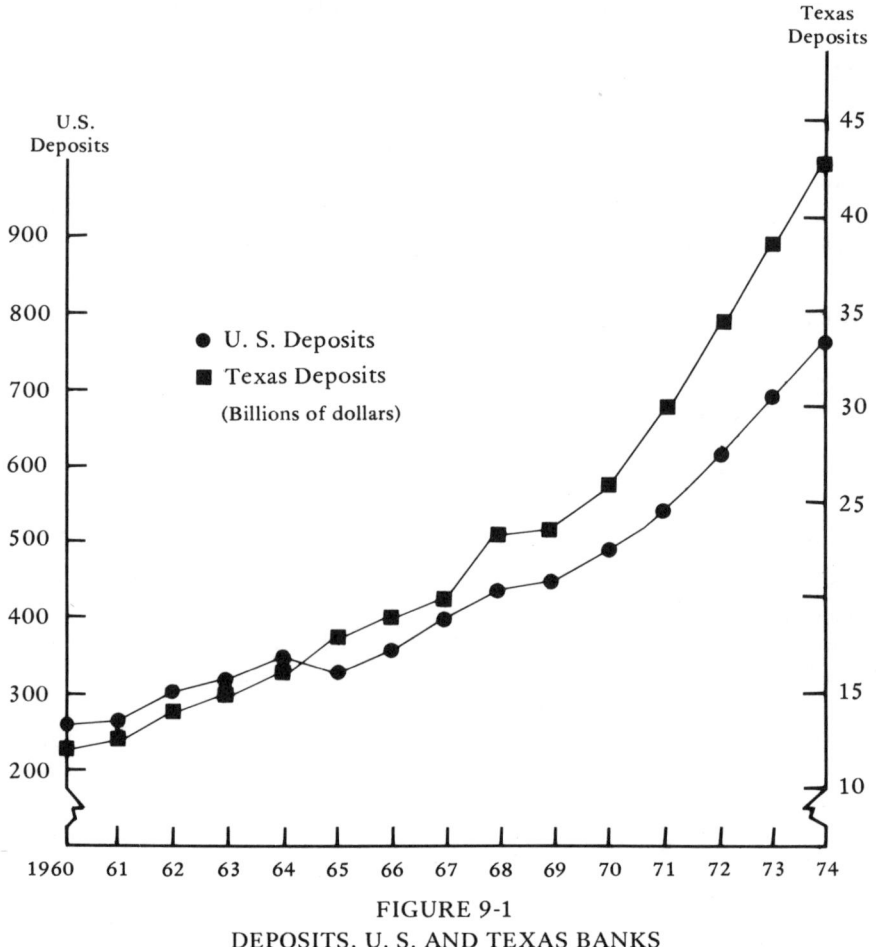

FIGURE 9-1
DEPOSITS, U. S. AND TEXAS BANKS

Source: *Texas Almanac and State Industrial Guide, 1976-77*, p. 466 and Board of Governors, Federal Reserve System.

WORKSHEET FOR FIGURE 9-1

Deposits Year	Bank, U. S. (Billions)	Bank, Texas (Billions)
1960	266.9	12.3
1961	288.0	13.4
1962	304.6	14.0
1963	320.7	14.8
1964	357.6	16.6
1965	333.8	17.8
1966	355.1	18.7
1967	398.2	20.8
1968	437.5	23.4
1969	440.0	23.7
1970	485.5	26.3
1971	542.9	30.0
1972	621.5	34.7
1973	687.6	38.6
1974	753.6	42.5

Source: *Texas Almanac and State Industrial Guide*, 1976-77, p. 468 and *Statistical Abstract of the United States*.

With regard to the specific question of the functions of the commercial banking system in Texas, there are two views as to what constitutes the product market for commercial banks. One viewpoint is that commercial banks are single product firms. The advocates of the single product view do not believe that commercial banks compete with other intermediaries because the basic product of commercial banks is demand deposits and the transfer of those deposits by check. Non-bank intermediaries do not now have the ability to provide checking accounts in Texas.

The alternative view holds that commercial banks compete with a number of other financial institutions, including savings and loan associations, the lending activities of life insurance companies, credit unions, and finance companies. Observers generally agree that banks are isolated from competition in the market for short term business loans of small size. In the field of consumer credit, loans on cash values of life insurance, loans by finance companies, and credit unions are alternatives to commercial bank loans and credit.

The boundaries for geographic markets for banking services in Texas are especially difficult to determine. A bank in Houston or Dallas may have clients for its services from the immediate area and also participate in the national market for business loans.

According to the Texas Banking Code, "No state, national or private bank shall engage in business in more than one place, maintain any branch office, or cash checks or receive deposits except in its own banking house."[11] Texas law has always prohibited the existence of branch banks. The anti-branching law has had two major effects on the nature of commercial banking in Texas. First, Texas banking resources show evidence of fragmentation which causes some large firms to go outside Texas for their credit needs. The second effect, related to the first, has been the establishment of bank holding companies in Texas.

There are fewer large banks in Texas compared with some other states. In Texas, only 17 percent of the commercial banks have deposits in excess of $20 million. New York banking statistics show that almost 50 percent of their commercial banks have assets greater than $20 million, and in California the figure is 45 percent.[12] Among all fifty states, Texas ranks very low in concentration of deposits. When concentration is defined as the percentage of the states' bank deposits held by the five largest banks, Texas ranks forty-sixth with 21 percent. The states ranking below Texas were Arkansas, 20 percent; West Virginia, 18 percent; Iowa, 17 percent; and Kansas, 16 percent.[13] These states are not well known for their industrial development or high personal income.

In 1970 amendments to the Bank Holding Company Act of 1956 caused the expansion of bank holding companies in Texas. Bank holding companies are corporations formed to acquire stock in banks for the purpose of controlling those banks. If a holding company buys controlling interest in two or more affiliate banks, it is designated a multibank holding company. By the end of 1972 there were fifteen registered multibank holding companies in Texas with a total of seventy-one affiliated banks. The deposits of affiliated banks stood at 31.6 percent of all Texas bank deposits in 1972.[14]

The impact of multibank holding companies in Texas is the generally beneficial effect of mobilization of bank capital and bank lending power. Another possible result concerns portfolio diversification and rests on the assumption that bank holding companies control affiliates in many different parts of the state.

Because bank holding companies acquire banks located in many different regions, individual banks within the holding company organization can assume more risk than independent banks of the same size. This could mean several things: (1) a higher percentage of individual

TABLE 9-2
20 LARGEST COMMERCIAL BANKS IN TEXAS
(As of September 30, 1975)

75	74		Assets ($000's)	Deposits ($000's)			Loans ($000's)		
					75	74		75	74
1	1	Republic National Bank (Dallas)	3,112,149	2,137,894	2	1	1,521,169	1	1
2	2	First National Bank (Dallas)	2,923,644	1,919,048	3	2	1,416,549	2	2
3	3	First City National Bank (Houston)	2,869,985	2,140,519	1	3	1,338,905	3	3
4	4	Texas Commerce Bank (Houston)	2,395,332	1,674,328	4	4	1,159,507	4	4
5	6	Mercantile National Bank (Dallas)	1,149,254	890,554	6	6	547,263	5	6
6	5	Bank of the Southwest (Houston)	1,127,623	919,502	5	5	475,813	6	5
7	7	Fort Worth National Bank (Fort Worth)	876,194	657,082	7	7	459,140	7	7
8	8	First National Bank (Fort Worth)	754,637	613,988	9	9	402,195	8	8
9	9	Frost National Bank (San Antonio)	732,596	615,965	8	8	317,844	10	9
10	11	Houston National Bank (Houston)	561,617	435,550	11	11	219,588	11	11
11	10	Allied Bank (Houston)	545,977	457,724	10	10	349,009	9	10
12	13	Austin National Bank (Austin)	477,693	404,630	12	13	184,150	14	16
13	12	National Bank of Commerce (San Antonio)	456,599	366,811	13	12	217,962	12	12
14	16	El Paso National Bank (El Paso)	376,712	323,076	15	14	151,802	22	23
15	18	Capital National Bank (Austin)	371,628	330,915	14	17	176,581	18	17
16	15	State National Bank (El Paso)	366,764	310,780	16	15	178,936	17	15
17	21	Texas Bank & Trust (Dallas)	349,152	283,909	18	21	179,220	16	18
18	25	First National Bank (Midland)	347,421	304,370	17	24	179,655	15	20
19	17	Houston Citizens Bank & Trust (Houston)	340,367	276,078	19	16	208,685	13	13
20	19	First National Bank (Amarillo)	337,777	269,816	20	18	166,572	19	22

Source: State Call Report and Federal Deposit Insurance Corp.

bank assets devoted to loans, (2) an increased commitment to longer-term loans, and (3) a generally greater willingness to assume risk.[15] Table 9-3 shows some important multibank holding companies based in Texas in 1975.

Texas farms and ranches have increased their average size and mechanization in recent years. Along with these changes have come increased use of bank credit for financing increased productivity. One study indicates that "farms have approximately doubled their indebtedness over the preceding decade, while on a per farm basis the use of credit has more than tripled."[16] The demand for credit by the agricultural sector has grown faster than the availability of rural banking resources in Texas. Multibank holding companies have the resources to increase the flow of credit to agriculture.

Savings and Loan Associations

For many years, in Texas and in other states, savings and loan associations were rather uncomplicated intermediaries, channeling savings deposits into residential mortgages. The intermediary is important because of the emphasis that our culture places on owner occupied homes. Allocation of funds to finance the increasing demand for individual family housing continues to be an important issue with bearing on the community's growth and stability.

In a secular climate of price inflation, it is an unusual institution which borrows short, mostly from individual households, and lends long. Given the demand for housing and the interest rate movements during the business cycle, one would expect a rapidly growing institution, but an institution whose growth rate is vulnerable to changes in the national monetary policy.

When short-term interest rates are low in relation to long-term rates, the savings and loan associations operate profitably. Profitability depends on differentials between short-term and long-term interest rates which occur when the level of economic activity is low, associated with business recession. During recessions, individuals tend to hold their savings in liquid form and passbook savings rise, reducing short-term rates. Long-term interest rates decline but not as much as the reduction in short-term rates. On the other hand, when the economy is strong or near full employment, both short and long-term rates rise and the spread between them may narrow or even disappear. For the savings and loan associations, prosperous times cause their cost of money to increase faster than the return on their earnings assets. As

TABLE 9-3

MULTIBANK HOLDING COMPANIES IN TEXAS

Name	Location	Rank	Subsidiaries	Deposits (Millions)	% State
Allied Bancshares, Inc.	Houston	9	13	770.5	1.98
Austin Bancshares Corp.	Austin	15	2	302.3	.77
Briscoe Ranch, Inc.	Uvalde	22	2	60.6	.15
Dynamerica Corporation	Richardson	25	2	13.8	.03
Farmers & Mechanics Trust Co.	Childress	24	3	30.0	.08
Federated Capital Corp.	Houston	7	6	914.8	2.34
First Abilene Bankshares, Inc.	Abilene	28	3	141.9	.36
First Bancorp, Inc.	Corsicana	20	5	92.3	.24
First City Bankcorp. of Texas, Inc.	Houston	2	23	2,689.8	6.91
First International Bancshares, Inc.	Dallas	1	23	3,219.4	8.26
First Security National Corp.	Beaumont	16	10	275.3	.73
First Texas Bancorp, Inc.	Georgetown	23	4	49.2	.13
First United Bancorporation, Inc.	Fort Worth	10	9	754.5	1.93
Frost Bank Corporation	San Antonio	11	5	611.2	1.57
Galbank/United States National Banc.	Galveston	19	2	98.2	.25
Mercentile National Bank/Equitable Company of Texas	Dallas	8	4	847.5	2.17
National Bancshares Corporation of Texas	San Antonio	12	4	388.4	1.00
Pan National Group, Inc.	El Paso	13	5	386.5	.99
Republic of Texas Corp./RNB	Dallas	4	3	2,402.8	6.17
Security Bancshares, Inc.	Waco	26	2	9.1	.02
Southwest Bancshares, Inc.	Houston	5	15	1,420.4	3.65
Texas American Bankshares, Inc.	Fort Worth	6	9	1,173.8	3.02
Texas Commerce Bancshares, Inc:	Houston	3	24	2,478.7	6.38
Trans Texas Bancorporation, Inc.	El Paso	14	4	360.0	.94
U. S. Bancshares, Inc.	Brownwood	21	3	67.8	.17
Victoria Bancshares, Inc.	Victoria	17	7	159.7	.40

Source: Federal Reserve Branch Bank, *Computer Printout on MBHC*, Houston, 1975.

earnings decline, savings and loan associations cannot increase the dividend rates, depositors divert funds to more profitable assets, and the supply of home mortgage funds dries up.

In the United States, assets of the savings and loan associations have grown from about $9 billion in 1945 to $243.6 billion in 1972.[17] Until recent monetary policy adversely affected the savings and loan associations, these institutions progressively improved their share of the market for specialized mortgage lending. In the United States, savings and loan associations held about 29 percent of residential mortgages during the mid-fifties, increasing to about 49 percent in 1972. The proportions in Texas are probably similar.[18]

Savings and loan associations can be chartered by the Federal Home Loan Bank Board or by state agencies. In Texas, the Savings and Loan Department regulates state-chartered institutions. All but a few institutions have their deposits insured by the Federal Savings and Loan Insurance Corporation, an entity similar to the Federal Deposit Insurance Company which insures the depositors of commercial banks.

In Texas in 1972, 33 associations were state chartered, mutually owned; 171 were state chartered, stockholder owned; and 78 were federally chartered, mutually owned.[19] Also that year, the Federal Home Loan Bank Board modified its rules to permit conversion of federally chartered mutual savings and loan associations to stock companies by assigning stock to depositors. What is involved in the conversion is a change from a depositor-owned association paying out profits in higher interest on deposits, to a stockholder controlled firm which is capable of paying out profits in higher interest on deposits, to a stockholder controlled firm which is capable of paying dividends to its shareholders. Regulations insure that all stock issued in conversion be distributed to eligible depositors pro rata with no preferential distribution to management permitted.

Conversion of federal mutual associations to stock associations is evidence of an attempt to provide more funds for home mortgages. If stock associations need funds, they may sell additional stock, building a larger equity base on which to receive deposits and extend loans. Such an institution which pays dividends and is unhampered by interest rate ceilings under law or convention, should be more attractive to investors. Proponents of the conversion plan believe that it will increase the flow of funds to the home mortgage market.

In the decade of the 1960s and in the first years of the 1970s, the number of savings and loan association offices in Texas did not grow much. Some change in number came from increases in branch outlets which are not permitted for commercial banks. In 1960 there were 232 offices in Texas. By 1965 the number of savings and loan associations had expanded to 166 and by 1972 the number had grown to 282.[20]

Some structural characteristics of the savings and loan industry in Texas are revealed in the size distribution of firms. In 1972 total assets of state and federally-chartered savings and loan associations in Texas were $10.99 billion. Over 9 percent of assets were held by the eight largest savings and loan associations in Texas.[21] Assets held by state-chartered associations were $7.826 billion and $3.157 billion for associations with federal charters in 1972.[22] Total mortgage loans granted by both state and federal associations in 1972 amounted to $9.048.[23] By 1976, the state's savings and loans held $16.9 billion in deposits, $19.9 billion in assets, $16.1 billion were mortgage loans.

Finance Companies

Financial corporations operating under various names such as loan broker, loan company, personal finance company, or consumer finance company, service a market for small loans to consumers in the Texas economy. The loans to consumers are in cash ranging in size from $5 to $3,000 and may be secured or unsecured. Finance companies are often lenders of the last resort when installment loans are not possible from other sources. In the national economy, finance companies were important sources of installment credit. In 1972, finance companies provided 25.2 percent of all installment credit, second only to commercial banks with 46.95 percent.[24] Installment credit for the United States economy, held by finance companies, amounted to $35.6 billion as of August 1973.[25]

The latest tabulated data for Texas finance companies show $1.01 million installment loans outstanding with a value of $662,634,147 as of 31 December 1975.[26] Total assets of finance companies in Texas were $1.2 billion in 1975.[27]

Securities Industry

The laws of the state of Texas contain a securities act providing for the regulation of the sale of securities and of dealers, agents, and salesmen by the creation of a Securities Commission and the appointment of a Securities Commissioner.[28] The registration process involves submission of statements about the issuing corporation's location, nature of business, financial condition, and a prospectus describing the securities. Securities sold interstate and registered with the Federal Securities and Exchange Commission (SEC) may be registered by "coordination." The term coordination means that securities accepted and registered by the SEC for national sale will also be approved by the state of Texas.[29]

The securities industry in Texas has grown rapidly in terms of registration with the State Securities Commission between the years 1963 and 1969. The volume of registrations declined to a low point in 1971 following the national market and rebounded in 1972 approaching the peak reached in 1969 (Figure 9-2).[30]

Growth and fluctuation in the volume of new applications for security registrations reflects changes in the demand for funds for investment in plant and equipment which are associated with change toward a more industrial and an increasingly sophisticated regional economy.

The dollar volume in Texas for mutual investment companies (mutual funds) in 1972 was $325.4 million which was the figure for original applications to the Securities Commission for registration.[31] Applications for renewal of registration for mutual investment companies operating in Texas were valued at $452.8 million in 1972.[32] Original registrations in 1972 represented a substantial increase over original registrations in 1970-71. Original applications for registration of all other corporate securities stood at $767.5 million in 1971-72, up from $501.7 million in 1970-71 in Texas.[33]

The dollar volume of total applications for registration is shown in Table 9-4. The data show substantial increase in both total and original applications for registrations in Texas over the last ten years. Also as shown in Figure 9-1, the pattern of fluctuation of the amount of registration of securities in Texas follows the national trend. In the data for Texas, the so-called Kennedy market of 1962-63, the "credit crunch" of 1966-67, and the "bear" market of the summer of 1970 are apparent. The patterns show that the Texas security industry is no longer an isolated or provincial market, but is integrated into the national market.

Licenses issued for securities dealers in the state of Texas have almost doubled in the period between 1967 and 1972; 5,708 in 1967 to 10,414 in 1972.[34] The change comes in two predominate categories, salesmen and corporate dealers.

Consumer Credit Unions

In Texas during 1972, credit unions were important sources of consumer installment funds. Texas credit unions ranked third among the fifty states in terms of savings shares and deposits with $1.53 billion, slightly behind second place Michigan with savings shares and deposits of $1.66 billion. The state of California ranked first among the fifty

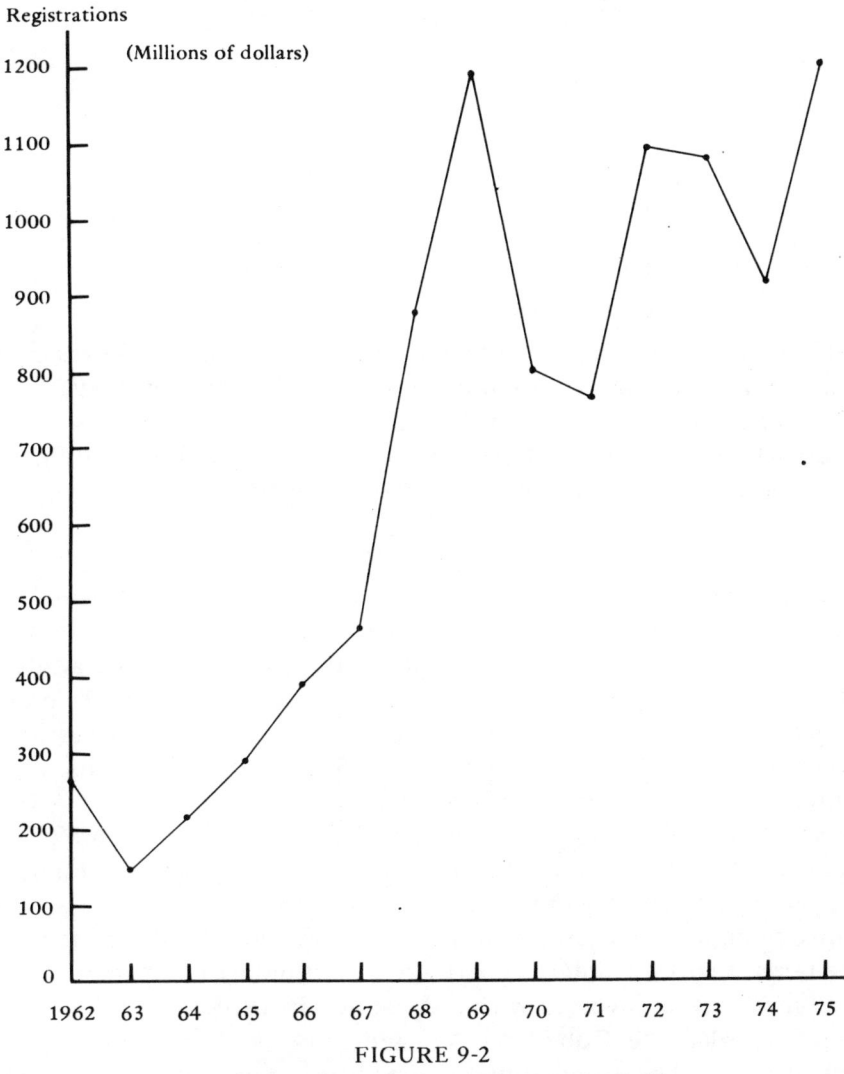

FIGURE 9-2
SECURITIES REGISTRATIONS IN TEXAS

Source: Texas Bureau of Business Research

WORKSHEET FOR FIGURE 9-2

Year	Original Applications (Millions of dollars)
1962	256.8
1963	151.4
1964	216.4
1965	283.3
1966	393.1
1967	462.2
1968	873.4
1969	1,197.9
1970	804.5
1971	760.4
1972	1,092.9
1973	1,080.2
1974	910.4
1975	1,200.0

Source: Texas Bureau of Business Research.

states with savings shares and deposits of $2.8 billion.[35] Texas credit unions with savings shares and deposits of $1.53 billion in 1972 may be compared with total deposits in Texas commercial banks of over $30 billion, savings and loans deposits of $9.169 billion, and finance company loans (at the beginning of 1972) of $685.6 million.[36]

Lending Activities of Insurance Companies

Lending activities of insurance companies may be divided into two categories. First, loans to life insurance policyholders based on their policy's cash value, and more importantly, the credit made available to the economy originating from the investment of insurance premiums and reserves. Representatives of the insurance industry estimate that policy loans amount to between 15 and 20 percent of life insurance in force. The value of ordinary life insurance in Texas in 1972 was $47.8 billion and policy loans probably ranged between $7.7 billion and $9.5 billion according to a 15 to 20 percent rule-of-thumb.[37]

More difficult to estimate is the amount of credit based on insurance premiums and reserves in Texas. Until 1963 the Robertson Law required that three-quarters of reserves of insurance companies operating in Texas be invested within the state. In 1963 the Texas Legislature repealed the Robertson Act and reserves are now exported to other states. The exact amount of credit extended by insurance companies to the Texas economy is not known. The amount of mortgages owned by life insurance companies operating in Texas was $7.4 billion in 1971.[38] Mortgages held by life insurance companies for the entire United States were valued at $73.4 billion in 1971, thus insurance companies in Texas held slightly more than 10 percent of all mortgage assets owned by all life insurance companies operating in the United States.

Insurance companies have also been active as sources of funds for farm mortgages in Texas. In 1950 life insurance companies provided $154.5 million to the market for farm mortgages in Texas. By 1960

TABLE 9-4

DOLLAR VALUE AND PERCENT INCREASE OF ALL APPLICATIONS AUTHORIZED FOR SALE DURING FISCAL 1962-1972
(Millions of dollars)

Year	Total Applications		Original Applications	
	Dollar Value	Percent Increase Over Previous Year	Dollar Value	Percent Increase Over Previous Year
1972	1,569.4	26.8	1,092.9	43.7
1971	1,238.0	3.0	760.4	-5.5
1970	1,201.6	-21.6	804.5	-32.9
1969	1,531.6	40.8	1,197.9	37.2
1968	1,087.7	69.4	873.4	89.0
1967	642.2	18.9	462.2	17.6
1966	540.1	40.2	393.1	38.8
1965	385.1	19.9	283.3	30.9
1964	321.1	28.8	216.4	42.9
1963	249.3	-30.2	151.5	-41.1
1962	357.3	1.6	256.8	4.4

Source: Texas Bureau of Business Research. Ernest W. Walker, "Securities Registration in Texas." *Texas Business Review*, November, 1972, p. 250.

the figure was $293.9 million, and by 1970 the figure rose to slightly under $1 billion.[39]

Additional Sources of Finance

There are several less known sources of industrial financing available to Texas businessmen. In this section some of these sources will be described along with three bills recently passed by the Texas Legislature encouraging the financing of industrial development in Texas.

Real Estate Investment Trust. The real estate investment trust (REIT) is a comparatively recent innovation among financial intermediaries. Federal Reserve Board statistics for the national economy are available for REITs only since 1968. In the United States, $200 million in mortgages were held by REITs in 1968 and the amount grew to $5.5 billion by 1972.[40] Assets of REITs in the United States were close to $7 billion in 1972.[41]

A real estate investment trust is an intermediary incorporated for the purpose of investing in real estate loans. The loans made by a REIT may finance construction or they may be short-term loans for permanent financing. Real estate investment trusts have enjoyed rapid growth in the nation, in Texas, and in other states because they do not pay corporate income taxes if 90 percent of their earnings are payed out in dividends to stockholders.

Tax-Exempt Revenue Bonds. According to Internal Revenue Service Ruling 1963-20, some non-profit corporations may be eligible to issue tax-exempt revenue bonds. These securities are sold at interest rates lower than the prime rate of interest and do not affect the credit of political subdivisions or require approval by a general election in the district. Tax-exempt revenue bonds may be used to finance "activities which are essentially public in nature" and such corporations must be approved by the government of the political subdivision.[42]

Small Business Administration Loans. Financing in Texas through the Small Business Administration (SBA) usually involves interaction with a local development corporation. The SBA offers several direct and participating programs which should be particularly attractive to the financing of profit or non-profit enterprises in rural Texas. To be classified as a small business and thus be eligible for a loan, the business must be independently owned and operated, have an average employment of less than 1,500 depending on its relative size with other firms in the industry, and meet revenue maximums depending on the industry.

Under the SBA 502 loan program, financing is available only if other means of finance are not available. The SBA will not make a direct loan in excess of $50,000; however, it will participate with other institutions up to $150,000. The SBA will guarantee bank loans to 90 percent of $350,000 whichever figure is less. Most of the SBA financing in Texas operates through a local development corporation or an industrial foundation. A loan from the SBA is made to the development corporation which in turn allocates the proceeds of the loan to the business or constructs a facility suited to the needs of the business.

An example of SBA financing was the recent loan guarantee to the

El Campo Economic Development Corporation and the Ferrotherm Corporation, a private firm manufacturing foundry tubing. The El Campo Development Corporation provided $65,400 and the SBA guaranteed 90 percent of a $370,000 bank loan. The funds were used to buy land and construct a facility employing thirty-five people.[43]

Legislation for Financing Industrial Development. In May 1971, the governor of Texas signed into law three bills with the common goal of encouraging industrial growth.

The first bill concerned state business development corporations, with the stated purpose "to promote, stimulate, develop, and advance the business prosperity and economic welfare of this state and its citizens; to encourage and assist through loans, investment, or other business transactions, in the location of new business and industry in this state."[44] The bill further provides for the formation of a state business development corporation when called upon. Lending institutions which are members of the development corporation then acquire capital stock in the development corporation up to 10 percent of the lending institution's legal loan limit.

On the basis of this bill, the South Texas Business Development Corporation has been formed and is comprised of about fifty individuals in twenty-six counties on the Texas Gulf Coast and with approximately $2 billion in funds potentially available for industrial financing in that area.

A second bill passed by the sixty-second session of the Texas Legislature is entitled the "Texas Rural Industrial Development Act."[45] This act directs the Texas Industrial Commission to make loans to local industrial development corporations in the "rural area of Texas." Such loans may not exceed 40 percent of the cost of projects which are to be determined by the local development corporation. Allocation of funds by the Commission originate from the "Industrial Development Fund" which is to be established by appropriations from the Legislature. Interest rates will be determined by the Industrial Commission without lower limit and certainly below the prime rate. The principal and interest paid on loans is to be returned to the State Treasury.

The final bill passed in 1971 is a law which authorized political subdivisions in the state of Texas to issue revenue bonds to be used to promote industrial and economic development.[46] The language of the legislation uses the term "public health" and implies that the bill is designed to help in financing local health care facilities in addition to other types of projects. Bonds issued under this law are to be repaid from revenue of the projects which they have financed. All facilities of a given project are eligible for funding including land, plant, and equipment. The Texas Industrial Commission is in full control of the lease agreement for the project. The public must be notified before the revenue bonds are issued and in the event that 10 percent of qualified voters file a written protest, a general election must be called. The constitutionality of tax-exempt revenue bonds to be used for land acquisition by a non-profit corporation has been affirmed in the state of Texas.

In all cases, the legislation described above is designed to keep Texas industrial financing competitive with other contiguous states which offer similar advantages either in regard to finance or to tax accomodations. As an example of the competition between states to attract new industry, the Board of Commerce and Industry in Louisiana, with the governor's approval, exempts new industrial plant and equipment, and additions to existing plant and equipment, from all state and local millages for a period of up to ten years. A publication of the Public Affairs Research Council of Louisiana compares tax exemptions and other inducements to new industry in eight southern states as of 1969.[47] In all other states compared, there were extensive provisions for the encouragement of new industry except for the state of Texas which was described by one sentence which was, "Texas cities may allow, by local option, tax exemptions."[48]

HISTORY OF THE TEXAS FINANCIAL SYSTEM

When the Republic of Texas joined the United States in 1845, the Texas Constitution was silent on the subject of banks. At that time, the new state had one bank at Galveston. Samuel May Williams had obtained a charter from the Legislature of the state of Coahuila at Monclova, Mexico, which established the *Banco de Commerica y Agricultura*. According to Carlson, "It is believed that this charter was granted by the Mexican authorities partly as a concession to the rebellious Texans."[49] The Commercial and Agricultural Bank of Galveston remained the sole banking establishment until about the beginning of the Civil War.

By 1868 there were at least 15 private banks in Texas. The Constitutions of 1861 and 1866 prohibited state-chartered banks and all banking activities were carried out in Texas by private and national banks. Between 1868 and 1893 private banks increased in number from 15 to 133. In 1894 there were 218 national banks in Texas.[50] An amendment to the Texas Constitution in 1903 allowed banks to receive a state charter and the provisions of the amendment were embodied by the Texas Legislature into state law in 1905. As of 20 December 1906, there had been 157 state banks chartered.[51]

Texas law provided for regulation of banking by the creation of the Department of Insurance and Banking in 1907. The Texas Legislature in 1909 set up a form of deposit insurance for Texas banks. However, the turbulence of the times, management practices, or depression in some agriculture prices caused many failures among the new state banking system. In 1921, the total number of Texas state banks organized was 1,359 and, during the same year, 334 of these banks closed and 68 failed. Texans lost more money as a result of bank failures than because of thieves in the period. By 1928, of 1,560 state banks organized in Texas, 810 closed and 228 failed.[52] The Depositor's Guaranty System may have encouraged reckless management practices in a number of Texas state banks and in 1927, the act was repealed. After many more bank failures in Texas during the depression of the 1930s, another plan for deposit insurance was introduced in the Texas Legislature but was abandoned after the establishment of the Federal Deposit Insurance Corporation which now insured almost all Texas banks. With the formation of the Federal Reserve System in 1914, many Texas banks became members and the district Federal Reserve Bank was located in Dallas.

In 1923, the State Department of Banking was created. Regulation of Texas insurance was separated and another agency created to regulate insurance companies. The Texas Legislature passed a number of laws to regulate the growing insurance business in the state. One significant act passed in 1907, known as the Robertson Insurance Law, required all insurance companies doing business in Texas to invest at least 75 percent of their reserves for Texas policies in Texas securities and Texas real estate. The law stated that securities purchased were to be deposited in the State Treasury or in certain banks and a 1 percent tax on gross premiums was to be rendered to the state. As the law became effective twenty-one companies withdrew from the state and soon after the deposit requirement was reduced.[53] The law has resulted in the creation of many Texas insurance companies. Several attempts to repeal or modify the Robertson Law were made over the years, but they did not succeed until 1963. Texas savings and loan associations have been regulated since 1913 when the Legislature passed laws creating the Texas Savings and Loan Department.

ADEQUACY OF THE TEXAS FINANCIAL SYSTEM

John R. Stodden, a member of the research staff at the Federal Reserve Bank in Dallas, has reported that the commercial banking system in Texas did not meet the credit needs of the larger corporations domiciled in or doing business in the state of Texas.[54] After interviews with representatives of eight of the state's larger corporations, thirty-four other firms were asked to participate in a study of their needs for credit resources and banking services.

The sample set of a total of 42 corporations represented firms among the state's 100 largest corporations in terms of assets and sales. The total sales of the 42 corporations were in excess of $19 billion per year and assets of nearly $18 billion.[55] Total employment of the firms in the sample was about four hundred thousand nationally, and in some cases, internationally.

More than 50 percent of the firms in the sample stated that their principal banking affiliation was outside the state, and about 80 percent of the sample's loans and credit arrangements were made in banking establishments outside Texas. According to Stodden, out-of-state banks held three times the value of the sample corporation's deposits compared with monies deposited in Texas banks.[56]

Earlier in this chapter, mention was made of the prohibition of branch banking in the state of Texas and the effects of unit banking on the structure of the state's commercial banking industry. The point was that although Texas ranked first among the states in number of banking establishments with 1,215 at the beginning of 1972, the state was fifth in deposits with $30.04 billion. With respect to measurement of concentration of deposits (the percentage of commercial bank deposits in a state's five largest banks), Texas ranked forty-sixth with 21 percent.[57]

The case is made that the reason for the dependence of intra-state firms operating on banking services located outside Texas is the size of those banks. Banks in Texas have comparatively lower lending limits because of their size, which is relatively smaller than some banks based outside the state. One-third of the corporations participating in Stodden's study reported that there were problems encountered with Texas banks because of low lending limits.[58]

In addition to the ability to meet the credit needs of large corporations, respondents were asked about the performance of Texas banks in general. Stodden reported that slightly more than half of Texas banks are competitive with banks out of state, in cost of borrowing and quality of service. And 7 percent said Texas banks are better. But a significant two-fifths believed that the state's banking system is absolutely uncompetitive.[59]

Seven percent of all business loans by Texas banks, or about $0.5 billion, were negotiated outside Texas in 1972.[60] If large, prime customers must go outside the state for credit accommodations, then the growth of the financial community in Texas and ultimately the entire economy of the state is inhibited. Stodden concludes that "banking resources in Texas are either inadequate or—probably because they are so thinly spread among small banks—inefficiently organized."[61]

Other earlier studies of the Texas commercial banking system conclude that the system could be more efficiently organized. Lawrence Crum's study of Texas banks between 1956 and 1965 finds the assets of Texas banks, as a proportion of the United States total bank assets, falling from 4.6 percent in 1956 to 4.05 percent in 1965 possibly indicating a loss of deposits from Texas banks.[62] A study of Texas banks by William Townsend in 1967 advocates branch banking as a means to increase the mobility of capital in Texas.[63] The Commission on Money and Credit stated in its report that:

The Commission recommends . . . the provisions of the National Banking Act should be revised so as to enable national banks to establish branches within "trading areas" irrespective of state laws, and state laws should be revised to provide corresponding privileges to state-chartered banks.[64]

The comments above pertain to commercial banks and some remarks are in order concerning the nonbank financial institutions. The primary function of nonbank financial institutions is to provide a means of channeling savings into investment goods and consumer durables. It was seen in the foregoing description of these nonbank financial institutions that they are highly specialized compared to the facilities offered by commercial banks. A very fundamental question arises as to whether the specialized nature of the nonbank financial institutions should be maintained or eliminated.

In December 1971, the president of the United States received a report from his Commission on Financial Structure and Regulation, which had been established to recommend changes in the nation's financial system. The Hunt Commission, named after chairman Reed O. Hunt, called for sweeping changes in the nation's financial system, and consequently the state's financial system. The president stated that the recommendations would:

> ... enhance the *"flexibility and efficiency"* of competing financial institutions by putting them *"on a roughly equal footing"* with regard to deposit powers, lending powers, and tax burdens.[65]

Specifically, the recommendations of the Hunt Commission are to:
- phase out interest-rate ceilings on savings deposits;
- permit savings and loan associations for the first time to offer checking accounts, credit cards, and other bank-type services;
- broaden savings and loan associations' lending and investment powers so they could, among other things, begin offering consumer loans and investing in corporate bonds and commercial paper;
- eliminate interest-rate ceilings on home mortgages backed by the Federal Housing Administration and the Veterans Administration;
- modify tax laws to remove a tax advantage savings and loan associations currently have in relation to commercial banks, and substitute a new "mortgage tax credit," available to both banks and savings and loan associations, as an incentive to mortgage lending.[66]

The results of all the changes recommended will be to reduce specialization of nonbanking financial institutions. In August 1973, the president sent these recommendations to Congress requesting legislation incorporating many of the reform measures suggested by the Hunt Commission.

Over the years the Texas financial system has changed, reflecting the state's movement toward an industrialized and mature economic region. The Texas financial system is in the process of taking on the characteristics of the national financial system. Such change has not been fully accomplished. Unit banking laws, loss of some banking business to other areas of the nation, and a political scandal involving a few financial institutions in the state are evidence that the development of the Texas financial system has not reached the same level of development as the rest of the nation. As change and innovation occur in the national financial system, these changes may be expected to be incorporated into the Texas financial system with less lag than in earlier times because of the progress made toward complete integration with the national system.

NOTES

1. "SMSA's Become More Important in Economy of the South-

west," *Business Review*, Federal Reserve Bank of Dallas, July 1973, p. 7.

2. Clifton McCleskey, *Government and Politics of Texas*, p. 15.

3. Ibid.

4. Herbert W. Grubb, *The Structure of the Texas Economy*, vol.1 (Austin, Texas: Office of the Governor, 1973), p. 33.

5. "Personal Income in Texas Accelerates to Rate Faster Than the Nation's," *Business Review*, Federal Reserve Bank of Dallas, May 1972, p. 8.

6. U. S. Department of Commerce, *Statistical Abstract of the United States*, 1975, (Washington: Government Printing Office, 1975), p. 468; Texas Savings and Loan League, *Annual Report of Savings and Loan Associations in Texas*, 1974, p. 6; Credit Union National Association, Inc., *Annual Report, 1976*, pp. 22-23; and State of Texas, *Analysis of Annual Reports of Licensees, 1974*, [Finance Companies], (Austin, Texas: Office of Consumer Credit Commissioner, 1975, p. 12.

7. Joel M. Yesley, "Defining the Product Market in Commercial Banking," *Economic Review*, Federal Reserve Bank of Cleveland, July 1972, p. 20.

8. *Texas Almanac and State Industrial Guide*, 1976-1977, (Dallas, Texas: Dallas Morning News, 1976), p. 466.

9. Ibid.

10. Texas Commerce Bancshares, Inc., *Texas Facts and Figures*, 1976, p. 3.

11. *Vernon's Annotated Civil Statutes*, art. 342-903.

12. Joseph M. Grant, "Sources of Financing for Industrial Expansion in Texas," *Texas Business Review*, April 1973, p. 85.

13. Texas Commerce Bancshares, Inc., op. cit., p. 7.

14. Peter S. Rose, "Bank Holding Companies in Texas: Benefits and Problems," *Baylor Business Studies*, 96th issue, May, June, and July 1973, p. 42.

15. Ibid., p. 46.

16. Ibid., p. 47.

17. United States Savings and Loan League, *Savings and Loan Fact Book, 1973*, p. 95.

18. Ibid., p. 35 and p. 38.

19. Annual Report of Savings and Loan Associations in Texas, 1972, op. cit., p. 5.

20. Ibid.

21. Ibid., p. 7.
22. Ibid., p. 6.
23. Ibid.
24. Credit Union National Association, Inc., op. cit., p. 14.
25. Board of Governors, Federal Reserve System, *Federal Reserve Bulletin* 59, no. 10 (October 1973): p. 54.
26. State of Texas, *Analysis of Annual Reports of Licensees,* 1970-1975, [Finance Companies], op. cit., p. 10.
27. Ibid.
28. *Vernon's Annotated Civil Statutes,* art. 581.1, 1-39.
29. Ibid.
30. Ernest W. Walker, "Securities Registration in Texas," *Texas Business Review,* November 1972, p. 250.
31. Ibid.
32. Ibid.
33. Ibid.
34. Ibid., p. 251.
35. Credit Union National Association, Inc., op. cit., p. 14.
36. Ibid.
37. Institute of Life Insurance, *The Life Insurance Fact Book, 1973,* p. 23.
38. Ibid., p. 81.
39. Federal Reserve Bank of Dallas, *Regional Economic Facts,* 1967, p. 105; and U. S. Department of Agriculture.
40. Thomas W. Adler, "Real Estate Investment Trust and the Commercial Bankers," *Journal of Commercial Bank Lending,* September 1972, pp. 22-23.
41. Ibid.
42. Joseph M. Grant, op. cit., p. 87.
43. Ibid.
44. *Vernon's Annotated Civil Statutes,* art. 5109.2, 1-10.
45. Ibid.
46. Ibid.
47. Public Affairs Research Council of Louisiana, *Industry Rates Louisiana,* pp. 90-92.
48. Ibid., p. 92.
49. Avery Luvere Carlson, *A Monetary and Banking History of Texas,* p. 1.
50. Ibid., p. 39 and p. 52.
51. Ibid., pp. 57-61.

52. Ibid.
53. Ralph Wright Steen, *Twentieth Century Texas*, pp. 109-10.
54. John R. Stodden, "Texas Banking: Their Small Size Costs Banks Business of Large Corporations," *Business Review*, Federal Reserve Bank of Dallas, October 1973, p. 6.
55. Ibid.
56. Ibid.
57. Texas Commerce Bancshares, Inc., op. cit., p. 7.
58. Stodden, op. cit., p. 6.
59. Ibid., p. 7.
60. Ibid.
61. Ibid.
62. Lawrence L. Crum, *Transition in the Texas Commercial Banking Industry, 1956-1965*, p. 11.
63. William S. Townsend, "Concentration and Competition in Texas Banking," *Texas Business Review*, December 1967, pp. 327-30.
64. Commission on Money and Credit, *Money and Credit*, p. 166.
65. *The Wall Street Journal*, 6 August 1973, p. 3.
66. Ibid.

TEN

TEXAS IN INTERNATIONAL TRADE
Dale B. Truett · Paul N. Bartlett, Jr.
Lila Flory

CONCEPTUAL BACKGROUND

Economists almost universally agree that the basis for trade between one geographical region and another or one nation and another lies in potential differences in the relative values of commodities produced and sold within each region. Thus, if a given country or region produces a large quantity of a certain commodity in comparison with its production of other goods, that particular commodity will tend to be relatively low-priced in the country or region in which it is produced. This may place the producing country or region in the position of a "comparative advantage" in production and trade of the commodity in question, and such an advantage may permit it to strike favorable bargains in international or interregional trade.

The notion of comparative advantage is cost-based, that is, the circumstances that enable a country to be in a relatively advantageous position for sale of a given commodity in international trade have to do with something that ensures the low-cost production of that commodity relative to others. Fundamentally, it can be argued that production will be relatively low-cost in cases where the resources needed for the production process are abundantly available in comparison with other resources. Thus, one might imagine two countries with approximately the same endowment of natural resources and climatic conditions but vastly different populations. If the labor supply of one of the countries was double that of the other, one would expect the labor-abundant country to be able to produce at lower cost those goods requiring a relatively large amount of labor input in their production process.

The way in which comparative advantage leads to international trade can be illustrated using a simple two-country, two-commodity economic model. If we take the two countries mentioned above, one of which we can characterize as labor-abundant and the other as labor-scarce, and allege that each country produces two commodities, steel and wheat, and that labor is the only relevant cost of production, we might imagine the cost configuration indicated below.

Country	Labor Requirement (man-hours)		Wage Rate	Domestic Cost (in wages)	
	per lb. Steel	*per bu.* Wheat		*per lb.* Steel	*per bu.* Wheat
Labor-scarce	3	6	$2	$6	$12
Labor-abundant	5	7	$1	$5	$ 7

Here, the labor-abundant country has low wages and tends to use more labor per unit of output in both steel and wheat production. Further, if the currency unit in both countries is the dollar and initially the exchange rate between the dollars of one country and those of the other is one for one, the rightmost two columns above give us the cost in terms of labor of a pound of steel and a bushel of wheat in each of the two countries. Note that the labor-abundant country can produce both steel and wheat for less dollars per unit than can the labor-scarce country. Still, it can be demonstrated that the former can gain by trading its wheat for steel produced in the labor-scarce country. Moreover, the labor-scarce country can also gain from this kind of an exchange.

Suppose there is full employment of labor in both countries. Since a pound of steel costs $5 in the labor-abundant country, one would have to give up 5/7 of a bushel of wheat production to get an additional pound of steel produced domestically. Thus, if it would be possible to get a pound of steel from the labor-scarce country for less than 5/7 of a bushel of wheat, the labor-abundant country would be happy to strike such a bargain. The question then arises as to whether the labor-scarce country would be willing to accept less than 5/7 of a bushel of wheat for a pound of its steel. At home in the labor-scarce country, a pound of steel only costs 6/12 bushel of wheat or, alternatively, an increase of one pound of steel production costs only 1/2 bushel of wheat production to be given up.

If the labor-abundant country were to offer, say, 4/7 of a bushel of wheat for one pound of the labor-scarce country's steel, both would find the exchange to be favorable, since: (a) the labor-abundant country would get a pound of steel for 4/7 bushel of wheat, which is 1/7 bushel less than it could get the steel for at home; and (b) the labor-scarce country would get 4/7 bushel of wheat for a pound of steel, more wheat than the 1/2 bushel that a pound of steel would exchange for at home. Both countries gain.

The implication is that the labor-abundant country should tend to specialize in wheat production and obtain some of its steel from abroad, while the labor-scarce country should tend to specialize in steel production, obtaining some of its wheat through trade. Such specialization will, however, alter internal costs through effects on domestic resource markets thereby placing limits on this tendency to specialize and trade. Because of this, one would not expect the labor-abundant country to produce only wheat or the labor-scarce country to produce only steel.[2]

One further point should be made in regard to the preceding illustration. The labor-abundant country traded away wheat because it had a comparative advantage in wheat, and the labor-scarce country traded away steel because it had a comparative advantage in steel. That is, the former could only produce steel at 5/6 the cost per pound in the labor-scarce country, but it could produce wheat at a much greater cost advantage, 7/12 of the cost per bushel in the labor-scarce country. Thus, the labor-abundant country had a comparative or relatively greater advantage in wheat. Likewise, the labor-scarce country was at less of a cost disadvantage in steel. This lesser disadvantage (6/5 in steel as opposed to 12/7 in wheat) is also called a "comparative advantage."

In a world of many commodities and many countries, it is not difficult to imagine arrays of comparative cost configurations which open up staggering, if not infinite, numbers of opportunities for gain from trade. Of course, the ultimate differences in relative production costs from country to country will not depend on labor cost alone but will include the effects of government regulations, monopoly power in the business sector, unions and collective bargaining, as well as each country's endowment of resources other than labor. Further, each country's trade pattern will be affected to a significant degree by the rate at which it makes technological innovations and the investment it makes in the education and training of its population.

Since the Keynesian revolution, economists have expanded their analysis of the gains from international trade to encompass the effects on the employment and national income of international flows of purchasing. Lord Keynes very convincingly demonstrated that any once-over injection into the national expenditure stream would affect national income and product by a multiple of itself, since those who received the initial amount would respend most of it, thereby creating another injection into the stream. This process would go on repetitively until enough of the flow had "leaked" into saving and imports so that the effect of subsequent respending approached zero.

The connection of the Keynesian analysis to international trade is that foreigners' purchases of a given country's exports constitute injections into the domestic expenditure stream while imports into the country are paid for by "leakages" from the domestic expenditure stream. Thus, both exports and imports play a role in the determination of the overall level of a nation's economic activity and, consequently, the level of employment and price stability or instability.

If a country's resources are fully employed, purchasing by foreigners will lead to inflation, but if a country is suffering unemployment, purchases by foreigners may constitute a welcome addition to the domestic expenditure stream. Similarly, in inflationary periods, a country might be glad to have some of its income spent on foreign products—imports—rather than used to bid up prices of domestic output; with unemployment it might prefer that people spend at home rather than abroad. However, this last point does not lead to a conclusive argument for import restrictions when there is domestic unemployment, since such restrictions have negative effects on foreign incomes and therefore the export sales of the country imposing the import restrictions. Clearly, if all countries were to shut off all trade in times of unemployment or depression, they would simply worsen matters by wiping out the gains from comparative advantage (The Great Depression being a case in point).

At the state, rather than national, level, the income and employment effects of international trade are obviously important but difficult to measure. Nevertheless, the U. S. Department of Commerce has attempted to quantify the employment effect of manufactured exports produced in each state, and these figures will be presented in a subsequent section of this essay.

IMPORTANCE OF TEXAS IN INTERNATIONAL TRADE

Texas' significant position in the overall international trade of the

United States is convincing evidence of the importance of such commerce to the economic well-being of the state itself. United States Department of Commerce data on export and import trade by Customs Region and District provide a good overview of international trade flows through Texas since all Texas ports of entry (land, sea, or air) fall into the Houston Customs Region report. Furthermore, the Houston Customs Region encompasses five Texas custom districts, three of which primarily handle ocean-going trade (Houston, Galveston, and Port Arthur), and two of which primarily handle trade by rail and truck (Laredo and El Paso). Figures for 1976 on the value of exports and imports passing through the Houston Customs Region and the Texas districts are presented in Table 10-1, along with comparative data for the United States and its other eight custom regions. It should be noted that whereas the Houston Region covers mostly Texas ports of entry, some of the other regions cover large numbers of states and are geographically extensive.[3] For example, the Boston Region includes districts in Maine, Vermont, Rhode Island, Connecticut, and western New York State, while the San Francisco Region includes the districts of Anchorage, Honolulu, Portland, Seattle, and Great Falls, Montana. What this suggests is that Texas ranks much higher among the states in terms of international trade flows than it does among the customs regions.

Table 10-1 shows that Texas, in terms of export value, ranks fourth among customs regions.[4] In 1976, over 10 percent of all United States exports left the country via Texas. Within the Houston Region, the Houston Customs District itself was the state's largest exporter, and over 95 percent of Houston District exports were taken out by ship. In fact, U. S. Department of Commerce data for 1976 show that only the seaports of the New York and New Orleans districts handled higher values of ocean-going exports than did Houston. Further, the Laredo Customs District was one of the most important landlocked ports of the United States (export value exceeded by Detroit and Buffalo, New York districts only) and was certainly the most important for United States–Mexico trade.

With respect to the value of imports into the United States, the Houston Customs Region ranked fifth out of the nine regions in 1976. As Table 10-1 shows, in 1976, Texas was a net importer, but by only some $150 million, while the United States as a whole was a net importer by $5.7 billion. Thus, foreign trade flows through Texas reflected a close balance between exports and imports, while the United

TABLE 10-1

U. S. EXPORTS AND IMPORTS, BY CUSTOMS REGIONS & DISTRICTS
(1976, ALL METHODS OF TRANSPORTATION)

U. S. Customs Regions & Districts	Value of Exports		Value of Imports	
	Millions of dollars	Percent of U.S.	Millions of dollars	Percent of U.S.
New York Region	19,369.6	16.8	21,884.0	18.1
Chicago Region	17,129.1	14.9	18,518.7	15.4
San Francisco Region	13,087.3	11.4	13,525.9	11.2
Baltimore Region	13,075.1	11.4	13,199.0	10.9
Houston Region	12,455.3	10.8	12,712.7	10.5
Houston District	5,622.5	5.9	4,466.3	3.7
Laredo District	2,963.8	2.6	1,427.6	1.2
Galveston District	2,240.2	2.0	3,017.2	2.5
Port Arthur District	1,049.2	0.9	3,151.8	2.6
El Paso District	597.7	0.5	649.7	0.5
New Orleans Region	12,201.7	10.6	9,308.4	7.7
Boston Region	8,661.9	7.5	12,087.0	10.0
Miami Region	7,297.5	6.4	8,010.4	6.6
Los Angeles Region	7,143.0	6.2	11,070.6	9.2
Other Categories	4,576.6	4.0	359.9	0.3
Grand Total	*114,997.2*	*100.0*	*120,677.4*	*100.0*

Source: U. S. Department of Commerce, Bureau of the Census, "Highlights of U. S. Export and Import Trade," Report FT 990, December 1976, Washington: U. S. Government Printing Office, 1977.

States as a whole was running a significant trade deficit.

Prior to the energy crisis and accompanying increases in the price of foreign crude oil, the Houston and New Orleans customs regions typically registered annual exports far in excess of their imports. In fact, for 1972 the Houston region showed an export surplus of almost $2 billion, while the United States ran a trade deficit of over $5.8 billion. The results of the energy situation are apparent in Table 10-1. By 1976, New Orleans was the only United States custom region with an export surplus, and Houston's former surplus position was wiped out by the importation of large quantities of high priced foreign oil through the Port Arthur, Galveston, and Houston districts.

Another significant facet of Texas' international trade is the growth of export and import flows since World War II. Trade through Texas increased significantly throughout the War, so that by 1950, exports and imports were at levels seven or eight times greater than 1940. Table 10-2 traces export, import, and trade balance statistics for the period 1950 through 1976.

Note that at the end of the 1950-55 period, exports from Texas actually slipped below their 1950 level while imports increased, and the trade balance slightly deteriorated. The data are reflecting the general slowing of the national economy during and after 1952. In 1951 there was a substantial spurt in Texas' exports, but this fell off with no real recovery until 1956. Thereafter, both exports and imports increased markedly, the latter at a faster rate but from a smaller

TABLE 10-2

INTERNATIONAL TRADE GROWTH OF TEXAS
(In millions of dollars)

Year	Exports	Index*	Imports	Index*	Trade Balance	Index*
1950	1,400	100.0	312	100.0	1,108	100.0
1955	1,419	99.9	430	137.8	989	89.3
1960	2,594	182.7	618	198.1	1,976	178.3
1965	3,137	220.9	858	275.0	2,279	205.7
1970	4,028	283.7	1,754	562.2	4,032	363.9
1975	12,885	907.4	8,853	2,837.5	4,032	363.9
1976	12,877	906.8	12,713	4,074.7	164	14.8

*1950=100. Index numbers reflect the percentage of increase of each item since 1950. When a given index reaches 200, the item has doubled.

Source: U. S. Department of Commerce, Bureau of the Census, *Quarterly Summary of the Foreign Commerce of the United States*, Report FT410, and *Highlights of U. S. Export and Import Trade*, Washington. U. S. Government Printing Office.

base. The result was an increase in the net trade surplus until the late 1960s, when dramatic increases in imports caused the net balance to stabilize at about $2 billion. This development probably reflects the overall growth in consumer markets of Texas and the Southwest during the 1960s.

Despite a growing Southwestern market for imports, the export surplus of Texas widened to over $4 billion in 1975. However, increases in crude oil imports and prices virtually eliminated the Texas trade surplus in 1976. Whether Texas will again become a net exporter will depend in large part on the future of international petroleum markets and development of alternative domestic energy sources. However, it is clear that the Houston region is likely to gain importance among United States customs regions as the growth of the Southwest continues.

COMMODITY COMPOSITION OF TEXAS EXPORTS

Table 10-3 presents data on the value of Texas exports by commodity for the year 1976. The data are classified by major commodity groups and selected subgroups. Although more than two-thirds of Texas exports are nonagricultural commodities, the range of nonagricultural goods is quite broad, and this causes an agricultural commodity classification (for example, foods, beverages, and tobacco) to be the largest single commodity export group. Within the foods group, the major export products are grains and cereals, accounting for over 20 percent of total Texas exports.

Texas is internationally known for its production of petroleum and mineral fuels, but these materials do not constitute a large share of the state's exports since most of the petroleum products leaving Texas ports are destined for the United States home market. Chemicals, another commodity group produced in large quantity within the state of Texas, do constitute a significant export. In 1976, almost 17 percent of Texas exports were chemical products.

Manufactured goods exported through Texas enter the foreign trade statistics through two major groups: manufactured goods classified chiefly by material; and machinery and transport equipment. Manufactured goods classified chiefly by material represented over 8.6 percent of Texas' exports in 1976, and included such products as tires and other rubber articles, paper goods, textiles, iron and steel, and metal manufactures. In the machinery and transport equipment category, the most important products were nonelectrical machinery

TABLE 10-3

TEXAS EXPORTS BY COMMODITY, 1976

Commodity Description	Value (In millions)	Percent of Total
Grand Total	12,325	100.0
Agricultural	3,559	28.9
Nonagricultural	8,766	71.1
Foods, beverages, tobacco	2,856	23.2
Grains & cereals	2,618	21.2
Crude materials, except fuel (inedible)	915	7.4
Raw cotton	302	2.4
Mineral fuels, lubricants, etc.	435	3.5
Chemicals	2,078	16.9
Manufactured goods classified chiefly by material	1,057	8.6
Machinery & transport equipment	4,460	36.2
Nonelectrical machinery	2,819	22.9
Transport equipment	906	7.4
Miscellaneous manufactures	354	2.9
Other	170	1.4

Source: U. S. Department of Commerce, Bureau of the Census, *Highlights of U. S. Export and Import Trade,* Report FT990, December 1976, Washington: U. S. Government Printing Office, 1977.

and transport equipment. The bulk of the latter consists of motor vehicles and their parts.

The Department of Commerce periodically surveys the origin of exports of manufacturing establishments and reports the value and employment generation of such activities by state.[5] However, only total value and employment figures are reported, and the commodity composition of manufactured exports is not easily obtained at the state level. Standard Department of Commerce sources do not provide state origin data on agricultural goods exports.

Because of severe limitations on statistical information, it is possible only to speculate regarding the extent to which the export data in Table 10-3 reflect the composition of the nation's export goods produced in Texas. A substantial share of the grains and cereals exports probably represents Plains States output, which is shipped to Texas ports. In the case of cotton, however, it is likely that much of the exported product leaving Texas is also Texas-produced.

Manufactured products present a difficult analytical problem since even the total value figures presented in the State Export Origin Reports are not particularly helpful. For example, the export origin data for 1971 show that approximately $1.6 billion worth of manufactured exports were produced in Texas. This figure is substantially less than Table 10-4 indicates in miscellaneous manufactures, machinery and transport equipment, and manufactured goods classified chiefly by material for that same year. Furthermore, the state origin series is based on the Standard Industrial Classification, a classification substantially different from the commodity groupings found in United States foreign trade statistics, and the former includes such lines as chemicals and allied products, petroleum and coal products, and processed raw materials.

When adjustments are made for such problems of comparability, it is reasonable to conclude that something less than two-thirds of the manufactured products exported through Texas ports actually are produced in Texas. Studying Table 10-3, one can conclude that it is likely that a good proportion of the petroleum and chemical products exported from Texas are produced in the state, but at least 50 percent of the other manufactured goods simply pass through Texas on their way to foreign ports. Except for California and Washington, Texas is still the largest producer of manufactured exports west of the Mississippi. In the nation as a whole, Texas ranked sixth among the states in production of manufactured exports in 1971. In descending order, the other five principal exporting states were Michigan, Ohio, Illinois, New York, and California. The state of Washington was virtually tied with Texas in 1971, exporting $1.65 billion of manufactured goods.[6]

With respect to export-related employment, Texas reflects the overall national pattern with something less than 5 percent of the state's manufacturing employment of 694,000 related to exports in 1971. Indeed, the Department of Commerce reports on export-related manufacturing show that there is a very close correlation between the share of exports in the total value of manufactured output and the percentage of the manufacturing work force in export-related activities. Only Washington's exports were more than 8 percent of total manufacturing shipments, constituting 16.2 percent in 1971.[7]

COMMODITY COMPOSITION OF TEXAS IMPORTS

Whereas exports leaving the United States through the state of Texas are in large proportion agricultural commodities, over 90 percent of the imports that enter the state are nonagricultural goods (see Table 10-4). These include a broad range of manufactured goods and crude materials. Nonferrous metal ores are the largest category of nonfuel raw materials imports into Texas, and manufactured goods imports are dominated by iron and steel products, electrical machinery, and transportation equipment. These three manufactured product groups made up 22 percent of Texas' foreign imports in 1976.

The origin of Texas' imports is easy to determine from the commodity composition of imports. For example, the bulk of the agricultural goods come from Latin America, and coffee is the major agricultural import. Oil imports are from Venezuela and the Middle East.

TABLE 10-4

TEXAS IMPORTS BY COMMODITY, 1976

Commodity Description	Value (In millions)	Percent of Total
Grand Total	12,749	100.0
Agricultural	842	6.6
Nonagricultural	11,906	93.4
Foods, beverages, tobacco	931	7.3
Raw coffee	401	3.1
Crude materials, except fuel (inedible)	377	3.0
Nonferrous metal ores	226	1.8
Mineral fuels	7,397	58.0
Manufactured goods classified chiefly by material	1,250	9.8
Iron and steel	588	4.6
Machinery & transport equipment	1,818	14.3
Nonelectrical machinery	434	3.4
Electrical machinery	679	5.3
Transport equipment	1,545	12.1
Miscellaneous manufactures	450	3.5
Other	526	4.1

Source: U. S. Department of Commerce, Bureau of the Census, *Highlights of U. S. Export and Import Trade*, Report FT990, December 1976, Washington: U. S. Government Printing Office, 1977.

The nonferrous metal ores originate for the most part in Mexico and the Caribbean, and the mineral fuels are also of Latin American or Caribbean origin. The iron and steel imports are from Mexico, Japan, and Europe. The bulk of the machinery comes from Japan and Europe, as do most products classified under transportation equipment.

The broad range of the state's imports reflects the growing consumer market of the southwestern region of the United States. About one-fourth of all imports are foodstuffs or manufactured materials. As the region's industrial activity expands, it can be expected that the volume of raw materials imported will increase.

TRANSPORTATION FACILITIES

Less than 3 percent of Texas imports and exports are carried by air, in spite of the fine Dallas-Fort Worth, El Paso, Houston, and San Antonio international airports. In 1976 almost 70 percent of foreign goods entering Texas were carried in waterborne commerce. The remaining 30 percent of exports, and approximately 20 percent of imports were accounted for at landlocked ports of entry on the Mexican border.[8]

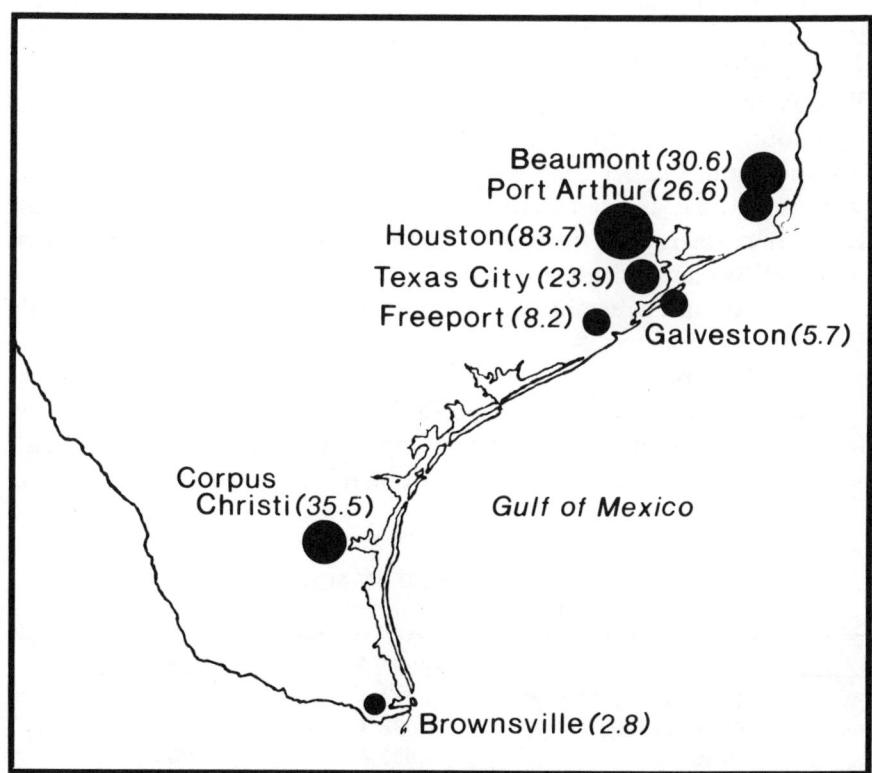

FIGURE 10-1
MAJOR DEEP WATER PORTS OF TEXAS:
TOTAL SHIPPING HANDLED BY PORT FOR CALENDAR YEAR 1975
(figures in million short tons)
Source: Based on data from U. S. Army Corps of Engineers, *Waterborne Commerce of The United States*, 1975, Washington: U. S. Government Printing Office, 1976.

Information is available on the flow of commodities through Texas seaports, since the U. S. Corps of Engineers gathers and publishes such data. Figure 10-1 presents a map of Texas ports, showing comparative shipping tonnages for the year 1975. The state's major deepwater ports are Orange, Beaumont, Port Arthur, Houston, Galveston, Freeport, Port Comfort, Port Aransas, Corpus Christi, Port Isabel, and Brownsville.

The Houston-Galveston-Texas City complex handles by far the largest total tonnage, although the Beaumont-Port Arthur and the Corpus Christi-Port Aransas areas also account for substantial shares of total waterborne shipping. It is important to note that the shipping data of Figure 10-1 include both domestic and foreign commerce and, indeed, are in many cases heavily weighted by large volumes of internal traffic moving within each harbor area. Still, it is true that those ports handling large volumes of total shipping are also those which handle major amounts of foreign commerce.

Import and export tonnage for the eight ports which are most important in Texas' foreign waterborne commerce are presented in Table 10-5. It is clear from these data that each port has its own particular commodity composition of trade which makes it either a substantial net exporter or a substantial net importer in tonnage terms. The only exception is Houston, which handles about the same amount of exports as imports.

The Commodity list shown in Table 10-6 helps to clarify this situation. For example, the large net import tonnage of Corpus Christi harbor is heavily weighted by the tremendous amount of aluminum

TABLE 10-5

FOREIGN COMMERCE HANDLED BY MAJOR TEXAS PORTS
(1975, 1.000 Short Tons)

Port	Imports	Exports
Houston	18,273.4	18,000.8
Corpus Christi	13,038.1	5,195.6
Beaumont	6,037.8	3,960.9
Galveston	854.4	3,092.0
Port Arthur	8,197.1	2,158.5
Brownsville	1,461.1	492.6
Freeport	3,142.0	971.3
Texas City	5,662.6	531.6

Source: U. S. Army Corps of Engineers, *Waterborne Commerce of the United States*, 1975, Washington: U. S. Government Printing Office, 1976.

TABLE 10-6
PRINCIPAL TEXAS IMPORTS & EXPORTS BY PORT, 1975
(In rank order)

Port	Principal Exports	Principal Imports	Port	Principal Exports	Principal Imports
Houston	Wheat, corn, sorghum grains, basic chemicals, rice, coke & petroleum asphalts, machinery (except electrical), lubricating oils & greases, miscellaneous chemicals, iron and steel pipe & tube, soybeans, phosphate rocks, vegetable oils, nitrogenous fertilizers, plastics, animal fats & oils.	Crude petroleum, iron ore & concentrate, liquified gases, basic chemicals, iron & steel pipe, iron & steel plates & sheets, iron & steel shapes, molasses, motor vehicles, parts & equipment, basic chemicals, fabricated metal products	Galveston	Wheat, dry sulphur, sorghum grains, cotton, rice, wheat flour & semolina	Sugar, bananas & plantains, crude petroleum, plywood veneers, nonferrous ores
			Port Arthur	Coke & petroleum asphalts, wheat, lubricating oils & greases	Nonmetallic minerals, crude petroleum
			Brownsville	Sorghum grains, residual fuel oil	Residual fuel oil, distillate fuel oil, iron & steel plates & sheets, nonferrous ores
Corpus Christi	Sorghum grains, wheat, basic chemicals, crude tars	Crude petroleum, aluminum ores, nonmetallic minerals, pig iron	Freeport	Basic chemicals, rice, plastics, nonferrous metals	Crude petroleum, basic chemicals
Beaumont	Wheat, dry sulphur, corn, soybeans, coke & petroleum asphalts, sorghum grains, basic chemicals	Crude petroleum	Texas City	Crude tar, gas & oil products	Crude petroleum, basic chemicals

Source: U. S. Army Corps of Engineers, *Waterborne Commerce of the United States, 1975*, Washington; U. S. Government Printing Office, 1976.

ores unloaded there annually. Galveston's net export position, on the other hand, is due primarily to grain and cotton shipments and exports of dry sulphur. The interested reader can similarly establish the relationship of the commodity pattern to the net export or import tonnage of each harbor by comparing Tables 10-5 and 10-6.

By 1975, commodity exports leaving the United States at points along the Texas–Mexico border and various other ports constituted a flow of over $5.1 billion. Imports from Mexico exceeded $3 billion per year, giving the United States a net surplus on trade with Mexico of over $2 billion.[9] This trade activity between Texas and Mexico is greatly facilitated by the railway and highway networks on both sides of the border.

For both rail and highway traffic, the most important border cross-

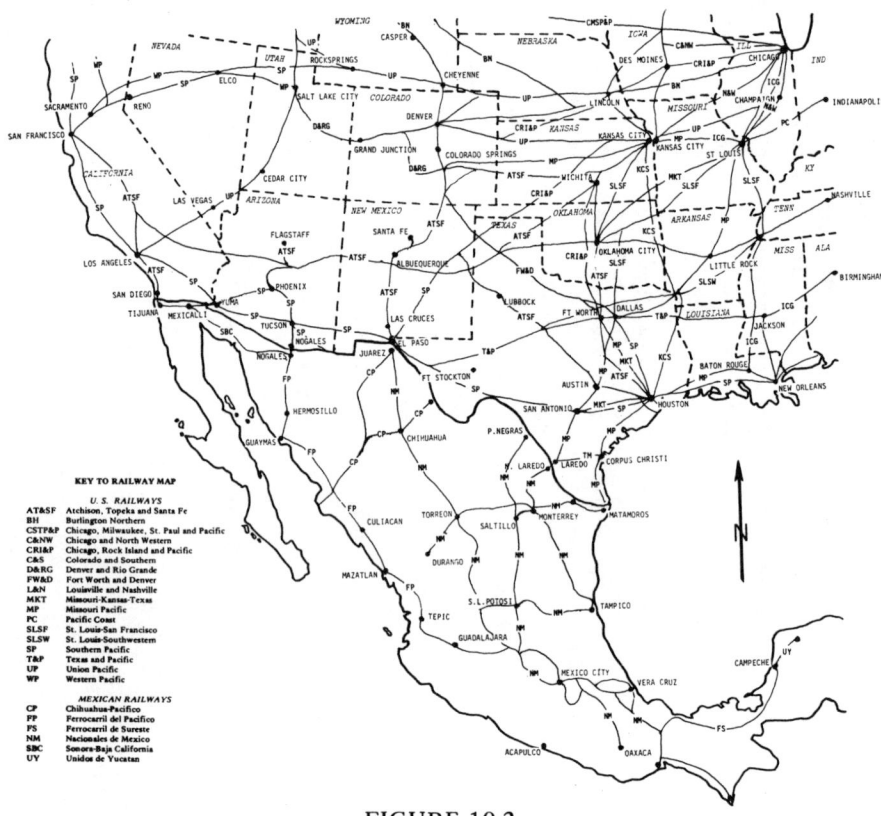

FIGURE 10-2
U. S. – MEXICO RAILWAY NETWORK

Source: Based on information from Mexico's Banco Nacional de Comercio Exterior and recent maps and atlases.

ing points are Laredo (Nuevo Laredo), Eagle Pass (Piedras Negras), Brownsville (Matamoros), and El Paso (Ciudad Juarez). Figure 10-2 illustrates the Texas railway network and its connections into Mexico. Note that in addition to the aforementioned border cities, rail freight also enters and leaves Mexico through Presidio (Ojínaga), Del Rio (Ciudad Acuña), and McAllen (Reynosa). With respect to highway freight, Laredo is the most important connecting point because Interstate 35 and Mexico's Route 87 to Monterrey and Route 57 to Mexico City provide an important direct link between central Texas and Mexico's industrial heartland (see Figure 10-3).

Foreign trade data for Mexico reveal that over 60 percent of the country's imports are purchased from the United States and that about half of these goods enter through Nuevo Laredo.[10] A like

FIGURE 10-3
U. S. – MEXICO HIGHWAY NETWORK

Source: Based on information from Mexico's Banco Nacional de Comercio Exterior and recent maps and atlases.

proportion of Mexico's exports are shipped to the United States, but only about a third of these enter through Laredo. Thus, Laredo is very much a net exporter in the United States-Mexico trade. The net result of this difference between the flow of Mexican goods through Laredo to Mexico is that, typically, the Laredo customhouse shows four-fold United State's sales to Mexico as Mexican sales to the United States.

The commodity composition of the trade through Laredo is significant, since a large proportion of the total movement in both directions consists of manufactured goods. In this respect, the Laredo trade differs from the Brownsville-Matamoros trade, in which agricultural goods are the primary Mexican export and industrial goods are the primary United States export. Brownsville, on balance, is a net importer in United States-Mexico trade.

It is quite likely that as Mexico continues to industrialize, the two-way trade in industrial products through Laredo-Nuevo Laredo will increase substantially, and it can be expected that capital goods and intermediate goods will continue to constitute a large proportion of the flow of products into Mexico, while manufactured consumer goods will grow as a proportion of Mexican sales to the United States. Of course, the strategic position of Laredo with respect to both the United States and Mexican rail and highway networks insures that it will continue to be the most important crossing point for this trade.

FINANCING OF INTERNATIONAL TRADE

Experts in the financial community are basically in agreement regarding the participation of Texas banks in international trade. First, the prevailing belief is that international trade will play an increasingly important role in the Texas economy. In the 1950s and 1960s, the Texas business community appeared to have limited interest in developing foreign markets; accordingly, financial institutions offered meager encouragement for international trade ventures. During the 1970s, this attitude toward international commerce has been replaced by one of keen, aggressive interest.

The growing interest of financial institutions in Texas' international trade has led to the creation of subsidiaries of six major U. S.-owned international banks in Houston. In fact, Houston has recently become the center of Texas' international financial activity, and the subsidiary banks (known as Edge Act Banks) have experienced tremendous growth since 1971.[11] Whereas international trade advice was difficult to obtain in Texas a decade ago, the Edge Act Banks offer extensive expertise on all phases of foreign commerce. Consequently, even many small Texas businesses are awakening to this largely unexplored area of trade.

During most of the 1960s and seventies, Texas had very few billion-dollar banks, in terms of assets. Basically, this reflects Texas' history as a unit-bank state in which it is impossible to expand an individual banking firm to the size and power found in the leading United States financial centers. It was not feasible under such circumstances to compete in international finance with the larger United States banks that in many cases had assets of many billions of dollars and could devote substantial internal resources to the maintenance of international trade and foreign exchange departments.

An important development of the early 1970s that greatly influenced the activity of Texas banking institutions in international finance was the rise of a large number of bank holding companies, known as bank corporations. By 1977, Texas had ten bank groups with assets of over $1 billion each (see Table 10-7). These banks and bank corporations had reached a level of size and sophistication that was making them very important participants in financing the state's international trade. A comparison of Table 10-7 with Table 10-8, which shows the asset size of the twenty largest United States banks in 1976, reveals that none of the largest Texas banks have assets approaching those of the real giants of United States banking (note the enormous assets of the top three in Table 10-8). However, the two tables also show rather clearly that a number of Texas banks are not at all small in relation to the banks at the lower end of the nation's top twenty. For these large and growing Texas institutions, size is not likely to be a significant obstacle to future expansion in international activities.

The increased activity of Texas banks in international trade is frequently attributed to the enhanced climate for international business generally. The availability of insurance and guarantee programs covering foreign operations must be considered a prime factor in this growth process. Briefly, the major United States insuror of export sales is the Foreign Credit Insurance Association (FCIA).[12] There are two types of insurance policies on credit sales: (1) a short-term policy generally extending up to six months on consumer goods, and (2) a medium-term policy of up to five years where capital goods are involved. The merchant may obtain comprehensive protection encompassing both

TABLE 10-7

TEXAS BANKS AND BANK CORPORATIONS RANKING
AMONG THE 100 LARGEST IN THE UNITED STATES
(As of December 31, 1976)

Name and Location of Bank	Assets (Million dollars)
First International Bancshares (Dallas)	7,167
Republic of Texas (Dallas)	6,521
First City Bancorp. of Texas (Houston)	5,256
Texas Commerce Bancshares (Houston)	5,196
Mercantile Texas (Dallas)	2,820
Southwest Bancshares (Houston)	2,292
Texas American Bancshares (Fort Worth)	1,934

Source: Federal Reserve Branch Bank of San Antonio

TABLE 10-8

THE TWENTY LARGEST U. S. COMMERCIAL BANKS
(As of December 31, 1976)

Name and Location of Bank	Assets (Million dollars)
BankAmerica Corp. (San Francisco)	73,913
Citicorp (New York)	64,282
Chase Manhattan Corp. (New York)	45,638
Manufacturers Hanover Corp. (New York)	31,483
J. P. Morgan & Co. (New York)	28,766
Chemical New York Corp.	26,614
Bankers Trust New York Corp. (New York)	22,249
Continental Illinois Corp. (Chicago)	21,975
First Chicago Corp. (Chicago)	19,834
Western Bankcorp (Los Angeles)	19,672
Security Pacific Corp. (Los Angeles)	16,401
Wells Fargo & Co. (San Francisco)	12,969
Marine Midland Banks, Inc. (Buffalo)	10,719
Crocker National Corp. (San Francisco)	10,711
Charter New York Corp. (New York)	10,209
Mellon National Corp. (Pittsburgh)	9,353
First National Boston Corp. (Boston)	8,499
Northwest Bankcorp (Minneapolis)	8,358
First Bank System, Inc. (Minneapolis)	7,844
National Detroit Corp. (Detroit)	7,553

*Includes bank holding companies.
Source: Board of Governors of the Federal Reserve System, courtesy Federal Reserve Branch Bank of San Antonio.

commercial and political risks, or he may choose a policy for political risk only. Premiums are based on the length of credit, whether or not there is security, and the country to which goods are being shipped. The recipient of the goods is normally required to place a minimum down payment of 10 to 20 percent, and then the exporter can obtain insurance from FCIA on the balance.

Also of great assistance in facilitating foreign transactions is the Export-Import Bank (Eximbank). This agency works in conjunction with FCIA and in many instances will underwrite a transaction which FCIA would not accept. In particular, Eximbank guarantees have been afforded numerous projects which incorporate foreign investment with export transactions in capital equipment. Texas bankers have praised the aggressive leadership of Eximbank in supporting the growth of the state's international trade and financial sectors.

It is obvious that the state of Texas is extremely important in the international trade of the United States. Texas' historical position as a net exporter to the rest of the world has added substantially to the international position of the United States, and the state's consumer marketplace constitutes an important outlet for foreign-made goods. Even in the aftermath of the energy crisis, Texas foreign trade remains without a significant deficit, due to dramatic increases in exports.

The commodity composition of Texas exports basically reflects the resource base of Texas and that of the Plains States. Because of this, agricultural-grain products and chemical products loom heavily in the value of state export sales. On the import side, the variety of goods brought in is extensive, since Texas and the surrounding states constitute one of the nation's most substantial and rapidly growing consumer markets.

At the present time, much of Texas' international commerce is financed by non-Texas banking institutions. This has been brought about because of federal laws which permit large Eastern and West Coast banks to maintain international subsidiaries in Texas and also because state banking laws prohibit banks in Texas from carrying on branch operations. However, some of the larger Texas banks and also many of the bank holding companies which they have founded have recently become more active in international trade financing.

In the future, it can be expected that international commerce will be one of the major engines of growth for Texas. Texas will continue to be a substantial exporter of several commodities (cereals, chemicals, certain petroleum products, machinery and equipment) which are in great world demand. Further, the flow of imports into Texas will grow along with the state's population and industrial base. Finally, Texas will obviously continue to be the gateway for the United States–Mexico trade. This trade is expected to grow substantially as Mexico joins the ranks of industrialized nations during the last quarter of the twentieth century.

NOTES

1. This section briefly summarizes introductory materials on economic analysis of international trade which are presented in greater detail in most of the popular texts on economic principles. The reader may wish to consult one of the following for further study: Paul A. Samuelson, *Economics*, 9th ed. (New York: McGraw-Hill, Inc., 1973), chapter 34; or Richard T. Gill, *Economics and the Public Interest*, 2nd ed. (Pacific Palisades, California: Goodyear Publishing Company, Inc., 1972), chapter 13.

2. The reader may notice that the specificied 1:1 exchange rate initially would make it possible for importers in the labor-scarce country to buy both steel *and* wheat at the lower prices prevailing in the labor-abundant country and resell at home at a profit. However, this one-way trade would cause a deficit in the balance of payments of the labor-scarce country, and the value of its currency would fall. If, because of such a deficit and alteration in the exchange rate, it takes 1.5 dollars of the labor-scarce country to get one dollar's worth of merchandise from the labor-abundant country, then to import a pound of steel from the labor-abundant country would cost $5×1.5= $7.50 and to import a bushel of wheat would cost $7×1.5=$10.50, in terms of dollars of the labor-scarce country. With this exchange rate, only wheat would be imported into the labor-scarce country. The reader can verify by similar reasoning that such an exchange rate would ensure that only steel could be profitably imported into the labor-abundant country, which would spend just $0.67 of its currency to get one dollar's worth of the currency of the labor-scarce country.

3. Several landlocked ports of entry, Denver, Oklahoma City, Tulsa, Albuquerque, and smaller New Mexico cities, are included in the Houston Customs Region, but the volume of trade through these

ports is a very small percentage of the total trade for the region.

4. The balance of the statistical information presented in this section is based on the U. S. Department of Commerce Report, "Highlights of U. S. Export and Import," Report FT-990, December 1976 and previous issues.

5. See U. S. Department of Commerce, Social and Economic Statistics Administration, Bureau of the Census, "Survey of the Origin of Exports of Manufacturing Establishments in 1971," in *Current Industrial Reports* (Washington: U. S. Government Printing Office, 1973).

6. Ibid.

7. Ibid.

8. "Report FT-990," op. cit. All percentages are of total dollar sales.

9. Ibid.

10. See: Mexico, Secretaria de Industria y Comercio, Direccion General de Estadistica, *Anuario estadistico del comerico exterior de los estodos unidos mexicanos*, (Mexico, D. F., 1974 and later years).

11. Edge Act Banks find their authority in the 1957 and 1963 revision of regulation K of section 25-a of the Federal Reserve Act, which allows United States commercial banks to form such financing subsidiaries. The 25 July 1977 issue of *Business Week* (p. 105) reported that seventeen major foreign banks also set up representative offices in Texas in recent years.

12. The reader who desires an intensive analysis of this topic is referred to J. Fred Weston and Bart Sorge, *International Managerial Finance*, (Homewood, Illinois: Richard D. Irwin, Inc., 1972) chapter 4.

ELEVEN

A FISCAL PROFILE OF TEXAS
Daniel C. Morgan, Jr.

In the late 1970s two Texans might be discussing the fiscal state of their state. One is delighted: "Our state government is levying practically no taxes on us and is still acquiring almost more revenue than it can spend and our cities have high bond ratings and none of those problems plaguing the old cities of the East and North." The other is dejected: "Our taxes have shot up so fast in the last two decades that it looks as if they may go out of orbit when we use up those surpluses, which we're doing right now." Is this merely the view of an optimist against that of a pessimist?

Over the last twenty to twenty-five years America's system of fiscal federalism has been changing dynamically. Perhaps the dominant features of this change are these: (1) the public sector has been growing faster than the private sector; (2) within the public sector, the state-local portion has grown much faster than the federal portion; and (3) the fiscal relationships among the levels of government have been shifting rapidly. Between 1954 and 1976 total government spending rose from 26 1/2 percent of the nation's gross national product (GNP) to over 34 percent. While federal government expenditures were increasby 21 percent over this period, state-local expenditures were increasing by 49 percent. Table 11-1 presents some of the magnitudes of revenues, rather than expenditures. We see state-local revenues rising from $31 billion in fiscal 1955 to $208 billion in fiscal 1974, an increase from 8.2 percent of GNP to 15.3 percent. We see federal grants increasing from $3 billion or 10 percent of state-local revenue in 1955 to $42 billion or 20 percent of state-local revenue in 1974.

A Fiscal Profile of Texas 245

It is estimated that by the close of fiscal 1977 we shall have surpassed $70 billion or nearly 27 percent of state-local revenue. Table 11-1 shows property taxes declining from more than 34 percent of state-local revenues in 1955 to less than 23 percent in 1974. Table 11-2 shows us how rapidly employment has risen in the public sector, both in absolute numbers and in relation to private sector employment. Between 1955 and 1973 it was state and local government that was

TABLE 11-1

SOURCES OF REVENUE OF STATE AND LOCAL GOVERNMENTS
ALL 50 STATES, 1955 AND 1974

Source of Revenue	Amount (Billion dollars)		As percent of GNP		As percent of total revenues	
	1955	1974	1955	1974	1955	1974
Federal grants-in-aid	3.1	41.8	0.8	3.1	10.0	20.1
Taxes	23.6	131.2	6.2	9.7	75.7	63.0
Property	10.7	47.8	2,8	3.5	34.3	22.9
General sales & gross receipts	3.1	26.3	0.8	1.9	9.9	12.6
Selective sales	4.8	20.2	1.3	1.5	15.2	9.7
Individual income	1.2	19.5	0.3	1.4	3.9	9.4
Corporation income	0.7	6.0	0.2	0.4	2.4	2.9
Other	3.1	11.4	0.8	0.8	10.0	5.5
Charges & miscellaneous	4.5	35.2	1.2	2.6	14.3	16.9
Totals	31.3	208.2	8.2	15.3	100.0	100.0

Source: Emil M. Sunley, Jr., "State and Local Governments," Chapt. 9 in *Setting National Priorities: The Next Ten Years* (Washington, D.C.: The Brookings Institution, 1976).

TABLE 11-2

FULL-TIME EQUIVALENT EMPLOYEES, 1955 AND 1973

"Industry"	Number (In millions)		Percent of total employees	
	1955	1973	1955	1973
All "industries"	54.9	75.9	100.0	100.0
Federal government*	1.7	2.0	3.1	2.6
State and local governments**	4.1	9.1	7.5	12.0

*Excludes military and employees of government enterprises. **Excludes employees of government enterprises.
Source: Department of Commerce, *National Income and Products Accounts*, Table 6.4 and *Survey of Current Business* (July, 1974), Table 6.4. The computations and form are borrowed from Sunley, "State and Local Governments" cited in Table 11-1.

the source of this growth and not the federal government. While federal civilian employment hardly increased, state-local employment rose 122 percent. As a percentage of total employment, federal civilian employment declined from 3.1 percent in 1955 to 2.6 percent in 1973, while state and local employment rose from a 7 1/2 percent share to a 12 percent share.

We discover similar magnitudes in Texas. It is probably correct to say that government is our biggest industry, just about any way we choose to measure. This is so even in terms of income generated. (Table 11-3 documents this, comparing Texas with the entire nation.) We see that in Texas, 18 percent of labor and proprietors' income (a close proxy for "income generated" or "value added") derives from government (federal, state, and local combined). No industry for which Texas is famous—oil and gas, chemicals, petrochemicals, cattle, cotton, rice, fruits and vegetables, transportation, electronics, aerospace, banking and insurance, timber, tourism—is close to this figure. For example, oil and gas and other minerals ("mining" in Table 11-3) generate just over 4 percent of Texas income, and the entire agricultural industry generates only 2 1/2 percent. The only way another in-

TABLE 11-3
PERCENTAGE DISTRIBUTION OF LABOR AND PROPRIETORS' INCOME
BY INDUSTRIAL CATEGORY, UNITED STATES & TEXAS, 1975

"Industrial" Category	Percent of Total Income	
	U. S.	Texas
Farm	3.3	2.5
Manufacturing: Durables	15.7	11.2
Manufacturing: Nondurables	9.1	9.0
Mining	1.3	4.2
Contract Construction	5.3	7.0
Wholesale and Retail Trade	16.2	19.2
Finance, Insurance and Real Estate	5.2	5.5
Transportation, Communication and Public Utilities	6.9	7.7
Services	15.5	15.5
Other Industries	0.3	0.4
Government	17.5	18.0
Federal Civilian	[4.2	[4.2
Federal Military	2.1	3.8
State and Local	11.2]	10.0]

Source: U. S. Department of Commerce, *Survey of Current Business,* April 1976; cited in *1976 Annual Financial Report of The State of Texas, Volume I,* for the fiscal year ended August 31, 1976, Bob Bullock, Comptroller of Public Accounts, p. 1.

dustry can equal government is to combine all "manufacturing" industries or to combine all wholesale and retail trading enterprises, and even then the totals barely exceed government. One might protest that when the federal portion is removed from this total, government falls from 18 percent to 10 percent of total Texas income. But even a brief perusal of Table 11-3 is sufficient to instruct that this 10 percent is big business, and its finance is big finance.

Establishing a method to classify the disparate fiscal systems of states (in order to compare them) has long been a question.

ACIR'S FIVE SIGNIFICANT FEATURES OF STATE–LOCAL REVENUE SYSTEMS

One method of comparison has been suggested by the Advisory Commission on Intergovernmental Relations, or ACIR. This commission was created by Congress in 1959 to monitor the operations of the American federal system and make bipartisan recommendations for improvement, and it has evolved as one of the most highly respected authorities in the area. ACIR says that the questions it has found to be of greatest concern regarding state-local tax systems are 1) tax burden and tax'effort, 2) distribution of burden among the income classes, 3) diversification or the mix of the sources of revenue, 4) relative roles of state and local governments, and 5) integration of equity features into the system (such as food exemption in the sales tax and "circuit breaker" in the property tax). Table 11-4 has been constructed to give first approximation answers to ACIR's questions, comparing Texas' fiscal system with a composite of fifty state-local systems.

Table 11-4 suggests that 1) taxes in Texas are low, both per capita and as a percentage of personal income; 2) the yield is derived in a manner similar to that of the average state in some ways, such as reliance on federal aid, property taxes and general sales taxes, but different in that Texas employs no individual or corporate income tax; 3) the state government supplies about the same total tax revenue in Texas as it does in the average state—nearly three-fifths; 4) the burden pattern is regressive by conventional measures of progressiveness, as it is in most states; and 5) Texas equity-integrating features do not differ significantly from most states—there is a food exemption from the sales tax and no "circuit breaker" in the property tax system.

Texas' low taxes and taxing effort imply low expenditures for public services. Federal aid is insufficient to bring expenditures to the national average, and the Texas tax base, presently outpacing that of the average state, is not high enough to enable the low rates necessary to produce an average yield. To illustrate, here are the public expenditures per capita for 1975:

	Total	Education Total	Local	Highways	Welfare	Health & Hospitals
U.S. average	$1,077	$412	$289	$106	$128	$88
Texas	838	363	249	100	73	69

MAXWELL SCHOOL'S COMPARISON OF FISCAL SYSTEMS

A new technique for classifying the unique fiscal systems of the fifty states has been developed by David Puryear, Ray Bahl, and Seymour Sacks, all of the Maxwell School of Syracuse University. This method groups the fiscal systems of states according to the division of financing responsibility among the three levels of government (federal,

TABLE 11-4

FIVE SIGNIFICANT FEATURES OF STATE-LOCAL REVENUE SYSTEMS
TEXAS VS. AVERAGE OF FIFTY STATES, 1975

	Texas	U.S.
1. Burden and effort		
A. Per capita state-local taxes	$515.00	$664.00
B. Taxes as % of personal income	10.6%	12.3%
2. Source of state-local general revenue		
A. Federal aid	20.7%	20.6%
B. Taxes		
Property	22.1	22.6
General sales	14.0	12.8
Income (individual & corp.)	0.0	12.3
Other	23.2	14.3
C. Charges and miscellaneous	19.9	17.4
3. State government percentage of total taxes	57.7%	56.7%
4. Incidence (Basis: by one-year family income)		
A. Progressive		5 states
B. Proportional		15 states
C. Regressive	X	30 states
5. Equity features, high-yield taxes		
A. Food exempt from sales tax or income tax credit?	Yes	25 states
B. Circuit breaker property tax relief?	No	25 states

Source: Advisory Commission on Intergovernmental Relations, *Significant Features of Fiscal Federalism 1976-77 Edition, Vol. 11-Revenue and Debt* (Washington, D.C.: March 1977), M-110-Table A.

TABLE 11-5

CLASSIFICATION OF STATE FISCAL SYSTEMS:
NONWELFARE EXPENDITURES OF STATE AND LOCAL GOVERNMENTS
1972

	Expenditure Responsibility		
	High State	Moderate State	Low State
High State Financing Responsibility			
High Expenditure Per Capita	Alaska Delaware Hawaii Vermont		
Moderate Expenditure Per Capita	Idaho Utah West Virginia	Louisiana New Mexico	
Low Expenditure Per Capita	Kentucky South Carolina	Arkansas Mississippi North Carolina Oklahoma	
Moderate State Financing Responsibility			
High Expenditure Per Capita	Montana Wyoming	Arizona Maryland Oregon Washington	Minnesota Wisconsin
Moderate Expenditure Per Capita	North Dakota New Hampshire	Connecticut Pennsylvania	Florida
Low Expenditure Per Capita	Maine Rhode Island	Alabama Georgia Tennessee Virginia	Iowa
Low State Financing Responsibility			
High Expenditure Per Capita			California Nevada New York
Moderate Expenditure Per Capita		Colorado Kansas Nebraska South Dakota	Illinois Indiana Massachusetts Michigan Missouri New Jersey
Low Expenditure Per Capita			Ohio TEXAS

Notes: High, moderate, and low designations for each category relate to whether the state government placed in the top 15, middle 20, or bottom 15 among states. State expenditure responsibility is the state government's share of total state and local direct expenditures. State financial responsibility is the share of total state and local expenditures financed by the state government. Per capita expenditures is total state and local expenditures per capita.

Source: Metropolitan Studies Program, Maxwell School of Citizenship and Public Affairs, Syracuse University. Calculated from various data sources. Presented in Table 7 of Advisory Commission on Intergovernmental Relations, *Federal Grants: Their Effects on State-Local Expenditures, Employment Levels, Wage Rates* (Washington, D. C., GPO, February 1976), A-61.

state, local); division of expenditure responsibility among the three levels; and level of expenditure, combining the state and the local levels of government.

"Financing responsibility" refers to the percent of state and local expenditures financed by each of the three levels of government. The federal financing measure consists of the federal grants to local governments. The state share consists of direct state expenditures and grants to local governments minus local government's payments to state governments and federal grants to state governments. The local financing measure equals direct spending to local governments and payments to state governments minus state grants to local governments and direct federal-to-local grants. Each financing measure is designed to deal with the originating source of finance. "Expenditure responsibility" describes final authority for the spending of the funds. Thus, in a typical state, the "expenditure ratio" for the state government would compute very high for highways but much lower for both education and health, where it would be divided with local government.

The new Maxwell School technique groups Texas among the lowest fifteen states in expenditure per capita, in financing responsibility of the state government, and in expenditure responsibility of the state government. Texas is ranked among the eleven states which are the most "local government dominated." The others, as Table 11-5 shows, are California, Nevada, New York, Illinois, Indiana, Massachusetts, Michigan, Missouri, New Jersey, and Ohio—populous, urban, and high-income states. Many will be surprised by this finding and by Table 11-5's mapping of the Maxwell School findings. The inference is that Texas' closest fiscal relatives today are not its four neighboring states, the Southern states, or the oil and gas producing states. By this technique, Texas' closest relative may be Ohio.

TEXAS TAXES

Perhaps the most distinguishing feature of the Texas fiscal structure is how comparatively low its taxes are. Table 11-6 shows this for 1974, a year in which Texas ranked forty-third in state-local tax per capita and state-local tax per $1,000 of state personal income. Tax per $1,000 of income is a conventional measure of burden and effort; according to it, the only states beneath Texas in 1974 were North Dakota, Missouri, Indiana, Ohio, North Carolina, Illinois, and Arkansas. In per capita taxation the only states below Texas were Kentucky, Mississippi, Alabama, North Carolina, West Virginia, New Mexico,

TABLE 11-6

DIRECT STATE AND LOCAL GENERAL EXPENDITURES FROM OWN REVENUE SOURCES PER $1,000 OF PERSONAL INCOME AND PER CAPITA, BY STATE, FISCAL YEAR 1974

State	Per $1,000 of Personal Income		Per Capita	
	Amount	Rank	Amount	Rank
U. S. Average	$148	—	$ 742	—
Alaska	318	1	1,848	1
New York	209	2	1,202	2
Hawaii	194	3	1,049	3
Vermont	190	4	762	17
Wyoming	174	5	801	14
Nevada	171	6	942	4
Wisconsin	169	7	805	13
Washington	165	8	840	9
Minnesota	163	9	832	10
Arizona	162	10	725	21
California	162	11	880	5
Massachusetts	162	12	851	7
Maryland	160	13	870	6
Oregon	158	14	748	18
Louisiana	156	15	613	32
Utah	152	16	612	33
Colorado	151	17	741	19
Michigan	150	18	828	11
Maine	149	19	596	36
South Carolina	149	20	565	42
New Mexico	146	21	556	45
Mississippi	146	22	509	49
Delaware	145	23	844	8
Montana	143	24	656	29
Pennsylvania	140	25	701	22
Florida	139	26	651	30
New Jersey	139	27	815	12
Idaho	138	28	588	39
West Virginia	137	29	545	46
Virginia	137	30	657	28
Georgia	137	31	590	38
Tennessee	136	32	558	44
Rhode Island	135	33	680	24
Alabama	134	34	513	48
New Hampshire	134	35	614	31
Oklahoma	133	36	566	41
Connecticut	131	37	777	16
Iowa	130	38	699	23
South Dakota	128	39	605	35
Kansas	126	40	674	25
Nebraska	126	41	664	26
Kentucky	126	42	506	50
Texas	126	43	562	43
Illinois	126	44	731	20
North Carolina	124	45	522	47
District of Columbia	121	46	790	15
Ohio	120	47	607	34
Indiana	119	48	594	37
Missouri	118	49	569	40
North Dakota	115	50	658	27
Arkansas	108	51	422	51

Source: Emil M. Sunley, Jr., "State and Local Governments," *Setting National Priorities: The Next Ten Years* (Washington, D. C.: The Brookings Institution, 1976), Table 9-9.

Tennessee, and Arkansas. Over the last two decades Texas has remained at or below 80 percent of the average state in state-local tax per $1,000 of state income. It would appear that this relative burden or effort is declining. Between 1 July 1973 and 1 January 1977, Texas was not among the thirty state governments increasing tax rates; in fact, Governor Dolph Briscoe has taken pride in promising and delivering "no new taxes" during his terms of office.

Such burden estimates may be slightly complicated by the matter of "exportability" of taxes between states. Whether in fact taxes can be exported is something of a dispute among economists, but it would seem plausible that from any budget constraint states would attempt to maximize collections from out-of-state residents. The Texas revenue system has generally been believed capable of exporting a higher percentage of its yield than that of the average state. The primary reason is the state's relatively high reliance on severance taxes on the oil and gas industry. With federal regulation of interstate natural gas prices at levels below profit-maximizing points, it has appeared easy to pass on a significant portion of such taxes without doing full tax damage to Texas producers and consumers. If this estimate is correct, Texas taxes are lower relative to other states than official figures suggest.

The relatively heavy Texas reliance on severance taxes and the light reliance on income taxes is further indicated by Table 11-7 which presents the distribution of total revenue sources for both the state and local governments, comparing Texas with the composite state. We see a blank in the column for Texas' individual income tax as Texas is one of six states without some form of individual income tax. (The others are Florida, Nevada, South Dakota, Washington, and Wyoming. Three states have only limited-version individual income taxes: Connecticut taxes capital gains and dividends, Tennessee taxes only interest and dividents, and New Hampshire taxes interest and dividends and levies a commuter tax.) Texas also levies no corporation income tax, along with Nevada, Washington, and Wyoming. This is true at a time when income taxes are beginning to produce one third of the tax revenues of the states levying them, a very high percentage measured by the standard of history. So it is hardly surprising that Texas has low total taxes.

But Texas taxes are also low compared with those which all states levy. One of these is the gasoline tax. Each year the Texas gasoline tax is lowest per gallon of the fifty states or else is tied for lowest.

For instance, on 1 July 1976, the Texas tax was lowest in the nation, at five cents per gallon. Most states were levying eight, eight and one-half, or nine cents, and some were levying ten or eleven cents per gallon. The general sales tax in Texas is also low by comparison. If one looks only at the rate of this tax, which is 4 percent for the state government and 1 percent for cities which opt to piggy back (and most do), the Texas sales tax appears only medium-low among the states. But the base may be the nation's narrowest: food and medicine are exempted from the tangible personal property base; practically all personal services are excluded; and transportation, lodging, water, and telephones are exempted. If one subscribes to a full consumer burden theory of sales tax incidence, Texas has the least regressive sales tax in the nation. Finally, another "tax," Texas' college tuitions, fees, and student charges, is among the lowest in the nation. The propriety of this practice is fiercely debated by academicians but only tepidly by Texas politicians.

TABLE 11-7

PERCENTAGE DISTRIBUTION OF STATE AND LOCAL REVENUE FROM OWN SOURCES, TEXAS & ALL 50 STATES, 1975

	Texas	All 50 States
State government		
General sales, gross receipts	15.1	13.7
Excise and business receipts	13.9	10.2
Individual income	–	10.4
Corporation income	–	3.7
Licenses and franchises	5.1	3.5
Other (including severance)	9.0	2.8
Charges and miscellaneous	10.7	9.2
Local government		
Property	27.3	27.6
Other (including city sales tax)	4.4	6.2
Charges and miscellaneous	14.4	12.7

Source: ACIR, *Significant Features of Fiscal Federalism 1976-77*, Table 26.

Texas does severely tax tobacco. Since 1966, the Texas tax per pack of cigarettes has been among the highest of the states. At eighteen and one-half cents per pack in 1976, Texas narrowly lagged New Jersey and Connecticut. These state taxes are in addition to federal taxes. The median state tax in 1976 was twelve cents per pack. In a typical year the Texas state government collects a higher percentage of its revenues from tobacco taxes than 96 percent of other state governments.

High tobacco taxes suggest that Texas might follow its fundamentalist heritage and tax on a sumptuary principle. This is the case with other states of the Confederacy, which levy the nation's highest alcoholic beverage taxes. Yet Texas alcoholic beverage taxes are only about median-high, well below those of Alabama, Mississippi, North Carolina, South Carolina, Georgia, Florida, Virginia, and Arkansas.

Just how low the Texas tax burden or tax effort is depends only on the measure one prefers. The methods and studies have been numerous—according to personal income, value-added, wealth, sales, and "representative tax systems," all with and without economic and demographic variables controlled.[1] The conclusion is invariably the same: the Texas burden is comparatively *very* low. A recent study by the Advisory Commission on Intergovernmental Relations finds Texas' "tax effort" to be lower than any of the states but Oklahoma (lowest), Nevada, and Arkansas, and at the same time possessed of more "untapped tax capacity" than any other state except Ohio.[2]

THE ROLE OF FEDERAL GRANTS

What has been the role of federal grants in Texas' fiscal structure relative to their role in other states? This question is a surprisingly difficult one, and an important Advisory Commission study has recently completed an extensive attempt to answer it.[3] ACIR concludes that federal grants do increase the level of public spending in the state rather than merely substituting for state and local finance. It finds Texas to be among the top ten states in "participation" (high response residuals) with no matching, low matching, and formula types of federal aid programs, and among the middle thirty states with project, state recipient, local recipient, and high matching grants. The study finds that federal grants raise employment levels in high participant states, and Texas is an above-average recipient state.

THE ROLE OF POSITIVE GOVERNMENTAL INDUCEMENTS

Southwestern and Southern states are known for their positive governmental inducements to industrial and commercial location. Historically, Texas has not been prominent in these practices, at least at the state level of government. The most prevalent inducements are state industrial finance authorities, local industrial bond financing, tax concessions, statewide development corporations, and local private development corporations.[4]

State industrial finance societies are state agencies that grant credit directly to new or expanding industry or guarantee the repayment of loans made by private lenders. Among Texas' neighboring states, Oklahoma led the way in 1960 with a constitutional amendment granting authority to make industrial loans to private firms. There were few state imitators; Texas did not follow.

Local industrial bond financing programs, on the other hand, have been important to Texas' competitor-neighbors. These programs authorize local governments to issue revenue bonds and/or general obligation bonds to obtain funding for acquisition of industrial facilities or for improvement of existing facilities. The governments then lease these facilities to private firms. Interest from the bonds is exempt from federal income tax, and since the facilities are governmentally owned, they are generally exempt from local and state property taxation. Though Texas has not, her surrounding states have all adopted variants of industrial bond financing.

Many states either grant tax concessions to industry or allow their municipalities to do so. Louisiana has received the greatest national attention for its extensive program of exempting new industry from all state and local property taxes for ten years. Other Southwestern states adopted quite limited versions of the Louisiana program. However, Texas did not, at least not openly, for to do so would have been to violate the state constitution. An illicit approach to tax concessions under the Texas constitution—the device of undervaluing property— is openly practiced in Texas and surrounding states.

The statewide development corporation, employed by Arkansas, operates under the state charter but employs private funds. Texas has not openly employed this institution, but does operate with public funds, groups whose purpose is "development." An example is the Texas Industrial Commission.

The local development corporation is a private inducement program which has become widespread in Southwestern states, including Texas. It is often established by local chambers of commerce under state charter and permits private funds to be pooled for industrial development. Generally, these corporations are reticent about making funds available to new concerns that are expected to compete with firms already located in the area.

REGRESSIVITY OF THE COMPOSITE STATE–LOCAL SYSTEM

If one aggregates all of the state and local taxes, what in terms of family income, computed for a one-year time period does the Texas burden add up to? The answer, as seen in Table 11-8, can be influenced by varying the incidence assumptions employed, the income definition, and so on, but the primary conclusion will probably hold: that the overall tax system of Texas is slightly more regressive than that of the average state while its burden on the income classes is lower across the board. Assuredly, the state's after-tax distribution of income differs insignificantly from its before-tax distribution.

The variable which would most alter Table 11-8's figures is employment of an alternative theory of property tax incidence. Tax incidence deals with the effects of taxes on real incomes. A tax is thought to change the price of things people buy and the things they sell, thereby redistributintg real income. The property tax is actually an amalgam of several types of taxes. Immense controversy centers on how this amalgam works and therefore on how property tax yields should be allocated to the various family income classes. The issue here is whether the property tax is a consumer burden or a capital burden. The effect of the alternative assumptions has been estimated as follows for a tax yielding 5 percent of overall personal income:[5]

Family Income Class	Consumer Burden	Capital Burden
$ 0 - $ 3,000	13.0%	7.0%
3,000 - 5,000	8.0	5.4
5,000 - 10,000	5.9	3.6
10,000 - 15,000	4.9	2.6
15,000 - 20,000	4.7	2.9
20,000 - 25,000	4.4	3.7
25,000 - 50,000	4.4	5.7
50,000 - 100,000	3.7	14.1
100,000 - 500,000	3.5	22.4
500,000 - 1 million	3.0	24.5
$1 million and over	2.1	18.2
All incomes	5.0%	5.0%

Shifting incidence assumptions is unlikely to greatly affect Table 11-8's conclusions regarding Texas' position relative to other states, though it would slightly affect the relative burden of the family income classes.

THE STATE GOVERNMENT

"State-local government" is anything but a single entity. There are between 3,000 and 4,000 local governments in Texas—counties, school districts, municipalities, special districts, and others—more than almost any other state in the nation. Comparison and generalization about these units is hazardous. But one government is more important in terms of fund-raising than these thousands combined, and that is the government of the state of Texas. Perhaps the best way to commence a discussion of the state of Texas is to excerpt a letter of transmittal to Governor Briscoe:[6]

> *The state's fiscal year ending August 31, 1976 was, again a record year for both revenues and expenditures for state government. Revenues of $8.05 billion supported expenditures of $6.4 billion, leaving a net cash balance of $1.6 billion. This cash balance was also a record figure and, as in 1975, almost $200 million more than the cash balance at the beginning of the fiscal year....*
>
> *Respectfully submitted,*
>
> *Bob Bullock*
> *Comptroller of Public Accounts*

Any state governor would have been delighted to receive such a report, particularly after receiving reports of ever-higher cash balances, such as those of the Texas state government: $474 million in 1971, $574 million in 1972, $916 million in 1973, $1.26 billion in 1974,

TABLE 11-8

STATE-LOCAL TAX BURDEN AS A PERCENTAGE OF FAMILY INCOME
(TEXAS VS. 50-STATE AVERAGE) 1974

	(Tax Burden as percent of gross income, family of four)					
	$5,000	$7,500	$10,000	$17,500	$25,000	$50,000
All States	11.3	10.0	8.9	8.5	8.1	7.8
Texas	9.3	7.5	6.1	5.6	4.6	3.5

Source: Stephen Lile, *Family Tax Burdens*, prepared for Kentucky Department of Revenue, December 1957; reproduced in ACIR *Significant Features of Fiscal Federalism 1976-77*.

$1.45 billion in 1975, $1.64 billion in 1976. These closing balances were occurring while total state expenditures were increasing from $3.4 billion in 1971 to $6.2 billion in 1976, or by 82 percent in only five years.

One might protest that this increase was only slightly higher than the rate of inflation, but it must be recalled that all this transpired during the most depressed period since the 1930s in a state that possessed no income tax or property tax (the state government's property tax is nominal only today) and the nation's most narrowly-based sales tax. Increased federal assistance is only partially responsible for the high receipts. The federal government assumed the majority of welfare activities, and federal funds increased by 75 percent between 1971 and 1976, but state government tax collections doubled for the period.

Table 11-9 presents the full picture of finance of the state of Texas from 1971 through 1976. We see that tax collections generally contribute about 60 percent of the state's net revenues while federal funding contributes between 25 and 30 percent. Traditionally, the general sales tax is the biggest revenue raiser and its share has been accelerating, from 31 percent in 1971 to 38 percent in 1976. Recently, however, the sales tax has been rivaled by the severance tax. Oil and gas production taxes yielded 15 percent of state taxes in 1971, they exceeded 20 percent in fiscal 1976, and in mid 1977 their share was continuing to expand. This is so even without severance taxes on minerals such as uranium and lignite, which many legislators are presently pressing for.

Federal funding's total share has changed little since 1971, but its direction has changed from highways to alternative functions. This is one of the reasons Governor Briscoe and the sixty-fifth Legislature felt compelled to increase state governmental funding, though opinions differed widely as to the correct magnitude of increase. In fiscal 1976, the state of Texas granted over $2 billion to its local governments, but all but 4 percent was to local school districts. The state government's feeling seems to be that since local governments receive federal grants and revenue sharing plus the 1 percent piggyback on the state sales tax for the cities, this is nearly adequate for state aid when one takes account of the immense assistance to public school districts.

To what should the state's relative prosperity be attributed? Clearly, much is explained by the relatively rapid economic growth of the state. History will probably record 1975 as the year when Texas overtook the average state in per capita income. Unadjusted money

TABLE 11-9

PERCENTAGE DISTRIBUTION OF TOTAL REVENUES BY SOURCE STATE OF TEXAS, 1971-1976 (FISCAL YEARS)

	Percent of Total					
	1971	1972	1973	1974	1975	1976
Tax Collections by Major Tax						
Sales tax	31.7%	35.2%	35.8%	37.2%	37.6%	37.8%
Oil & gas production taxes	15.2	13.1	13.0	17.1	19.7	20.3
Motor fuel taxes (gasoline, diesel, LPG)	16.7	15.2	14.9	12.9	11.7	10.9
Cigarette & tobacco taxes	10.2	9.9	9.5	8.2	7.8	7.2
Motor vehicle sales tax	4.9	7.1	7.6	6.5	6.0	6.9
Corporation franchise tax	6.6	5.5	5.2	5.1	4.9	5.5
Alcoholic beverages taxes	3.5	3.4	3.2	2.9	2.8	2.5
Insurance occupation tax	3.0	2.8	3.0	2.8	2.7	2.6
Inheritance tax	1.8	1.7	1.8	1.7	1.4	1.5
Ad Valorem (property) taxes	3.2	2.6	2.2	1.7	1.3	0.9
Utility taxes	1.1	1.0	1.1	1.1	1.3	1.5
Telephone tax	0.9	0.9	0.9	0.9	0.9	0.9
Total Tax Collections	100.0%	100.0%	100.0%	100.0%	100.0%	100.0%
[Total Taxes, Absolute Amounts]*:	$1.995	$2.344	$2.583	$3.026	$3.370	$3.913
Revenues by Source						
Tax collections	57.6%	58.5%	58.1%	60.5%	59.4%	59.4%
Licenses & fees	7.2	6.8	6.6	6.2	5.6	5.2
Interest income	2.9	2.8	3.0	3.4	3.8	3.6
Federal funding [Total]	[29.1]	[28.7]	[29.1]	[25.7]	[26.8]	[26.9]
[Federal Funding (total) Absolute Amounts]*:	$1.007	$1.150	$1.293	$1.283	$1.524	$1.775
Highways	8.0%	6.0%	4.9%	4.4%	4.7%	4.7%
Health	0.4	0.5	0.4	0.4	0.6	0.6
Welfare	14.0	15.2	13.6	11.2	11.9	11.8
Education	4.5	4.8	4.8	4.8	4.5	5.0
Revenue sharing	0	0	2.9	1.9	1.7	1.5
Other	2.2	2.2	2.5	2.9	3.4	3.3
Land Income: Rents, Royalties, Sales	2.2	2.0	2.0	3.2	3.2	3.7
Other Revenue Sources	1.0	1.2	1.2	1.0	1.2	1.2
Total Net Revenues	100.0%	100.0%	100.0%	100.0%	100.0%	100.0%
[Total Net Revenues, Absolute Amounts]*:	$3.461	$4.483	$5.017	$5.916	$6.937	$8.047

*Amounts in billions.
Source: *1976 Annual Financial Report of the State of Texas, Volume 1, for the fiscal year ended August 31, 1976,* Bob Bullock, Comptroller of Public Accounts (November 1, 1976, Tables IV and V.

income per capita in Texas was still only 92 percent of the national average in 1977,[7] but after cost of living adjustments were made, the figure became 105 percent of the United States average.[8] The relatively rapid growth rate moved the Texas share of the nation's personal income from 5 percent in 1969 to 5 1/2 percent in 1975,[9] and this relative growth rate appears unabated even as the nation moves out of its severe depression. In the first months of economic recovery in early 1976, Texas personal income grew at a 15 percent rate compared with the nation's 11 percent.

How much of this above average growth derives from government itself? One popular hypothesis is that the federal government is a key factor in the relative gains of the "Sunbelt States," which include Texas.[10] Some explain it in terms of the success of Texas' politicians in capturing important committee positions in Congress, the Lyndon B. Johnson presidency, being "insiders," capitalizing the benefits of Texas importance in presidential nominations and elections, emphasizing the dangers of killing off existing federally-supported programs, projects, bases, and such. Others argue "power elitist" theories, that is, that the federal government, influenced by power groups, favors Texas, the South, and the Southwest in an attempt to foster development where labor is weakest and where attitudes are least humane.[11] The latter hypothesis would appear more plausible for the Sunbelt states as a group than for Texas. In 1975, the federal spending in the average Southern Sunbelt state was $1,356 per person as compared with the federal tax (total) per person of only $1,188; by contrast the figures for Texas were $1,296 for spending and $1,264 for taxes.[12] Proponents of the hypothesis would challenge this conclusion at least so far as defense spending is concerned.[13] Whatever may be the case for Texas as an entity, the hypothesis proponents could make a strong argument regarding certain cities or areas, for example, the San Antonio and Fort Worth areas are relatively heavily dependent on defense.

If we accept the conclusion that the relative prosperity of the state government is only partially explained by the state's economic growth and that in turn this growth is not explained by the influence of the federal government, then other factors must be important. Dominant among them is the state government's heavy reliance on its severance taxes. At a time when fossil fuels are expected to diminish or disappear, it is natural to wonder whether Texas leans too harshly on its oil and gas industry relative to its other industries and trades. As we saw in Table 11-3, the state's economy, despite the popular impression, does not depend primarily on oil and gas. Interestingly, a study during the 1960s concluded that oil and gas were overtaxed by the state relative to Texas' other industries. It analyzed only the impact of the Texas tax burden, rather than incidence (following economic shifting), assuming each of the following as a possible criterion for taxation: value-added, profits (before and after federal tax), gross receipts, assets, equity (assets minus liabilities), and combinations of the foregoing. By all criteria, the chemical industry was clearly undertaxed, as was agriculture (though data for agriculture were particularly weak).[14] No similar study has been performed for the 1970s. Immense changes have occurred in the Texas economy since the 1960s, the dynamic growth of government among them. While the 1960s study neglected government as an industry, it would be instructive to see how the answers would differ if government itself were regarded as "fair game" for taxation. While there are legal and political obstacles, the logic for taxing government should be appreciated in a state that has chosen to levy its taxes on businesses rather than individuals. The rationale is very well understood in cities like Austin and San Antonio where such large percentages of economic income and property value are exempt from taxation because they are classified as federal, state, or local government. Studies of this type force us to ask why we are taxing, what our principles are, who is being exploited by whom, and why data are being denied us.

LOCAL GOVERNMENTS

From a political perspective, the problems of Texas' local governments have centered on the property tax and on school finance reform, the two frequently being linked. The linkage derives from the *Rodriguez* case and the public's dissatisfaction with both the burden and the equity of Texas multitude of local property taxes.

On 21 December 1971, a three-man federal court ruled that

> ... *The current system of financing public education in Texas discriminates on the basis of wealth by permitting citizens of affluent districts to provide a higher quality education for their children while paying lower taxes ... this court concludes ... that the plaintiffs have been denied equal protection of the laws under the Fourteenth Amendment.*
>
> Rodriguez et. al., v. San Antonio Independent School District, et. al.

The decision said that constitutionally the quality of a student's public education should not depend on the property values of the school district in which his or her parents reside, particularly in a state where "districts" have been held meaningless and students have been forced to attend school. The United States Supreme Court rejected 5-4 that Texas was violating the Fourteenth Amendment by these practices, but in its decision admonished Texas and told it in essence to improve. In terms of tax and yield, the consequences of Texas' system at the time of Rodriguez are reproduced in Tables 11-10 and 11-11. Many Texans interpreted the Rodriguez issue to be a test of the legitimacy of the property tax itself. During the 1970s, Texas' opinion that the property tax was the one most in need of reform reflected that of the entire nation.[15]

About 60 percent of total Texas property taxes are raised for public schools; $1.6 billion out of a total property tax yield of $2.8 billion in 1976. Texans see property taxes rising rapidly as the state government enjoys "no new taxes." Representative Wayne Peveto, chairman of the Legislative Property Tax Committee, strikes a responsive chord every time he declaims that property taxes have mushroomed. Even so, by national standards Texas' average property taxes are relatively low, as Table 11-12 indicates. Yet one understands what Chairman Peveto is talking about as the average effective property tax rates on FHA-insured family homes inch above the national average on a statewide average basis.[16] This is not true for commercial and industrial property, however.

Property taxation plays such a crucial role in Texas finance that some discussion of its fundamental structure is in order.[17] Under Texas law all property not specifically exempted is taxable on an "equal and uniform basis" and "in proportion to fair market value." However, most property used for governmental, religious, charitable and educational purposes is fully exempted. Moreover, state law exempts part of the value of 1) all homesteads for state tax purposes and some county tax purposes, 2) at local option the homesteads of the elderly for local tax purposes, and 3) property owned by disabled veterans. A form of partial exemption is granted certain "agricultural lands"—taxation at "productivity value" as opposed to market value.

Texas property tax jurisdictions do not make a pretense of following the constitutional-statutory presumption of assessment and taxation in accordance with actual market value. Fractional assessment is recognized by administrators and taxpayers and even by the courts.

TABLE 11-10

THE RELATIONSHIP OF SCHOOL DISTRICT PROPERTY VALUES,
TAX EFFORT, AND YIELD PER PUPIL FROM LOCAL TAX, 1968 SAMPLE
(PRIOR TO RODRIGUEZ CASE)

Market Value of Taxable Property Per Pupil (1)	Actual Tax Rate Equalized Per $100 Value (2)	Yield Per Pupil From Rate of Column (2)	Hypothetical Yield From Equal (highest) Tax Rate
Below $10,000	$0.70	$ 60	$ 108
$10,000 - $30,000	.72	162	292
$30,000 - $50,000	.55	213	519
$50,000 - $100,000	.38	262	918
Above $100,000	.31	585	2,358

Source: Joel Berke, Anthony Carnevele, Daniel Morgan, Ron White, "The Texas School Finance Case: A Wrong in Search of a Remedy," *Journal of Law & Education*, 1(October 1972), Tables III, IV.

TABLE 11-11

RELATIONSHIP BETWEEN DISTRICT WEALTH,
TAX EFFORT AND TAX YIELD, BEXAR COUNTY 1968
(PRIOR TO *RODRIGUEZ* CASE)

School District by Market Value Per Pupil (1)	Equalized Tax Rate Per $100 (2)	Local District Yield Per Pupil From (2) (3)
Edgewood ($5,960)	$0.42	$ 26.28
Harlandale ($11,345)	.51	59.13
North Side ($20,794)	.52	108.13
San Antonio ($21,944)	.62	136.05
North East ($28,202)	.56	173.46
Alamo Heights ($49,478)	.68	343.00

Source: Joel Berke, Anthony Carnevele, Daniel Morgan, Ron White, "The Texas School Finance Case: A Wrong in Search of a Remedy," *Journal of Law & Education* 1(October 1972), Tables VII, VIII.

TABLE 11-12
STATE-LOCAL PROPERTY TAX COLLECTIONS, PER CAPITA AND PER $1,000 OF STATE PERSONAL INCOME, 1975

State and Region	Per Capita Amount	Per Capita % Annual Increase Since 1967	Per $1,000 of Income Amount	Per $1,000 of Income As % of U.S. Average	State and Region	Per Capita Amount	Per Capita % Annual Increase Since 1967	Per $1,000 of Income Amount	Per $1,000 of Income As % of U.S. Average
U. S. Average	$242	7.9%	$45	100	*Southeast*	(112)	(8.1)	(25)	(56)
New England	(316)	(9.5)	(60)	(133)	Virginia	157	10.4	30	67
Maine	231	7.9	51	113	West Virginia	101	7.0	23	51
New Hampshire	315	8.6	65	144	Kentucky	95	6.6	22	49
Vermont	299	11.1	66	147	Tennessee	117	8.3	26	58
Massachusetts	430	10.6	75	167	North Carolina	118	9.1	50	58
Rhode Island	270	9.1	50	111	South Carolina	101	11.6	24	53
Connecticut	352	9.1	55	122	Georgia	162	10.9	34	76
Mideast	(247)	(8.6)	(40)	(89)	Florida	162	5.2	31	69
New York	369	9.3	60	133	Alabama	53	5.7	13	29
New Jersey	413	10.8	66	147	Mississippi	97	7.6	26	58
Pennsylvania	163	7.1	30	67	Louisiana	85	5.8	20	44
Delaware	128	8.4	20	44	Arkansas	90	7.1	22	49
Maryland	213	6.3	36	80	*Southwest*	(159)	(6.2)	(34)	(76)
District of Columbia	197	7.0	28	62	Oklahoma	117	4.4	26	56
Great Lakes	(255)	(7.7)	(46)	(102)	TEXAS	191	7.4	39	87
Michigan	292	9.7	50	111	New Mexico	95	5.7	24	53
Ohio	202	5.8	37	82	Arizona	233	6.0	47	104
Indiana	231	6.3	44	98	*Rocky Mountain*	(233)	(5.1)	(45)	(100)
Illinois	281	8.5	45	100	Montana	304	7.5	62	138
Wisconsin	271	7.6	52	116	Idaho	160	5.0	33	73
Plains	(239)	(5.2)	(46)	(102)	Wyoming	283	5.0	55	122
Minnesota	231	3.1	43	96	Colorado	214	3.9	39	87
Iowa	263	5.8	50	111	Utah	152	2.9	35	78
Missouri	184	7.1	36	80	*Far West*	(283)	(7.8)	(50)	(111)
North Dakota	192	3.8	34	76	Washington	230	9.5	41	91
South Dakota	267	5.8	57	127	Oregon	277	8.0	53	118
Nebraska	281	4.6	53	118	Nevada	253	3.6	44	98
Kansas	253	6.1	46	102	California	373	7.5	63	140
					Alaska	215	14.9	32	71
					Hawaii	150	7.8	25	56

Source: ACIR, *Significant Features of Fiscal Federalism 1976-77*, Tables 76, 77.

Large quantities of "taxable property" escape taxation for a variety of reasons. Many types are believed to be impractical to tax, for example, intangibles and household furnishings. Taxation of personal property such as automobiles is practicable, but a majority of jurisdictions do not levy on it. Insurance companies and saving and loan companies are usually allowed deductions (probably unconstitutional) and have become immune from taxation.

Significant ratios regarding Texas practice were derived from a 1975 sample study of the Legislative Property Tax Committee:
1. The "valuation ratio" was 60 percent, meaning that 40 percent of taxable property value is lost to undervaluation
2. Average valuation ratios of the districts ranged from 11 to 81 percent
3. Valuation ratios were lowest in West Texas and South Texas
4. Ratios varied by types of property:
   a. 58 percent for industrial
   b. 39 percent for rural
   c. 71 percent for residential
   d. 77 percent for commercial
5. Lower assessed value-to-true value ratios were found for high-value properties than for low-value properties

These findings were consistent with earlier studies, such as those of Censuses of Government, Charles Bartlett, and Ralph Nader. Table 11-13 presents conclusions of the 1972 Census of Government. (The 1977 Census is currently underway.) We see Texas ranking between thirty-fourth and fortieth in conventional measures of quality of property tax assessment.

One can see why there is a concern about intra-government coefficients of dispersion; for within a taxing district equals should be equally assessed and taxed. The concern over high inter-area coefficients derives primarily from Texas' system of public school finance.

Since 1949, with the passage of the Gilmer-Aiken Act, property tax values have played an important part in the distribution of state aid to local school districts. Following the passage of House Bill 1126 during school year 1975-76, the relative value of a district's "full taxable property" was important in determining the amount of state aid it would receive. Each district benefitted from keeping its state-estimated full taxable property value low relative to the other districts. Unfortunately, the relatively richer districts have somehow managed to perform better than the poorer districts. Such appears true in the present officially sanctioned estimates of the Governor's Office of Educational Resources (GOER). GOER's audit of prevailing values invited utility, railroad, and pipeline companies to submit their own values and relied for its oil and gas values on existing appraisals widely understood to be unacceptable in the actual marketing of properties. Legislation for the purpose of making bona fide, independent appraisals has been thwarted by owners of timberland, ranchland, minerals, pipelines, utilities, and railroads.

TABLE 11-13

SELECTED INDICATORS OF THE QUALITY OF PROPERTY TAX ASSESSMENT IN TEXAS, 1972 CENSUS OF GOVERNMENTS, FOR 1971

	Median State	Texas	Texas Quality Ranking Among States
1. Uniformity of assessment, single family nonfarm house			
a. Intra-area coefficient of dispersion	22.5	25.7	38th
b. Inter-area coefficient of dispersion	14	19	34th
2. Ratio of assessment to sales price			
a. All types of property	30.5	17.1	39th
b. Single family urban homes	32.6	18.0	40th

Source: U. S. Bureau of the Census, 1972, Vol. 1, *Taxable Property Values and Assessment-Sales Price Ratios.*

The Advisory Commission on Intergovernmental Relations has repeatedly documented the poor quality of assessment practice in Texas. In its 1974 publication *The Property Tax in a Changing Environment*, ACIR presented its findings on the improvement in quality of property tax assessment in each of the fifty states. Texas was one of four states which was tagged as making "no significant progress" for the 1963-73 decade. These were matters such as adoption of full value assessment standard, statewide reassessment to bring levels up to legal ratios, control of statewide reassessment programs, assessment ratio studies, establishment of state and/or appeal agencies, supervision of or assistance to local assessors, training and certification of local assessors, state assessment of complex properties, consolidation of assessment jurisdictions, adoption of circuit breaker systems, and many more.

On a more hopeful note, it must be recalled that Texas property taxes in the past have been below those of the nation generally so that the inequities may not have been so egregious as implied. Moreover, the pressure for improvement is rising, as public school finance reform appears intractable without it. Despite the present gloom on this matter—the sixty-fifth Legislature adjourned without school finance reform or significant property tax reform—the situation today appears more equitable than at the time of the *Rodriguez* decisions. The skeptic need only compare the distribution of revenue per pupil among the districts of diverse wealth shown in Table 11-14 with the pre-Rodriguez situation (shown in Tables 11-10 and 11-11).

The most hopeful note on local governments in Texas is the position of its central cities relative to the Northeast and Midwest. The media have popularized this fact to the degree that one would think that Texas cities have run away from the nation's other cities, and the only question remaining is how to explain it in terms of an abundance

TABLE 11-14
DISTRIBUTION OF TEXAS SCHOOL DISTRICTS MARKET VALUE, SOURCE OF REVENUE, AND TOTAL REVENUE PER PUPIL, 1975-76

Market Value Per (ADA) Pupil	No. of Districts	Source of Revenue, Percentage Distribution			Total Current Operating Revenue Per Pupil ADA
		State	Local	Federal	
Under $50,000	77	65%	19%	16%	$1,081
$50,000 - $80,000	207	59	35	7	1,147
$80,000 - $110,000	207	46	47	7	1,275
$110,000 - $140,000	132	49	47	5	1,303
$140,000 - $170,000	93	46	50	5	1,331
$170,000 - $200,000	59	41	55	4	1,386
$200,000 - $230,000	52	36	57	6	1,538
$230,000 - $260,000	42	27	71	3	1,585
$260,000 - $290,000	35	44	50	5	1,624
Over $290,000	186	18	80	2	1,864
State totals: $2.54B.	1,090	52%	40%	8%	$1,218

Source: Texas Education Agency, *The Briefer for Texas School Finance Studies*, Vol. V, No. 1 (Austin: April 25, 1977), p. 13.

of energy and space, a dearth of taxation, an absence of organized labor, the pro-business attitude, warm weather, support by federal government, the world movement back to food, or whatever.

The present must never be assumed for the indefinite future. An excellent illustration is New York City. In 1956, the *New York Times Magazine* devoted an entire issue to New York City. The assessment of one writer, unchallenged within the issue or by the "experts," was:

> This island will, for as many years as can be seen ahead be the hub . . . the magnet which attracts . . . the finest . . . the best . . . the busiest . . . the most modern . . . the most luxurious . . . the choicest . . . the biggest . . . the most fabulous. . . . Ours is a town of superlatives.

Twenty years later articles were being published that described the city as dying. In 1956, Buffalo, Newark, and Detroit would have

TABLE 11-15

TEXAS LARGE CENTRAL CITIES SECTORAL EMPLOYMENT CHANGE SINCE 1958 COMPARED WITH OTHER U. S. CENTRAL CITIES

City	Percent of Base Year				
	Manufacture 1958-72	Retail Trades 1958-72	Wholesaling 1958-70	Selected Services 1958-70	Local Gov't 1960-72
Austin	192.5	205.7	242.8	220.9	182.1
Dallas	159.0	137.4	146.4	217.8	177.7
Fort Worth	103.3	103.8	122.2	145.7	105.5
Houston	161.2	171.7	167.5	282.1	140.2
San Antonio	146.6	143.1	n.a.	177.6	156.6
U. S. Average	123.5	141.1	143.5	182.6	134.6
Average "old" city	86.1	83.8	82.1	135.4	119.8
Average "new" city	196.6	161.0	180.9	247.7	150.2

"Old" central cities include Chicago, Baltimore, Boston, Detroit, New York, Cleveland, Pittsburgh, Buffalo, Cincinatti, Jersey City, Louisville, Milwaukee, Minneapolis, New Orleans, Newark, Philadelphia, Rochester, St. Louis, Washington, Providence, St. Paul, Kansas City, San Francisco, Oakland, Los Angeles.

"New" central cities include the five Texas cities, Albuquerque, Atlanta, Charlotte, Ft. Lauderdale, Miami, Phoenix, San Diego, Tampa, Orlando, Tuscon, Hollywood, St. Petersburg.

Source: David Perry and Alfred Watkins, "To Kill A City: A Critical Reevaluation of the Status of Yankee and Cowboy Cities," University of Texas at Austin symposium, "Political Economic Studies of the Sunbelt," February 10, 1977, Austin.

laughed at a forecast that in 1976 they would see further tax hikes as counter-productive, the only solution to be to literally beg for help. Yet it would appear that each of these four and most of Table 11-15's other old cities have experienced the same economic and demographic evolution: immigration of poorer, less educated people to their central core; emigration of middle income, better educated families to both suburbia and exurbia; and the loss of manufacturing jobs, sometimes initially compensated for by public sector jobs.[18]

This pattern may be discernible in Texas cities today. There is a floodtide of immigration of poor families with many children; San Antonio and cities south of it may be among America's poorest cities despite high bond ratings. Even the Dallas-Fort Worth area appears to replicate the familiar central city-suburb controversy of the "older" cities: jobs and tax bases have been shifting to the suburbs for many years. Houston appears to have little outward shift of tax base, and it has recently become a city of great interest to public sector analysts. The danger signals are now being flashed; for instance, we are reading that the students of Texas' largest school districts score far below the national average on the Iowa educational skills tests, in large part because only 37 percent of the pupils are Anglo. The fiscal situation of Texas cities is really not essentially different from that of the nation, for it shows the problems of all cities with rapid growth and the tensions of cities with severe poverty.

NOTES

1. See, for example: Advisory Commission on Intergovernmental Relations, *Measures of State and Local Fiscal Capacity and Tax Effort* (October 1962, M-16); ACIR, *Measuring the Fiscal Capacity and Tax Effort of State and Local Areas* (March 1971, M-58); John S. Akin, "Fiscal Capacity and the Estimation Method of the Advisory Commission on Intergovernmental Relations" (Discussion paper for Institute for Research on Poverty, University of Wisconsin at Madison, October 1972); Glenn Fisher, "Determinants of State and Local Expenditures," *National Tax Journal*, XIV (December 1961); Allan D. Manvel, "Differences in Fiscal Revenue-Sharing System," *National Tax Journal*, XXIV (June 1971); ACIR, *Financing Schools and Property Tax Relief* (January 1973, A-40), Tables 35-40; and Kenneth Quindry and Richard Engels, *State and Local Revenue Potential 1972* (Atlanta, 1974).

2. ACIR, *Financing Schools and Property Tax Relief* (January

1973, A-40), Tables 39, 40.

3. ACIR, *Federal Grants: Their Effects on State-Local Expenditures, Employment Levels, Wage Rates* (February 1976, A-61).

4. For three good discussions see Joe S. Floyd, Jr., "State and Local Inducements for Industry," *National Tax Journal*, XVIII (March 1965); W. A. Johnson, "Industrial Tax Exemptions—Sound Investment or Foolish Giveaway?" *1962 Proceedings of the National Tax Association*; and Texas Research League, *Statewide Industrial Financing* (Austin, 1962).

5. Charles Schultze, Edward Fried, Alice Rivlin, and Nancy Teeters, *Setting National Priorities: 1973 Budget* (Washington: Brookings, 1972), pp. 445-47.

6. *1976 Annual Financial Report, Volume I*, (Austin, Texas: Bob Bullock, Comptroller of Public Accounts, 1 November 1976).

7. Laura Lehner, *Comparative Standard of Living Indices* (New York: Economic Development Bank, undated).

8. Department of Commerce, *Survey of Current Business*, April 1976.

9. Robert Bretzfelder, "Contrasting Developments in the United States During Recession and Early Recovery," *Survey of Current Business*, April 1976.

10. See, for example, "Federal Spending: The North's Loss Is The Sunbelt's Gain," *National Journal*, 26 June 1976, pp. 878-91; "The Second War Between the States," *Business Week*, 17 May 1976; Perry and Watkins, "To Kill a City" (following).

11. David Perry and Alfred Watkins, "To Kill a City: A Critical Reevaluation of the Status of Yankee and Cowboy Cities," (University of Texas at Austin symposium, "Political Economic Studies of Sunbelt Cities", 10 February 1977).

12. C. L. Jusenius and L. C. Lederbur, "A Myth in the Making: The Southern Economic Challenge and Northern Economic Decline," unpublished manuscript (Office of Economic Research, Economic Development Administration, U. S. Department of Commerce, November 1976), Table 11.

13. Sources and presentation not yet to be released.

14. Cadwell L. Ray, "An Analysis of Value Added Taxation with Special Reference to the State of Texas," Ph.D. dissertation (University of Texas at Austin, August 1967); also see Daniel Morgan and Cadwell Ray, "Business Taxes in Texas," mimeographed (1965).

15. For the research findings of Opinion Research Corporation of

Princeton, New Jersey, "Public Opinion and Taxes," see Appendix B of ACIR, *Financing Schools and Property Tax Relief*.

16. See ACIR, *Significant Features of Fiscal Federalism 1976-77*, Tables 71, 72.

17. Much of the following three paragraphs borrows heavily from the four-article series by Craig Foster, "The Texas Property Tax System," *IDRA Newsletter* (San Antonio and Austin: Intercultural Development Research Association, 1976-77).

18. The point and the following paragraph borrows from the analysis of Bernard Weinstein and Robert Firestine, "Industrial Dispersal and a Growing Metropolitan Economy," *Texas Business Review*, LV (February 1977), pp. 27-31.

TWELVE

THE TEXAS ECONOMY IN SPACE
Lorna A. Monti

Division of labor occurs throughout Texas. The basic industrial section of Texas stretches along the Gulf Coast and up into East Texas; the "general purpose" part of the state which provides government, trade, services, and general manufacturing occupies Central and North Texas; agriculture, oil and gas production, and their trade centers appear across South and West Texas and the Panhandle. Most Texans live in the eastern half, where water, heavy industry, and the general purpose economies of North and Central Texas are.

The economic activities of the different areas of Texas vary because of resources, markets, and concentrations of interdependent economic activities. Manufacturing requiring heavy inputs locates near those inputs and frequently near water transportation. Other manufacturing locates near markets. Some non-manufacturing activities, by their very nature, cannot exist apart from the populations served. Examples are medical care, education, and retail trade. Other activities can operate across distances if communication is good, but benefit from concentrations of similar services in one place. Financial and design activities are good examples.

The early Texas farm family's tradition of spending a day in town for shopping, marketing, banking, or voting illustrates the concentration of services and their separation from agricultural production and consumption. Later development of manufacturing that required location near water or other resources increased division of labor by place. Still later, the relative growth of services in recent decades increased the proportion of economic activity that is not bound to a specific location. The division of labor by place within Texas and between Texas and the rest of the country is an important and dynamic feature of the Texas economy; a complete description requires a description of the location of economic activities by regions.

FUNCTIONAL REGIONS IN TEXAS

The regions of Texas specialize in economic activities because of historical and current economic forces. Within each region, regardless of specialization, people travel to shop, work, acquire services, and entertain themselves. These trips delineate functional regions in which most trips begin and end inside the boundaries. Several delineations of Texas economic regions exist, depending on the evidence used to determine the interdependence of counties, the common units that are grouped to form regions.

Charles P. Zlatkovich has analyzed traffic flow data to determine self-contained groups of counties whose major traffic flows are with each other. His delineation produced thirty-eight regions:

Dallas County is the terminal county for the largest region, containing 35 counties and a total population of 2,905,413 (or about 26 percent of the state population). This region is large enough to contain three subregions, with Dallas, Tarrant, and Smith as the subregional terminal counties. The largest of these is the Dallas County subregion, which contains 17 counties and about 61 percent of the population of the region. Twelve counties and about 32 percent of the regional population fall into the Tarrant County (Fort Worth) subregion. The Smith County (Tyler) subregion contains six counties and about 7 percent of the regional population.

The Harris County region, which contains the Houston and Galveston-Texas City SMSAs, is the second largest of the regions. Houston is the focus for this region, which covers 20 counties and has a population of 2,386,816. The third largest region is Bexar County region, with 23 counties and a population of 1,133,027. Both the San Antonio and Laredo SMSAs are included in this region. Webb County (Laredo) is the terminal county for a subregion containing three counties and about 7 percent of the regional population.

More than 57 percent of the population of the state lives in the three largest regions. The other 17 regions dominated by Texas

SMSAs contain more than 36 percent of the state's population. Among the larger regions not dominated by Texas SMSAs are the regions subordinate to Victoria County (Victoria) and Caddo Parish (Shreveport)....[1]

These self-contained regions are natural market areas indicating the distances from which specialized services could expect to draw customers. They indicate the useful boundaries of advertising, as well as reasonable boundaries for administration of public services such as health centers and higher education. Regions dominated by metropolitan areas comprise 93 percent of the population of the state so that, in effect, the important market and planning areas consist of metropolitan areas and their dependent counties.

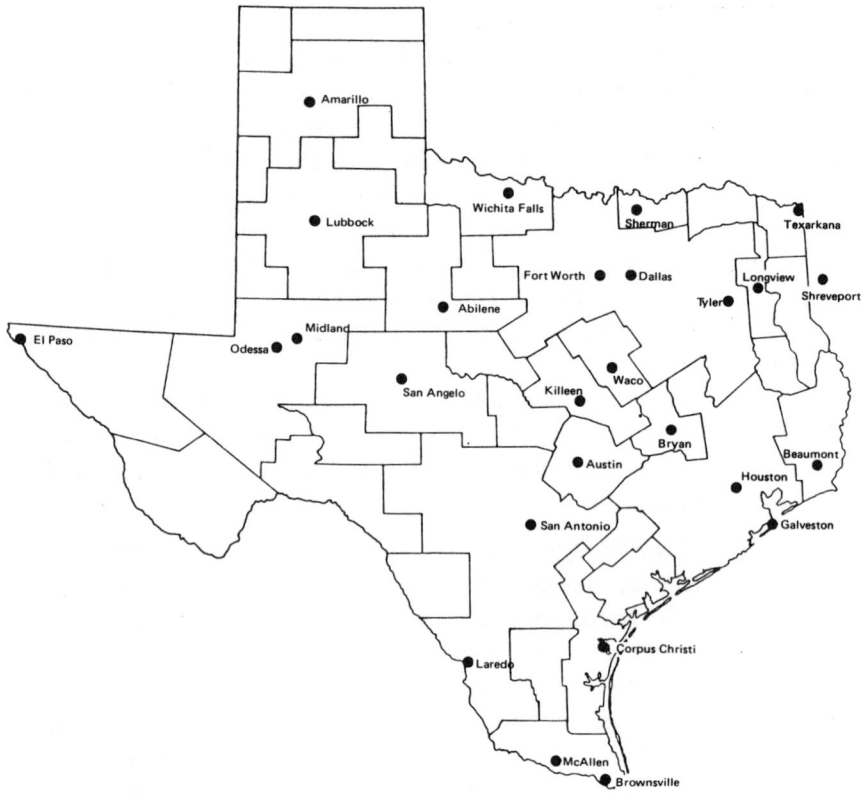

FIGURE 12-1
TEXAS HIGHWAY TRAFFIC FLOW REGIONS

Source: Charles P. Zlatkovich, *The Identification of Functional Regions Based on Highway Traffic Flow Data*, Research Report 1 (Austin: Bureau of Business Research, 1977): 27.

Functional Regions in Texas

The delineation of regions by traffic flow data produces smaller regions than other methods. Methods employed by the Bureau of Economic Analysis (BEA) of the U. S. Department of Commerce produce seventeen economic regions in Texas.

... Boundaries were drawn so that each region has all of the economic components, in varying proportions, that are found in the national economy ...

Each BEA area consists of an urban center and the surrounding counties in which economic activity is focused, directly, or indirectly, on the activity of the center. Each area combines place of residence and place of work of the labor force as nearly as possible so there is a minimum of commuting across area boundaries.[2]

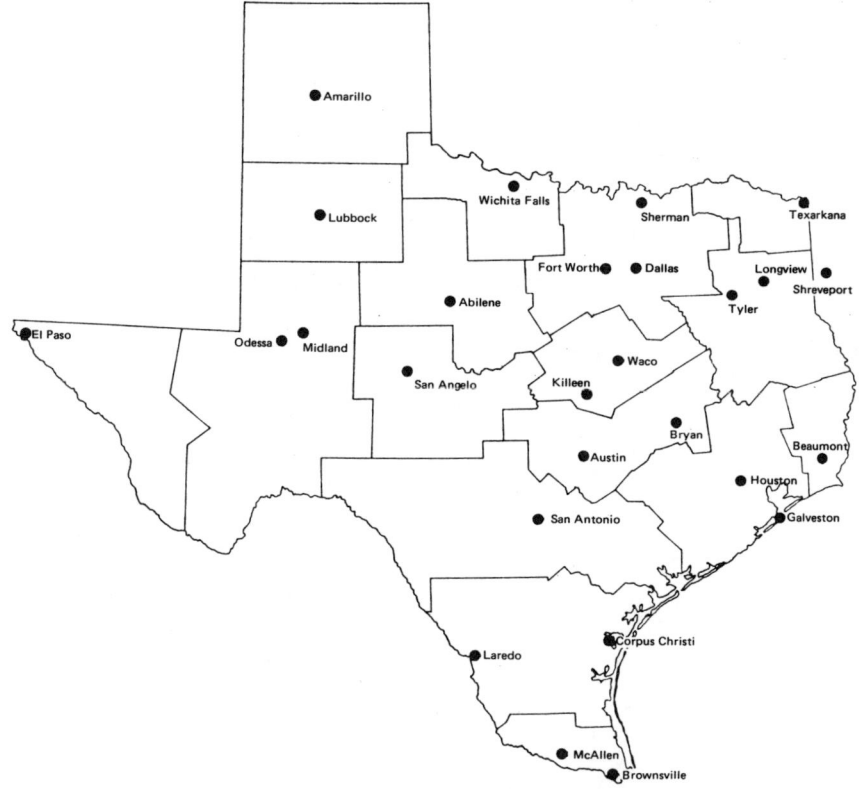

FIGURE 12-2
BUREAU OF ECONOMIC ANALYSIS ECONOMIC AREAS
Source: Charles P. Zlatkovich, *The Identification of Functional Regions Based on Highway Traffic Flow Data*, Research Report 1 (Austin: Bureau of Business Research, 1977): 29.

The BEA regions are defined much more broadly than the traffic flow regions. The BEA regions, do, however, incorporate the concept that emerged from the traffic flow analysis. The important regions of Texas consist of metropolitan or other urban areas and their surrounding counties. Both the BEA regions and the traffic flow regions indicate that close economic ties exist across state borders into New Mexico, Oklahoma, Arkansas, and Louisiana, although Figures 12-1 and 12-2 stop at the state borders.

A third delineation of Texas counties into regions was performed by David L. Huff and Diana R. DeAre using 1970 commuting patterns and newspaper circulation (Figure 12-3).[3] Their regions are also metropolitan centers and surrounding counties. The number of

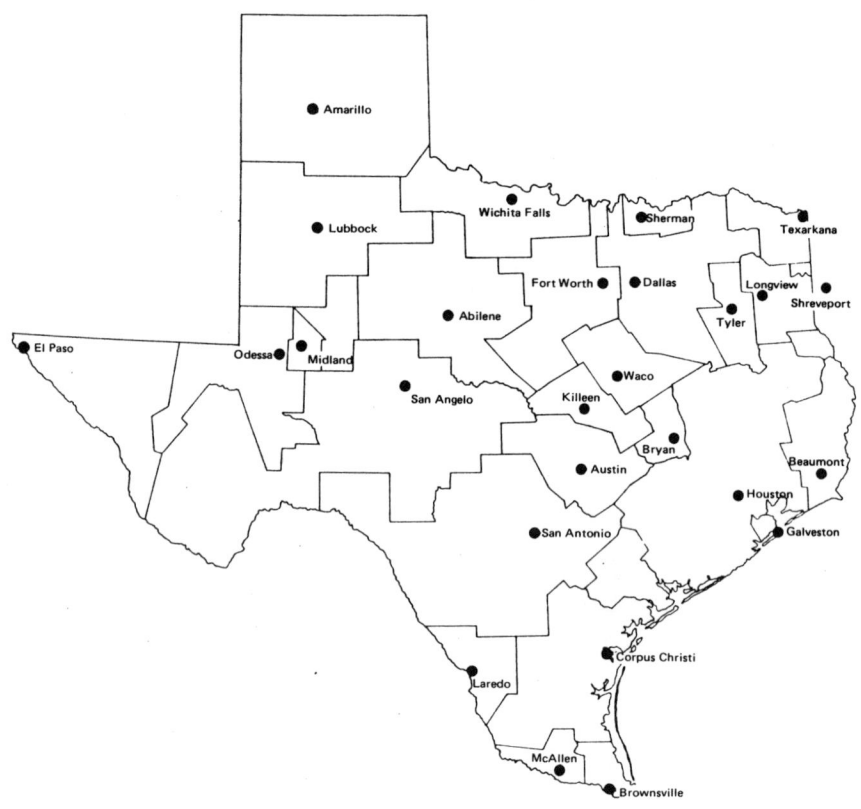

FIGURE 12-3
HUFF–DEARE PRINCIPAL INTERACTION FIELDS
Source: Charles P. Zlatkovich, *The Identification of Functional Regions Based on Highway Traffic Flow Data*, Research Report 1 (Austin: Bureau of Business Research, 1977): 31.

regions—twenty-eight—was determined by the selection of the metropolitan areas and two non-metropolitan urban areas, Victoria and Big Springs, as centers. Their method separated Dallas from Fort Worth by assumption, which leads to a different form of regions than that produced by the highway traffic flow data or the BEA regions.

The three delineations indicate that Texas is divided into functional regions around its metropolitan areas and that the connection of outlying counties to the metropolitan areas will vary with the form of identification used. Highway traffic patterns and newspaper circulation patterns do not coincide. The top five regions—those traffic flow areas surrounding Dallas-Fort Worth, Houston, San Antonio, Austin, and Beaumont—include approximately two-thirds of the state's population. These areas share the eastern half of the state, evidence that most of the people and their economic activities are in the eastern half of Texas—the half with the water. Fewer people are involved in the oil and gas production and agriculture that characterize West Texas.

THE PATTERN OF INCOME GROWTH IN TEXAS

An examination of income growth by sources of income reveals that the population concentrations in the eastern half of Texas are connected in a kind of urban string, similar to that along the East Coast of the United States. Figure 12-4 shows Texas counties identified by sources of personal income with above average percentage increases between 1969 and 1973. The map reveals that most counties with rapidly-growing sources of income owed that growth to trade and government income. The trend in the eastern half of the state is for growth to occur around cities, and along the corridors between them.

> . . . *Texas cities are stretching toward each other to form a horseshoe that leaves Houston going north, sweeps up to Dallas-Fort Worth, and returns by Interstate Highway 35 to San Antonio. A second, but connected, chain of counties characterized by increases in trade and government income follows the border from Brownsville to Del Rio with a branch over to Corpus Christi....*[4]

This pattern is the result of productivity trends in the economy. Increased productivity in goods-producing industries and movement of workers into people-oriented activities (including health and education) means that income growth is associated with increased trade and government incomes rather than increased incomes in basic goods

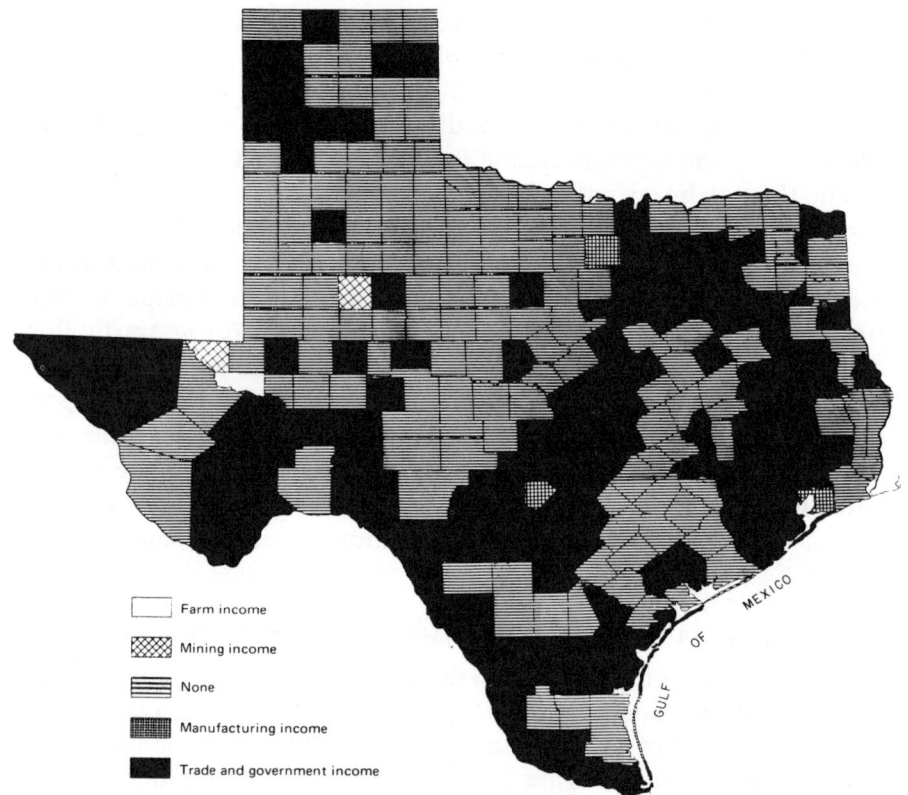

FIGURE 12-4
TEXAS COUNTIES BY SOURCES OF PERSONAL INCOME
WITH ABOVE-AVERAGE INCREASES, 1969-1973

Source: Lorna Monti, "Location of Economic Activity in 'Post-Industrial' Texas and the U. S.," *Texas Business Review* 50 (August 1976): 179.

producing industries that support and generate growth. The pattern of chains of counties implies that growth spills from county to county along major transportation routes and around metropolitan areas.

DIVISION OF LABOR BY AREAS OF TEXAS

Analysis of regional and growth patterns in Texas reveals that the state is organized into regions dominated by metropolitan areas. This kind of spatial organization occurs in all regions. Geographers and regional analysts call these regions nodal regions, implying that they are functional regions focused on metropolitan nodes. It is possible to combine these nodal regions by similarity to reduce the number of economic regions in Texas for ready discussion. For purposes of discussion, Texas is divided into seven economic regions: Panhandle, North Texas, East Texas, Gulf Coast, Central Texas, West Texas, and South Texas. The Panhandle contains Lubbock and Amarillo; North Texas contains Wichita Falls, Sherman-Denison, and Dallas-Fort Worth; East Texas contains Texarkana, Longview, and Tyler; the Gulf Coast contains Beaumont-Port Arthur-Orange, Galveston-Texas City, Houston, and Corpus Christi; Central Texas contains Waco, Killeen-Temple, Austin, Bryan-College Station, and San Antonio; West Texas contains Abilene, San Angelo, Midland, Odessa, and El Paso; and South Texas contains Laredo, McAllen-Pharr-Edinburg, and Brownsville. The boundaries between the areas will change according to the way in which dependent counties are assigned to major metropolitan areas, but the general characteristics of the regions can be described by the economies of the metropolitan areas. The names used here correspond to the Standard Metropolitan Statistical Areas defined by the Bureau of the Census.[5]

Panhandle. Lubbock and Amarillo, the metropolitan areas of the Panhandle, are trade centers for the irrigated farming and cattle ranching of the Texas High Plains area. Wholesale and retail trade are more important to these plains cities than to the state because they are service areas for the surrounding agricultural counties. In recent years, both areas have experienced manufacturing growth in electronics, apparel, and copper refining, but the contribution of manufacturing to the area's economy remains below the state average.

Lubbock and Amarillo are stable cities with moderate growth. Amarillo has experienced growth due to natural increase in recent years, although Lubbock has experienced some in-migration. Potential depletion of the Ogallala Aquifer, on which the irrigated farming depends, clouds the future of both these two cities and the High Plains agricultural area they serve.

North Texas. North Texas metropolitan areas are diversified manufacturing and trade centers. Dallas-Fort Worth serves the entire South Central United States. Wichita Falls and Sherman-Denison are both satellites of Dallas-Fort Worth and centers for subregions of North Texas. Neither Wichita Falls nor Sherman-Denison experienced growth in the first half of the decade; Sherman-Denison lost population and Wichita Falls balanced net out-migration with natural growth for a slight total increase. Both Sherman-Denison and Wichita Falls have increased manufacturing income, while military expenditures, formerly an important part of the economic base, have declined in importance, precipitously so in Sherman-Denison. Wichita Falls manufacturing includes apparel, oil field equipment, plate glass, and electronics. Sherman-Denison manufacturing includes food processing, apparel, paper and cotton products, and electronics.

Dallas-Fort Worth, like its smaller neighbors, experienced moderate growth at a rate close to the national average in the early 1970s, which implies that most growth occurred through natural increase rather than through migration. The employment pattern of the area is one of above-average concentration in trade; slight specialization in finance, insurance, and real estate; and a diversified manufacturing base with emphasis on transportation equipment and apparel.

As a general diversified center, Dallas-Fort Worth depends on economic developments in the South Central part of the country and on national economic activity. It is not dependent on a particular industry. Economic indicators for the United States economy in general and for the South Central part of the country in particular will provide a guide to economic conditions in the metropolitan area and its related counties.

East Texas. The East Texas metropolitan areas of Longview, Tyler, and Texarkana are part of the manufacturing belt that covers the northern and eastern United States. Of the three areas, Tyler experienced strong growth in the early 1970s through a large proportion of in-migration, Longview experienced moderate growth through natural increase, while Texarkana balanced out-migration with natural increase. The manufacturing of the area varies from apparel, petrochemicals, steel, to oil field equipment. Federal employment is important in Texarkana.

The varied manufacturing and heavy concentration in East Texas make the economic prospects of the area a mix of the Texas Gulf Coast dependence on the oil and gas industry and petrochemicals, with the dependence of manufacturing areas in general on fluctuations in the national economy. Forecasts for East Texas require disaggregation of the manufacturing activity by industry to disentangle national, regional, and industrial effects.

Gulf Coast. The metropolitan areas of the Gulf Coast—Beaumont-Port Arthur-Orange, Houston, Galveston-Texas City, and Corpus Christi—comprise the center of the Texas oil and gas and petrochemical industries. The industrial complex is more than oil refining and chemical manufacturing, for equipment, pipelines, business services, real estate, and finance must also be included. Those parts directly related to oil and gas may fluctuate independently of developments in the national economy, as they did during the 1974-75 recession, while manufacturing serving other industries, as does much petrochemical production, will fluctuate with the other industries.

Houston grew rapidly in the early 1970s, largely due to migration from other areas. Galveston-Texas City had less migration and a more moderate rate; Beaumont experienced out-migration and a very moderate growth rate, as did Corpus Christi. Houston's relative prosperity was largely a result of the increased oil and gas exploration and drilling, much of it in West Texas, that increased as the recession took hold. The contrast between economic conditions in the rest of the country and those in Houston made that city the symbol of prosperity and growth in the South and West. A more cautious approach would be to say that Houston's most significant industry follows a different pattern from that of the nation. The economic indicators that are relevant for Houston and its neighboring metropolitan areas are those that relate to drilling rigs in operation, worldwide anticipated purchase of equipment, and oil and gas production. International industry developments are more important to Houston than to other areas of Texas. Analysis of Houston and the other Gulf Coast areas requires disentangling regional, industrial, national, and international effects. This is the most complex of the economic regions in Texas.

Central Texas. Due to increases in manufacturing, a corridor is growing in Central Texas from Waco to San Antonio, through Killeen-Temple and Austin, an area of state government, education, and military bases. The trend is most pronounced in Killeen-Temple, and less so at the ends of the corridor in Waco and San Antonio. To the east, Bryan-College Station also participates in the trend. The advantages of these cities are low land costs, an easily available labor force, access to the major markets of the Houston and Dallas-Fort Worth regions, and freedom from the congestions of larger metropolitan areas. The characteristics of the "Sunbelt" are more readily apparent in the Central Texas corridor than in the Houston and Dallas areas that characterize the South and West to people from other parts of the country.

The manufacturing industries are diverse, including mobile homes, apparel, office furniture, electronics, packaging, and a multitude of specialized products. The heavy industries of East Texas and the Gulf Coast—oil refining, steel, equipment building, and petrochemicals—do not appear in the corridor. The corridor consists of market oriented manufacturing for which the availability of space and labor force, particularly female labor force, is important.

In the early 1970s most of the corridor cities grew with the middle corridor cities of Austin and Killeen-Temple growing very rapidly through in-migration. The outlook for the corridor will depend on maintenance of the government, education, and military bases and continued attraction of manufacturing. The attraction of manufacturing will be dependent on both national economic patterns of the United States South Central region that the corridor serves. The corridor is growing by developing the kind of diversified manufacturing and trading that Dallas-Fort Worth has provided for some time.

West Texas. In West Texas, San Angelo and Abilene combine regional trade and service with military bases, Midland and Odessa produce oil and gas, and El Paso manufactures apparel while supporting some military and mining employment.

El Paso is the most independent metropolitan area in Texas because it is so far from the population centers of the state. Air traffic patterns are oriented to Los Angeles rather than Dallas, and the Huff-DeAre regionalization identified as much area in New Mexico as in Texas in the El Paso economic region. El Paso grew very rapidly in the first part of the decade, largely through in-migration. Prospects for El Paso depend on the health of its manufacturing, border relations with Mexico, and maintenance of its government employment.

Midland and Odessa combine oil and gas production with the services and equipment manufacturing that supports drilling. The two cities' fortunes rise and fall with energy production while population growth depends on increases in drilling. Midland and Odessa are even more tied to trends in the oil and gas industry than Houston.

Abilene and San Angelo grew moderately in the early 1970s, as did most of the areas that serve as regional trade and service centers. Both serve as centers for the livestock and farming areas surrounding them. Recently, both cities have also participated in the growth of manufacturing characteristic of the Central Texas corridor, but to a lesser degree. The two cities are a mixture of traditional trade and service centers for agricultural areas and the government-manufacturing trend characteristic of Central Texas.

The West Texas economy is really four economies, one participating in the growth of manufacturing in the South and West, one serving traditional livestock and farming, one producing oil and gas and one providing military bases. Prospects for the area depend on the prospects of all four.

South Texas. The South Texas areas of McAllen-Pharr-Edinburg, Brownsville, and Laredo share the problems of a region with low incomes, high unemployment, and continued uncertainty due to conditions along the border with Mexico.

In the first half of the decade, official population estimates showed net out-migration for Laredo counteracted by a large natural increase to create a strong rate of growth. Brownsville and McAllen-Pharr-Edinburg grew very rapidly through large natural increases. Frequently, however, official statistics are difficult to interpret for border cities because of what is believed to be a large but unrecorded influx of illegal immigrants. Many suggest that birth and death records are also distorted.

The South Texas cities are trade centers for the agricultural areas that surround them and for Mexican nationals. Manufacturing is concentrated in food processing that supports the agriculture, apparel, and electronics. The outlook for the South Texas cities is clouded by devaluations of the Mexican peso and possible restrictions on movement across the border. Illegal immigration of workers from Mexico is controversial because precise knowledge about the effects of this flow, and restricting it, is lacking. South Texas faces the most uncertainty of the economic regions of Texas.

TEXAS TIES TO NATIONAL PATTERNS

A national trend called the "Sunbelt" burst into public consciousness in the mid-1970s. This phenomenon could be defined as the recognition that states in the South and West were gaining population faster than states in the North and East. Jon Nordheimer wrote, "As the United States prepares to enter its third century, a restless and historic movement is taking place, shifting people away from the northern states that have been the base of population and power since the nation's infancy."[6] The size of the discrepancy in growth between South-West and North-East varies with sources as the definition of Sunbelt and the base year of comparison vary from writer to writer.

Actually, the South and West have been growing faster than the North and East since 1899.[7] Population has dispersed from the original concentration in the Northeast to fill the country more evenly. Manufacturing that needed to be close to markets or to a source of labor supply, or both, followed. The Sunbelt phenomenon is an acceleration and recognition of the long-term trends, strengthened by different regional impacts of the economic trauma—the oil embargo and the recession—that occurred in the first half of the decade.

Texas as a whole experienced less dislocation than the rest of the country during the 1974-75 recession because of the importance of the oil and gas industry in Texas, the benefits of the continuing shift of population, and the lower share of manufacturing in the Texas employment pattern than in the nation. Because manufacturing employment is more volatile over the business cycle, states with heavy shares of manufacturing employment experience higher unemployment rates in recession.

Figure 12-5 shows a classification of BEA economic regions in Texas and the rest of the country by the predominant economic activity in the area. Most areas contain some of each kind of activity, but classification is by predominant activity. The map reveals the relation of Texas to the United States.

> ... The Northeast, as well as part of the Southeast, is a manufacturing area. The rest of the country is characterized by agricultural, government, or mixed specialization. The Northeast manufacturing belt originally coincided with the concentration of population in the nation; so both the people and the manufacturing that supported their needs were in the same place. Throughout the twentieth century, both population and manufacturing have dispersed.[8]

Texas appears on the national map as a bridge between the manufacturing belt that covers most of the East and extends one finger into East Texas and the agriculture, government, and mixed orientation of the West. Both of the major economic areas of Texas, Dallas-Fort Worth and Houston, are classified as "other," or mixed types of economies. Neither area has the concentration of manufacturing that characterizes the East, but neither is sufficiently low in manufacturing as to be classified as government or agriculturally based. In a way, Texas contains a microcosm of the division of labor within the country as a whole; manufacturing and population are most heavily concentrated in the North and East, while agriculture and government are more important in the South and West.

Another view of the relations between Texas and national patterns is produced by examination of air travel patterns as seen in Figure 12-6. Dallas is a node for the South Central part of the country, a function complementary to its role as a regional trade, service, and general manufacturing area.[9] A self-contained region centered in Dallas extends over most of Texas, Oklahoma, Louisiana, and Arkansas.

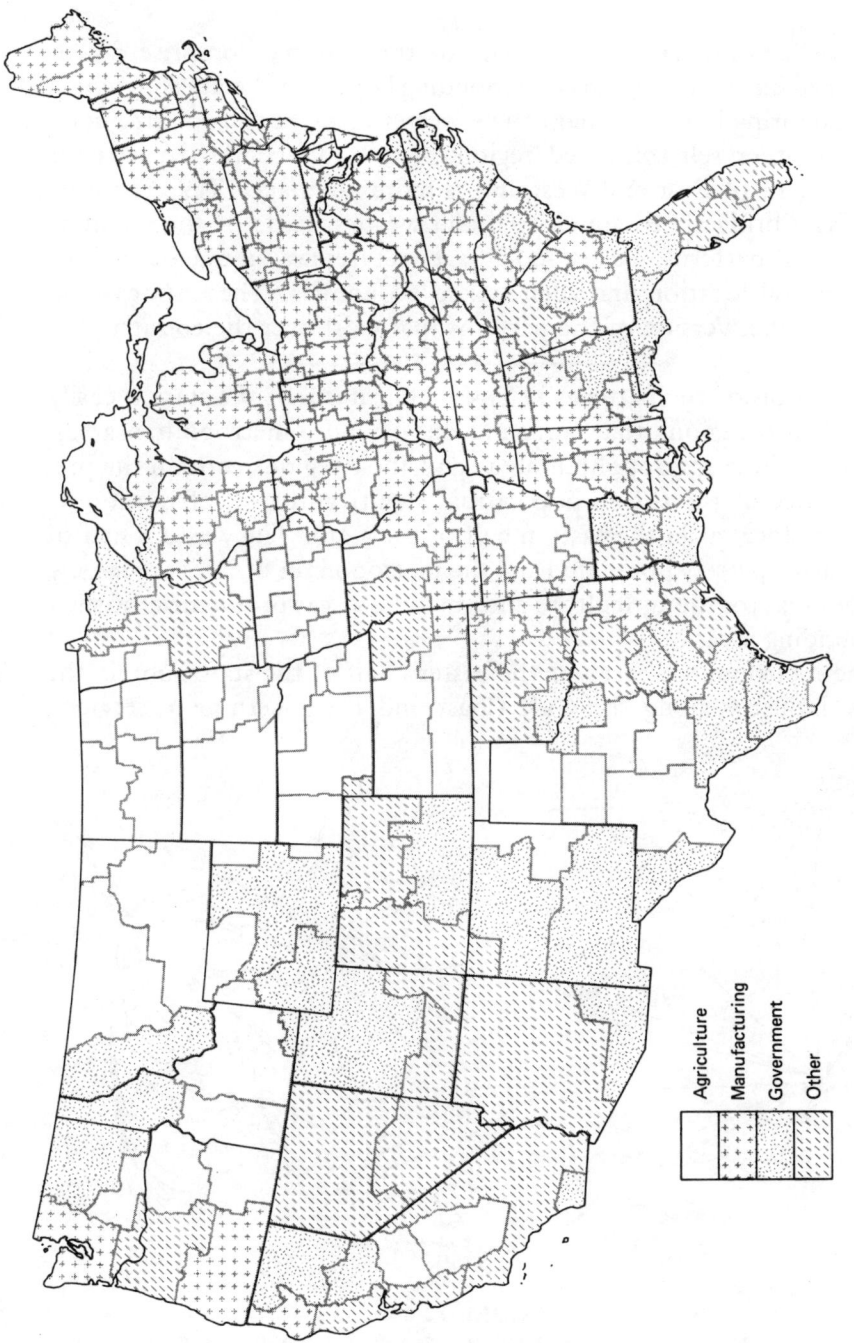

FIGURE 12-5
BUREAU OF ECONOMIC ANALYSIS ECONOMIC AREAS BY INDUSTRIAL GROUP, 1973

Source: U. S. Department of Commerce, Bureau of Economic Analysis

The northeastern and eastern part of the country comprise a self-contained air traffic region corresponding largely to the areas in which manufacturing is predominant. The western part of the country comprises another self-contained region. The Dallas-centered pattern is independent of East and West and is more compact. Texas appears again as a bridge between eastern and western parts of the country. In national patterns, Texas and adjacent states are unique because of their central location and their mixed economies. These states comprise a smaller version of the patterns that exist over the country.

Examination of the patterns in Texas indicates that the state is easily divided into regions that surround one or more metropolitan areas. A few of these metropolitan areas and their regions contain the preponderance of the state's population; significantly, all of the top regions are located in the eastern half of the state. The western half of the state is sparsely populated and the metropolitan centers are largely service areas for the agriculture and the oil and gas production of their surrounding areas.

The metropolitan areas of the eastern half of the state contain the heavy industry along the Gulf Coast and the government, services,

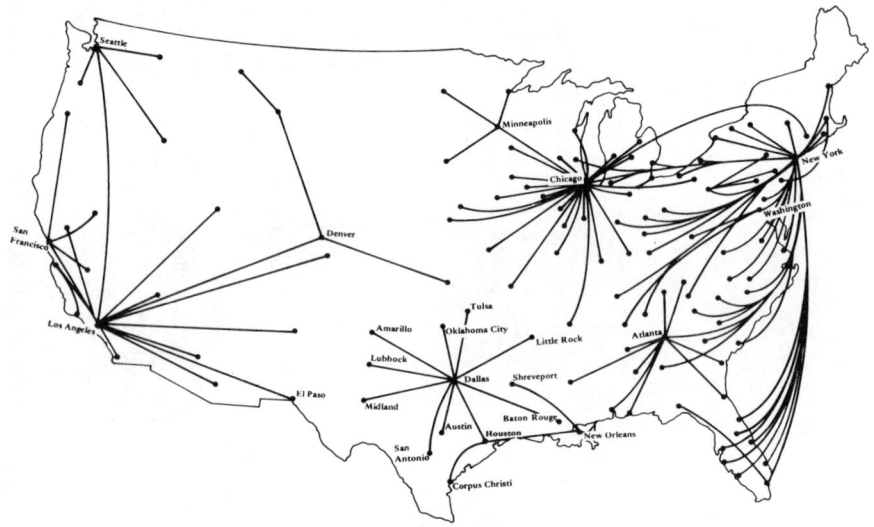

FIGURE 12-6
PRIMARY AIR PASSENGER TRAFFIC FLOWS, 1975

Source: Charles P. Zlatkovich, *Intermetropolitan Relationships: An Examination of National Air Travel Patterns*, Research Report 3 (Austin: Bureau of Business Research 1977): 2

trade, and diversified manufacturing that run from the Dallas-Fort Worth area through San Antonio. The Panhandle, West Texas, East Texas, and the Gulf Coast produce characteristically Texas products—livestock, grain, cotton, oil and gas, petrochemicals, and oil field support equipment. North and Central Texas produce the whole range of goods and services required to support a population. South Texas diverges somewhat from this generalization because it is both a trade center for its agriculture, and a wholesale-retail trade area due to the Mexican border. The large population centers are divided between the general government-service-trade-manufacturing function that is performed in Dallas-Fort Worth, the Central Texas corridor, and San Antonio-Galveston-Texas City, and the basic industrial function that is performed in Beaumont-Port Arthur-Orange, Houston, and Corpus Christi.

The patterns within Texas are part of the larger national pattern. The Dallas-Fort Worth area is a regional trade and service center for the South Central United States. The East Texas manufacturing section is a continuation of the manufacturing belt that covers most of the north and east of the country. The agriculture and governments of West and South Texas mark the beginning of such areas that extend to the Pacific Coast. Because of its central location, Texas repeats the national patterns, with the exception that its basic industry is concentrated in oil and gas production, oil refining, petrochemicals, and related support industries.

NOTES

1. Charles P. Zlatkovich, *The Identification of Functional Regions Based on Highway Traffic Flow Data*, Research Report 1 (Austin, Texas: Bureau of Business Research, 1977), pp. 11-13

2. U. S. Department of Commerce, Social and Economic Statistics Administration, Bureau of Economic Analysis, *Area Economic Projections to 1990* (Washington: Government Printing Office, 1974), p. 2.

3. David L. Huff and Diana DeAre, *Principal Interaction Fields of Texas Metropolitan Areas* (Austin, Texas: Bureau of Business Research, 1974).

4. Lorna Monti, "Location of Economic Activity in 'Post-Industrial' Texas and the U. S.," *Texas Business Review* 50 (August 1976), p. 179.

5. For background material for area descriptions see the following:

U. S. Department of Commerce, Bureau of the Census, "Estimates of the Population of Texas Counties and Metropolitan Areas: July 1, 1974 and 1975," Series P-25, No. 637, October 1976;

Carol T. F. Bennett and Charles P. Zlatkovich, "Midland-Odessa: An Economy Based on Energy," *Texas Business Review* 51 (March 1977), pp. 58-61;

Carol T. F. Bennett and Charles P. Zlatkovich, "San Antonio: A Military, Trade, and Service Center," *Texas Business Review* 51 (forthcoming, July 1977);

Lorna A. Monti, "Capsule Economic Analysis: How to Design an Economic Profile of Your area," *Texas Business Review* 50 (May 1976), pp. 104-108;

Lorna Monti and Charles Zlatkovich, "Killeen-Temple: A Magnet Area," *Texas Business Review* 50 (October 1976), pp. 231-34;

Charles P. Zlatkovich and Carol T. F. Bennett, "El Paso Economic Profile," *Texas Business Review* 51 (January 1977), pp. 4-7;

Charles P. Zlatkovich and Carol T. F. Bennett, "Amarillo and Lubbock: The Hubs of the Panhandle-Plains Region," *Texas Business Review* 51 (June 1977), pp. 125-29.

6. Jon Nordheimer, "Sunbelt Region Leads Nation in Growth of Population," *New York Times*, 8 February 1976, p. 1.

7. Leonard F. Wheat, *Regional Growth and Industrial Location* (Lexington, Massachusetts: Lexington Books, 1973), p. 10.

8. Lorna Monti, "Location of Economic Activity in 'Post-Industrial' Texas and the U. S.," op. cit., p. 177.

9. Charles P. Zlatkovich, *Intermetropolitan Relationships: An Examination of National Air Travel Patterns*, Research Report 3 (Austin, Texas: Bureau of Business Research, 1977), p. 2.

THIRTEEN

THE FUTURE IS NOW
Robert H. Ryan

Nothing is new under the Texas sun. The elements that will give substance to the future are here today. But in this last quarter of the twentieth century, the familiar elements are being recast into some very new shapes.

Reading the future has always seemed an exercise in arrogance. Yet today, analysts are applying new forecasting techniques and new generations of computers to masses of information, and offer glimpses of the Texas to come that are remarkably convincing. Economic forecasts are often seen as being only a bit more credible than soothsayers' readings from tea leaves, chicken entrails, or stars. But the multifaceted economic crisis the world has faced in the seventies has made forecasts, credible or not, among the most popular brands of reading matter.

In the mid-seventies the population of Texas passed the twelve million mark. By 1990 the total may exceed fifteen million; one recent forecast points to nearly sixteen million. Those 1990 figures are somewhat more than the current population of the Netherlands, a country smaller in area than Texas' three largest counties combined. The comparison suggests that Texas will still have plenty of growing room. By 1990, however, most of the Texas population will be crowded into an area no larger than the Netherlands and in some ways more congested. Texas metropolitan areas will account for more than ten million of the total population; most of the rest will be found in cities of substantial size. Already, half the people of Texas live in the Houston-Galveston area or along the Dallas-San Antonio urban strip.

URBANIZATION: A MILLION MORE TRASH CANS

During the first half of the seventies, Dallas-Fort Worth, now the largest metropolitan area in Texas, increased by only forty-two thousand residents through inmigration, but far more than that through the birth of new natives to the area. The high birth rate in Texas has kept its population considerably younger than the national average, a factor that magnifies the school tax needs but also somewhat depresses the market for housing.

Nevertheless, within ten years Texas standard metropolitan statistical areas will have almost a million more families than they do today—and a million more trash cans. The result will be a set of familiar problems raised to a new order of magnitude and new problems beyond imagining. Among other changes, the decade will necessarily bring some reordering of the local governments that now shingle the state with overlapping jurisdictions, competitive claims for tax support, and duplicative administration. The decade will also bring a shift toward professionalism in city management.

CONSTRUCTION: A TEN-YEAR CENTURY

Though population growth continued during the mid-seventies, housing construction was deeply depressed and the housing stock fell even further behind needs. By the time economic recovery had restored consumer buying power and confidence in 1976 and 1977, the cost of new housing had soared beyond the reach of many Texans. Meanwhile the obsolescence of available houses became a painful issue, with most existing homes seriously underinsulated and even extravagant in their demands on the energy supply.

Necessity may force the building industry to telescope into the next decade more progress than has been made in the last century, for many conventional building techniques have outlived their usefulness. The eighties will call for new approaches to construction; not only mass production of building modules but the application of modular techniques to storage space; integrated household appliances; more effective soundproofing for a noisier age; new construction products based on wood, glass, synthetic foams, plastics, metals—and waste materials. The high cost of transportation as well as building will mandate that more families will have to jam their living quarters into less space. Tall Texans may find their heads closer to the ceiling. High-density living may likely bring a new set of psychological problems and the need for more rigid social structures and less permissive attitudes toward maverick individualism.

EDUCATION: THE UNFULFILLED PROMISE

Paralleling the need for more efficient housing in years to come is the requirement for better education. The nineteenth-century utopian belief that all problems would be solved by free schooling for all has withered in the heat of dissatisfaction with the education system. The necessary concern with the rights of individuals and of minority groups has diverted attention and money from the primary goals of education. In response to political pressures, school systems have too often taken the low road, diluting the quality of their programs rather than facing the uphill fight that educational excellence always represents.

The defense has been made that the public schools have been overtaxed by the increased student loads since World War II. By the mid-seventies, however, enrollments were tending downward. Today there is at least a potential surplus of qualified teachers and adequate school space. There is little excuse left for compromises in the quality of schooling.

MANUFACTURING: A CHANGING MIX

A main support of Texas' population growth is the expansion of manufacturing. By 1980 Texas factories will probably be turning out four times their 1960 output. This does not mean, however, that they will be producing four times as much of the same products. Their output is changing radically.

Food products, for example, have increased in volume to feed a growing population. More important, each pound of processed food has become more valuable, not just through monetary inflation but because of more elaborate preprocessing and packaging.

Chemicals, Texas' most important export products, are expanding in variety. The chemical industry is especially involved in developing products to help solve environmental and health problems.

Electrical equipment, Texas' fastest growing factory output, is being designed to make more effective use of dwindling energy supplies.

In short, there is hardly any class of manufacturing in Texas that is not rapidly changing to accommodate itself to a new economic world.

AGRICULTURE: THE DISAPPEARING FARMER

With one agricultural revolution still incomplete, another is under way.

Since 1900 the Texas farm has been mechanized and the farmer himself mobilized. Except for a limited number of working hours, today's farmer has disappeared from many farms. Instead he commutes to his home in the nearest town and may be employed in an industrial plant there. The coming farm revolution will bring more efficient production, higher-level output, and continuing escalation of land prices.

TRANSPORTATION: WILD BLUE TRAFFIC JAM

The Texas skies are increasingly crowded, with multijet airliners and small craft competing for space in landing patterns and take-off queues. Urban expressways planned in the 1950s for long-term adequacy are now perilously crowded, while rail lines network Texas from border to border with scarcely a passenger train in sight. Texas' pressing need for expanded transportation capacity is clear enough, even though no state is better provided with long-distance transportation lines.

TRADE: KEEP CIRCLING THE BLOCK

The shift in Texas retailing and consumer services from downtown to suburban shopping center may have been inevitable. With the rise of the automobile and the decline in public transportation, even small cities have decentralized. Downtown businesses planned too little and late for adequate customer parking. (In most large cities automobile parking is a questionable use of expensive space.) The resulting proliferation of shopping centers, planned and random, has resulted in the appearance of more efficient and attractive retailing facilities than in any central business district—but also some of the most dismally disfigured stretches of street frontage in the world.

LEISURE: BOOM IN RELAXATION

Texans will have more money and time than ever by 1980. The combination of leisure time and affluence will stimulate interest in many familiar activities and probably in some new brands of inactivity. Spectator sports and the lively arts should flourish. In the seventies, the Texas economy has felt the real impact of the leisure boom in sales of boats, vacation homes, mobile homes, recreational equipment, and real estate.

ENERGY: BOTTOM OF THE BARREL

Suburbanization and the development of recreational areas well removed from cities are clearly threatened by the developing shortage of energy resources. Texas petroleum output passed its peak in the early seventies, yet demand for fuel and electricity continue to grow. The resultant higher costs for energy and government conservation measures will require a wrenching revision of personal and public priorities. With too little gasoline available for all members of a family to disperse in their own individual automobiles, the likelihood is increasing of families being obliged to travel together—or to stay at home together.

The Sunbelt climate of Texas may delight refugees from the Snowbelt in winter, but Texas summers have been made bearable only through the use of immense quantities of air-conditioning. Even white-collar workers are already finding it beyond their means to keep their homes at seventy-two degrees in August; in the future their collars may be more wilted than ever.

COMMUNICATIONS: GOODBYE, CENTRAL

Like the mule-driving dirt farmer, the telephone switchboard operator garlanded with wires and plugs is virtually extinct. The rise of electronic telecommunications may help solve some of Texas' transportation problems. The use of more elaborate telephone, closed-circuit television, and telefacsimile services will eliminate the need for much travel. Electronic fund transfer, inventory control, and other business services will make every shopping center a central business district.

RESOURCES: EARTH, AIR, FIRE, WATER

Managing the basic elements of the environment—keeping them available for future use and reasonably unspoiled by wastes—must be a chief concern of Texans from now on. But Texans have always been marked by a happy combination of ingenuity and serendipity, making the most of what they have and finding what they need, often by chance. Pre-Columbian Indians found on the South Texas coast a happy hunting ground with a climate that required no clothing. At the beginning of this century, as demand for petroleum was rising, Texans found it—initially in a water well. It cannot be doubted that the remainder of this century and the years beyond will bring surprises as well as predictable developments. With imagination and energy, Texas can be the better for both.

CONTRIBUTORS

STANLEY A. ARBINGAST, formerly director of the Bureau of Business Research, is Professor of Marketing, Resources, and Geography at The University of Texas at Austin, where he has taught since 1949. He obtained the B.S. degree from Winona State College and the M.A. and Ph.D. degrees from the University of Washington. He is the past editor of *Texas Business Review* and *Texas Industrial Expansion*. Dr. Arbingast has served as president of the Southwest Social Science Association and of the Associated University Bureaus of Business and Economic Research. He has written numerous articles dealing with economic matters, particularly in Texas, and is co-author of the *Atlas of Texas* and the *Atlas of Mexico*. He has just completed a three-year term on the Executive Committee of the Travel Research Association.

PAUL BARTLETT is Associate Professor of Business Law and Economics at The University of Texas at San Antonio. He is a member of both the Texas and the American Bar Associations and has served as consultant to several Texas law firms. Dr. Bartlett specialized in government and business interelationships and antitrust law and economics. Before coming to The University of Texas at San Antonio, he was Associate Professor in the College of Business at New Mexico State University, where he was twice elected Outstanding Professor in the College.

ALLEN COMMANDER, Vice President for Public Affairs at the University of Houston and the University's first director of the Energy Institute, received his B.S. degree from McNeese State University and his M.A. and Ph.D. from The George Washington University. He is a graduate of Johns Hopkins University's Institute for International Development and Harvard University's Institute for Educational Management. Commander has served as Foreign Service Officer for the U.S. Department of State and on ad hoc committees of the National Association of State Universities and Land-Grant Colleges; and the American Council on Education. He is a presidential appointee to the National Advisory Council on Extension and Continuing Education. He has been active in matters pertaining to energy as they relate to the state of Texas.

THOMAS R. DeGREGORI, Professor of Economics at the University of Houston, received the B.A. and M.A. degrees from the University of New Mexico and his Ph.D. from The University of Texas at Austin. He has taught at and served on the faculties of the University of Khartoum in Sudan, Case Institute of Technology, and the University of Houston. From 1969 to 1971 he was chairman of the Department of Economics at the University of Houston. Dr. DeGregori has published numerous articles dealing with economic development. He is the author of the book, *Technology and the Economic Development of the Tropical African Frontier* and co-author of *Economic Development: The Cultural Context*.

LILA FLORY is Assistant Professor of Economics at The University of Texas at San Antonio. She has published in the area of macroeconomics and is currently doing research in the areas of labor union behavior, banking, and managerial economics.

WILLIAM S. FRANKLIN is Associate Professor of Economics at The University of Texas at San Antonio. His research and teaching interests are in the areas of labor and manpower economics, with particular reference to manpower development in the construction industry. His work has been published in *Industrial and Labor Relations Review*, *Industrial Relations*, *Labor Law Journal*, and *Business and Economic Dimensions*, and in monograph form by the U.S. Department of Labor. Dr. Franklin received the Ph.D. degree in economics from The University of Texas at Austin in 1972.

ANTONIO FURINO is Professor of Economics in the College of Business of The University of Texas at San Antonio and directs the Center for Studies in Business, Economics, and Human Resources of the College. Prior to his present position, Dr. Furino was director of the Regional Analysis Division of the Alamo Area Council of Governments, an inter-governmental agency chartered by the state of Texas to assist local governments of a multi-county region in planning and in federal grants applications. A resident of Texas for nineteen years, Dr. Furino holds a Doctor of Jurisprudence from the University of Rome and a Ph.D. in economics from the University of Houston.

ROBERT W. GLOVER obtained the B.A. degree from the University of Santa Clara and the M.A. and Ph.D. degrees from The University of Texas at Austin. He is Acting Director of The Center for the Study of Human Resources at The University of Texas at Austin. Dr. Glover has published a number of articles in the labor and manpower area and is co-author of *Compensation of Texas State Employees* and of *Training and Entry Into Union Construction*. He has served Texas agencies on several consulting projects dealing with manpower and labor in the state.

JARED E. HAZLETON received his B.B.A. from the University of Oklahoma and the Ph.D. from Rice University. He has been on the faculty of The University of Texas at Austin since 1968, having previously served as banking services officer for the Federal Reserve Bank of Boston. He is a Professor of Public Affairs in the Lyndon B. Johnson School of Public Affairs. Dr. Hazleton has published numerous articles and is the author of five books and monographs.

ALLAN G. KING holds the B.A. from City College of New York, the M.S. and Ph.D. from Cornell University. He has been on the Economics faculty at The University of Texas at Austin since 1971. Dr. King is the author of several publications dealing with manpower. He served as Research Associate with The Center for the Study of Human Resources. Currently he is Associate Director of the Population Research Center at The University of Texas at Austin and Deputy Editor of the *Social Science Quarterly*.

LORNA A. MONTI received the Ph.D. degree in economics from The University of Texas at Austin in 1970. She was Instructor in the Department of Economics at the same institution from 1970 to 1973.

From 1973 to 1976 she was Research Associate of the Bureau of Business Research, and was Acting Director of the Bureau from 1976 to 1977. She was named Associate Director 1 September 1977.

DANIEL C. MORGAN, JR. is a Professor of Economics at The University of Texas at Austin. He obtained his B.B.A. and M.A. degrees from The University of Texas at Austin and the Ph.D. from the University of Wisconsin. Dr. Morgan has been employed by the Dow Chemical Company and has served on the Economics faculty of the University of Tennessee. He has published three books and numerous articles in the area of public finance.

LOUIS J. RODRIGUEZ, vice chancellor and provost at the University of Houston at Clear Lake City, previously served as dean of the School of Professional Studies at the same institution. Prior to coming to the University of Houston, he served in private industry, was dean of the School of Business Administration at Nicholls State University, and dean of the School of Business Administration and vice president for Academic Affairs at The University of Texas at San Antonio. Dr. Rodriguez, a former Alcee Fortier Distinguished Professor of Economics at Nicholls State University and a 1976 Fulbright Scholar to the Universidad de la Republica in Montevideo, Uruguay, has published thirty articles dealing with economics and education and is the co-author of a book, *The Economics of Education*. He received his B.A. from Newark College of Rutgers State University and his M.A. and Ph.D. from Louisiana State University.

ROBERT H. RYAN has been associated with the Bureau of Business Research as Consulting Editor since 1951 and since 1954 has also been a member of the College of Business Administration faculty at The University of Texas at Austin where he is Assistant Professor of Business Communication. He holds the B.A. degree in English from The University of Texas at Austin. Mr. Ryan was formerly Editor of the *Texas Business Review*, *Southwest Resources Handbook*, and *Texas Economic Indicators*. He has served as Industrial Economist on the staff of the Southwest Research Institute in San Antonio. As an economic consultant, he specialized in population and industrialization studies used in the planning of transportation, public utility, and financial services.

Contributors

MARY C. SCHIFLETT is Director of Publications for The Energy Institute and Senior Research Associate for the Institute of Labor and Industrial Relations in the College of Business Administration, University of Houston. She holds the B.A. and B.S. degrees from Southern Methodist University and the M.A. from the University of Houston. She has served the U.S. Department of Commerce, the Dallas Chamber of Commerce, Republic Oil Supply Company, Houston Oil Company, and McGraw-Hill Publishing Company writing primarily for *Business Week*. Most recently, she has written in the areas of the intersection of labor and the humanities, women in the labor movement, legal incentives and barriers to solar enery, and policy and manpower issues within the oil, gas, and petrochemical industries.

THOMAS J. STANLY, head of the Department of Agriculture at Stephen F. Austin State University, holds the B.S., M.S., and Ph.D. degrees from Louisiana State University. He served in faculty and administrative capacities at Nicholls State University and has a number of publications in the fields of agricultural economics, education, and college administration. Dr. Stanly is a past president of the National Association of Colleges and Teachers of Agriculture. He served on several National Academy of Science committees concerned with instruction in agriculture, natural resources, and biological sciences. Dr. Stanly has been awarded the Honorary State Farmer Degree by the states of Louisiana and Texas.

VERNON E. SWEENEY, JR. obtained the B.S. and M.A. from the University of Houston and the Ph.D. from The University of Texas at Austin. He has been employed by Truckline Gas Transmission Company, Inc., and Dow Chemical Corporation. Dr. Sweeney was on the faculty and served as chairman of the Department of Economics and Finance at Nicholls State University. His publications include an input-output model for the state of Louisiana. Currently he is chairman of the Department of Economics at Sam Houston State University.

DALE TRUETT is Professor of Economics at The University of Texas at San Antonio. He has done extensive work in price theory, international trade, and economic development, the latter with special reference to Mexico. In addition, Dr. Truett has served as consultant to the United Nations Industrial Development Organization, the Mexican national steel industry, and numerous private corporations engaged in international trade.

JOHN V. ZUCKERMAN is Professor of Organizational Behavior and Management, College of Business Administration, University of Houston. He was formerly deputy director of The Energy Institute at the University. Dr. Zuckerman previously served in faculty and administrative capacities at the University of Southern California, and was deputy director of the Bureau of International Business Operations of the U.S. Department of Commerce and director of Industrial Relations at Ampex Corporation. Dr. Zuckerman holds the M.A. and Ph.D. degrees from Stanford University.

BIBLIOGRAPHY

THE THEORY OF ECONOMIC DEVELOPMENT AND THE CHALLENGE OF A DEVELOPMENTAL POLICY

Allen, Ruth A. and Barton, Sam B. *Wages Earners Meet the Depression.* Austin, Texas: The University of Texas, Bureau of Research in the Social Sciences, Study no. 15, 1935.

Ayres, C. E. *The Theory of Economic Progress.* Chapel Hill, N.C.: The University of North Carolina Press, 1944.

Bancroft, Hubert Howe. *History of Texas and the North Mexican States.* San Francisco: The History Company, 1890.

Barr, Alwyn. *Reconstruction to Reform: Texas Politics 1876-1906.* Austin, Texas: University of Texas Press, 1971.

Bishop, Curtis Ken. *Lots of Land.* Austin, Texas: Steck Co., 1939.

Butler, Andres W. *Transportation in Texas 1820-1860.* Master's thesis, University of Houston, 1952.

Carter, Hadding. *Doomed Road to Empire: The Spanish Trail of Conquest.* New York: McGraw-Hill, 1963.

DeGregori, Thomas R. *Technology and the Economic Development of the Tropical African Frontier.* Cleveland, Ohio: Case Western Reserve University Press, 1969.

Drummond, Lorena, ed. *Texas Looks Ahead.* Austin, Texas: University of Texas Press, 1944.

Foster, George M. *Culture and Contact: America's Spanish Heritage.* Chicago: Quadrangle Books, 1960; Viking Fund Publications in Anthropology no. 27.

Gard, Wayne. *Rawhide Texas.* Norman, Oklahoma: University of

Oklahoma Press, 1965.
Gordon, Wendell C. "Foreign Investments." *Business Review* 9 (Fall 1962).
Haley, James Evetts. *The XIT Ranch of Texas and the Early Days of the Llano Estacado.* Norman, Oklahoma: University of Oklahoma Press, 1953, 1967.
Holden, William Curry. *Alkali Trails, or Social and Economic Movements of the Texas Frontier, 1846-1900.* Dallas: The Southwest Press, 1930.
May, Frances B. *Economic Statistics of Texas, 1900-1962.* Austin, Texas: University of Texas, Bureau of Business Research, 1964.
Montgomery, Robert H. *The Brimstone Game: Monopoly in Action.* New York: The Vanguard Press, 1940.
Sowell, Andrew Jackson. *Rangers and Pioneers of Texas,* 1884. Reprint New York: Argosy-Antiquarian Press, 1963.
Spratt, John S. *The Road to Spindle Top, Economic Change in Texas 1875-1901.* Dallas: Southern Methodist University Press, 1955.
Thrall, Homer S. *A History of Texas.* New York: University Publishing Company, 1885.
Webb, Walter Prescott. *The Great Frontier.* Boston: Houghton Mifflin, 1951, 1952.
———. *The Great Plains.* New York: Ginn and Company, 1931.
Wheeler, Kenneth S. *To Wear A City's Crown: The Beginning of Urban Growth in Texas 1836-1865.* Cambridge, Massachusetts: Harvard University Press, 1968.
Zeigler, Robert E. *The Workingman in Houston, Texas, 1865-1914.* Ann Arbor: University Microfilms 1973 (microfilm of a Texas Tech University thesis).
Zimmerman, Erich. *World Resources and Industries: A Functional Appraisal of Agricultural and Industrial Materials.* New York: Harper Brothers, 1933, 1951.

TEXAS—THE ENERGY ECONOMY

American Petroleum Institute. *Petroleum Facts and Figures.* 1961 ed.
American Petroleum Institute. *Petroleum Facts and Figures.* 1971 ed.
Ford Foundation Energy Policy Project. *Exploring Energy Choices.* 1974.
Grubb, Herbert W. *The Structure of the Texas Economy,* 2 vols. Office of the Governor, Office of Information Services, March 1973.
Hook, John Raymond. "Texas Energy Contribution to the Nation."

University of Houston, The Energy Institute, 1974.
National Petroleum Council. *U.S. Energy Outlook, A Summary Report.* December 1972.
Office of the Governor, Division of Planning and Coordination. *Electric Power in Texas.* November 1972.
Railroad Commission of Texas. *Annual Report on the Oil and Gas Division.* 1970.
Ryan, Robert H. "Texas Energy Industries." *Texas Business Review,* June 1972.
Shell Oil Company. *The National Energy Problem: Implication for the Petrochemical Industry.* February 1973.
Thompson, Russell G., et al. "Texas Energy Statistics and Forecasts." University of Houston, The Energy Institute, 1974.
United States Congress, The Joint Committee on Atomic Energy. *Understanding the National Energy Dilemma.* August 1973.
United States Department of Commerce, Bureau of the Census. "Summary Statistics." *1967 Survey of Manufacturers* I (December 1971).
United States Department of Commerce (in cooperation with the U.S. Social and Economic Statistical Administration, U.S. Department of Agriculture, and the U.S. Water Resource Council). "Date by States." *OBERS Projections,* I (September 1972).
United States Department of the Interior, Bureau of Mines. "Fuels." *1960 Minerals Yearbook,* II (December 1961).
United States Department of the Interior, Bureau of Mines. "Fuels." *1970 Minerals Yearbook,* II (December 1971).
United States Department of the Interior. *U.S. Energy Through the Year 2000.* December 1972.
United States Department of the Interior. "United States Energy Fact Sheets by States and Regions." 1971.
United States Federal Power Commission. *Electric Power Statistics, 1960-61.* December 1962.
United States Federal Power Commission. *Electric Power Statistics, 1970-71.* December 1972.
United States Federal Power Commission. *1970 Federal Power Survey.* December 1971.

THE AGRICULTURAL ECONOMY OF TEXAS
Books
Faculty and Staff, The University of Texas. *Texas Looks Ahead,* vol.

1. Freeport, New York: Books for Libraries Press, 1944.
King, Jack G. and Quimby, J. Roy. "History of Grain Sorghums in Texas." In *Texas Almanac and State Industrial Guide, 1972-1973*, pp. 418-19. Dallas: A. H. Belo Corporation, 1971.
Steen, Ralph W. and Donecker, Francis. *Texas: Our Heritage*. Austin, Texas: The Steck Company, 1962.
Texas Almanac and State Industrial Guide, 1976-1977. Dallas: A. Belo Corporation, 1975.
Wortham, Louis. *A History of Texas*. 5 vols. Fort Worth, Texas: Molyneaux Company, 1924.

Documents

Annual Report Commercial Fertilizer, July 1, 1975 to June 30, 1976. Agricultural Experiment Station Miscellaneous Publication 1279. College Station Texas: Texas A&M University, no date.
1975 Cash Receipts From the Sale of Texas Farm Commodities. Texas Department of Agriculture and United States Department of Agriculture, Texas Crop and Livestock Reporting Service, Austin, Texas, 1976.
Food and Fiber Facts. Prepared for Texas Food and Fiber Abundance Council by Texas Agricultural Extension Service and Texas Agricultural Experiment Station. College Station, Texas: Texas A&M University, no date.
General Soil Map of Texas, 1973. Department of agricultural Communications, part II, MP 1034. College Station, Texas: Texas A&M University, 1973.
Godfrey, Curtis L., Carter, Clarence R., and McKee, Gordon S. *Land: Resource Areas of Texas*. Texas Agricultural Extension Service, Texas Agricultural Experiment Station Bulletin 1070. College Station, Texas: Texas A&M University, no date.
Graves, James W. *Effects of 1966 Cotton Adjustments in Texas*. Texas Agricultural Experiment Station, MP 842. College Station, Texas: Texas A&M University, 1967.
Griffiths, John F. and Orton, Robert. *Agroclimatic Atlas of Texas*. Texas Agricultural Experiment Station, part I—Precipitation Possibilities, MP 888. College Station, Texas: Texas A&M University, 1968.
United States Bureau of the Census. *Statistical Abstract of the United States: 1976*. 97th ed. Washington, D.C., 1976.
1975 Texas Field Crop Statistics. Texas Department of Agriculture

and United States Department of Agriculture, Texas Crop and Livestock Reporting Service, Bulletin 136, Austin, Texas, 1976.

1975 Texas Livestock Statistics. Texas Department of Agriculture and United States Department of Agriculture, Texas Crop and Livestock Reporting Service, Bulletin 135, Austin, Texas 1976.

1975 Texas Poultry Statistics. Texas Department of Agriculture and United States Department of Agriculture, Texas Crop and Livestock Reporting Service, Bulletin 132, Austin, Texas, 1976.

1976 Texas Small Grains Statistics. Texas Department of Agriculture and United States Department of Agriculture, Texas Crop and Livestock Reporting Service, Bulletin 94, Austin, Texas, 1976.

What Texas Agriculture Means To You. Texas Department of Agriculture, Austin, Texas, no date.

Interviews

Jones Cecil. Department of Agriculture, Stephen F. Austin State University, Nacogdoches, Texas, 5 November 1976.

Perkins, Don. Rite Care Poultry, Inc., Nacogdoches, Texas, 14 December, 1975.

Addresses

Pope, L. S., dean of Administrative Affairs, College of Agriculture, Texas A&M University. Address to the Nacogdoches Farm and Ranch Club, Nacogdoches, Texas, 6 December 1973.

THE FINANCIAL SYSTEM OF TEXAS
Books

Carlson, Avery Luvere. *A Monetary and Banking History of Texas.* Fort Worth, Texas: The Fort Worth National Bank, 1930.

Commission on Money and Credit. *Money and Credit.* Englewood Cliffs, N.J.: Prentice-Hall, Inc.; 1961.

Crum, Lawrence L. *Transition in the Texas Commercial Banking Industry, 1956-1965.* Austin, Texas: Bureau of Business Research, 1970.

Federal Reserve Bank of Dallas. *Regional Economic Facts.* 1967.

Institute of Life Insurance. *The Life Insurance Fact Book, 1973.* New York, 1973.

McCleskey, Clifton. *Government and Politics of Texas.* Boston: Little, Brown & Company, 1971.

Public Affairs Research Council of Louisiana. *Industry Rates Lou-*

isiana. Baton Rouge, Louisiana: Public Affairs Research Council of Louisiana, 1971.

Steen, Ralph Wright. *Twentieth Century Texas*. Austin, Texas: The Steck Company, 1942.

United States Savings and Loan League. *Savings and Loan Fact Book, 1973*.

Reports and Government Documents

Credit Union National Association, Inc. *Annual Report, 1973*. Madison, Wisconsin, 1973.

State of Texas. *Analysis of Annual Reports of Licensees, 1971*. Finance Companies. Austin, Texas: Office of Consumer Credit Commissioner, 1972.

Texas Commerce Bancshare, Inc. *Annual Report, 1972*. Houston, Texas, 1972.

Texas Savings and Loan League. *Annual Report of Savings and Loan Associations in Texas*. Austin, Texas, 1972.

Periodicals

Bower, Leonard G. "Personal Income in Texas—Accelerates to Rate Faster than the Nation's." *Business Review*, May 1971.

Grant, Joseph M. "Sources of Financing for Industrial Expansion in Texas." *Texas Business Review*, April 1973.

Kelly, William H. and Rose, Peter S. "Market for Bank Services Changes in Texas." *Business Review*, April 1971.

Mettlen, Robert D. "Savings and Loan Associations—Past and Future." *Texas Business Review*, April 1971.

McClelland, Edward L. "Concentration Projected to Increase in Texas." *Business Review*, February 1973.

"Registered Holding Companies in the District Number 115." *Business Review*, June 1972.

Rose, Peter S. "Bank Holding Companies." *Baylor Business Studies*, May, June, and July 1973.

Steele, H. Ellsworth and Boston, Robert O. "Factors Influencing the Growth of Credit Unions in Southern Industry." *Southwestern Social Science Quarterly*, September 1963.

Stodden, John R. "Texas Banking: Their Small Size Costs Banks Business of Large Companies." *Business Review*, October 1973.

INDEX

Abilene, Texas: 279, 282
Advisory Commission on Intergovernmental Relations: identification, 247; its most important state-local fiscal questions—how Texas fares, 247, 248; its study of federal grants in state-local finance, 258
aerospace industry, Texas: 8
agricultural specialties: fish farming, 188; greenhouse and nursery products, 188; horses, 188; recreation, 174, 188; timber, 187
agricultural restrictions: 177, 192-193
agriculture: 78, 93, 169-195; agribusiness, 34, 171-72; cooperatives 171, 180; exports, 192; finances, 189-90; future, 272, 279, 286, 291; grain sorghum, 171, 184, 185, 192; hogs, 181; importance to the state, 169-71; irrigation, 188, 189; off-farm sector, 190-92; poultry, 171, 182, 183; principal products, 177-88; resources, 173-77; sheep, 181; unions, 151-54; vegetable crops, 187; wages, *See* farm and ranch; wheat, 186
Aid to Families with Dependent Children (AFDC): 127
Air Control Board of Texas: 93
Akin, John S.: 269
Alamo Planning Regions: 114, 119

Alaska: North Slope, 89; pipeline, 10
Amarillo, Texas: 279
apparel: 166, 279-83
apprenticeships: 98, 101, 102, 104, 132
Apprenticeship Outreach Program (AOP): 131
Arab oil embargo: 82, 89
Army Corps of Engineers: 59
assets, Texas financial system: 198-99
Atomic Energy Commission (U.S. Joint Committee of): 78
Austin, Texas: 279, 281, 282
automobiles: trend in use of, 83; effect of changes, 85-86; efficiency goals, 91
Ayres, Clarence E.: 14

Bahl, Roy: 248
Ball, Charles: 38
Bank Holding Company Act: 202
Bankhead-Jones Act: 55
Basing point system: 8
Baytown, Texas: 58
Beaumont-Port Arthur-Orange, Texas: 279, 280, 281, 187
Bexar County: 273
Big Bend: 52
Big Spring, Texas: 277
Big Thicket: 73
Birmingham, Alabama: 8

Blackland Belt: 49
Boulding, Kenneth: 43
"bracero" program: 130
branch banking: 202
Bretzfelder, Robert: 270
Briscoe, Dolph (governor of Texas): "no new taxes," 252; letter from comptroller, 257; highway expenditures (and 65th Legislature), 258; GOER (Governor's Office of Education Resources) audit of Texas property tax values, 266
Brownsville, Texas: 238, 279, 283
Bryan-College Station, Texas: 279, 281
Building and Construction Trades Councils: 131
Bullock, Bob (comptroller): fiscal report to Governor Briscoe, 257; income generated, by governments and industrial categories—Texas vs. U.S., 246
Bureau of Apprenticeship and Training: 131
Bureau of the Census, Standard Metropolitan: 279
Burnet-Llano Basin: 51

Caddo Parish, Louisiana: 274
California: 10
cattle: 4, 169, 170, 171, 177-80
central cities—Texas relative to other U.S. cities: 267-69
Central Texas: 272, 279, 282, 287
chemical and allied products: 163
Civil Rights Act of 1964: 130
climate: 158
coal: amount used in 1960, 79-80; use in Texas, 81, 82; coal-fired boilers, 84; use in 1980-85, 85; other, 31, 32
Coastal Plains: 47
Colorado River: 50
commercial banks, by size of deposits, assets: 203
communications: 293
Community Action Agencies (CAAS): 105

Community Action Programs (CAPS): 105
comparative advantage: 222
composition of annual income in Texas: 23
Comprehensive Employment and Training Act (CETA): 107, 108, 109, 111, 119, 126, 129, 132
Concentrated Employment Program (CEP): 107
conservation: 82-83; measures to decrease consumption, 84-85; and increased efficiency, 86; voluntary or mandatory, 83, 87; as relief for energy problems, 91; technological priority, 94
construction: 290
conversion of energy in Texas: to agriculture, 78; chart, 81; technological assessment of solar conversion, 94
Cooperative Area Manpower Planning System (CAMPS): 107
copper refining: 279
Corpus Christi, Texas: 279, 280, 287
corridor, Central Texas: 281, 282, 287
cotton: 4, 50, 169, 170, 171, 183-84, 192
credit, agricultural: 189-90
credit unions: 209-10

dairying: 180
Dallas County: 273
Dallas-Fort Worth, Texas: 9, 11, 279, 280, 282, 284, 287
Davis Mountains: 51, 52
DeAre, Diana R.: 276
DeGregori, Thomas R.: 14
demand forecast for Texas 1980: 83-84
Democratic Party: 7, 8, 9
Denmark: 1
Department of Commerce: 230
deposits, Texas and U.S. banks: 200-201
development obstacles: 36

East and West Cross Timbers: 50
East Texas: 272, 279, 287

East Texas Field: 48, 63
economic development: 1, 2, 12-13
economic growth: 1, 9-12
economic indicators for Texas and the United States, 1950-75: 21
Economic Opportunity Act (EOA) of 1964: 104, 105, 107
Edge Act banks: 238
education: 37, 263, 267, 281, 282, 291
Edwards Plateau: 51
Eisenhower, Dwight D.: 9
El Capitan: 52
El Paso, Texas: 237, 279, 282
electrical and electronic machinery: 166
electricity: power generation by fossil fuels, 84; solar tower at University of Houston, 94; solid waste, 95
electronics: 279, 280, 281, 283
energy: amount, 77; consumption, 77, 83; crisis of 1977, 87; efficiency 1960-85, 86; flows, 78, 79, 81; forecast in 1980, 82; Institute, 78; residential and commercial, 79, 81, 84-86; solar, 94, 95
—United States: amount of, 77; shortage, 88
English, second language: 119
environmentalists and the conservation movement: 10-11
expenditure, governmental: 248, 249, 250, 259
exploration and discovery, proposed Energy Commission regulation of incentives: 92, 93, 94
Export-Import Bank: 241
export surplus: 229

fabricated metals: 165
Fair Labor Standards Act: 128
farm and ranch: acreage, 172; income, 172, 177, 182, 189; integration, 171; investment, 189; number of farms, 172; part-time, 172, population, 170, 173, 174; wages, 173, 174, 177
federal and state funds for manpower and related services: 109-10
federal funding, to Texas: 258, 259
Federal Power Commission: 64, 82, 90
Federated Commercial Clubs of Texas: 16
female-headed households: 121, 122, 127
finance companies: 207
Firestine, Robert: 271
Fisher, Glenn: 269
Floyd, Joe S.: 270
food and kindred products: 160
food processing: 280, 283
forecasts: 289
Foreign Credit Insurance Association: 239
foreign investment: 6, 14
forests: 33; Texas forest resources, 55
Foster, Craig: 271
Foster, George M.: 41
frontier: 3
furniture and fixtures: 163

Galveston, Texas: 58, 236
Galveston-Texas City, Texas: 273, 279, 280, 281, 287
Garner, John Nance: 8
General Land Office, Texas: 93
George-Barden Act of 1946: 98
geothermal reservoirs, Texas: 94
GI Bill of Rights: 104
Gordon, Wendell: 5, 14
government: 34, 272, 281, 282, 286
Governor Sterling: 65
Grand Prairie, Texas: 50
grants-in-aid, federal grants, all governments: 245
Great Plains: 50
Green Thumb programs: 127
growth: economic growth factors, 25; government relative to private, 244-47; state-local government, relative to federal, private, 245, 246; economic growth of Texas explained by "government"? 258, 261; of taxes, 244-46; of property taxes in Texas, 262-65

Guadalupe Range: 51
Gulf Coast: 272, 279, 286, 287

Hardin, Garrett: 46
Harris County: 273
Hayes, Rutherford B.: 7
health: 18, 30, 36, 37, 38
higher education: 98, 103, 104
Highland Lakes: 51
Hill Country: 51
Houston, Texas: 8, 9, 12, 273, 279, 280, 281, 282, 287
Houston Customs Region: 226
Houston-Galveston, Texas area: 11
Houston Ship Channel: 58
Hueco Mountains: 52
Huff, David L.: 276
human capital: 4, 5
Hunt Commission: 217-18
hydroelectric: amount used 1960, 80; growth, 82

income generated, by industrial category: 246
income in Texas: origin, 23, 38; per capita, 8-18, 22, 23, 25, 38; personal, 21, 24, 36, 197, 198, 277, 278
indicators of economic growth: 17, 18
industrial financing legislation: 213-14
industrial location inducements Texas, relative to other states: 255, 270
industry as energy consumer: 78; oil as boiler fuel, 79; effective utilization, 80; potential adjustment in consumption, 84; largest user in Texas, 85; flows and forecasts, 86; efficiency goals, 91; multiple energy industrial systems, 92
infant death rate: 30, 36
insurance lending: 210-11
international trade: exports, 228, 229, 230; importance, 225; imports, 228, 231; other, 239; state export origin reports, 231; Texas' international trade, 228; tonnages, 234; with Mexico, 236
interstate highway: 35, 277

Interstate Oil Compact Commission: 74
investment, agriculture: *See* farm and ranch, investment
iron oxide: 70
Irrigation Act of 1889: 57
irrigation agriculture: *See* farm and ranch, irrigation

Job Corps: 105, 107, 108, 111, 119
jobs in energy in Texas: 78
Johnson, Lyndon B.: 8
Johnson, W. A.: 270

Keynes, John M.: 225
Killeen-Temple, Texas: 279, 281, 282

labor: agriculture, 170, 172, 174; employment, 197; markets, 122, 125, 138-40
labor unions: agriculture, unions in, 151-54; growth of, 142-48, 154-55; history in Texas of, 140; membership of, 141-48; patterns of unionization, 144; public employee unionism, 148-51; role of, 126-38
land: cropland, 174; farm & ranch, 174-77; forage & pasture, 174; landscape, 158; reserves of oil, Texas, 89; use & regulation in Tex., 93-94; value, 173
Laredo, Texas: 238, 273, 279, 283
Laredo Customs District: 226
legislation: natural gas, 90, 91; to encourage investment, 95
Legislative Budget Board of Texas: 93
leisure: 292
lignite in Texas (coal): 82; liquefaction and gasification of, 94
Lile, Stephen: 257
liquid hydrocarbon: 66
livestock and products: *See* agriculture, principal products
livestock expositions: 179
Llano Estacado or Staked Plains: 50
local governments of Texas: *See* property taxes
Longview, Texas: 279, 280
Los Angeles, California: 282

Lower Rio Grande Valley: 49
Lubbock, Texas: 279
lumber and wood products: 162

Manford Act: 148
Manned Space Center, Houston: 8
Manpower Development and Training Act of 1962: 104, 107
manufacturing: 17, 28, 157, 159, 272, 280, 287, 291
Manvel, Allan: 269
mass transit: 91
Maxwell School, Syracuse University: 248-50
McAllen-Pharr-Edinburg, Texas: 279, 283
Mexican border: 277, 282, 283, 287
Mexican labor: 151-52
Midland, Texas: 279, 282
military expenditures: 279, 281, 282
mineral fuels: 62
minorities: 102, 121, 122, 126, 128, 130, 131, 132
Minority Women Employment Program (MWEP): 131
Morgan, Daniel: 244, 263, 270
multibank holding companies: 205

National Alliance of Businessmen: 119
National Commission for Manpower policy: 108
National Defense Education Act of 1958: 104
national economy, effect of increased oil prices and cutback in petroleum production: 89
natural gas: use in Texas, 79-82; supply, 84; as a petrochemical feedstock, 90, 91; exploration, 90-91; U.S. reserves, 91
natural resources: 5, 31, 41, 42, 44, 45, 46, 52, 54, 61, 71, 158, 293
Neighborhood Youth Corps (NYC): 105
New Careers programs: 105
New Mexico: 282
New Zealand: 1

nonelectrical machinery: 165
non-ferrous minerals: 32, 33
non-fuel minerals: 69
Nordheimer, Jon: 283
North Central Plains: 49
North Texas: 272, 279, 287
nuclear power in Texas: 82
nursery products: 188

Odessa, Texas: 279, 282
Office of Economic Opportunity (OEO): 105
offshore leasing: 82
Ogallala Aquifer: 50, 279
oil field equipment: 280, 282, 287
oil imported to Texas: from other states, 79; and from outside the country, 83; availability of imported oil, 85; dwindling resources, 87, previous attitude, 88; Texas as net importer, 95; other, 232
oil and gas production in Texas: crude oil production, 89; currently nation's leader, 87; drop by 1985, 84; effects of cutback, 89; exports, 83, 84; natural gas 1980 and 1985, 90; price effects and reserves, 90; supply forecast of Texas, 83, 84; tax income from, 93; other, 16, 17, 81, 272, 280-82, 284, 286, 287
oil, non-energy uses: 79
oil utilization in Texas: 79-82, 84
oilseed crops: 186-87
Old-Age Assistance: 127
Operation Headstart: 105
Operation Mainstream: 105, 127, 129

Panhandle: 272, 279, 287
paper and allied products: 162
Perry, David: 270
petrochemicals: Texas part in, 77; as industry in Texas, 9, 87; processing plants, 88; natural gas as feedstock, 91; as Gulf Coast industry, 93
petroleum refining and related industries: 164
Pine Belt: 48

Piney Woods: 47, 55
Pittsburgh plus system: 8
political integration, importance of: 5, 6
population: 17,18, 21, 22, 25, 26, 29-30, 36, 38, 46, 82, 84, 85, 196, 197, 289
population, farm: See farm and ranch, population
Populist Party, and Populists: 7
Port Arthur, Texas: 9
Post Oak Belt: 48
poverty: by education, 37; rates, 36; war on, 98, 104
precipitation: 56
primary metals: 165
printing and allied products: 163
property taxes of Texas: 261-67
programs for disadvantaged: 126-31
Public Employment Program (PEP): 105, 106, 108, 131
public lands of Texas: 53
Puryear, Bahl, Sacks: 248-50

Quindry, Kenneth: 269

rail, highway traffic: 236
Railroad Commission: 65, 82, 92
Ray, Cadwell: 270
Rayburn, Sam: 8
Real Estate Investment Trust: 211, 212
Red River: 50
refinery capacity, Texas: 77, 87, 89
regions: administration, 274; air travel, 284; Burean of Economic Analysis, 275, 284; functional, 273; Huff-DeAre, 276; marketing, 274; nodal, 278; top five, 277, traffic flow, 273
Republican Party, and Republicans: 7, 9
research and development: 86; policies, 88; technological, 94; funding, 95
reservoirs: 59
residual wastes: 46
resources, agricultural: See agriculture, resources
revenue sharing, Texas: 259

rice: 185-86
right-to-work laws: 9, 141
Rio Grande Valley: 13
Rio Grande Plain: 49
Roosevelt, Franklin D.: 8
rural-urban shift: 17, 27

Sacks, Seymour: 248
San Angelo, Texas: 279, 282
San Antonio, Texas: 273, 279, 281, 287
savings and loan associations: 204-7
Sayre, Joseph D.: 16
secondary and tertiary recovery of oil: 89
securities industry: 207-9
Sherman-Denison, Texas: 279, 280
Shreveport, Louisiana: 274
Small Business Administration loans: 212-13
Smith County: 273
Smith Hughes Vocational Education Act: 98
socio-economic characteristics of Texas planning regions: 118, 120
soils: 53
South Central United States: 280, 282, 284, 287
South Texas: 272, 279, 287
spending, United States government in Texas: 8
Spindletop: 41, 62, 70
Standard Industrial Classification: 231
Standard Metropolitan Statistical Area: 25, 38
"Start-up" training: 129
state and local governments in Texas: 245, 246, 247, 250-54
state of Texas government: 258-61
state-local taxes: 248, 256, 257
Stockton Plateau: 51
stone, shell, clay, glass, and concrete products: 164
structural unemployment: 104
sulphur: 70
Summer Youth Program: 119
Sunbelt states: 260, 283

Index

Sunley, Emil M. Jr.: 251
Supreme Court, *Phillip's* decision 1938: 90

Tarrant County: 273
taxation, energy tax structure in Texas: 93-94
tax-exempt revenue bonds: 212
taxes, farm and ranch: 190
taxes in Texas: 248, 250-54, 262-64
technology and the arts: 3; and values, 3; and development, 3, 4; diffusion of, 5, 6
Texarkana, Texas: 279, 280
Texas as petroleum processing and marketing center: 88
Texas banks: 238, 239, 240
Texas City, Texas: 58
Texas coastline: 49
Texas economy: effect of natural gas, 88, 91; effect of oil price increase, 89; impact of tax structure, 93; natural resources enhancing wealth, 95
Texas Education Agency: 100
Texas financial system, history of: 214-16
Texas High Plains: 279
Texas Industrial Commission: 34, 35, 38
Texas Industrial Congress: 16
Texas land area: 33
Texas labor market statistics: 116, 117
Texas Panhandle: 50
Texas Planning Board: 17
Texas planning regions: 114, 115; demographic characteristics of, 119
Texas Public Employees Association: 149-50
Texas Rehabilitation Commission: 103
Texas seaports: 234
Texas State Advisory Council for Technical-Vocational Education: 100
Texas, total area: 47
Texas Water Conservation Association: 60
Texas Water Development Bd.: 59, 60

Texas Water Plan: 60, 61
textile mill products: 161
Tilden, Samuel: 7
timber: 47, 171, 187
tool using: 2
trade: 272, 279, 280, 282, 283, 287, 292
Trans-Pecos Texas: 51
transportation, use of energy: 79, 80, 81; adjustment in consumption, 84; utilization in Texas (flows and forecasts), 86; national use, 88; more efficient modes, 91; mass transit, 91; other, 166, 233, 292
Tyler, Texas: 279, 280

Underground Water Conservation District Act of 1949: 58
unemployment: 22, 25, 36
U.S. Bureau of Mines: 61, 82
U.S. Department of Commerce: 63
University of Texas: 94
Upper Rio Grande Valley: 52
uranium: 32
urbanization: 1, 2, 277, 290
Utility Commission of Texas: 92-93
utilities, Texas: use of energy, 91

Victoria, Texas: 274, 277
vocational education: 98, 104, 128, 131, 132
Vocational Education Act of 1963: 98
Vocational Education Amendments of 1968: 99
vocational rehabilitation: 98, 103, 104

Waco, Texas: 279, 281
wastes: 43
water: 27, 33, 34, 56, 72, 177
Water Planning Act of 1957: 60
Water Quality Board of Texas: 93
Watkins, Alfred: 270
Weinstein, Bernard: 271
wealth, distribution of: 3
Webb County: 273
Webb, Walter Prescott: 3, 14
West Texas: 49, 63, 272, 279, 282, 287

Wichita Falls, Texas: 279
wildlife: 33, 175
wind power: 94-95

Zimmermann, Erich: 5, 14
Zlatkovich, Charles P.: 273

Soc
HC
107
T4
D94